To
Jean Wright

Semper Fi

Russ Long

*Mekong Drillship*

*Mekong Drillship*
*Russ Long*

**VANTAGE PRESS**
New York

FIRST EDITION

All rights reserved, including the right of
reproduction in whole or in part in any form.

Copyright © 1999 by Russ Long

Published by Vantage Press, Inc.
516 West 34th Street, New York, New York 10001

Manufactured in the United States of America
ISBN: 0-533-12910-6

Library of Congress Catalog Card No.: 98-90805

0 9 8 7 6 5 4 3 2 1

To all those oil explorationists who have traveled to the exotic ends of the earth in search of new hydrocarbon discoveries. They enjoyed many exciting and thrilling experiences, but they also spent many lonely months and years facing varied dangers away from their families and lovers. Too often those times were spent under circumstances such as those endured by the hero in this story who dragged himself through many layers of dirt and degrading pursuits to accomplish his avowed purpose. They all deserve our greatest admiration and respect.

*Mekong Drillship*

# Prologue

Hong Kong's newest towers sparkled beautifully in the afternoon sun, and the slick little company jet moved briskly down the runway toward the open sea. Harold Blanton was always happy to depart the congested confines of that vibrant city's airport, for he knew, as a former Vietnamese War fighter pilot, it was a tight fit for any plane. Taking off toward the northwest on that runway brought planes much too close to the apartment-covered mountain for comfort. Fortunately, in the southeastern direction, there was a slot between the islands that encouraged a gentle climb away from the clutter of ships in the bustling port; then out over the open waters of the South China Sea.

Harold brushed back his curly blond hair as he sat in a comfortable leather seat in the rear of the cabin, mentally reviewing the data they had collected during their two-week stay back in Vietnam. Seated across from him was World Oil's chief accountant, Jack Franz, a formidable accountant who was their expert on international finances. They had been in Ho Chi Minh City, the former capital of Vietnam, researching possibilities for signing an exploration agreement with the Vietnamese State Oil Company. Harold had introduced Franz to his old wartime hangout in that city, the Majestic Hotel. "Saigon," as he remembered it. Now he and Jack were on their way home after researching the documents needed for an agreement with that government.

Bill Hanby, World Oil's Far East manager in Tokyo, had considered the trip important enough to send Harold's party by company jet. Also, he wanted to make sure Harold was back in town to host World Oil's Tokyo reception being held that evening. At that social gathering they would disclose their exploration intentions to the leaders of the Pacific Rim governments, and to directors of the most important commercial establishments of the Far East.

In front of them in the confined jet cabin were two World Oil company auditors who worked and traveled out of their Houston home office. They were returning from two weeks in Thailand, where they had reviewed the numbers of the company's exploration progress. They had also been assigned the task of surreptitiously asking pointed questions of the proper authorities in the Thai government about their intended future relations with Vietnam. They had arranged to stop through Hong Kong to meet Harold with their information. The other pair of seats were occupied by well-logging technicians returning from a survey offshore from Jakarta in the West Java Sea, and happened to be headed to Tokyo.

The door to the pilot's compartment was closed for takeoff, and since they had no stewardess, they were tending to their own seat belts. There were sandwiches and iced refreshments in the chests strapped down near the front of the compartment, so they were to help themselves.

Harold leaned across the aisle as their plane climbed out through the gap and remarked, "Jack, look outside. Flying past this busy city of Hong Kong always gives me a thrill. It's like a hive of bees down there. There's construction everywhere you look, and the harbor is as congested as the airport. I remember that ride up the cog railway to the top of Victoria Peak. The business district is such a cosmopolitan and civilized place, and yet it is surrounded by some of the worst squalor on earth. They're constantly scraping away those red mountains to make room for more apartments. Look at all those little fishing boats tied together along the docks!"

"I see them on this side too," Jack replied, "and there are a lot more of them back to the north, along the Kowloon coast. Some of those kids living there grow up without ever setting foot on the dry land, I've heard."

"I suppose you're right. They just ran out of space too soon; or the government won't accept them as citizens. Maybe if we find a lot of oil in this part of the Pacific Rim their chances for better living conditions will improve."

"Let's hope so. Now, since we missed our lunch and have some altitude, I think I'll find me one of those sandwiches before the technicians eat 'em all. Do you want anything?"

"No, thanks. I had a big breakfast, and if Andy Cheston has my tux back from the cleaners as he promised, I'll be running to the Dai-Ichi Hotel as soon as we arrive in Tokyo. It'll be quite a show, entertaining all those bigwigs. I hear the Japanese foreign minister is going to be there."

"I wonder if I'll get to meet him. Maybe I shouldn't eat now either, Harold, but I'm hungry. As exploration manager, you'll be in charge of introductions in the receiving line, won't you? Do you have your list of ministers and chairmen handy?"

"Yes, it's here, but I don't have all of the names memorized. That's what I must do now on our way back to Tokyo. That, and work on the pronunciation. Maybe Bill Hanby will take me off the hook if I stumble, since he knows most of the guests socially. He's a great guy to work for. I just hope I don't screw up in front of our board chairman, Gil Eason. A gaff there could shorten my World Oil career very quickly."

"Not to worry. He's been well advised of your capabilities and knows you don't take any bullshit. Sure you don't want something to munch on?" He tossed the question back over his shoulder as he labored up the short aisle of the climbing plane; but Jack Franz was never to reach the food chest by the pilot's door.

A blinding flash suddenly ripped a giant gash in the metal skin across the top of the cabin, and Harold watched in awe as Jack's body seemed to float slowly away, and he hardly heard the scream. Then it dived through the opening and into the void beyond. In apparent slow motion, it was followed by the front seats with the astonished men still strapped in them. It was as if a giant hand had broken the plane apart at the wing roots, and given it a sharp spin toward the infinite.

Harold was dazed and shocked, slowly realizing the tail section had separated from the front of the plane. He could see the nose and wings slowly swirling as they drifted away in the bright blue afternoon sky. The tail section then tilted gently downward, and began fishtailing toward the sea below. Faster and faster it fell, increasing its rotation toward an inevitable death in the sea, far below.

Harold had one last fleeting thought: to wish he had explained more about those sons of bitches in Saigon to Andy Cheston when they spoke on the phone this morning. Then he wouldn't have to learn about and face their underhanded dealings himself.

Nothing more mattered for him now. The great splashes of the plane parts into the South China Sea went seemingly unnoticed by man, and only the sharks and sea snakes remained to search for sustenance in the sinking debris of those troubled waters.

# One

Andy Cheston paused nervously beside the potted raintree plant guarding the main entrance of the Tokyo Imperial Dai-Ichi Hotel. He was gazing anxiously at the occupants of arriving limousines as they pulled up the steep slope of the hotel drive, looking carefully to see if he could recognize his friend. He had already phoned several times for Harold Blanton at their apartment, but there had been no answer. That was strange, because his plane was due back hours ago. As exploration manager, Harold's absence from this World Oil formal reception may even be considered an insult by their ministerial-level visitors who may not think it was unavoidable. Andy was becoming genuinely worried about his roommate, knowing his normal strict adherence to schedules.

They were gathering in Tokyo at the famous hotel for the gala reception from countries around the Pacific Rim at Harold's personal invitation in the name of World Oil. Many of them would consider Harold their host, even though several higher ranking company officials were present from the United States.

A slight prickle of fear began to crawl down Andy's spine, and he willed it to go away. Something must be seriously wrong, but there was no time to think about that. He'd have to soothe the feathers of World Oil's upper management himself until Harold arrived. Perhaps his plane had been held up by weather in Hong Kong. It was the only explanation he could think of.

As a well dressed couple emerged from a limousine, he could see them dimly silhouetted against the lighted backdrop of the Diet Building across the moat of the Emperor's Palace. They were Japanese, for he wore tails and she was in a resplendent kimono. The reception would be a fashion parade, all right. A line of vehicles was awaiting their turn to enter the portico and deposit passengers in front of the protected ballroom entrance. It was too slow a process to watch.

Andy tugged at the hem of his formal jacket to be sure it was in place, then patted the maroon cummerbund and again straightened his bow tie. He was nervous. Mentally he ticked off the guest list. He must get back inside, because Wellman would be missing him. James Wellman, his assistant, had been assigned the responsibility of making sure every place card was in its proper position, and arranged strictly according to design by protocol. He might need some help, and he felt conspicuous standing here like a company doorman. It was late, and he could not wait outside for his immediate boss, Harold, any longer.

"Yes, Doctor Cheston?" The colorfully uniformed doorman gave him his full attention as he approached.

"Are you sure there have been no phone messages?" Andy asked. "We are about to have a social disaster."

"No, Doctor Cheston, no one has made a call for you," the ornamented doorman spoke politely.

"OK, thank you. Please get a message to me inside if you hear from Doctor Blanton. It's very important," Andy stated firmly.

He turned and stepped inside, and was pleased to hear the mixed hum of voices and music. His eyes automatically swept the room to assure himself all was in order. Already there was a crowd around the bar, and soft danceable music filled the hall. It annoyed him that Harold had not told him earlier, when they talked by phone, what the important business was that had prolonged his stay in Hong Kong. Perhaps it was related to the new Vietnamese venture.

Even so, he thought grumpily, Harold could have called back to tell him he was going to be late. He knew how important this reception would be to the future Pacific Rim operations of World Oil. But such calls were not always easy to make. Maybe the company driver, Jimmy-san, hadn't made it to the airport in time. Not likely, Andy thought, wiping his sweaty palms against his trousers. He had always been a careful driver, but still . . . . There could be a thousand reasons for the delay, so quit worrying, he told himself.

Turning his attention to the brightly lighted interior, he skirted the crowd grouped around the reception line and moved toward the speaker's table. He had no wish to inform their Tokyo director, William Hanby, of Harold's absence just yet. Then he saw James Wellman, his fellow explorationist, talking intently with a group of the Japanese Idimitsu Oil Company geologists on the other side of the dance floor, which was beginning to grow crowded. He turned away from checking the table and headed in James' direction.

As he approached he tried to pick up their trend of conversation, but heard them conversing in Japanese. James had learned a few words of the local language, and was popular among their Japanese friends because of his congenial quiet way and staid intelligence. Andy had noticed, though quiet he may be, how things got done when Wellman was around.

James smiled as Andy paused beside him, a set of Thai star-sapphire studs flashed at his shirtfront. On him they went almost unnoticed, because he was so unobtrusive and he normally almost melted into the woodwork. He needed to be drawn out more, Andy knew.

"We missed you, sir. How's the weather out?"

Andy knew what he really was asking was, Is it bad enough to stop aircraft landings? "It's nice enough to have a party here, isn't it? Perhaps it's bad elsewhere," he answered.

James nodded briefly, and formally introduced Andy to those members of the group he did not already know. Andy focused on retaining names, for he knew it was good manners, especially in a foreign land, to call people by their name if at all possible. It was important for them to make a cooperative impression in their host country.

He and James were at ease with each other since they had worked together on projects in several Far Eastern locations over the years. The common problem throughout their professions of competition and cooperation between geologists and geophysicists did not affect them. Each had a great respect for the other's abilities and professional ethics. They were both eligible bachelors, and had spent many memorable nights out on the town together, seeing what they could stir up in a myriad of Eastern cities, so they were far from strangers.

Both of the explorers had also seen duty in the service in Vietnam. Andy was Army, and a lot of his close friends hadn't returned. James' buddies in the Marines were pilots, and had fared a little better. Now they were back in the Far East, fighting a battle of a different sort—developing international commerce for a major oil company that had intentions of carving out a large piece of the Pacific Rim commercial pie.

This formal party was a celebration hosted by World Oil to announce their entry into a new oil exploration program in the Far East. The Board of Directors of the company had come from Houston to announce their immediate decision to explore for hydrocarbons in the offshore waters of Vietnam. They believed the future giant oil discoveries, outside the Middle East, should result from exploration and production around the Pacific Rim. World Oil had based their future plans on that premise, and meant to obtain the lion's share of that new progressive market.

Quickly, Andy's eyes scanned the crowded room. He was pleased to note that all of the directors were present and greeting the guests, from

Chairman Gilbert Eason, and, Company President Phillip Harrison, right on down through the vice presidents to the new Tokyo director, William Hanby.

Hanby was busy arranging the receiving line so all the directors would be certain to meet their important and distinguished guests. Andy had known Hanby for several years, having worked with him throughout the countries bordering the South China Sea, and he was well aware of the importance of protocol at these functions. His years of service in the U.S. Consular Corps and in Far Eastern politics made him a good choice to direct World Oil's technical staff in this area. He knew enough to work his magic behind the scenes, and leave the technical operations to his competent staff.

As Andy watched Hanby smoothly conduct the introductions in the receiving line, he couldn't help but grin. Bill could out-tact most diplomats, and still hold his own in technical discussions around the directors' table. Although he was not an explorer, he was an excellent judge of personnel, and good at assembling a team of geologists and geophysicists who could provide reports and maps necessary for selling programs to higher management.

All was set for the scheduled impending arrival of the prime minister, so Andy and James excused themselves from the Japanese group to make one last round, making certain none of the place cards had been moved by the beehive of servers who continuously circled tables, adjusting settings and centerpieces. They had gone to great lengths to ensure that each minister and his wife, or feminine guest, was seated in the proper location as dictated by rank.

The principal table was for the Japanese Diet ministers in attendance with their ladies, plus the ambassadorial level personnel of other countries who had flown in for the occasion. They represented those nations with oil interests bordering the western Pacific and the eastern Indian Oceans. Hanby had jokingly told him earlier that they held the reins of commerce, and those seated on the floor below were there to make the wheels turn.

All were gradually entering into more spirited discussions as they became better acquainted and made good use of the parading waiters' offerings on their well stocked trays. Andy noted the guests were gradually separating into their own circles of friends and nationalities. The Japanese were concentrating at the end where the bar was set up, while the Chinese gathered in little knots toward the stage near the orchestra. There they chatted quietly and sipped their soft drinks.

One small isolated and unfriendly group of Vietnamese men and quiet "dates" kept to themselves near the middle of the dance floor. It was as though they wished to speak privately. Each was accompanied by a well dressed young lady, and this was troublesome for Andy, for it was not the custom of Vietnamese to bring wives to such functions. He wondered what they could be discussing and why they were so separated from the others, since they were their "star" guests at this function.

He recognized some of the Vietnamese technical personnel. His eyes focused on a man at the center of their cluster. It was the renegade of their young oil group, Dong Huan Chou, of course. He was easily recognized, with his head of bushy black hair and his acne-scarred face. He hid his gaze behind aviator-sized dark glasses, which made it difficult to tell where his attention was focused.

Andy suppressed a feeling of intense dislike for Dong Huan Chou. He was a repulsive character, and looked like the typical black marketeer who had roamed the Saigon streets during the late war. In their dealings with the Vietnamese cartel, Dong always seemed to be at odds with the recommendations of his group, but somehow he held his own as assistant energy minister. He undoubtedly had friends in high places.

Suddenly Dong's shaded eyes seemed to focus across the room as his heavy glasses tilted upward. Andy turned to see what had caught his attention. Tim McAllister, a prim, concise, small gentleman from the U.S. East Coast, suddenly caught Andy's eye. Tim, World Oil's Tokyo administrative manager, was the only one in the huge ballroom who seemed to be moving through the crowd with any purpose. Why should that be of interest to Dong?

Andy watched as McAllister moved directly to the rear of the receiving line, where he spoke for a few moments with Bill Hanby; then he threaded his way among the guests, obviously seeking someone. His gaze met Andy's, and he hurried toward him. Instinct warned Andy that something important was on his mind.

McAllister was a serious administrator who had progressed upward through the accounting ranks by his ability to concentrate on business; he was never deterred by personalities. He did not stop on his way to converse with any of the groups as he threaded his way, even though he knew many of them from his business contacts. Obviously, he had something much more serious to discuss or attend to.

Andy nudged James, nodding for him to notice the approaching Tim. When he arrived, he was a little out of breath, as though he had just wrestled a great problem to the ground, and lost.

"Andy, James, we have a seating problem. The prime minister is arriving very soon, but his secretary just called to say his wife has become ill, and cannot attend."

He paused a moment to get his breath. Is that all? Andy thought with relief. He had been sure it was something to do with Harold's ill-timed absence.

"That's a shame, Tim, but how can we help you?" Andy responded.

"Bill Hanby asked me to have you rearrange the seating at the speakers' table to fill the vacancy she will leave beside Chairman Gil Eason. That means a big, quick shuffle all around. Either that, or we invent some qualified replacement as Eason's dinner partner. Someone who will fill the protocol prerequisites. Can you handle that?"

"Sure," Andy replied lightheartedly. "We'll just call up a club on the Ginza and have them rush a mama-san geisha right over. Preferably one whose eyes have been corrected, speaks fluent English, and whose skin is silky like a swansdown baby's backside. No trouble at all," he joked.

Tim stared at him unresponsively and said nothing. Andy drew a deep breath.

"We'll take care of it one way or another, Tim. Tell Hanby we accept the responsibility," Andy replied belatedly, seeing that Tim would not respond.

Tim's gaze held Andy's for a long moment. He had a strange, unbelieving expression, as though he would never understand the corporation's explorers.

"OK, you've got the word, so now you can handle it," he said slowly and rather sharply as he turned and almost ran away, looking back once to see if anyone was going to respond to the order. He seemed pleased to have that problem out of his hands, but his belated grin told Andy they were still friends.

Andy turned to James, "Well, we had better get moving. Now we really do have a job."

"Whatever we do will put someone's nose out of joint," James spoke mournfully. "It has to be someone socially acceptable—that means Oriental, and someone who speaks English, so she can keep Eason occupied in case the prime minister doesn't have anything to discuss."

Andy viewed the crowd as he and James moved quickly along behind the speaker's chair. Together they reviewed the names on the elaborately scripted cards. When he glanced toward the crowd, there was the Vietnamese, Dong, still obviously watching attentively in their direction. Why was he so interested in them and their actions?

"There's no one—" Andy began. Then his gaze lifted to the reception line. A smile tugged at his lips.

"There is our answer," he said. "Look at that beauty just coming through the line. Boy, she's a knockout!"

"And check the way Eason is talking to her. They seem pretty friendly," James pointed out.

"I wonder why he wouldn't rather have her for a dinner partner than some porky Japanese mama-san dropping rice all over her kimono with chopsticks. Let's find out who that old gentleman is behind her," Andy said.

"If he's not her grandfather, he ought to be ashamed of himself," James added quickly.

"That wouldn't be too unusual for this part of the world," Andy responded, not bothering to smile.

"She would fill the bill, if she has the proper credentials, and she has already impressed Eason," James grinned.

"I've seen a lot of girls around here, and always wondered where the good-looking ones went," Andy agreed. "This one is really different, and she must have been hiding out—or the old man keeps her hidden."

Andy was thinking as he watched the lady, that it must be because she's a lot taller than most, and she picked up a lot of poise and conversational gestures from somewhere. She has Oriental polish even without a kimono, he thought.

"I'd say she has the credentials without even asking. I've got to get over there and meet her," Andy stated.

"It's agreed then. I'll go find out who they are, and get the chief's consent to have her join him for dinner."

"Good. While you do that I'll get a card ready, and we won't have to change but one," Andy replied.

A few minutes later, James was back, flushed with excitement.

"She's the granddaughter of the old fellow, all right. Her name is Lin Jin Hoe. Her grandfather is the head of one of our most useful shipbuilding companies. He has headquartered here and in Hong Kong ever since he was forced out of Saigon."

"Does Hanby know them?" Andy asked.

"Yes, and they are high enough in the social circles to merit a seat at the main table. We need to impress Mr. Hoe anyway, if we want to do business in this part of the world. He's one of the few who can operate in Japan, Hong Kong, and Singapore, and still retain contacts in Vietnam. She and her grandfather are already ticketed at the main table."

"A knockout like her should be at the center table anyway!" Andy remarked, admiring the length of her shapely legs as he watched her move elegantly across the room. "And she walks in high heels better than most women do in sneakers."

Lin Jin Hoe wore a silver lamé sheath that reached the floor, but was split on both sides so her sometimes exposed shapely legs could move her safely on rather high silver heels. The orchid she wore was huge, probably imported, and it had a deep purple color. It really stood out on the silvery background. It must be taped to her smooth, bare shoulder.

"So you think you'd like to meet her?" James asked.

"It has been a while since I've seen a gook chick I'd really like to know. What impresses me most about her is the way she moves—like a tigress. It's as though she's stalking something, but she doesn't let it show."

James couldn't help but laugh at Andy's abnormal enthusiasm, so he quickly agreed, "You'll get to meet her, then, and I'll change the cards."

"I guess I've had too many 'nightclub-type' girlie introductions in Nam. Just be sure you don't ever tell my twin sister what I said when she comes to Tokyo visiting. She'd disown me if she knew I even looked at an Oriental girl seriously, let alone dated one."

"Doesn't she like Orientals?" James asked.

"Yes, working in their grape vineyards, but they don't fit into her California social set. She thinks I should only date her sorority sisters."

Carefully holding a pen, Andy deftly lettered the new place card, and handed it to James.

"Here, you locate this properly, and I'll break the news to Miss Lin Jin Hoe that she has been promoted. I hope she considers it an honor," he said, as he left to seek out a proper introduction.

There'd be a chair vacant at their own table, Andy thought, if Harold didn't arrive. He'd have been happy to have her occupy it. But then, he sighed, he'd be talked about by all the expatriate wives, and word might even get back to his sister in the States.

Within a few moments Andy had joined a group where Miss Hoe's grandfather was deeply engrossed in trade discussions with other businessmen, presumably shippers. He soon arranged to be introduced to the gentleman by an acquaintance.

"Honorable Li Hong Hoe, may I present Doctor Andrew Cheston, senior regional geologist of our hosts. He is to be stationed here in World Oil's Tokyo office," his friend stated as he made the introduction.

"I am pleased to meet you, sir," Andy replied, bowing slightly. His gaze shifted to the beautiful woman beside the old man. He coughed slightly, waiting. After many compliments about the beauty of the ice carvings over the bar and the enormous spread of flowers surrounding the dance floor, Mr. Li Hong Hoe got around to introducing Andy to his granddaughter.

"Doctor Andrew Cheston, this is my favorite and most beautiful granddaughter, Lin Jin Hoe. She resides now with my family here in Tokyo. She had recently graduated from college, and I hope to entice her to work in my office." He was now all smiles, and obviously the doting grandparent. "She has just arrived from Hong Kong, where she lived with her mother after their departure from war-torn Vietnam."

Hong Kong? The word rang a bell, and suddenly Andy remembered Harold Blanton still had not arrived. He'd really fouled up this time, and Hanby would be upset. Andy was delighted with the introduction, because Hoe's remembering his name meant the impression he had made was a favorable one. Judging from the warmth of their greetings, he was sure their decision to invite her to sit with their chairman and the prime minister was a proper one.

"I have a humble request to make in the name of our chairman, Mr. Eason." Andy turned to speak to Li Hong Hoe with a smile. "With your kind permission," he addressed the elder, "it would be an honor if you would allow your granddaughter, Lin Jin, to join Mr. Eason at his table for dinner." Andy felt the tightening in his gut, for he knew his request sounded too stilted.

He tensely waited for her rejection, but Lin Jin smiled. Her acceptance was ensured as she looked directly and deeply into Andy's eyes. His spine turned to jelly under her intense, unflinching gaze. This black-haired girl was really a cat. A cat with great black eyes. Her manner was positive, without being pushy. He caught his breath. She really had something he could admire. He wasn't even considering being careful. That could come later, when his loving twin sister arrived to visit him in Tokyo.

The dinner arrangement was acceptable to Li Hong Hoe, for he had been advised only that he and his granddaughter were to be seated somewhere at the head table. Andy excused himself, assuring Miss Hoe he would come to escort her to the table when the dinner service gong sounded.

Andy then returned to their group, and to talk to James Wellman.

"I see you made a good choice in selecting Eason's dinner partner," he complimented Andy as he nodded toward Li Hong Hoe. "Who is going to take Harold's seat now?"

"I don't know. We'd better save it for him. I was sure he'd be here by this time," Andy said, his gay mood suddenly melting. "We'll have to find someone to sit with us in Harold's chair later if he doesn't arrive, I guess. He's going to miss the whole show, damn it! He's needed here to meet these people officially."

The party was going well. The guests had been given time to make a circuit of the floor to observe and remark at the elaborate decorations. Gradually the orchestra music was toned down to signify a momentary end to the dancing, and the great gong sounded its call for guests to find their dinner partners and their proper protocol seating location. Andy hurried away to find the lovely Lin Jin Hoe, and escort her to Gilbert Eason's group.

She was not a short woman, as were so many Orientals. She was only a couple of inches shorter than he. Her hair was a silky solid black, long and straight, hanging almost to her waist. The long strand of black jade beads she wore lay luxuriously on the lamé sheath, falling almost to her black belted waist. Her earrings matched the jade, and she carried a small, beaded black bag. Her perfectly sculptured face was framed by short bangs. In all the multitude of beautiful women dressed in their very best, Lin Jin Hoe was not hard to select as one of the most stunning. She was awaiting his arrival.

Chairman Eason was engaged in conversation with the prime minister and several other business leaders, including the American ambassador. Andy remembered that Lin Jin had not met the ambassador and his wife, and he wondered how their seating arrangement would meet with the wife's pleasure. For a brief moment he wondered if she was like his twin, who held a grudge against socializing with any Orientals. Then he remembered she was a diplomat's wife, and would never show any dislike, especially in this country.

Andy met the chairman of the board at one side and presented Lin Jin, whom Gilbert Eason remembered and immediately welcomed by name, saying how delighted he was that she could join them for dinner. He then presented both of them to the group, and the conversation continued to include her without so much as a pause. Andy was relieved to note that she fit into the noted group with complete acceptance, just as though she had come with the prime minister himself. They began to move off toward their table, and Andy excused himself to return to his group.

As he was leaving, Lin Jin turned and said simply, "Thank you, Doctor Cheston," with a warm smile and a quick touch of her hand to his arm.

His heart melted, and he felt as though an electric charge had found him. I must see this lady again, he thought.

James stood near the table they had selected for themselves and their Idimitsu friends. When Andy arrived, they were already seating themselves. Since they had no place cards, they were doing their best to arrange a boy-girl order without leaving anyone to talk in English among a group who spoke only Japanese. Andy politely suggested a shuffling of chairs to get some of the Japanese wives together so they could speak and be understood. They all smiled and bowed as though they knew what he had done.

The group had just settled down when he saw Tim McAllister hurrying out of the side office again. He was moving with a purpose, even quicker than before.

"Here comes Tim with another message, it looks like," he said to James. "Now, I wonder what momentous changes will be dictated."

When Tim swept up to the group, he frowned and motioned for Andy to join him at one side. His eyes looked glazed, and his hands were shaking uncontrollably. Something was affecting him seriously.

"What's the matter, Tim?" Andy asked, as he held his elbow firmly to steady him.

"We've had a horrible disaster. I just got the news by phone from the embassy. Our company plane blew up just after it took off from Hong Kong." He gasped, and continued, "The whole plane's gone." He was out of breath. "Our entire crew is missing!" His whole body shook, and it was getting worse as he held on to Andy's arm.

Andy Cheston stared at Tim in disbelief. He had never been so shocked in his entire life. His stomach muscles clinched, and he fought against the shock. "Oh my God!" he panted. His thoughts reeled around him as he reached unsteadily for the back of a nearby chair. His brain struggled to regain control of his body. He'd lost many friends in the Vietnamese War, but there you were ready for casualties, and expected them. Here, they were living in the civilized world, and such tragedies were not normal. He mentally pictured himself as though from far off, grabbing himself around the shoulders. There must be a way his mind could hold on to the present so he could understand what was happening.

If the plane blew up, and everyone was missing, then all of the company people including Harold Blanton were gone. Now who would carry out the company's exploration? He must get a hold of himself, Andy thought. This was not the time to go to pieces. He would have to mourn the loss of these friends later. Now he must decide if there was any immediate action to be taken.

Tim was completely breathless, gasping for air. He could hardly speak as he sat down. "There were six company people on the plane, with a pilot and copilot," he finally stammered. "The embassy is sending over a confirming fax to the ambassador by special messenger. He should be here soon."

"I was sure Harold must be having troubles of some kind, but I never suspected anything like this. Where did it happen, and how did you find out?" Andy asked in rapid succession, already knowing the answers.

"The Aeronautics Company called our office and Hanby's home, then the hotel and the embassy. They had a hard time finding anyone, because we're all over here. The embassy finally realized that someone could locate a company rep here with the ambassador, at the Dai-Ichi." Tim was overcome with emotion.

"Were there any survivors?" Andy asked.

"No, nothing. A fishing trawler saw the plane blow up about fifteen minutes out of Hong Kong, and reported it by radio to the British Coastal Patrol. The pieces were scattered all over the South China Sea. They must have just reached cruising altitude." Tim got the message out slowly.

"Harold was on it, and our accountant Jack Franz, and two auditors visiting here from Houston who were working that hush-hush job in Thailand. Also, Harold told me on the phone there were two men coming with them who logged our well at the rig drilling offshore from Jakarta. They were returning from testing the new discovery there."

Andy's brain was going a mile a minute, as he glanced up to see if they were creating a disturbance. The dinner entrée was being served at the head table, but suddenly he caught a glimpse of the black haired assistant energy minister from Vietnam, Dong Huan Chou. He was watching them so intently that the waiter was having to wait to serve his plate. Why was he so interested? was Andy's fleeting thought. Did he know or expect something?

"They'll get us a passenger list and a cargo manifest in the morning." There were tears in his eyes as he tried to go on with the expression of his thoughts. "What should we do? We must notify their families."

"We need to pass the word to Hanby first," Andy said, "but it's not the time for this news to be spread around to this whole group." He considered Tim's condition. "I'll go advise Hanby quietly now, but let's not upset the entire party, right in the middle of their entrée."

He moved away from the group with McAllister, signaling Wellman to join them. After a fast explanation, James quickly seated himself in the nearest chair.

"I can't believe it. What would make a plane explode in midair, besides a bomb?" Tears began to roll down his cheeks.

Andy said, "Get a hold of yourself—we can't break up now; and take care of Tim for a while. I'm going to speak to Hanby," as he headed for the speakers' table.

Andy wondered to himself if there was an opposition group so strong they would go to terrorist lengths to disrupt the company's newly organized Far East operations. Why would it pay for anyone to do such a thing? On the surface, everyone had been so cordial, but then things were not always the way they were presented, or appeared to be, in the Orient.

# Two

The dusty black Mercedes eased through the gateway into the compound of the old Dong Huan Chou family estate, and stopped on the gravel patio opposite the main heavy teak doors. It was just after dark, and the dim light flickered on over the entryway. Dong was at home after his exhausting trek. He lived in the area of Cu Chi, to the north and beyond the Tan Son Nhat International Airport from what the locals used to call "Saigon."

Only the white painted rocks separated the gravel paddock from the single step up to the entryway beneath the overhanging portico. The light was a single neon bulb that glowed weakly above the door. When privacy was required in the compound beyond that furnished by the high block fence, there were heavy wooden gates that could be moved along their tracks to seal the narrow entrance. The ancient estate-house was protected much like a fortress.

While the guards from the exotically decorated Spirit Houses tended the gates, the chauffeur and guard from the front seat of the Mercedes quickly left their places to tend to their duties of handling doors and providing the security that they deemed necessary in this location.

Dong smiled inwardly as he thought proudly of the not-too-distant past when his estate had been used as a secret command center by the Vietcong. He felt differently here at home from the pensive mood he had been in at the World Oil reception in Tokyo. His white linen suit's wrinkles showed the wearing effect of a day spent in offices with little air-conditioning. There he felt the pressure of his work, but here at home he answered to no one. His spirits began to soar, for he knew he had accomplished the NLF's purpose.

The fields of an ancient estate surrounded the villa, and the rice paddies extended down to the klong. They lay atop a network of tunnels which, some say, ran for hundreds of miles up-country. Their connections through the dank and sometimes water-filled underground chambers had enabled the Vietcong forces to survive the bombing and artillery fire of the war. Now they were mostly caved in, unkept, and largely reclaimed by the constant seepage of groundwater brought by the heavy rains.

The destitute people who remained on his estate scraped out a meager existence from the land. When the North Vietnamese cadres had come, Dong Huan Chou had been accepted as one of their own. They left him in charge of the estate and promoted his education and later his high government position. Now his laborers were content to live in their hovels and tend the paddies for their pitiful share of the lush crops. It was enough for the former Khmer Krom just to eat their *banh cuon* (boiled dumplings of rice flour with pork), with mushrooms and onion spices covered with *nuoc mam* (fish sauce). They might even leave a tiny gift at one of his elaborately decorated Spirit Houses, as their beliefs prescribed.

Dong was proud that his Spirit Houses were larger than the usual worship places. They had been converted from guard houses on the outside corners of the compound, and now they were sometimes pressed into double service when he deemed extra guards were needed.

Life was hard for the peasants since the war, but anything was better than being sent to the dreaded reeducation camps. In those awful penal colonies, anyone suspected of opposition to the government worked on farms while being taught the Communist line of Marx and Lenin. They lived under starving conditions for years, with little hope of release except by death. It was the Communist way of making positions in the local economy for the cadre brought from the north and Hanoi to supervise postwar production. There the bodoi administered their lessons, with terrible beatings being the proper manner of instruction. Dong had been known as an outspoken supporter of the new system.

Throughout the war, Dong had dealt in the black market. He bought his way into the necessary government schools afterward, thereby attaining a high stature in the underground. That had carried over to gain him his promotion to his position in the commerce of the present government. He gloried in the knowledge that his personal friend was the wartime secretary of the Vietminh, or the Communist Party in Saigon. This friendship had served him well.

He would never admit, even to himself, that the Vietcong victory had not turned the country into the instant economic "Garden of Eden" they had assured the people their hard-won peace would bring. Even the infrastructure left by the Americans had quickly gone to ruin.

Dong reminded himself that oil production offshore would make the greatest difference in their economy. It was their key to becoming a world power—one that would be respected for its riches. And he, Dong Huan Chou, would be there to get his cut when they "carried off the flag," for he was the assistant minister of energy. He would one day be promoted, and the Vietnamese must establish the production themselves, and for their own account, he thought grimly.

It was a cool evening for Vietnam, and a gentle breeze tried but failed to stir the humid air. A crack of light appeared at the door, which was then quickly opened wide by his yeoman and servant clad in a thin, white flowing baba.

"Good evening, master," Tan Tran said in a quiet voice.

"Come, Tan Tran; I need you," he commanded as he left the car.

The wiry little man was dressed for the weather in a loose baba, and he hurried out to carry Dong's heavy briefcase. He gave a grunt when it proved to be much heavier than expected. It was really a silvery aluminum suitcase, twice the thickness of a normal briefcase. Dong always kept it near him, for it was where he secreted his valuables.

The servant toted it carefully toward the entryway, as the chauffeur and guard from the front seat of the Mercedes quickly flanked the door. After a short conversation with the driver, Dong continued inside. The Mercedes pulled quietly away, to be hidden from prying eyes somewhere in a rear shed.

Dong did not smile as he preceded Tan Tran through the heavy entry door into the reception foyer of the estate mansion. He envied his servant's comfortable pajama-type suit, as it looked cool and was entirely appropriate for the climate. Also, he knew it could hide a multitude of pockets, such as storage for a weapon, or a grenade, if one were so inclined.

Dong was glad to be at home at last, as he made his way toward his den. He removed his dark glasses as he went. It had been a hard day, and it was still far from being finished.

"Bring me my drink," he directed in Vietnamese to no one visible.

He was met by a pretty young servant girl, dressed in a light robe. She knelt and took his shoes while he stepped into slippers, and then accepted his coat as he gave her a pinch and a quick lascivious pat. She meekly bowed her way to a corner and disappeared through a string-bead draped doorway. Dong continued through French doors into his inner lounge and office, still followed closely by his yeoman carrying the aluminum case.

He paced slowly and thoughtfully into the interior sitting room of his villa, holding his dark glasses by one temple. He clearly considered this his villa, though his rights had actually come through his stepmother, Ibu. She had owned the estate when she became his father's second wife. He, himself, had earned the fetid wartime friendships that paid for his retention of those rights, only because it was decreed by the Vietcong.

Dong carefully seated himself on the cushioned rattan sofa against the wall and across the large room from the French doorway. In front of him was a low work table, faced by two sturdy chairs. Soon a well dressed and beautiful girl in a bright red gown appeared with a silver tray containing crystal glasses with lemon and ice, an inch and a half of a clear liquid, and a bottle of Schweppes tonic. He greeted her by name.

"Vu Thi, have you missed your lover this week?" he asked, expecting no answer.

She gave her most seductive smile as he directed her with a nod to place his drink on the low table, for he did not trust her to pour. Dong did not trust anyone where matters of his health were concerned. Only the wise and those who were meticulously careful continued to live near the top of this dung heap they called a government. Dong had been cunning, and had edged his way well up into the controlling echelon of the Cong. And he had plans to go much higher. That was where great wealth could be achieved.

He settled into the soft cushions of the bamboo divan, then permitted himself to relax. He had returned from an important business trek to Japan where he had been invited as the representative of the energy minister. Now he was tired, but he must remain alert, for he had an important task to complete this evening for the NLF. He was inwardly very proud of the international incident he had arranged.

Vu Thi made an effort to snuggle beside him on the divan, but he waved her roughly away and turned his attention to call Tan Tran. He was aware Vu Thi left in a fit of pique as he spoke to his yeoman in the local dialect. He told him of his trek to Tokyo, about the people he had met, and of related activities. He dwelt on the disruption caused by the notice that had been received by World Oil's leaders during the formal reception with the prime minister and the ambassador.

"Tan," he directed, "I will have visitors at eleven—important visitors. Permit only the leader, Thanh Cong, to enter this room, and see that the guards remain alert outside in the compound."

"Yes, master," Tan Tran replied, returning to his desk.

Dong checked first to see that his personal weapons were where they should be. Dropping the dark glasses into a drawer under the table, he inspected the clip of the automatic pistol resting there. It was full. He felt a certain thrill when he touched the cold gold inlaid metal shaft of the stiletto tucked away beneath the side cushion. One could not be too careful, he mused.

Realizing that Tan Tran had not left the room, he became angry. His servant was not quickly heeding his orders. He was aware that when a Mercedes left a Central Bank after a late evening stop, the likelihood of its being followed by robbers was great. He must be cautious and keep his guards on alert.

"Tan, go now and recheck the security in the entry compound. Also, see that you search my guests well to ensure their 'cleanliness' when they arrive."

Tan was small, and looked innocuous in his baba, but Dong knew his searches were quick and efficient. He moved like a shadow, but always felt every extra lump with a knowing touch.

"Yes, master," Tan replied as before, but now he quickly exited through the French doors. Soon he returned and settled silently at his desk in the far corner, pretending to read the figures in his ledgers.

The heat felt stifling under the pair of lamps in the room as Dong began to sweat. A fan whined wearily in one corner. There was not enough electricity to run the air-conditioner. It was now completely dark outside— a night with no moon, and what little breeze there was had gone. Dong suffered in silence, and he could occasionally hear the heavy tramp of the booted guards as they passed on the gravel in the compound. Dong waited impatiently, for his visitors were overdue.

His attention was attracted by the tinkle of the new ice cubes as Vu Thi set a fresh glass on the table. He gave her a leering smile, and rubbed his hand down her thigh as she passed near to him.

"Vu Thi, await me in the bedroom," he said in the local dialect in an attempt for forgiveness. "There, take the other glass with you."

He stared with a lustful smile, for he enjoyed watching as she walked away. He was aware of her pique, but he had Cong business to complete. Vu Thi knew her job, and she fulfilled its requirements well, having gained her skills in the back streets of Saigon at the end of the war. The old campaign posters rattled on the wall when the oscillating fan turned past them, and the faded picture of Mao was framed in its place of honor.

Dong waited and listened, hearing only the buzzing of the insects. As the fan droned on, Tan Tran made a constant ticking rattle of an abacus as he thumbed through a stack of papers. The constant movement disturbed Dong. He considered directing his servant to be quiet.

"Tan, advise Mother Ibu that I will see her now," Dong spoke louder instead, for he felt a certain tension brought on by his incomplete business arrangement.

Tan Tran rose immediately, and left by a side entry. Dong went on with his drinking and the review of notes. His lifelong habit of writing had served him and the Cong well. He was proud that the historical files kept in the secret tunnel below were always in readiness to make reports to his leaders.

"Ibu will come soon," Tan Tran replied as he returned to his table.

"Bring the silver case to me," Dong commanded sharply.

Tan Tran placed the case on the table, and silently worked it open. Dong knew that his silence did not indicate lack of observation. He was confident his servant was highly capable, for he kept him informed of all happenings around the compound. Only Ibu could give Tan Tran directions when the master was away.

"Come, Tan," Dong said, after mixing his drink to his satisfaction. "See the beauty of the earth that I have brought from the bank this night. This ingot will pay the NLF Party's just debts for a job well done."

He brought out a carefully wrapped block. Removing the cover, he asked, "Isn't this lustrous nugget beautiful? I love the sight of its golden yellow. Just to pass my hands across a kilo of gold such as this makes me certain I'll never be considered a *parvenu*." He was no upstart. His family would one day be one of the richest in all Vietnam. He grinned, gloating greedily in his reverie.

"Indeed, master; gold is beautiful in all forms. In the ingot it has added value of easy portability. The news indicates the terrorists did their job well, and they should be pleased with the payment," Tan Tran replied, honored that he was being considered.

"Yes, they must be paid well, for they may have other services to perform in the future. I wish this settlement could somehow be avoided, for this ingot would fit well into my collection below."

At a swishing of the beads, he looked up. Ibu entered slowly from the rear door, hobbling carefully around the sparsely furnished room. It was almost as though she were in a coma. Obviously she had been highly medicated, to ease the pain from her perpetually aching bones. Dong thought how good it was of him to furnish her with the white powder that took away the great hurt. It was plain that her mind was still in firm control of her actions, however, for her eyes, though narrowed, were still bright.

There was only one comfortable seat in the room where Dong sat with his work spread before him. The pair of formal sturdy chairs were for business guests, who were to be made uncomfortable by intention. Mother Ibu made her way carefully and painfully onto one of those, which was not ideal for her comfort. Dong did not feel a need to stand or to show respect.

"Show me what you have brought, Dong Chou," she said brusquely, speaking in the local dialect. She leaned as near as possible to the case sitting open on the table before him.

He delayed for a few moments, for effect. Picking up the block from its neat balsa wooden box, he handed it carefully to Ibu. It was heavy for her to hold with her arthritic hands, but she cradled it lovingly. Her eyes gleamed as she rubbed her hands along the deeply molded letters in its casting. To watch the old woman hold the fortune gave him a warm glow inside. In this light, it was a lustrous golden yellow.

"It is a shameful thing to pass on such wealth, even in a good party cause," stated Ibu, lost in thought.

Dong only nodded, his face carefully masking his thoughts.

Ibu continued, "From long and distressing experience, I know that such quantities of gold really have no home. It is only of value if one owns it; and then only when well hidden. Or, it may be for the payment of great debts. From your expression I see that you love the yellow metal as much as your ancestors did. I am grateful you thought to show it here, even if this is only its temporary resting place. It gives me joy at my age. Just to feel it brings memories."

Rubbing the ingot once more, she carefully placed it back into the silver case. Ibu had seen what she came for, and nodded for Tan Tran to follow as she hobbled out of the room as slowly as she had come.

Tan Tran returned almost immediately with a large securely sealed envelope. He handed it respectfully to Dong.

"Ibu requested you guard this packet most carefully. She asked that it be stored safely in your sanctuary of files below," Tan Tran stated.

Taking the envelope, Dong noted that it had been sealed with a heavy tape. The lettering across the front was in Ibu's own failing hand, and said in English, "Not to be opened before my death, by the head of the Hoe family." It was sealed with wax, and her chop in bright China-red ink.

He wondered what bit of secret family gossip Ibu believed she must retain recorded in such a manner. Could she not even confide its contents to her son? He was half inclined to rip it open and read the contents. Then he decided it was better to humor the old one in her remaining years, or weeks. Her life had been a harsh one.

Dong put the envelope away carefully in the top section of the briefcase. Then he placed the gold bar back into its wooden box in the open side of the silver case, but only after his hands had again caressed it longingly, just as Ibu had done.

"Gold," he said to himself, "is the mistress of all those who would aspire to a long reign of power and greatness." His friends had told him this amount would buy a large house, even in Middle America. Perhaps someday he would be allowed to go and see for himself.

"Tan, later this night we must make a visit to the tunnel and store Ibu's treasure and my notes where they will be safe from thieves." He thought to himself, it is regretted that I cannot hide away this gold treasure as well without incurring the wrath of the NLF.

He heard the front gates slide back and the crunch of gravel as a vehicle was admitted to the compound. From the sound of the motor he knew it was a light truck or van, probably a service vehicle from the Tan Son Nhat Airport. His contact worked for an aircraft maintenance company, which gave him access to airfield hangar areas both in Saigon and in Hong Kong.

The vehicle stopped near the portico, outside the heavy teak entry door. Two car doors closed, and footsteps on the driveway indicated two men were entering. Dong was sure others stayed on guard inside the truck. They were probably his contact's working cohorts here in Vietnam, having driven here from the airport on their evening tea and smoke break, and to act as his guards. Dong listened carefully as Tan Tran quickly went to the entryway inside the front door. Soon he had seated one on a stark bench as he escorted the taller of the two through the French doors. He indicated a chair for him to occupy as he closed the doors. Dong sat silently waiting.

The visitor was dressed in coveralls that had a service patch on one sleeve, with a discolored ring on his back showing where a logo had been removed. His clothes smelled ripe from his having worked in the sun all day.

"You are Thanh Cong?" Dong spoke gruffly. He had met the man before, and considered him of a lower class. He was a *con lai*, a half-breed, and his features were coarse and dark. He really needed no proof of who Thanh was. He only wanted to see proof that the deed arranged by him had been carried out successfully. He prided himself that he never forgot a face.

"I am. We met, and you hired me over a week ago to do this job in the manner we discussed."

"What proof have you brought of your success?" Dong demanded, as he looked carefully to see what Thanh was producing from the two zippered plastic bags he carried. They were not bulky, or they would never have passed Tan Tran's inspection.

"These should be adequate proof of my work," Thanh replied.

He handed Dong a sheaf of newspaper clippings from Hong Kong that concerned the explosion of the private plane. He thumbed through them, confirming the information with his own knowledge. It blew up about 100 kilometers east of Hong Kong, when the plane exceeded 15,000 feet of altitude. There were pictures of the plane, probably from some newspaper file, and accounts of the plane's crew with obituaries of the World Oil employees.

The two engineers were on their way home from a well test in the South China Sea, and the two auditors had spent three weeks in Bangkok. The only one of interest to Dong was the exploration manager, Harold Blanton. He had been making a circuit of the company's South China Sea producing offices. His stay of two weeks visiting the Vietnam State Oil Company in Ho Chi Minh City was prominently mentioned.

The article speculated that World Oil was contemplating the opening of an office there. It went on further to state that Vietnam was the unpicked plum for oil exploration of the entire Pacific Rim. Dong knew what the article surmised was correct, for he had attended the meetings where Blanton had sold his energy minister on the arrangement for a future contract. When he finished reading, he looked up expectantly.

Thanh Cong then drew a heavy glass ashtray from the zippered bag. It was etched with the logo of World Oil, and had the name of their contract aircraft operator imprinted. This he proudly presented to the assistant minister, who took it and examined the words carefully.

"You removed this from the plane?" Dong asked. "They should be ashamed of such a display of opulence—such wasteful spending of money for the few capitalist dogs who would fly in their private jet."

"I did the work alone, and there were no clues left, for I did not report to work that day," Thanh stated.

The display had irritated Dong, and he slammed the heavy glass aside.

"These things I have seen. Any Saigon thief could have obtained them," stated Dong with a rush. "Let me see some proof that you were the one who set explosive in their plane. That I need before I pay you the two hundred *luong* in gold as we agreed. Do you have such proof?" he demanded loudly. Dong was upset that this *con lai* would think he was interested in seeing only papers and ashtrays.

"Here is the real proof, Minister Dong," stated Thanh proudly. He reached carefully into the second zippered bag, and produced an envelope. From it he removed a small brass plate. "Show me," Dong demanded impatiently, reaching out.

"It is the registration plate detached from inside the company plane. I removed it while placing the altitude-sensitive device behind the pilot's compartment on the day before their departure."

Dong took the plate carefully, and held it up to the dim light. He read and reread the lettering as Thanh Cong continued. This was truly good proof he had worked there.

"I was most careful that no one could connect me with any maintenance done on the plane. It was a project cleanly executed, and the altitude trigger worked perfectly, as you know. Now I have come to collect the balance of the payment as we agreed."

Thanh Cong was obviously nervous, for his pay would depend on how certain Dong and the NLF organization were that he would cause them trouble if he was not paid. He must retain some of the balance of power.

Dong continued to finger the plate carefully. The NLF would tolerate no error in such costly business. He wanted no later claimants to come stalking his compound. Finally he reached a satisfied conclusion, and placed the light bronze plate back into the envelope. He then resealed it and placed it under the wooden box in the case. Setting the box on the table, he carefully removed the 200 *luong* brick of gold. He caressed it gently as he laid it on a scarf.

Thanh Cong nervously eyed the grim Dong; then he reached forward and picked up the ingot. He weighed it carefully in his trembling hands, and read the printed markings. Retrieving a cloth from his plastic case, he carefully wrapped the kilo nugget, and secured it with a broad rubber band. Then he placed the gold deep within his bag, and slid the zipper closed. Rising to depart, he buried the bag deeply inside the loosened collar of his coveralls. It was literally close to his heart.

"I will hold myself in readiness for additional tasks, should Your Excellency need the services of my combine again," Thanh Cong nervously stated, trying to play the part of a strong leader of a group.

Dong dismissed him with a wave of his hand. "You will be contacted, as before, if you are needed."

Almost as an afterthought, Thanh Cong picked up the plastic bag with the heavy ashtray. He wrapped it as well, and placed it inside his coveralls on top of the gold. Then he passed quickly to the entry room, and followed Tan Tran to the great teak door. He motioned to his driver on the bench, and they quickly went directly to the van, not bothering to look back as the heavy door was closed behind them.

Dong placed the clippings and the wrapped brass plate into the silver case and closed the latches. They made a sturdy sounding click as they slid into place. He then carried the case with him as he removed the pistol from his belt, and proceeded to the entry door where he handed the case to Tan Tran.

Dong felt sad as he peered through the door's peephole. He saw the autobus swing around toward the exit, and his two guards with their guns in hand appeared. Slowly they pulled back the heavy wooden gates. The sections made a creaking noise as they slid on their rusty tracks, and soon they were open wide enough for the small vehicle. With a sewing-machinelike whine of its motor, it started through the gates.

Suddenly, a large six-by-six truck slammed head-on into the exiting vehicle, just as its cab passed free of the gate. A tremendous burst of gunfire originated from above the cab of the big truck, shredding the front seat of the smaller vehicle. Both men inside it were killed instantly.

At the first firing of weapons, the house guards on the portico rushed inside, pushing Dong aside to close the heavy doors across the entrance to the main house. Tan Tran, from somewhere within his baba, had produced his own Uzi. He cradled it carefully across one arm, as though it were a good friend. He stood behind his master, ready to react. But there was no need for them to join the melee.

Through view holes, Dong saw the smoking van thrust violently back into the compound by the bigger truck, and the two men jumped from the rear door of the little bus. Each had an Uzi, blasting aimlessly, as they ran away to escape the van and seek shelter against the wall. Any protected place would be better than staying there on the open gravel surface, facing the heavy machine gun firing from the six-by-six.

There was no safe place. The gun mounted above the cab of the big truck, which completely filled the narrow entrance, now swept the compound. The two men were their only remaining targets. The back of the van was beginning to burn with flames leaping high, and Dong's gate guards already lay in pools of blood beside the rusty gate tracks.

Only fifteen seconds had passed since they had started out the gate, and now six men were dead. All this occurred in spite of Dong's considered opinion that his compound was safely guarded. He watched to see what would happen next.

A few moments of deafening silence eerily ensued as the firing ceased. He could actually hear the crickets chirping by the klong across the road. There was no other sound, and no movement. All the dead echoes faded away.

Suddenly, a man burst from the side door of the big armored truck and quickly squeezed in between the cab of the burning autobus and the block wall holding the wooden gate. He leaned into the shattered van on the side away from the driver, and frantically pawed at the dead body of the man in the front seat. Thanh Cong would never move again, but he was holding the treasure.

The attacker pulled a heavy plastic zippered bag from inside the bloody coveralls of Thanh Cong, and dashed back toward the six-by-six, just as an Uzi opened up with fire from a Spirit House in the outer corner of the compound wall. Soon another gun joined the firing from the opposite corner. The big truck slowly backed away. Its metal shields gave it good protection against such a puny attack, and the engine roared as it picked up speed.

Dong swore aloud as the big truck swung away unhurriedly into the rough country track, and soon was out of range of their weapons. The raiders had succeeded in completing their robbery, and easily escaped unharmed.

Dong realized he had only been a spectator, for the gold the raiders sought was no longer his. His obligation to the Cong had been dispatched. He had watched the entire scene develop with a critical eye. Then he thought, Was it possible the bandits had made a mistake in their great rush?

The van, which was burning and smoking, looked as if it would explode at any moment. The roar of the big engine faded quickly as the truck sped down the rough trail toward the main road. Then there was silence, except for the faraway crickets. Nothing moved around the compound.

Dong reacted quickly. He left the silver case with Tan Tran as he jerked the wooden door aside. Hurrying across the compound, he could see the bodies of the guards in pools of blood as he ran. There were pockmarks everywhere around the entry door, which had been well marked by the stray firing of the big truck's mounted machine gun.

He waved his automatic pistol at the portico guards, indicating they should stay at their posts, but they stumbled out in a daze to see the results of the melee. They were stunned and helpless, undoubtedly thinking of the deaths of the other guards, who were their close relatives.

Dong ran headlong to the smoldering van, and leaned into the shattered side window of the little vehicle. It smelled strongly of acrid gasoline fumes, and it continued smoking. He must hurry, for there was something he must know that was more important to him than the possibility of an explosion. He dug deeply into the blood soaked coveralls of Thanh Cong. There he found something very heavy wrapped in a cloth, and secured with a large rubber band.

Dong slipped the package into his robe's pocket, and fled quickly. He was not a moment too soon, for a flame leaped up around the engine. Then it spread with a swoooosh to the gas line and then to the tank. It was a spectacular explosion, followed by a huge fireball that engulfed the area. The gates were afire, but Dong didn't care. He had beaten them. He had the gold. They had mistaken the heavy glass ashtray for his payment.

When he met Tan Tran back at the great door he noted that his Uzi had mysteriously disappeared. He had reverted from protector to being his bookkeeper again.

"Give me my silver case," Dong demanded.

Taking it back to his table, he spread it there again to examine its contents. He felt better after he had buried the 200 *luong* gold nugget back into its wooden box, under the clippings.

"Tan, I think we must visit the tunnel now," Dong stated, as he produced a flashlight from a drawer.

Carefully locking the doors to the room, Tan Tran moved to the teak built-in bookcase. Feeling for a pin concealed behind a book, he carefully slid the case toward the center of the room, exposing the dark hole of a tunnel entrance. The beam of Dong's flashlight revealed the top bar of a ladder concealed within.

Tan Tran climbed down into the musty confine first, and lit a candle far below. Dong followed with his silver case. When they had carefully deposited its contents, they both returned to reseal the entry.

"Check the guards' postings, Tan, for we want no return visits. Make a temporary repair of the front gate, and see that the families have taken care of their dead. But first, advise Vu Thi I will see her in my quarters. It has been a busy and profitable day. I believe champagne will be in order. See that beer is provided for those guards who remain."

When Vu Thi entered his bedroom with the iced bottle, Dong smiled for the first time since his return from Tokyo. He was already undressed, and lay beneath the wattle-covered window with the lights dimmed and the fan turning slowly to stir the humid air. This night deserved a celebration, he thought, and the NLF would never know the payment of gold did not evaporate into a klong of the Mekong River. Their payment, meant to stop exploration by foreign oil puppets, had both done its job and yet stayed at home—to ensure the rich future of the Chou family.

# Three

It was almost noon, Pacific Coast time, when the big jet slammed down onto the left runway at the airport south of Candlestick Park near San Francisco. It had been a long and tiring week of heartfelt and tearfully expressed condolences. Andy Cheston felt like a zombie, for he was extremely tired. Officially he had gone through the motions of representing the company by attending Harold Blanton's hometown memorial service. In reality, he had been performing his own personal duty by visiting the family at the small town outside of Dallas. He had talked and mourned with his closest friend, Harold's parents, and other close relatives, for several hours.

Andy told them stories about where he and Harold had spent a lot of their time in the past years as they worked together in the countries of the Far East. Those were their happy times together, for there was no need now to dwell on the rough roads they had traveled and the foreign intrigues they had surmounted together. He wished to leave, and retain, happy memories.

The members of the family were also considerate of his feelings. They knew how close Andy was to their son. Harold was a fine man with a great future, so they realized what a loss to all it was for him to be snuffed out right at the blossoming of his successful career. His parents had worked hard and made their sacrifices to enable Harold to achieve an advanced geology degree from the University of Texas at Austin. It had not been easy or inexpensive for them. Now they had no regrets for that part, and only relived their many happier memories.

The memorial service had been an extremely short one, since there was no following trip to a cemetery. Many of Harold's other friends, both from the company and from his earlier home life, had assembled from near and far. Andy knew most of them from their previous joint activities, but there was barely sufficient time to say a regretful "hello." Then they were off, returning to their own homes or driving back to Dallas to catch a plane.

Andy stayed at the parents' residence for a couple of hours after the service, and told the family all he could of their last work together in Tokyo. He commiserated in their deep sympathy, which he felt for himself as much as for them. In actuality, it was their sympathy for him that was needed, for the two of them had been very close during the past years. He probably had seen a lot more of Harold than had any of his family. It helped him to know they were his friends from previous visits, and he would always be welcome in their central Texas home.

His tears were successfully held back until it was time to say good-bye to Harold's mother, and then neither of them could pretend any longer. The other relatives kindly left the two of them alone with their uncontrollable grief.

Harold's mother gave him a final tearful hug, and whispered in his ear, "Please don't stay away over there forever, where your loved ones can't reach you. We need to see you here—a family needs to touch one another often. You are the closest thing we have to our son now. We wish he had left a wife and children for us to love. Please come and visit us as often as you can, and make yourself a family before we lose you to a foreign life entirely. We love you too, Andy, and will pray for your return."

It was a plea he had heard other families make before, including his own. Now they were gone. When a person makes a decision to work overseas, he commits himself to being unavailable for help in any sudden family crisis back in the States. It is said that after five years overseas people no longer think in the same way, for they have a serious and a permanent commitment to another land and another culture, and memories of home and old friends become vague.

When it came time for him to depart, he shook Mr. Blanton's hand firmly. He placed his arm around his shoulder and told him, "I swear to you, sir, I'll find the person who caused Harold's death. I'll take care of him."

"Bless you, Andy. My prayers will be with you," Mr. Blanton said sadly. "Don't do anything foolish on our account."

Those parental words were in Andy's thoughts as the plane taxied the long route after landing into the San Francisco terminal. He had flown from Tokyo directly to Dallas without a stopover on the day following the company memorial services there. Of course there was no body to arrange to transport back home. The bomb must have been a big one, for they hadn't found even so much as an engine nacelle or a floating lunch tray. The memory of a great flash in the sky seen by the fishermen on a Chinese boat was all that remained to mark the location.

The services in Tokyo had been at the American church, and were conducted by the Consular Corps chaplain. All of the company personnel had been in attendance, of course, as well as most of the local people who had been at the World Oil reception at the Dai-Ichi Hotel the night they had received the terrible news. But the difference in the people was notable. They had been so gay and talkative that night at the party, and now at the mass, they were all in black, and spoke no more than a few words of condolence to each company employee.

He had seen Li Hong Hoe and his granddaughter, and after expressing their sympathy, they introduced him to Lin Jin's brother, Kim. He appeared to be a little younger than Lin Jin, and presented a nice appearance. She was extremely quiet that day and had spoken very little. She was still a knockout, even in mourning. Her sensitivity to his feelings was touching, and she seemed to know instinctively that Andy was closer to Harold than were any of the other company men there. Of course she knew they had shared an apartment together.

The big plane nosed into the gate finally. It had been a long taxi, and now he must get back to the present. He was glad he had been able to bring more comfortable clothing for the long plane ride, for he was tired of wearing the black suit every day. His plane for Tokyo was not to depart until late afternoon, so he had over four hours to spend at the airport. One thing he must remember was to stock up on scotch at the duty-free shop, because the supply in the apartment was dangerously low. He had hosted many extra condolence visits of friends during the past week.

He wondered, as he gathered his coat and briefcase, if his twin sister, Elizabeth, had been able to change her plans and come to meet him at the airport. She was so wrapped up in the social whirl of San Francisco that it was sometimes difficult to meet her, even for a short visit. He sincerely wanted to talk to her, for they had been close and loving siblings all their lives. Her strong caressing arms would be a welcome reminder of a much needed family tie.

Beth was married now. He was remembering the fancy wedding he was able to attend a few years back as a green college grad. She became Mrs. Elizabeth Jane Cheston Halstead, of the California Halsteads. Her husband, Hillary, made his money growing grapes and making wine, so naturally, they lived north of the bay, beyond Sausalito. She had met Hillary at a college sorority party for old grads, and they took to his social set from there.

Andy had called Beth after checking in the rental car in Dallas, but she didn't know if she could arrange to meet him on such short notice. She had said she would try, and all he could do now was hope she'd be there. He hadn't seen her since Thanksgiving of last year, when he and Harold had stopped over on their way to Houston. They had gone out on a yacht trip, ostensibly to fish. They had only caught sunburn, but, anyway, Beth's memory of Harold would be a pleasant one.

As he came out of the passageway, he felt a thrill when he saw his twin standing right up front, waving like crazy. She was obviously glad to see him, for she moved quickly toward the crush of people exiting the ramp. She was beautifully dressed, as usual, and today she had on an especially nice outfit. Beth didn't have to go to extra trouble to be gorgeous. It just seemed to happen for her.

"Hey, Elizabeth!" he shouted. "Here I am!"

Beth rushed to hug and hold him tightly, as soon as she could avoid the crush of grandparents meeting children, who seemed to be everywhere. He held her tightly, and she responded vigorously.

"Hello, Andy, darling," she said. "You must be dead . . . you look tired! Come over here out of the traffic and let me get a better look at you."

He led her out of the crowd near the gate, and then he realized that Beth was not alone. A luscious blond was following them, taking in the scene very carefully, and eyeing him as though she were going to bid on a horse.

"And who is your escort?" he asked, referring to the lady as he gave her a smile.

Beth stopped to introduce her as soon as the crowd would permit.

"Valarie, this is my twin, Andrew—Andy Cheston. He doesn't visit here too often anymore since he prefers to stay over there and 'work' with those Oriental girls. This is Valarie Rogers."

"Well, how do you do, Valarie. I'm happy to see Beth didn't have to come all the way out here alone."

Valarie responded to his offered hand by taking his in both of hers. It was just short of a hug, and Andy felt a quick tingle of recognition—of what, he wondered.

"Hello Andrew," Valarie replied in a deep drawl, uncharacteristic of the Napa Valley. "I'm very pleased to meet you. Now I'll know who Beth is always talking about."

She had a pleasant voice, and made a beautiful smile with her brightly painted red lips.

"She was on her way to an afternoon tea, so I talked her into letting me pick her up early," Beth interrupted. "I needed her for company, but really, I just wanted you to meet her," she concluded, being frank.

Now he understood why she was so uncertain about the time to come directly to the airport to meet him. Beth was always trying to introduce him to just the right girl—that is, the right girl from her viewpoint. And such a viewpoint would include looks, savoir faire, and social position.

Beth chatted on, "Andy, darling, you do look tired. Are you sure you can't change your plans and stay over? Valarie and I can skip the party, and celebrate your visit instead."

Andy noted that they certainly weren't dressed for an airport visit or for traveling.

"My luggage is already checked through, and I've missed too many days of work," Andy explained. "Let's go spend a couple of hours in the VIP Club lounge. They'll check me into the flight, and call when it's time to make the plane. That way we'll be free to talk."

"That's what we're best at," Beth injected.

"Good; then we might even discuss the grape crop in the Napa Valley. Let me see your feet, Beth. I want to know if Hillary has you stomping grapes."

Andy didn't feel much like humor, but he made the weak attempt. He wondered if Beth had picked Valarie out long ago to arrange a meeting, or if she was a "spur of the moment" catch.

They settled into a booth with a view of the planes flying past every thirty seconds or so, and the noise provided a regular interruption of their conversation. They were getting their words in quickly when they could be heard, and Andy was so tired that the drone was almost putting him to sleep.

The bar service was good, and soon they each had a Bloody Mary, complete with celery stalk. He was thankful it didn't have a little umbrella like the ones they insisted on serving in Japan. And their conversation continued.

Beth understood how he felt about the loss of his close friend, for she had met Harold on several occasions. She waited until they were settled, then she carefully expressed her deep sympathy—at the same time, giving her brother another great caress while patting his head down on her shoulder, as though she were his mother.

"Andy, Hillary and I are so sorry about Harold's death. We know how good a friend he was to you, and that you'll miss him terribly. We will too, in a different way. He was a nice man, and we always enjoyed his visits." Beth hung on to Andy tightly.

"Thank you, Beth. I'll miss him in more ways than one, for we thought alike and took our vacations together usually, not to mention our joint work. I assured his parents that I'd take care of the unfinished business there. Everyone will miss his coordination of our work for the company. Please thank Hillary for his concern, too."

She held him a few more seconds, and then the spell was broken. Beth moved back to her own section of the booth, and arranged herself for their friendly conversation to continue.

"And please accept my deepest sympathy," Valarie added.

She would have been bored with their talk of family happenings, except that she was showing an intense interest in everything Andy had to say. Occasionally she would ask a question about where he lived in Tokyo, and how his social life was there.

"Do you go to the American Club?" she asked directly.

She knew it was beside the Russian Embassy, so Andy knew she had traveled some in the Orient. It was certainly not a location most tourists would find on their own without proper introductions.

"Yes, it is a handy watering hole for our after-office breaks, so we go there often," Andy answered.

"It will be more important that you meet others there now without your apartment-mate." Valarie became abruptly quiet, and he realized that she knew she had injected a rude reminder.

Beth's questions about his Tokyo life were also specific. She wanted to know all about the parties there.

"Who are the women you can date there? Are there any single American secretaries, or female geologists?" She persisted, "Do the company men date the Oriental girls?"

"Well, some do, sometimes." It was hard for him to answer truthfully, because their ESP didn't permit him to lie very successfully.

It bothered Andy a little when she kept coming back to the same subject, and it was even worse when he tried to tell her about the table arrangement he and James Wellman had cooked up for the chairman of the board at their formal reception. Then she wanted to know how the American ambassador's wife regarded the replacement, and if Andy would consider her a bigot.

"Didn't Mrs. Ambassador think they should have found an American woman for the chairman's dinner partner?" Beth asked.

"She didn't discuss it with me afterward," he replied.

The more he thought about it, the more he thought Beth might be right—but then he remembered the look of Lin Jin, and how soft her hand had been when he left her at Eason's side that night at the reception. He'd have to arrange to see her again. Eason certainly hadn't objected to her color or her company.

Miss Valarie did not leave Andy much time to think. She occupied more and more of the conversation as the time quickly passed. By late afternoon, when Beth realized that they must be leaving for their party, he knew the entire life history of the statuesque blond. She was indeed well educated, and had a startlingly varied social life.

Just because the lady was their age and fit well into her San Francisco culture didn't mean she would go well with the international oil circuit — especially in the rough-and-tumble world of commerce in a foreign location. She just didn't quite have the color for it. At least not in the Orient. Andy's mind told him to be a bit leery of this overly friendly girl, for he could sense a trap.

Valarie was certainly one of the liberated American women whom one could often find frequenting night clubs and at parties. She might even go into the singles bars, if she liked. That was part of being liberated, he supposed. You'd never see a lady like Lin Jin in such a place alone. The women in the Orient were gentle and sweet, and trained from birth to wait on their men.

An American woman would never fit in as a family member over there. The macho American males he had seen going through the wars in the Far East, and picking up brides there, seemed to be quite content with their quiet home lifestyle. Of course, foreign wives never seemed to go out much. Maybe that was the difference. They were content to stay at home and rear their children. American women wanted a maid to do the chores at home while they met their husbands for lunch after they went shopping. Andy wondered if ever the twain could meet.

He could never see himself paired up with anyone from the West Coast—they just didn't travel well in his Far Eastern circle, mainly because the Pacific was such a big ocean. And every time he crossed it, his mind seemed to make a complete turnover, as if he had to think with the other side of his brain. Everything over there was different, and it wasn't all just the jet lag. He jarred himself back to the present, wondering if his ESP with his twin was slipping.

This Valarie Rogers was one you could never associate with the color yellow, even socially. She might accept "golden," if there was enough of it. Why, Andy wondered, had he resented his twin setting him up to meet this girl? She was a little too forward for his current circumstances, coming home from a funeral as he was. Suddenly he realized he was comparing this girl with Lin Jin Hoe—for no real reason.

The two hours passed quickly, and Beth said, "Andy, it's time we got on our way. If you won't come with us now, when can you return?"

"Not for a vacation for a long while, for our business is heating up. I'll throw my hat in some weekend soon, though," Andy answered.

Their departure scene was a reversal of the arrival, except that now he also kissed Valarie on the cheek, and she had an arm around his shoulder. After many promises to stop over in Sausalito soon if possible, the ladies were about to leave, when Valarie called to him.

"I'm coming to Tokyo in the next few months with my father. I just decided. Is it all right if we call on you to show us around the Ginza?" Then she added a little hesitantly, "I want you to show me one of those hot-bath massages I've heard so much about."

Beth laughed at her forward remark, and turned to make a big fuss of getting her purse and gloves together.

"We'll be staying at the Okura Hotel, and Dad will have a car for us," Valarie added, not explaining who "us" meant.

"Sure, just give me a call when you're settled in, and I'll see if I can get away from my maps for a half day," Andy replied.

Now that would take some arranging, to be busy when she came to Tokyo, or to be out of town. He wouldn't want to insult the girl. Even worse, he wouldn't want to upset sister Beth, assuming she was also in on this plan.

They all waved happily, and Beth called out, "See you next trip, somewhere."

The ladies disappeared amid the crowd of people hustling with their luggage to find another line to occupy. Andy, all talked out, retreated to find the duty-free shop. He always returned to Tokyo carrying liquid gifts, if possible. Then he was off to the bar, where he prepared himself for the long airborne evening, following the sun.

He had a busy schedule ahead. All of the work that had piled up during his duty-forced trip would be waiting on his desk. Now he must get his mind back on the company's work. He had to get his presentations ready for their meeting with the Vietnamese, but first he must sell a position to the World Oil management—one that he and Harold had developed. That shouldn't be a great problem, because their work had been predicated on previous recommendations, and the Board had approved the preliminary work. The real test would come when they saw how they would get along with agreeing on a contract in Ho Chi Minh City.

Something else was nagging at the back of his mind. His last phone conversation from Harold Blanton still bothered him. What was it he had said? He wished it had been on tape. It was something about a warning Harold had received in Hong Kong from a member of the Vietnamese

Petroleum Company staff, about connections for their future drilling activities. Their phone call had been interrupted before he could tell him any more. What had he meant? Was it something that would come out later as they pursued their normal field exploration activities? For now he could only wish he knew.

No matter what his future was as an explorer, he'd find the time to track down those responsible for the death of his friend, just as he had promised Harold's dad. His friend had had great ambitions for himself and for the company in exploring the Pacific Rim. He would have gone far with World Oil, probably eventually becoming a member of the Board. Now it was up to him personally to see that someone paid for cutting Harold Blanton's promising career short.

# Four

Andy Cheston was in a serious mood as he spoke to the dozen men of the exploration staff surrounding the cluttered table of their Tokyo office. They had all been through a difficult time, and now knew they needed to get back to basics and bury themselves in their work to forget.

"Gentlemen, we have almost finished a tremendous assimilation of geology in a short time, but we still have a lot more to complete. These maps and reports show both an honest and a technically correct description of the Mekong Delta area. This is the only group in the world who could have come up with such a data organization for the Vietnamese recommendation in so short a time. We're getting close to a final product, and we'll soon have a report we can sell to management."

He went on to review details of the better structures on the brightly colored geologic maps. Their charts and seismic cross sections appeared to be spread helter-skelter over the walls and tables of World Oil's largest Tokyo conference room. To the uninitiated, it would seem to be a scene of utter chaos, but actually those maps were the well-organized result of many months of geophysical and geological contouring, and their careful interpretation.

The staff had been stretched to the limit. Not only were they supervising the current operations in several Far East countries, and some of those also with new ventures, but now they also were working on the proposed Vietnamese contracts. The gray-haired Wally Brooks, chief geologist, leaned back in his chair and rested for the first time Andy could remember that whole day, and as he listened a pleased expression showed under his pushed-up glasses.

As the regional geologist, Andy's serious mood was brought on by the fact that they had been intensely busy without any break for two weeks following their company's air disaster and subsequent memorial services. The group had all been overworked, and their exhaustion was beginning to show.

"Gentlemen, the individual trees that make up the forest are about to appear as a result of our work," he remarked, "so let's call it a day now, and look again tomorrow morning after we've had a rest. Then we can see if there are any elephants hidden there."

"We can all agree with that. It's been a long and productive day," Wally stated. "I wish our new boss were here to join in the extra work. When do you think we'll find out who he'll be?" He aimed his question at Andy.

"I'll bet they'll replace Blanton with a green college graduate packed with lots of degrees and very little field experience," James Wellman injected. "That would seriously delay our report if we had to stop to educate a new man."

"Probably the directors consider that we're too busy to be bothered welcoming a new man right now. Hanby hasn't mentioned anything," Andy replied.

Everyone in the company realized that the Vietnam New Ventures Task Force had a tremendous assignment to complete, and little time to waste. They had industriously unified their expertise to complete a recommendation, well supported with basic data, and were designing a report they hoped would be accepted by Houston management. The decisions had to be made soon, or some other company would step in and pick up the blocks ahead of them.

What they really needed, Andy realized, was about four more experienced men to help with the interpretation of the sections into maps. As regional geologist, he was filling in for Blanton temporarily, but that was just a matter of keeping the wheels turning. Nobody had told him he was in charge, although the team accepted his natural leadership.

He saw James Wellman wearily push his mop of blond hair back on the top of his head and call the passing coffee Josan for a refill.

"What do you think of our work schedule, James?" Andy asked.

"I think we're all tired. Let's take a night off, and go at it again tomorrow when we're fresh."

There was a general buzz of agreement. Andy realized they had been discussing their interpretations all afternoon without a break, and they were exhausted.

"Sounds reasonable to me. Let's clean this mess up."

Andy's firm pronouncement came as a conclusion of the day-long review of their efforts, and their eyes and brains were giving out.

"Where do we go from here?" asked James, not yet quite willing to release his mental grasp of the day's work. "We have used every piece of data we've been able to scrounge, or dream up, and it still isn't a great interpretation. We won't have a viable drilling location until we reshoot our own seismic over the entire area. I don't trust this crap the Viets have furnished us. We've got to get better coverage."

"Even if the recording were good," Wally injected, "its exact location could be a mile or two off. We'll still need a couple of months to interpret our own data, and to integrate them into regional maps."

Andy knew they were right, but they would have to bid on the blocks based on present data. This wouldn't be the first time a company has been forced to go out on a limb to get a choice acreage position in an untested area. Their real problem now was to prove to themselves that there was a geologic basin in the Mekong Delta with oil accumulation possibilities. Andy held the back of his stiff neck as he continued to look down at the maps. He reasoned to himself that there was no way this basin shouldn't also have the necessary ingredients to cook up a lot of oil.

In summary of the day's efforts, Andy said, "I believe in this basin's possibilities, my friends, so tomorrow let's start to paint as rosy a picture for our management as possible. We know they are already inclined to buy it, or we wouldn't have been assigned to do this. Now they want us to justify the money they must bid to get over other companies' offers, and stay ahead of the local government. We know the Viets have some officials who want to do the drilling by contract, and try to use only their local talent to preserve their whole ownership."

The geological interpretation had all been done by their own staff—by these people around this room, and Andy had a hand in hiring most of them. He had reason to be proud of their efforts. The company's geophysicists could farm out a lot of their basic work, he knew, for the processing by giant computers was mostly done by seismic contractors. The geology, however, had to be interpreted here based on geophysics and well data, by far-sighted dreamers such as Wellman and Brooks. Based on their ideas, the company could lose big money on some big gambles, but they had to offset any such losses with giant oil strikes.

Good untested new venture areas were few and far between in today's global oil search. The major companies had to go after all available new areas. This basin in Vietnam was becoming available only because of the previous political and wartime restrictions. Many international oil giants were scrambling for a sizable interest in the blocks and, while no individual company could take the risk to explore and develop the entire basin, they all wanted their share.

The area was one that Harold Blanton had been scouting before his untimely death. Their energy minister in Ho Chi Minh City had been interested in getting technical assistance from the most experienced companies working in the Far East to evaluate the offshore area south of the Mekong Delta. At least, that was what many of the more well educated higher-ups in the new Vietnamese governing hierarchy were attempting to arrange.

Blanton had advised Andy privately that there were others in their government who were determined they could conduct the exploratory drilling alone. He had explained to them that deep water production is the toughest job in the world of oil search, and they had no personnel with previous experience in that field. Also, he described the meeting he had with the energy minister and his assistant, Dong Huan Chou. There had been very "heavy" discussions, with much of the talk in Vietnamese so he would not understand.

Harold had explained to Andy that neither the minister nor Dong realized, or admitted, that he would be starting a billion-dollar exploration project with no experience. It seemed so simple to them—you hire a seismic crew to provide the offshore maps, you hire a geologist to select a location, and then you hire a drillship to come in and produce oil into a tanker. It sails away to a refinery in Japan, and you collect a payment in good green cash for the black gold. It would be easy, and the resulting income would regenerate the economy of Vietnam. The American trade embargo be damned!

Short of that simple operation, all they were willing to agree on was that the Americans would furnish the money to buy the data and rent the ships, and they would keep control of the operations and the money. Harold had explained to Andy that Dong Huan Chou, the energy minister's assistant, was making noise about keeping his hand personally on the strings of their operation, should they get the contract. Harold had then made it clear that he personally would recommend that World Oil not enter into any such agreement. Andy wondered if that dissent, and failure to be intimidated, could have signed Harold's death warrant.

Andy realized that whoever presented the deal to their government would have to convince the powers in Vietnam that they needed more than money alone to succeed in offshore exploration. They would need expertise, and all the tact Hanby could muster. No company in the world was going to furnish that knowledge without a firm contractual hold on a portion of the resulting production. That would be their big selling job before signing a workable contract to operate in that area. He still didn't know who that salesman would be, but he must arrive here soon, for there were a lot of data to digest before the selling could begin.

If they actually did come up with an agreement to operate in blocks offshore from Vietnam, the fire-brand Dong would have to be sidetracked or outflanked, for he was an obvious avowed enemy of anyone trying to enter the business world of the Mekong Delta. But they couldn't allow anyone to run their exploration like a black market. Harold's last message must have been indicating that World Oil had to retain control of their own operations in Vietnam.

It had been a long and strenuous meeting, and they were all mentally exhausted. A pretty little Japanese secretary named Chisai entered the conference room, making no noise at all as she approached Andy across the carpeted floor.

"Mr. Hanby wishes to see you in his office before you leave today, Doctor Cheston. Thank you." Chisai spoke quietly as she handed the note to Andy, and bowed before she backed away out of the room. The note read the same.

"This is not an uncommon request, I trust," Andy said, as he handed the note to James. He again pushed back his hair, and read.

"He probably just wants you to wipe down his car before he takes off for the club," he grinned as he spoke.

There's something about being too serious for too many hours that brings out levity even in the most serious situation, and the hard workers had become giddy.

"I expect he wants to go over the schedule for tomorrow, because we'll have to do this presentation again soon, with him included. Then we'll get to put our opinions on the line for real," Andy answered seriously.

"Sooner or later we always have to sign our names to the reports," James replied.

It was a little strange, Andy thought, that James had not been included in this invitation if it were strictly a work-planning meeting, for they had conducted their efforts jointly for the most part, and were at equal staff levels. He took off walking briskly up the stairs to Hanby's office, one floor up.

Andy arrived a little out of breath. Chisai nodded sweetly when he entered, and picked up her phone. After a word, she gave him her agreeable smile again, and waved her carefully manicured hand toward the closed office door of her boss, William Hanby.

Chisai normally said very little to anyone, but she was in positive control of the office protocol, being the top of the pecking order for secretaries. She was capable of keeping company secrets safely to herself, including all salary and personnel recommendations.

As Andy entered the formal office, still breathing hard from his hurried trip, he found Bill Hanby seated in his big leather chair behind the polished teak desk. He was almost hidden behind a stack of reports and papers he was reading. On one corner was another stack of letters, presumably awaiting his signature or initials.

Every word that went out of the Far East office of World Oil passed across that desk, and Hanby read everything carefully. He had a mind like a giant file cabinet where he stored a mass of data. It was the mark of a capable manager, to absorb and retain all of the information concerning the operations under his direction. His decisions based on available information could make the stockholders of the company a lot of money, or lose it as quickly. His salary was arranged accordingly.

"Please have a seat," Hanby directed him, motioning to the leather chair opposite his. "We must get right to the business at hand, because the death of Harold has put the company, and me in particular, far behind the operating schedule Houston had set up for new ventures in this area."

"These past weeks have been a trying time for everyone here," Andy answered noncommittally.

"His death could not have come at a worse time, if there were such a thing. It's as if someone deliberately picked that time to put a monkey wrench in our schedule. And perhaps someone did."

Andy was listening intently, but he had nothing to add. The discourse continued after Hanby had relit his large pipe.

"But that's water over the dam. We are partly behind in our new ventures preparations because no one has been appointed as Exploration Manager, Far East to replace Harold. He was such a good man, and I depended on him so heavily to carry out much of the day-to-day company activity between our offices. Now I find myself snowed under with this mountain of paperwork."

"He was a fast worker, that's true."

"His efforts left me free to review our more far-reaching considerations, such as government contacts and politically related activities. Now I miss having those normal in-house messages handled for me. In a way, it has been good for me to get back into the mainstream, for I needed to review what a big job daily operations can be."

"Normal communications can keep us busy enough without new ventures," Andy replied.

Hanby swung back toward Andy in his swivel chair, puffing on his pipe.

"But, enough of that. As you can see from these stacks, I am getting further behind. If I don't get some help soon, I won't be able to find my desk." Bill had a slight smile on his lips as he spoke.

He continued his grin as he slowly relit his large briar pipe, as though he knew something that was about to please him.

"I'm sure it must be a tremendous burden," Andy said, after a long pause.

He did not know where this conversation was leading, or how he was expected to respond. When you're called into the boss' office, you never know if a bombshell is about to explode or if you are about to be made the head of the rest room cleaning committee. Andy tried to relax, but he was too ill at tease, so he sat forward in the soft leather chair. His feet were too far off the ground, so he inched farther forward.

"I need help," said Hanby, with a sudden burst of sincerity, "and I need it right away, for we have a meeting set up with the Viets in about five weeks. By one month from now we must know on what basis we can expect it to be profitable for us to invest in the Mekong Delta, for that is when we make our preliminary pitch to Houston."

"We're working to have our data all in order by then, and we'll make that deadline," Andy said firmly.

"I know you will, but, more important, we must also decide if we can trust the Viets to honor their agreements should we decide the Mekong area looks sufficiently prospective for the huge cash outlay our operation would require. I can't handle this burden of decision on my own."

"We'll do all we can to help, sir," Andy responded, still not knowing how he should reply.

Hanby swung around in his chair a little, still puffing, trying to make his pipe go, and spoke off into space.

"This will be the largest single company investment to be made anywhere in the world. It must be handled by top-notch exploration and production people. There is a lot of ground to be covered in a very short time. I have sent a man to do some reconnaissance for me on what we can expect from the Viets' inside planning. He is really our auditor, who was once an FBI man. But no one is supposed to know that—or that he is not just looking for errors in the bean count. Keep that under your hat."

"Do I know him?" Andy asked.

"His name is Kelly Johnson, and he has been nosing around the Far East, collecting information between Ho Chi Minh City and Hong Kong for three weeks now."

"I've seen him passing through the office, but haven't met him." Andy was both startled and pleased to hear the company had someone looking into the cause of their plane's bombing.

"You'll meet him soon. He's a capable investigator."

"I'm glad to hear that. We owe a debt to Harold, which will be repaid one day when the responsible people are located," Andy answered, and when Hanby sat thinking, he continued.

"We have most of the available data already in-house, sir, and I believe that by using some of the imported help from the adjacent area offices, and by working extra hours and weekends, we can bring it all together for a presentation to Houston by the middle of the month."

They'd even have to get extra secretaries to type the reports, Andy thought. He avoided commenting further about the FBI man and the covert investigation, but he was happy to hear that someone had started gathering background information on the Viet setup.

Hanby swung back toward Andy. "We'll have to do it on schedule, as best we can—there's no other choice," answered Hanby. "Gilbert Eason has talked to the energy minister of Vietnam, Ho Bac Minh, and he set up a meeting with their technical staff for the end of next month to go over the exploratory possibilities. If that is successful, a contract negotiation will be started at that time."

"Will we have authority by then to act?"

"We'll have to present our case to Houston first, and with their approval, return in time for the meeting in Saigon." He leaned back in his chair and relaxed as he blew a smoke ring toward the pile of reports. He was apparently lost in thought as he looked out over the darkening Tokyo rooftops.

Andy watched as well, and he was suddenly mentally immersed in all the doubts he had felt since his return from the memorial trip to Texas. As he watched Hanby pensively smoking his pipe, he thought of the time he had spent during that break in his work habits to search his own soul—to see if he was capable of going on with the work he had helped Harold Blanton outline and develop for the future of the Pacific Rim exploration. There was so little time to accomplish so much work, and he was examining his own self-esteem to determine if he could continue working on the job they had started together. It would be tough without Harold, for he was an inspiration.

If the job could be done, World Oil was the company to be working for, because they had the drive to finish what they started, as well as the monetary backing. If they had to complete all of their reviews and make recommendations locally in a couple of weeks, there would be no time to put polish on a presentation. They'd have to go with their raw data to Houston, where they would have even less opportunity to prepare themselves for their appearance before the powers that guided the destiny of their company. It would be a hassle. Andy's mind was reeling.

He was allowing himself too many self-doubts, he suddenly realized. Get a grip on your life—take control of your mind, Andy told himself. He fleetingly thought about who the dissenting person or persons were who hid themselves out there somewhere, and who had planned their people's deaths. Why would they be so intent to kill their production efforts offshore from the Mekong Delta? Who would have charge of finding out what group or person was behind that terrorist deed? Was one former FBI agent enough? He himself would somehow make sure the job was done before they were finished exploring here.

Finally, Andy interrupted their thoughts. "That will be a big job for the entire staff, Mr. Hanby. We will hardly have time to gather our maps and sections, let alone study the structural interpretations. Could we call in some of the other South China Sea exploration staff to help us for these two or three weeks before we have to present our results to Houston?"

"If that is necessary, let's do it," came the curt reply.

"They are already familiar with related areas, and could be a great help in assimilating data. One man from each of the adjoining countries would be a great help. A geophysicist from the Houston bullpen to help James with the seismic cross sections would be a big help also."

His musing tapered off, because it was apparent that Hanby was not really listening, and had sunk deeper into his own thoughts as he smoked his pipe and looked out into the sea of lights in the dark sky.

Suddenly Hanby's attention returned to Andy.

"I need help now to carry this program off—and I've called you here to advise you that our Board of Directors has approved my recommendation to get it. I advised them that you are the most qualified and most experienced person available to carry on Harold's work, and I want you to be the new Manager of Exploration for the World Oil Far East region." He paused, noting Andy's surprised reaction.

Andrew Cheston, World Oil Exploration Manager, Far East. That sounded pretty good to Andy, and he couldn't help smiling as he realized Hanby had really assigned him to the position. Andy was so overcome that he did not trust himself to speak.

"We had been considering you for managerial level promotion for some time already, and the terrorist downing of our aircraft just hurried the sequence along a little. You are the right person for the job, and fortunately, you happen to be here in the right place. We would have selected you no matter where you had been stationed, but it is convenient that you are already in Tokyo, and know this geologic province so well. You can continue your work, as you have already taken over much of the responsibility previously handled by Blanton." Hanby was smiling as he enjoyed the pleasure showing in Andy's eyes.

"Thank you very much," Andy said weakly, still churning over in his mind what this sudden promotion meant. He had not dared to hope he would be selected for the position.

"In fact, you have already been handling the job, and I delayed having this discussion because I wished to free you from daily reports to continue your maximum efforts on the Vietnam project."

"This may disrupt my thinking a bit, sir, so it's a good thing you waited until the end of the day."

"Your promotion is already effective, as of last month, in fact. I am especially glad that you already know more about the structure of the South China Sea than any other geologist on our staff." He stood and offered his hand to Andy. "So welcome aboard, Doctor Exploration Manager, and my congratulations," Hanby said formally.

Andy had a little trouble standing from the deep chair, but he accepted the extended hand, and shook it weakly.

"Thank you, sir, and I'm afraid Harold's boots will be large ones to fill."

He had received promotions before, but he hadn't expected this giant step. It had been assumed that some egghead from the research center would be imported to fill the important position left vacant when the plane went down.

"We discussed your background thoroughly, and we're sure you can handle the job. Just keep on with the way you have been working. And here—take some of these reports."

Andy could only reply, "The impact of this is almost staggering to me. I'll have to think about it a little. But it will be no problem to accept. Thank you; I'll do my best, Mr. Hanby."

"Call me Bill, and we'll get along just fine. I already know the quality of your work. Now we must concentrate on developing your staff."

Realizing the sudden shock of the promotion was disconcerting to Andy, Hanby went on with his discussion in order to let his friend recover from his rush of emotion.

"After you left for the States to attend the memorials and talk to the families, I had a meeting with Eason and the other directors who were visiting here. At that time we all agreed that you were the logical man for this critical post and in this particular situation. It promises to be a difficult one, because we must learn to get along with the Oriental people on their own turf if we plan to do business in this part of the world. You have the knowledge to continue this project to successful exploratory conclusion. Now we must make it work both politically and socially."

"I've always liked living in this part of the world."

"As exploration manager, you will be responsible for carrying out our program of new ventures, as well as the current drilling and exploring projects in the other Pacific Rim countries. World Oil is going to be spending even bigger money here in the future, and we must have a man who can look to the future of the area, as well as someone who intends to become a part of this business culture. You must be able to get along with the people of the Far East."

"My sister has already given up on my moving back to California," Andy replied thoughtfully.

"You must have a desire to live the culture of the Far East and to develop the oil production that is desperately needed by this Oriental society to augment the success of their other commercial ventures." He relit his pipe again, since, with all of his speech, he could not keep it drawing.

"They have a long way to go, and oil production is the best step in the right direction for a jump-start of their economy," Andy injected.

"Your promotion was not too difficult a decision for the company, because you had already been brought to the attention of the directors by your hard work and resulting successes. That had already placed you in line for a managerial position. I'm just sorry it has to come to you as a result of the terrorist activity against our staff, including our good friend, Harold."

"Harold had big plans for the future, it's true."

"You are young for such a responsible position, and it is always better to have a little more experience behind you when you step up to hold the reins. You have to drive your own buggy sometime, and this appears to be your time. The directors agree with me on your selection, and they will doubtless convey their own sentiments now that they know you have been installed."

It had been a long speech, and Andy realized Hanby was talking in order to let him regain some composure after his sudden shock. His stomach churned. What would be fitting for a new exploration manager to say?

"Thank you very much, sir—Bill," Andy said as he sat back in the chair, with some hesitation. "I didn't expect a replacement for Harold to be selected locally, but I'll do my best. I had a respect for him that went far beyond friendship."

This new position would require his greatest effort and deepest concentration. He was just beginning to realize how much his future would have to change from the old "humdrum, go-to-work-every-day" ethic. It was too soon to make snappy comments to his boss—better he should accept his good fortune for now with mild mannered thanks, and reserve the flamboyant comments for later.

"See me first thing tomorrow. We'll go over the coming week's schedule, and then you can get back to your work."

# Five

"Hey, Andy, have a look at the fancy formal invitation we just received," said Wally Brooks. "There's one there for you, too. It looks like the entire staff got one."

Wally was carefully reading the embossed card which had come in its hand-addressed envelope, as he handed the similar one to Andy.

Andy read, "Mr. and Mrs. William Handy request the pleasure of your company at a reception in honor of Andrew B. Cheston, Exploration Manager, Far East of World Oil...."

"Pretty fancy, Wally, engraved and everything," Andy commented. He waved the card at James, who had just brought in a new stack of maps. "We must be making money somewhere if we can afford one of the salon rooms at a hotel like the Okura."

"Yeah; I've already seen mine. They must want you to know you've been promoted if there'll be too many guests for it to be held at Hanby's apartment."

Andy realized there must be outsiders invited, and that meant other oil company personnel.

Wally looked up from his card and said, "Bill and Jill Hanby are going to introduce you to the social set of the Tokyo oil industry in style!"

"Yeah; I can hear my sister Beth now, saying I'm going to be one of those Far Eastern oil moguls." Andy assumed he'd already met most of the people who'd attend, or at least all of the husbands. He continued, "Now we'll meet the wives who really run the companies from behind the scenes."

Few promotions were ever gained, Andy knew, without the approval of the company wives.

"This is probably Jill Hanby's doings, because she has always been friendly toward you, even years ago when you were a junior geologist," said James. "They like looking out after young eligible bachelors, since they have no wives of their own."

"It's their motherly instinct toward the unattached males, and not entirely unappreciated," Andy replied.

"We'll have to get out our best bibs again, I guess," James said. "Those seem to be getting a lot of use lately."

"I'm not for that," added Wally. "But I guess Beatrice will enjoy seeing us dressed up." Wallace Brooks, with his gray hair, considered himself too old for company fancy-dress parties.

Andy remembered it was Jill who had suggested that James join him to live in the apartment where he and Blanton had lived. He really didn't need to live alone, especially now. The place was in a classy location, near both the American Club and the office. It had two bedrooms and baths, and was ideal for a pair of bachelors. A prize apartment was hard to find in Tokyo, especially in such a desirable location, so World Oil would never let it get out of their grasp.

The company also rented the adjacent unit, which was reserved for upper echelon visitors. Kelly Johnson, the FBI auditor, was leaving his things there at the moment, because he had been around for several weeks while he checked on the various subcompanies. Besides, someone had to keep an eye on the company's collection of wood-block prints displayed there.

"James, did you get moved into your new room OK?" Andy asked. "The doorman said he'd help if you needed anyone to carry bags."

Bachelors travel light, he knew, and James was not a big collector of artifacts, as were some world travelers. His only prized collection was his seashells. He was glad James was joining him, for the apartment had become a lonely place since Harold was gone. It helped Andy, some, that he spent almost all of his waking hours in the office.

"Yes, I'm all in there now. Hope you were in the bedroom you wanted. If not, we can swap, because it doesn't matter to me."

"I'll keep the one I'm in. Bedrooms are for sleeping, so the view doesn't matter that much," Andy answered with a grin.

\*   \*   \*

When the two friends arrived at the rear street entrance to the Okura Hotel, Jimmy-san, the driver, allowed the hotel doorman to handle their exit with his sedate greeting. The Crown Toyota then pulled away to park and await their return. They had come a few minutes late, and made their way to the reception salon near the top of the escalator.

"Good evening, Andy and James," said Jill Hanby when she met them at the salon entrance. "You are both looking very handsome." She gave

Andy a big hug complete with a kiss on each cheek, then awarded the same to James. "And Andy, my personal congratulations."

"Thank you. You are looking beautiful as ever tonight. That's a fancy dress you are wearing for a fancy occasion. I very much appreciate your doing this, but you should not have felt you had to go to such lengths for a lowly geologist," Andy stated, as he gave her his best smile.

"Bill and I wanted to," Jill replied, "We haven't had too much to celebrate lately, and we want to get you started in Tokyo society on the right foot." She too was all smiles. "Our heartiest congratulations are very richly deserved."

Andy blushed, and said nothing more. He was thinking to himself that he would have to stretch his abilities to live up to their great expectations.

Bill Hanby stood nearby smiling and nodding his approval, and showing no signs of being jealous of her motherly locutions. This was not to be one of those formal reception-line affairs, Andy was happy to note.

"Good evening to you both, gentlemen. I've already provided you with my words of wisdom," Hanby said as he shook their hands, "so, let's get on with the celebration. I think the entire crew deserves a party, so let's have one."

"Right!" James joked. "Bring on the dancing girls."

At one end of the room there were tables set out for dinner, which set the plan for the evening. It would be conversation and dancing, followed by a buffet dinner. A small combo played in one corner, and an area was left clear for dancing. Several couples drifted toward the area already. The bar was set up on the opposite end, and waiters circulated with glasses of champagne. World Oil was sparing no expense apparently, and they wanted their friends to know they really appreciated their deserving new Exploration Manager, Doctor Andy Cheston.

James and Andy already knew everyone there, for the early arrivals were mostly company personnel and their wives. Some secretaries mixed congenially with the young bachelors. There were friends from other companies with Tokyo offices coming in, and most of them brought their wives. A few of the young company "bucks" had Oriental dates, which made a nice mixture to converse with their Japanese guests.

A few of the ladies were attired in their exquisite Oriental kimonos with brocade obis, and it appeared World Oil would live up to their multinational ethnic reputation. The group was quickly growing, and Andy realized the party was going to be a large-sized affair. He made a mental note that he must let his boss know how much he appreciated such an elaborate introduction.

Andy had just enough time to order a drink when the couples started migrating toward him. Everyone offered him good wishes, expressing hopes for a successful economic venture. He knew their successes were tied together. No one person would be the winner if they found oil in their areas. The entire World Oil staff seemed pleased that one of their own had received the promotion to the prestigious position.

He was speaking with Ben Brodecki, chief accountant, and Tim McAllister with their wives, Teri and Pamela, when the latest arrivals caught his eye. It was Li Hong Hoe and his granddaughter, Lin Jin. This was a great surprise, and a thrill went tingling up Andy's spine. How nice to see the lovely lady again. How had Jill Hanby come up with their names for her invitation list?

He could not help but watch as she and her grandfather were ushered into the room by Jill Hanby. Lin Jin looked stunning this night, as she had been at the earlier company reception where they had first met. Except this night she was dressed more in an Oriental style.

She wore an ao dai gossamer gown, which had a very thin veiled white overlay, split to the waist on both sides. It covered black tightly fitted silk trousers, which some Oriental stylist had copied from the traditional Vietnamese dress. Andy wondered if she had dressed to impress him, since it was his party. She certainly had succeeded.

"There is a beautiful lady," said Teri Brodecki, calling the attention of the group to Lin Jin, who was moving into the crowd with Li Hong Hoe.

"She certainly is," replied Pamela McAllister. "If I looked like that, I'd dress like an Oriental all the time." There was a note of admiration in her voice.

Lin Jin's long black hair was draped over her high-necked outer top, and was almost as long as her sleeves, but the black, low cut interior bodice showed through distinctly. Outside of the overlay, she wore a simple gold chain and locket, and her tiny waist was accented with a thin gold chain for a belt. Andy wondered what she kept in her tiny gold purse. If there were coins in there, they had to be small ones.

Teri and Pamela were obviously well aware that James and Andy were watching Miss Lin Jin Hoe's entrance.

"She must be one of the most beautiful women to get out of Vietnam," Andy said without taking his eyes from her.

"They say the prettiest ones come from Hue, so she must be the exception that proves the rule. She's from Saigon, by way of Hong Kong, I heard," James explained. "I didn't see any like her when I was there during the war."

"Perhaps she did not have the chance to dress so well as she does now in her grandfather's house," Teri said with a smile. "I have talked with her a few times. She is very outgoing and friendly, unlike most Oriental girls. I find her easy to be around, and a most pleasant person."

Pamela added, "She's not at all self-conscious around strangers, as so many locals are. Her English is good, too. Right out of a Saigon Catholic School."

They went on with their conversation, but kept an eye on the Hoes. Lin Jin was smiling and chatting happily with Jill and Bill Hanby, and joined readily into the gaiety of the occasion. Li Hong Hoe was a good friend and long time business associate of World Oil. His shipyards had constructed many rigs to the specifications of the producing department, so he knew Hanby well.

Lin Jin soon saw Andy with the group in the center of the room. As they moved away from the entrance, she immediately steered her grandfather straight for the group that the Brodeckis and McAllisters had gathered around the guest of honor.

"Good evening, Doctor Andy Cheston." Li Hong Hoe grasped Andy's hand and shook it rather limply, giving him a respectful bow from the waist simultaneously.

Orientals called everyone "doctor" as a sign of respect for anyone with an advanced degree.

"My heartiest congratulations on your achievement of the most prestigious nomination to the high post of your esteemed company."

"Thank you, Mr. Hoe," replied Andy rather formally, as he made a slight bow in return.

"I am sure they will be greatly rewarded by your future exploration efforts, and by the production of much petroleum. We will look forward to your future successes, and to World Oil's rich rewards."

It was too flowery a speech for the occasion, but the Orientals were inclined to such efforts and never said anything in one word if two or more would do. Andy was embarrassed in front of all of the company people there. He tried to brush the compliments aside.

"Thank you very kindly, sir, but I haven't earned all this," he replied.

Lin Jin was only a step away, and she was not about to let him off the hook so easily. She took a step nearer, and spoke slowly and distinctly, as though the words came easily to her mind.

"We are so proud to know a gentleman who has been selected by your world-known company to direct their efforts in this great Pacific Rim market. We know they invest their money wisely. You must be astute, indeed, to conduct such an effort successfully."

She appeared to say just the right thing without visible mental effort. Many people have a facility for saying the wrong thing when a few words of compliment are required, Andy thought, but not Lin Jin. He suspected a little of her Hong Kong education was showing.

She took his hand in an apparent intent to shake it, but she ended up just holding it gently. The lightness of her touch did not go unnoticed by Andy, for he felt a thrill just feeling her cool palm against his. When he suddenly realized that she was showing no inclination to let him go, it was a magic moment in his life. There was a chemistry there that told him this instant was important, and he knew he did not mind the soft touch of her fingers on his palm.

"You are too kind," Andy answered weakly. "Let's go check out the music, and see what kind of hors d'oeuvres that waiter is offering with the champagne. Will you excuse us, please?"

He escorted her easily toward the dance floor. And just that simply, he spirited Lin Jin away from the group. Her grandfather was already entering into a polite conversation about the Pacific Rim economy with Tim and Ben. They would be at home with his discussion of such related numbers, which are the same whether done on a calculator or an abacus. He did not seem to expect his offspring to spend the evening at his side. Teri and Pamela were apparently accustomed to the prevalence of business discussions at the parties they attended.

James Wellman had already asked the Japanese secretary of Bill Hanby, Chisai, to join him on the dance floor. Andy steered Lin Jin to one of the side tables where they could rest their glasses. Then he invited her to join him in testing the combo's music with the group of young explorers already on the dance floor.

The musicians soon increased the tempo of the music, and it became as lively as Andy could wish. He wasn't sure his dancing was up to the steps their pace required. The others seemed to like the rhythm, so he'd try. After all, it was the company staff's night out.

Lin Jin was very easy to talk to, Andy soon realized. She spoke with so soft a voice that he had to listen carefully above the din. He didn't mind, though, for she showed a great deal of studied intelligence, reflecting a broad education. He soon learned more about her background.

"Did you go to secondary school in Saigon?" he asked.

"Yes, we did," she explained quietly, and they rested between dances. "Kim and I were educated by Catholic nuns in a Saigon school, followed by university training in Hong Kong. My mother had followed my grandfather out of Saigon during the latter days of the war."

Apparently, her mother, Thi Lan, had seen too many of the atrocities of that era during her teen years when Lin Jin was born. She and her brother, Kim Jin, had finished their schooling in Hong Kong where she had found a job as a private secretary in the shipping business upon graduation. Brother Kim had just finished college, and now he was looking for a position, but did not wish to enter one of his grandfather's establishments permanently.

"Your mother has a pretty name," remarked Andy.

"Yes, it means 'Little Orchid,' and she yet reminds one of a beautiful flower," Lin Jin answered.

It had not taken Grandfather Li Hong long to recognize that his granddaughter had a talent in the business world, and he requested that the family reunite in his Tokyo home. Thi Lan had refused to leave Hong Kong, so Lin Jin had moved to live in the Li Hong Hoe estate in Japan, and worked part time in his offices.

Andy enjoyed talking to Lin Jin, but not half so much as he liked the way she moved when they danced. He loved the way she felt. The slick black silk under the filmy white cover might just as well have been her skin. It revealed just enough to convince him that underneath there was a real woman. He must get to know her better!

Andy tried not to be too obvious, and he made every effort to circulate among the guests. In doing so, he found that he was unconsciously making an effort to see that Lin Jin met all of the company people there—especially the wives. Most of them he already knew, and he wanted them to have the opportunity to know an Oriental lady with regal taste. Too many of their opinions had been formulated by reading about "tea houses" and "August moons." He wanted an introduction to Lin Jin to be a part of their education, too, as it was becoming a most interesting part of his. He knew that they would meet very few Orientals like her.

Andy left Lin Jin's side only to dance with those wives of special friends he knew. It bothered him a little that overseas wives treat all of the company bachelors as they would their own sons, and as if they needed help with their social arrangements. Then if things got too hot for them to handle, they'd back off and deny everything.

Andy escorted Jill Hanby to the dance floor during one of the quieter numbers.

Jill said, smiling, "I'm happy to see that you appreciate the presence of a certain young lady tonight. She wanted very much to meet you again."

"And how would you know that, Madam?" Andy grinned back,

"I know, because she told me at a dinner party we attended a couple of weeks ago. I was having trouble there because I never could eat well sitting on the floor. Lin Jin was sitting near me, and I guess she noticed my discomfort, so we spent most of that dinner hour in conversation. Anyway, I'm happy to see the attraction is mutual."

Jill was a special friend of Andy's. They had known each other well enough that she recognized his likes and appreciations as well as her husband, Bill, knew his abilities. She showed an interest in the well-being of the men who worked for her husband, but she knew Andy best. He therefore was not offended by her personal remark. He rather appreciated having a lady around to whom he could speak frankly.

Words got whispered into the proper ear sometimes that could move mountains, but could never be conveyed to one's boss, even in a social conversation. In that circuitous manner, the meanings got passed to the ears of authority, but without the impropriety of a direct comment. Companies didn't run in such a manner officially, but wives established the "pecking order" of their company society.

"She really is a beautiful and intelligent girl, Jill. If you had anything to do with picking her to divert my mind from the agonies we have all gone through these past weeks, I thank you."

"I didn't exactly set you up, Andy. We just fixed it so it could happen, if you both wished it to."

"She is nice. I'd like to take a little time off to develop a friendship with her, but we are aware what work the next months will entail. The entire staff will be extremely busy, with no time for socializing. Anyway, I really thought it was her grandfather who was responsible for her being here," Andy concluded with a sly smile.

That got a laugh from Jill. They parted when Andy returned her to the group of couples surrounding the table his host had selected to entertain the ranking noncompany guests.

A few minutes later, Andy saw Jill talking to the headwaiter, and he knew instructions were being given for the entrées. They were to serve their own plates from a buffet, then arrange seating of their own selection.

He found his way quickly back to the group where Lin Jin was happily chatting with her new friend, Chisai, and the geologists. Just as the big gong reverberated its announcement that dinner was available, he approached Lin Jin and held her lightly by the arm.

"Lin Jin, would you join our little group for dinner?" he asked. "We have a table for eight staked out over here by the dance floor. Perhaps the music won't be too loud." He didn't remember if he had suggested they eat together before, but it certainly had been inferred.

Lin Jin smiled sweetly, and first looked around questioningly to find her grandfather before she answered. Seeing him occupied at the Hanbys' table, she quickly nodded her assent. Both she and Andy assumed quite correctly that the elder Hoe would be happier with a group nearer his own age and interests, and where they could at least refer to business.

The dinner discussion at their table was light and frequently interrupted by couples leaving for the dance floor. Chisai, whom James had asked to join them, was finding that she had a lot in common with Lin Jin. They were birds of a feather, Andy and James agreed.

The ladies kept up the light banter in Japanese among themselves and with the wives of the Idimitsu guests throughout dinner. Occasionally one of the husbands would explain to his wife what the men were saying in English, but for the most part it didn't matter so long as the food was good and the sake was flowing with the music. Andy worried that the ladies would feel excluded, but apparently they had arranged a congenial young group, all of whom liked to dance and were ready to devote this night to partying.

A dessert tray was presented to each individual after a superior meal, followed by a service of real imported coffee. The party was ending all too soon to suit the younger group, so it was easy for them to agree they should continue the dancing at a cabaret on the Ginza, and possibly take in a floor show.

"Why don't we all meet at the Golden Bee?" James suggested. Soon the entire younger set had made their plans to meet there after their genial host and hostess had said good night.

Andy turned to Lin Jin. Taking her hand, he said, "Lin Jin, it would please me greatly if you could join me with the group at the Golden Bee. James and I have a driver available tonight, so I can take you home later, whenever you wish. Perhaps your grandfather wouldn't mind if I borrowed you for another hour or so?"

She pressed his hand when he asked, and listened intently.

"I would be delighted to join you, Doctor Cheston. It sounds like fun, as long as we do not intend to visit the 'hot-bath' teahouses." Lin Jin gave a quick smile at her intended joke. "I must first advise Bapak Hoe that I have accepted your invitation, and will ride home with you later."

Apparently, Lin Jin had established her complete but respectful independence from the Bapak, or fatherly rule.

"Please call me Andy," he replied warmly. "We don't stand on formality with our dancing partners."

\* \* \*

They had dropped James and Chisai off at her apartment. "I'll find my way on home, Andy," James told them. "It was a very nice evening, and it was my pleasure to see you again, Lin Jin Hoe."

"Good night, James and Chisai. It has been most pleasant," replied Lin Jin.

"Thanks, James," Andy said. "It'll take Jimmy-san a while to get to Hoes' and back here, so I'll see you tomorrow. Good night, Chisai. I've certainly enjoyed the party, and I'll tell the Hanbys how much I appreciated them getting us all together."

It was getting on into the wee hours of the morning as Jimmy-san cruised toward the residential outskirts of the huge city. The cabaret visit had been as successful as the dinner party, and the group really did have a lot in common. They loved to party.

By the time Andy and Lin Jin were riding alone in the comfortable rear seat of the Crown Toyota, they were feeling both very tired and very much at ease. It was the effect of the great quantity of alcohol consumed, together with a lot of exercise. Andy was glad that Lin Jin lived a good distance away in the suburbs, because it gave him an opportunity to get to know her with more privacy than he had been able to achieve during the extended evening.

Since Lin Jin didn't seem to object, and since he had been holding her closely all evening while dancing, it was only natural that they should fit so comfortably against one another as they rode through the dark quiet Tokyo outskirts. This was the only time these streets were quiet, so it lent a certain magic to the night as they peered at the trees lining the avenues through the rings of mist around the distant streetlamps.

He found they no longer had anything that needed to be said to each other. It was contentment enough to feel the warmth of their nestled bodies as her silk sheathed leg lay alongside his. Her head found its place snuggled on his shoulder, and her long black hair streamed down over his arm as he held her hand. It was the only communication they needed. He suddenly realized that he was squeezing her hand too tightly, and the giant pearl ring must have been cutting her fingers. It went along with his thoughts.

The Crown Toyota nosed through the open iron gate of the rock-fenced Hoe estate, and stopped in front of the doorway. Jimmy-san left his seat and went around the car, waiting to open her door. Andy noted it was a huge stone house. Li Hong Hoe lived in the high-rent district, but then he owned a shipyard. It was what was expected of him, but not overly pretentious.

Their good-night kiss was almost an anticlimax after their hour-long loving ride. He regretfully stepped down from the car, and followed Lin Jin to the portico, where a lit lantern hung above the door. She seemed to melt into his arms. Andy wondered if this magic moment was only the result of too much liquor and too late an evening. Was she thinking the same? Would she still remember him so lovingly in the morning?

Right now he felt that he'd prefer not to end this evening at all. He also realized it was much too soon for such thoughts. They must maintain some semblance of decorum, if only for social appearances. Should he ask her for another meeting now? Or should he call her later—say, next week? But next week he'd be working and too busy.

Finally, and all too soon for Andy's way of thinking, their kisses ended. Did he dare speak to this lovely lady who was making her own needs and desires so obvious? He could get in over his head very easily. Would it compromise the company's business relationship with her family? He must risk that, even if his twin sister, Elizabeth, would certainly not approve. Lin Jin was so lovely.

"Lin Jin, I must see you again, soon," he said quickly. He was either short of breath, or afraid he'd change his mind and not speak. Had he kissed her that long? "I want to take you to dinner—soon. Can you accept a night out with me tomorrow evening—or, it will soon be light, so that's tonight?"

His mind was spinning around, balancing the necessity of keeping his work schedule in order and fighting against the influence of all that alcohol. Still he knew that he could no longer put off an arrangement to be with Lin Jin again, if she was willing. What would her grandfather think of such a dating arrangement? He supposed Mr. Hoe would respect any arrangement Lin Jin made, since she was well educated, and apparently completely in charge of her own life.

"I would love to go out with you, Andy-san," she replied softly.

Andy was thrilled when she used the term of endearment for the first time. It was almost like a dream. Too much alcohol, he realized.

"First I must speak to Bapak, however. Please call me later than twelve tomorrow, and by that time I should be able to accept properly for a later afternoon arrangement."

With that, she leaned quickly forward, retrieving her tiny purse from beneath his arm, and kissed him lightly, again on the lips. Then she slipped through the entry into the engawa, and as she stooped to remove her shoes, the heavy door closed with a quiet click. Andy knew he would dream well that night.

# Six

At midday the haze obscured the view of the mountains below, which Andy knew was normal for that area of the sky around Mount Fujiyama. He sat with William Hanby in the first-class section of the wide-bodied jet. They had just settled into reading their briefcase material and accepted a glass of champagne from the stewardess. Their departure from Narita Airport a half hour before, en route to Ho Chi Minh City in Vietnam, had been right on time. Andy peered intently past Bill and out their right-hand window. He was attempting to catch a glimpse of the famous volcanic holy mountain with its snowy cap. He knew it should show through the haze, above the layer of stratus clouds.

Only once had he seen the picturesque mountain from his apartment in Tokyo, through the crystal clarity of a cold air mass, and without any clouds. It is remarkable, he thought, how they come up with all of those beautiful clear picture postcards for calendars they sell to tourists. They make everyone believe that the neatly manicured Japanese gardens extend right up the slopes to the very top of the oft-climbed shrine.

"Look, Bill. There it is way out there. It's quite a disappointment from this viewpoint." It was thirty miles away or so, and about four miles lower. "From here it looks like a tiny Chinese coolie's hat sitting on a sea of cotton balls." The calendar artists would dismiss this shot.

"Yes, I've seen it a lot clearer. We'll have to accept an invitation to play golf there when things aren't so busy," Bill suggested.

"It looks a lot more impressive from the courses there on the flanks," replied Andy.

There was no reply. Bill sipped his drink, and it was obvious that he had more serious things on his mind.

"Andy," Bill said as he settled himself with his briefcase on his knees, "I'm glad we have this time to review our position before we face our new partners in Vietnam. You and your team did an excellent job of selling our presentation to the directors back in Houston, and I want to commend you on your part in that sales job. You certainly impressed them."

"Thanks; it went rather well. The data summary was neatly prepared, thanks to the coordination with the geophysicists by James. It gave us the background for the financial projections by Ben Brodecki. He kept their data churning in their computers for a lot of nights."

"I know you all put in a lot of work, and it paid off."

"It was a team effort to get all of the exploration and engineering and financial projects together under the same tent. We hardly had a chance to coordinate a recommendation before we were presenting it to Chairman Eason's committee. Of course, the members had already pretty much made up their minds." Andy knew this was nothing new to Bill.

"Our directors are nobody's fools, and if you can sell any deep water drilling deals to them, and make it appear to be to our company's advantage to risk a hundred million or so on a joint deal with the Vietnamese government, then it should not be any trouble to convince the Viets they should accept the use of our money," Bill stated firmly.

"I'm sure they'll be happy for us to invest that amount to boost their economy. What worries me more is how we go about retaining control of the operation. They may want to set the contracts up so they can take the money and run," Andy explained.

"That's true; I'm sure they will," Bill replied. "I'm glad you were making the presentation in Houston. It gave me a chance to listen for once, and to think objectively about our recommendations." Hanby continued to sip his champagne.

"I'm afraid it wasn't as polished as it could have been," Andy said.

"For the time we had, it was great. We have to make sure that the company's rewards will be worth our risk there. The Viets expect us to put up all the money and direct the efforts required for exploring. The only risk they are taking is that we will really push to make them accept only the contract we propose, and exclude others, including locals. If they sign with us it will cut out any other contractor competition for a considerable period of time."

"They could hardly expect us to come in without a tight contract," Andy replied.

"I hope they see it that way." Bill continued, "We'll be in on the ground floor in their country, and with a head start on production. We'll stand a good chance of making a lot more profit if we find oil there."

"It's still only a one-in-ten shot to make a discovery on our first well, with a little better odds on subsequent efforts," Andy reminded him.

"Our main problem, assuming that we find oil, is running an operation that will be conclusive. We must remain in control of the business once the crude appears and is aboard a tanker on its way to market. People have a way of becoming greedy when they see a profit accumulate. We'll have to see that safeguards against such changes in our contracts are clearly spelled out," Bill stated.

"World Oil is not so big a company that it can afford to fritter away the kind of cash this operation will require," Andy answered. "It'll be over a year before we can get into production, at best. Therefore, we have to concentrate on long-range goals."

"We have already felt the sting of their business associations when we lost our plane. I'm not so sure all of their factions are convinced we're welcome to come into their arena with American dollars and do the operating."

"It's only the dollars they want. We'll have to be damn careful to see that they don't arrange to toss us out on our ear once we have made the investment such as seismic coverage and geological evaluation, and drilled the first discovery well," Andy stated.

"That's something I want to talk to you about, Andy." Bill was obviously deep in thought, because he sipped his drink again and almost missed the tray when he set it down. He leaned nearer to speak softly. "I've had a man working on that plane crash. This is top-secret info, so don't spread it around to anyone. You'll need to know soon, though, because your work will be affected."

"Is it someone I'd know?" asked Andy in a whisper.

"Yes. It's Kelly Johnson. I spoke to you of him before. He's along on this trip for that reason. He's sitting in the back with Brodecki and Wellman and the rest of our group. He was actually hired from the FBI as an investigator. Not only is he a qualified auditor, but he is also well trained in snooping where it is needed. He has made several trips through Hong Kong recently, following up on the trail of the work Harold Blanton was doing there. Frankly, it is work you will soon be deeply involved in."

"That will suit me fine," Andy said. "I'm determined that somehow the deaths of our friends are going to be avenged. It may take a long time, but there will come a day of reckoning for that bastard, whoever he may be."

"Let's not be in too big a hurry. Perhaps time will furnish clues that would not be available on a short-term basis." Hanby produced his pipe, and looked around to see if he would be allowed to light it there. Thinking the better of it, he replaced it in his pocket.

"I might as well tell you now that we should be thinking about opening an office in Hong Kong to conduct this operation in Vietnamese waters.

It may happen that we can't operate freely from Ho Chi Minh City, especially since the man who set up the bombing was traced back to there by Kelly. He must be well up in the government, for he knew all of Harold's plans."

"That's not too surprising," Andy said. "Things in Saigon are probably no different now from what they were during the war with all the black market. They weren't so good in Saigon then, even under the Americans."

Andy was thinking that we should have learned a thing or two from the French, and let them fight their own bush war. We'll be a lot better off now if we can conduct our business with them around the conference tables of their official governmental offices, and with responsible, educated personnel. Their big problem is they have sent all of their former college level people to the reeducation camps, and replaced most of them with northern incompetents. This was hard for him to explain to Bill, since he hadn't been there.

"I'm glad to hear you are not afraid to go back to Saigon in spite of your war experiences. It appears their officials hold no grudges against the men who were there during the fighting. We'll try to minimize any references to your previous knowledge of poisoned bamboo spikes and claustrophobic tunnels experienced in their country. Try to put that all behind you for now, and concentrate on business level associations."

"I'll try, but that may be hard to do completely, because I know what they're capable of," Andy said, as he searched his briefcase for a sheaf of notes on his upcoming presentation.

"We'll set up a meeting with our staff in our hotel tonight after we get settled in, and go over the presentation we plan to make to their energy minister. I suppose he has very few experienced or overly educated men in his employ, and absolutely nobody with any drilling experience. They've rubbed up against the Russians a bit, but that's no help. We'll have to speak explicitly and very clearly, or they are not likely to understand us. When we get to the money part, such as will be presented by Brodecki, I'm sure then they'll come alive, and both listen and understand only too well."

"We may be surprised by the knowledge of some of their young men," Andy said. "They may have rehired some of those who chose to leave with the American forces. They could have been educated at universities in the States, and returned to join in the economic revolution they have promised."

He thought of the black-shaggy-haired, bushy-eyebrowed assistant minister, Dong Huan Chou, who attended the reception the night they had heard of the company's plane disaster. He had dark, inset, unsmiling eyes that seemed even more menacing because of the constant frown he wore on his pocked face.

"It wouldn't surprise me if Dong Huan Chou wasn't one of those. He seemed to be the type who would scramble for a position where there was money to be made. I wonder who he knew to get to be assistant energy minister," Andy mused.

"That would be hard to tell. Probably someone connected with the horde from the north who moved in at the end of the war. He might even have been working for them as an agent all along."

"Anyway, I didn't like his looks. I think I had seen him before when the war was on in Saigon, but I'm not sure. I didn't have that much to do with the black market. We'll probably get the chance to meet him again tomorrow," Andy said.

"We'll all be a lot smarter tomorrow when we hear about how they react toward our offer. I'm sure they will be sharp bargainers, and no matter what we offer they'll want more. We just have to make sure we don't leave a lot on the table for some other company to come in and snap it up." Hanby closed his briefcase and placed it on the floor. Then he moved across Andy into the aisle and stretched.

"I need to talk to Brodecki, and with Kelly, so I'm going in the back. I'll send Wellman up. You can 'buy' him a drink while the money handlers and I go over a few things for tomorrow's program."

While alone for the moment, Andy was thinking these next few days were going to be a wearisome time. But he may as well get used to it, for these negotiations may last for weeks. The company was depending on Hanby to strike a deal with the Vietnamese that would be fair both to them and to World Oil, but he would be the one who was expected to carry out the exploration. He wondered if the Viets could be trusted to stick by any contract they might sign. His experience with them to date indicated they would stir up a lot of trouble in his future.

James Wellman strolled into the first-class compartment a few minutes later. He stepped his long legs across Andy, and dropped into the window seat.

"I hear you want to speak to me about bartending duties," he stated with a knowing smile.

"No," Andy replied. "That was Bill's idea. Maybe he thought you needed a drink, or that you hadn't picked up your cash advance for this trip." It was an inside joke, so they both smiled.

"Actually, he just wanted my seat so he and old 'bean-counter' Brodecki could go over the figures he expects to present to the Viets tomorrow," James joked.

"Bill tries to make his plane rides productive."

"Yeah; they want to count their money. Do you think they'll send a limo to meet us at the airport, with a sleigh and Santa suits?" James gave a sly grin.

"You believe they'll think we have a sack of presents to give them?"

"I'll bet they think we're going to be the best thing they've seen since Christmas. Or is it Tet? They'll believe our briefcases are stuffed with hundred dollar bills," James answered.

"Maybe we can avoid giving them the family jewels if we're careful. At least not both of them," Andy replied. "Pull up a tray, and we'll get that lanky stewardess with the short skirt to bring the bar cart and leave it where we can reach it. By the time we get to Saigon we'll be ready to accept any deal they offer."

He waved to the girl who was passing with a tray on her way to the galley. She already knew what he wanted.

"No, I think I'll just have a gin and tonic to avoid the dreaded fever, and let it go at that. It sounds like Bill is planning to put us through our paces until late tonight. We'll have to be on our best behavior." James talked big, but it was just his relief gimmick from his steady hard work habit.

Andy smiled. He had been so busy lately that he had little time to observe how James' love life had been progressing. Tall and boyish, he had little trouble making contacts with sweet young things, but they both had been spending all their available hours on map preparations. Still, one does have to go out to eat occasionally, and to sleep sometimes.

"Haven't you been to the Ginza for a hot bath and massage lately?" Andy asked. "I've heard they're very relaxing after a long day in the office."

"You know where I've been spending my time," James replied with disdain. "We haven't been more than fifty feet from one another for the past three weeks." James craned his neck to look out the window. There was nothing to be seen there but sun above the clouds, which was normal for this altitude. He pulled down the window screen.

"What's out there?"

"Nothing but clouds. I don't know why they put windows in planes anyway, since you can't see anything," James said.

Their drinks arrived, and after a long sip, Andy asked, "Whatever happened to the thing you had going with Chisai? You were escorting her around pretty well after the party at Hanby's. Did Jill set you up with her, or did that just develop naturally?" He gave James a wry smile.

"That was quite an evening, but it just developed for me the same way your date with Lin Jin did for you."

"It looked like you had planned the whole encounter ahead of time. You must not look for meat where you get your potatoes, as the old saying goes."

Andy smiled, and they both knew he was joking. They also knew that it was one of those serious-type jokes, for there is no quicker way to disrupt the effectiveness of an office staff, so you don't date the secretaries. Right now, they had no time in their schedules for poor performances.

"What about you, Andy?" James replied with a questioning glance. "How many times have you been out with Lin Jin since that party weekend?"

"Not many. We've been too busy."

"Jill sure had an eye out for your social life, and she picked a nice one for you. I wonder how she knew you two would get along?" They were good friends, and personal questions were not unwelcome.

"She has a knack of keeping up with her friends, and Jill knows me," Andy answered.

"I know you saw her again on the next day, but if you've seen her again since then, it must have been the result of serious planning." In response to Andy's grin, James went on. "Care to tell me about it?"

The jets droned as a thoughtful interlude ensued. Finally Andy said, "Yes, it turned out to be an exciting weekend." He told James about their late night, loving ride. Andy was enjoying thinking back over the weekend. It brought a warm glow into his chest and made his voice more gentle.

"Was that the end of it?" James asked.

"No. I made a date with her for the next day, and we met at her grandfather's club for a late lunch. Then we returned to their sitting room and talked for hours beside a hibachi. She told me how she and her brother, Kim, came to be educated by the nuns in French and English schools of Saigon."

"You can tell she's had a good education. When did she move to Hong Kong?"

"There's something funny about that. Her mother left Saigon early in the war. Lin Jin doesn't seem to know much about why. She and Kim went with her to Hong Kong, then returned. They stayed with a relative there and attended the Catholic schools until their grandfather insisted they leave.

He's a smart old bird. But all the time we talked, I was wondering how sister Beth would fit Lin Jin into her San Francisco social life."

"Does Elizabeth know you have an Oriental girlfriend yet?" James asked. Before Andy answered, he knew he need not have even wondered. The question was not too far out of line, for he had met Beth on several occasions.

"I think not. Beth and I seem to have grown apart in our thinking. When we were both in school it didn't seem to matter, but now I realize she has become a first-class bigot. She and her social circle can't accept anyone with any color. Sorry to talk about my twin in a negative way."

The stewardess came by and checked their drinks, but they were fine. James was listening obediently, so Andy went on.

"Our conversations continued for hours. Her family came and went, almost ignoring us as though it were common to have a 'round-eye' making himself at home in their parlor. It's a funny thing about a Japanese house—you never know where the doors are supposed to be, for any rice-paper panel can slide open at any time. For Orientals, privacy is more of an understanding than a physical requirement."

"It sounds like you had a pleasant day, since you remember the details of it so well. Did she ever let you go home, or did you offer to spend the night?" James asked with a smirk.

"Oh, that wasn't the end of it. When it began to get dark out, we had tea served by her grandmother. We saw little of the old lady, because she seemed a bit frail. I think she felt it her duty to make an appearance. You know she didn't go to the Hanbys' party. Anyway, after the tea, Lin Jin and I escaped back to the company car. She suggested a quiet restaurant off in a suburb. It took a long time to drive there, so we became even better acquainted en route."

"It sounds like a successful introduction to love."

"To make a short story even shorter, I'm sure Lin Jin was getting the impression that I'd be back to see her. I explained that we had a serious work schedule ahead, and any interests we might develop would have to be put on a back burner."

"Yeah, you've got it bad," James said with a boyish grin. "I can't wait to see Beth's expression when you show up for dinner with Lin Jin on your arm, and she just happens to have her friend, Valarie, along. That should create a fireworks display good enough for the Tet celebration."

"I'll try not to let that happen. We don't want to start another civil war." Andy was a little worried, though, as he thought of the possibilities. If things continued along these lines, their confrontation was bound to happen sometime.

They finished their drinks. Bill Hanby walked up the aisle and stood beside Andy.

"How's the other side of the tracks doing?" James asked lightly.

"They're fine. They probably didn't want to watch the movie anyway," Bill replied, knowing he had interrupted their solitude.

"Well, I'll get on back to my seat then, and let you get some rest before we arrive." James exchanged places with Bill, again stepping around Andy. "We'll see you on the ground then, and hope the Viet Petros have arranged at least a cycleshaw for our transportation."

Bill settled into his seat with a squirming, restless motion. Finally he turned to Andy.

"I've been talking to the FBI. Kelly wants to get together with you in Saigon for some extracurricular touring. He knows his way around the world, but not around Saigon so well. He wants to go over some possibilities with you, and to check out some leads on the ground. He thinks he has good insight into the group who planted the device that exploded on our plane. In fact, he thinks he knows who they were, past tense. He was specific about the 'were,' because he believes they may no longer exist. Now he is trying to locate the persons who directed their work." Bill gazed steadily at Andy. "Do you think you could help him in a covert operation?"

Andy looked intently back at Bill Hanby and said, "My best friend was killed on that plane. Anything I can do to find out who those bastards were, I'll do."

Hanby settled back in his seat. "I guess we all feel the same way. Aside from our dedication to the company and its programs, the men on that plane were our friends. We're not going to just forget what happened to them. So why don't you stroll back and get better acquainted with Kelly Johnson. He may have some information you will need to know."

"OK." Andy stood up and stretched. "We should be arriving in about an hour. I'll go back and hear what Kelly has to say. We'll have to watch our step while we're there, because I know whoever we're looking for will also be watching us. I'll be back before we land."

Andy made his way past the curtains and into the rear section, and found their company group sitting together. Kelly Johnson had a stocky, quiet appearance, not one who would stand out in a crowd. In fact, he looked like an auditor, Andy thought. He would demand respect if he asked a question, but he was not overly intimidating. He certainly didn't look like FBI. He saw Andy coming, and with a nod he rose and wandered farther back in the cabin. They settled into a pair of seats in a quiet corner where they would not be disturbed or overheard.

"It's good to see you again, but sorry about the circumstances." Kelly pulled out a small notebook. "I've been collecting data for the company on the bombing of our plane, while ostensibly checking our offices as an auditor, and looking at data related to the Saigon negotiations you are going to conduct."

"I'm glad to hear that the company is officially looking into the explosion," Andy said. "I really didn't think Eason or Hanby would let it pass without an investigation, especially when we desperately need to know which side the local authorities are on."

"Bill Hanby told me you were cleared for this. There's little we can do officially, of course," Kelly stated. "What we do about the terrorists may not end up being an official action, if you follow me."

Andy's heart gave a leap, for here was a man who thought as he did.

"Whoever caused that terrorism needs to be punished, one way or another," Andy spoke grimly. "A person can feel very strongly about such things when his best friend has been killed."

"I'm sure you are right," Kelly spoke softly. "I'm going to need some assistance in Saigon to carry out the investigations." Kelly turned a page in his notes.

"Just let me know what I can do."

"Hanby tells me you are well versed in the activities there, or were during the war. Let's hope things haven't changed too much, and that we can still be free enough of their surveillance to allow a little snooping. I have Hanby's permission to ask you to help in this covert operation, without spreading the information around, even to our close friends in company circles. I'm sure you understand what I mean, for one never knows how far our efforts might go afield. In that case, it may be safer for our friends not to know all that transpires. Do you think you want to get yourself involved in such skulduggery?"

"I have been hoping someone like you'd get here to look into this action for the company," Andy replied.

Kelly had tried to make it very clear that now was the time to opt out, before the plane landed in Saigon.

"Do I make myself perfectly clear?" he insisted.

"Yes, perfectly," replied Andy. "I've thought this over carefully. You can count on me for whatever action it takes." Andy knew he was committing himself firmly.

"Good," replied Kelly. "Now, one more thing. During my last visit to Hong Kong, I made some contacts at the airport. It turns out that all the maintenance of private aircraft there is handled by a company called International Maintenance, Inc. They have crews who have Vietnamese connections. Thus far I have not been able to come up with names, but I'm sure they did the actual bomb installation."

"What are the chances of finding out who they worked for?"

He turned several more pages in his notebook. "I'll hope to get that information while we are in Saigon. Then we will go ahead and see where their involvement might lead."

Andy had a lot of questions, and before they reached Saigon he became satisfied that Kelly was a skillful and dedicated agent who would do his best to find all of the answers they needed. He was certain they could work well together, for each had a deeply ingrained common purpose. It was to eliminate the enemy of their company who had killed their friends.

As they started their descent into Saigon, Andy returned to his own seat, and tried to mentally prepare himself for their reception by the government representatives. He couldn't help but wonder what would be the attitude of the lower working echelon of the local Vietnamese Energy Ministry. How would they be treated?

Would it be all smiles and cooperation with open arms, being viewed as saviors bringing money to develop a sagging economy, or would they be seen as a group of interlopers who were trying to steal Vietnam's wealth? He would have to be on guard to properly perform his function as exploration manager, and at the same time concentrate on his commitment to assist Kelly as his determination had dictated.

# Seven

The screech of the tires announced the touchdown of the heavy plane against the humid runway. The big jet taxied slowly on the bumpy asphalt up to the international terminal at Saigon's airport, Tan Son Nhat, just as the sun sank through the clouds at the horizon. A profusion of uniformed men surrounded the ramp. It was dead calm outside, and the heat was stifling. It had been raining, for a few of the airport crewmen wore slickers. Others just accepted the rain as a normal occurrence, which helped cool their thin shirts.

There were two seasons in Ho Chi Minh City, Andy thought, hot and dry, or even hotter and raining. Most of the people standing on the observation deck of the terminal held umbrellas as protection against a drizzle as they faced the quickly disappearing red ball of the sun.

The World Oil team gathered at the bottom of the ramp of steps, where an official representative of the Vietnam State Oil Company arrived to greet them. It was Pham Xuan Bach, whom Andy had met before, and he introduced himself as the assistant to the president of the oil company. This meant that he had been assigned to take them to their hotel, and see that they made it to the conference room tomorrow morning where their official meetings were to be held.

Pham Xuan Bach was a short little man with heavy glasses, and his light, linen shirt was drenched either with perspiration or rain. He was all smiles, though, and was assuring everyone there would be no trouble with the customs officials if he could just collect the passports. They would be returned at the hotel, which would be the old Majestic. Andy knew it well.

From the hotel rooms, he explained, they would be able to look out at the magnificent view of the broad Saigon River. It was an American officer's quarters during the war, and now was primarily occupied by thuong gia, or traveling traders. Andy had stayed there many times during the war. Now, however, he realized it would be entirely different under the government's management.

Everyone was gazing inquiringly at the airport facilities, trying to figure out where Bach was leading the group. Actually the group was just moving out of the push of the crowd. Soon, the hustle and bustle of the other passengers wandering toward the terminal began to clear the area. Only then did a procession of black sedans appear, inching toward the group among the carts and bicycles that seemed to be running everywhere.

Pham Bach carefully positioned his visitors into specific cars according to rank, as his protocol list had dictated. William Hanby and his second in command, Manager of Exploration, Far East, Andrew Cheston, were directed to the first and longest limousine, where Bach would be their guide.

He further explained that they would be seeing some of the sights of Saigon on their "chay rong rong" through the city.

The stocky little guide explained that the luggage would be taken care of, and would reach them at their hotel. That suited everyone just fine, for geologists and geophysicists never travel without their tubes of maps and heavy briefcases in their personal possession. In their experience of avoiding the loss of their valuable works, they never checked their reports if there was any way to keep them in sight while traveling. Andy watched Kelly as he boarded a car. He noted that he was making careful observations as to how the unescorted passengers were being checked by customs. He suddenly wondered if Kelly was carrying any kind of weapon, and what they would do if they found one. But it was a chance they could not take, being here on official business.

The entourage was finally settled in the parade of vehicles, and when Pham Bach was satisfied, he returned to his seat. They then started off in a rush, horns blaring, making no effort to avoid the masses of humanity on the narrow paved road after they had left the airport gate. There seemed to be crowds of people standing everywhere along the road, the same as inside the airport.

Just to make conversation, Andy asked, "Pham Bach, what were all those people waiting for at the terminal? Surely those masses couldn't be leaving on airplanes."

"Most were there with some member of their family, hoping that possibly today they might squeeze aboard a flight, becoming emigrants," relied Pham Bach. "Even when their papers are finally cleared, there is no guarantee that an exit from the country will be permitted soon."

"Your English is very good, Pham Bach," Hanby said. "Where did you go to school?"

"I studied business management at Georgetown University in Washington," was his proud reply.

He didn't mention how far he had progressed toward a degree. He then continued with a running explanation of the scenery as they passed.

"The government is keeping up the maintenance of the airport, which had been left in miserable condition by the Americans."

Andy observed that only one runway was in operation, and many of the service vehicles had grass growing through the cracks of the asphalt beneath them.

Their Mercedes was air-conditioned; however, there seemed to be some trouble with the system, and only the driver was comfortable. Andy was glad he wore only a light cotton shirt. As they traveled down the red laterite roads, he pointed out some of the features to Hanby that had been missed by Pham Bach.

"Bill, they have some beautiful girls here," explained Andy. "Many of the women used to wear ao dais, which have long sleeves for protection against the sun. Most of the younger girls prefer T-shirts or even sleeveless blouses these days, it seems. The ao dai is now usually seen only on clerks in the fancier shops, right, Pham Bach?"

"That is so true, Doctor Cheston. See the old men with their sunken eyes who huddle shivering under blankets? They have malaria," said Pham Bach, as they sped by. "Half the people here have it. Those who have jobs can buy medicine, but most jobs are temporary, and last only a day or so each week."

Andy knew most of the educated men had been sent to reeducation camps to work on the farms, and the women didn't really matter here. They were only a commodity to be used, either in the fields or in bed. It was a chauvinistic society of the worst kind.

He was sad to see the faces of the malnourished children as they roared past in their eloquent procession. His stomach turned as they passed near the markets, and they got a strong whiff of the way the common people really lived.

As they passed, they could see their shops and stalls had few goods on their shelves for sale. Pham Bach dismissed the outrageous prices as a result of materials being smuggled into the country via the Mekong Delta. Ho Chi Minh City was the second capital of Vietnam, but Saigon was the noisy river town where commerce was king, and people lived by their wits. Andy knew their pickpockets were brazen, and extremely adept at their trade. One always kept his hand on his wallet in a crowd.

"Here we are approaching the Roman Catholic Cathedral," Pham Bach noted, interrupting Andy's thoughts. "It conducts masses every day."

Their guide was still sweating profusely, but there was no escape from his stench. Anyway, the "round-eyes" probably smelled the same to him.

Bach continued, "And that is our beautifully decorated City Hall, which is the meeting location of the People's Committee of Ho Chi Minh City." He seemed very proud of it. "It administers over four million people, and Saigon is growing rapidly, since it is the center of our commercial development." He winced when he realized he had officially used the old city name, and Andy wondered if he would correct himself. He didn't.

Andy had too many memories of the scenes they were passing to share his thoughts with anyone who had not been there at that horrible time of history. He wondered how James was putting up with his review of Saigon.

"Ahead is the National Museum, where are collected the most important Vietnamese artifacts, both those of war and of peace, such as the bronze plaque from the former American Embassy building."

Making the comment did not seem to bother him, for his American schooling had not replaced all of his Communist indoctrination.

"We are crossing Dong Khoi Street, which is where there still exists night life, but no longer with the aggressive bar girls of the night who lived here to entertain the American soldiers during the war."

He went on to explain that prostitution is now illegal. He failed, however, to tell the mission of the sharply dressed young ladies who cruised by on their motorbikes, making lewd suggestions to all who would look.

"Many visitors like to shop here," Pham Bach continued. "We have mother-of-pearl and tortoise shell for ladies." He was becoming enthusiastic. "Also there is liquor, bronze gongs, drums, and oil paintings, all good; and Cuban cigars. There is fine Russian caviar—we have many Russian Soviet oil expert visitors." He was obviously into the sales setups for visiting dignitaries, and undoubtedly had experience directing people to shops operated by his relatives who would save his commission for payment later.

Andy was almost ill when he saw the men, both old and young, who sat bent over on the curbs. He realized why, and he had seen the same thing hundreds of times. Occasionally, one could be seen with a syringe in the act of shooting liquefied opium, which is much cheaper than heroin.

"That is illegal, you know, to do drugs here," said Pham Bach. "The government has rehabilitation centers where addicts can get acupuncture to help them dull the dreadful pain of withdrawal." Andy wondered if he was speaking from personal experience.

"Bill, what do you think? Can we operate here?" Andy asked. Did Bill Hanby realize what they were getting into? He was talkative when we left the airport, but now he had slumped into a numb silence.

"Hmmm," was his only reply.

"This is the completely refurbished Rex Hotel, which was bachelor officers quarters during the war. It was decided you should stay at the Majestic Hotel, because rooms there are larger and the view is better," Pham Bach droned. "And here is the Vietnam State Oil Company office, where we will convene our meetings tomorrow." He failed to mention that it was formerly the American Embassy. Perhaps he thought it would be embarrassing.

Andy just wanted to get out of the mass of hopeless struggling people, and to prepare himself for their new venture into this tainted land. He could never be happy here, for it contained too many ghosts. But he must put those thoughts behind him, for they had a new operation to plan, and to sell to this government. First they must find out if they could meet them on even ground, and trust any agreements they might make. Only then could their own efforts go forward in a businesslike manner.

As they trooped up to the reception desk of their hotel, Pham Bach directed Bill and Andy to the counter of a pleasant, well dressed girl, who spoke in excellent English. She handled their papers efficiently, but would not engage in any extracurricular talk. Her efforts must have been strictly supervised by someone watching from behind the scenes. Andy wondered, where had she come from? What district? How many difficult times had she overcome to acquire such a prestigious position? She furnished no clue regarding the answers to those questions.

In their economy, women were less than nothing. Beauty was fleeting, because of their inability to take care of even simple hygiene over a period of time. Pretty girls were to be used and discarded, like a cheap commodity.

When they were finished with the hotel card, Andy and Bill moved to one side.

"This girl either has a very highly positioned family, or is the lover of a well placed government official," Andy explained.

"So that's the way it works, eh?" Bill replied, and he looked ill.

Andy wondered how Lin Jin and her family had lived in the outlying district of Saigon, and how they could have managed to get out of this hellhole. It was at the same time when Lin Jin's grandfather, Li Hong Hoe, who was Japanese, had been developing his shipyards. Their family setup was a complicated one, but obviously of some financial importance to the economy of the region.

Lin Jin and her brother Kim had, indeed, been fortunate to have escaped the terror of a warring Saigon at an early date. He wondered if he would ever know what had happened to them during that era. She had spoken of her mother only fleetingly, saying she and Kim had returned to attend school after Thi Lan had escaped and they had obtained a British passport in Hong Kong. He was becoming more and more determined that they must operate their offshore drilling from a base outside the country.

Neither Kim nor Lin Jin had ever spoken of their father, except to say they didn't remember him. Obviously he was a topic that was not discussed. Many young men her father's age had been killed in the war, and Andy assumed their father had been one of those. Given the status of the country at her birth, the possibilities of his identity were many, some unspeakable.

As Pham Bach prepared to take his leave of the group, he said, "Please call me George, for that is what they named me in the United States school."

He could have told us that sooner, Andy thought.

"Thank you for meeting us, George," Hanby told him. "What should we do tomorrow morning about our transportation? We can get taxis. Or will your drivers return?"

"Your transportation has been arranged, so have no dismay. They will await you at eight. Will you need them this evening?"

"No, George. We're all tired, and have our program to review. So, thanks again, and good night." He made a curt bow.

"Andy, let's see if we can get a quick shower and then meet with the group in the bar at eight for a quick drink and sandwich. Then we'll go over our program once more to be ready for tomorrow. You and Kelly may want to get your feet on the ground later."

Hanby had spoken precisely. It was more of an order, and it demonstrated that Bill also recognized they had a division of priorities in Ho Chi Minh City.

# Eight

It didn't look like the Saigon American Embassy to Andy anymore. The Vietnamese had converted it into an office building, taking care to preserve the systems built into the facility, such as air-conditioning and security. Still, it did not appear as he remembered it when he had occasions to pass through here during his war days, even though some of the furniture seemed to be the same.

The entire group of World Oil visitors were ushered into the State Oil Company's conference room, and directed to seats with name cards hand lettered on both sides, which were positioned in front of each chair.

"Permit me to welcome all of you in the name of the Vietnam State Oil Company," President Nguyen Muoi said. "I trust your airport reception made your arrival convenient. Also, I hope your hotel accommodations are satisfactory, and that you had a good night's rest. My assistant, Pham Xuan Bach, whom you call George, tells me your luggage was delivered safely."

Nguyen Muoi's English was very good. He wore a freshly pressed linen shirt, which showed no evidence that it had ever been worn outside in the heat.

"My name is Nguyen Muoi, which is usually too difficult for Americans, but you may please call me Moe, as I was named in the Petroleum Engineering School at the University of Oklahoma. We have interpreters here, as you can see, but you may find they are unnecessary, since most of our technicians have had education in the United States. They speak and comprehend well in your language."

Twenty-some men were gathered around a large table in the main conference room of the State Oil Company. Their office location told a lot about the economic expectations that had been placed on this venture by the Vietnamese government.

Moe spoke in a sharp monotone, as though the speech had been given many times to groups of men of different nationalities in similar conferences. He welcomed the visitors, mentioning each by name and position to show he knew everyone, and was well in control of the meeting.

He concluded by saying, "We wish to make our guests comfortable.

We hope your coordination with us will result in agreements that will be advantageous both to World Oil and to the Socialist Republic of Vietnam."

As he spoke, he glanced toward his guests, who were seated in a row of descending rank down one side of the polished table. The opposing seats were occupied by the staff of the State Oil Company, commencing with the assistant energy minister, Dong Huan Chou. The interpreters and tea girls stood ready for service behind their chairs.

"We will be joined later by our minister of energy, Dr. Ho Bac Minh. He is represented at this meeting by his assistant, Dong Huan Chou."

All during the introduction, Dong had been sitting sour-faced, staring intently at first one of World Oil's men and then another. Andy knew he was memorizing their faces.

The president had adequately set the stage whereby we were matched one-on-one for the negotiations, Andy thought. He wondered if James, sitting to his right, realized that they would not be overwhelmed in numbers of technicians, at least. He may be speaking the technical language of geophysics only to himself.

It is difficult to communicate ideas of a specific geologic and structural nature to a large group all at once, especially if you know they don't have a technical background. They nod and smile when spoken to, but may not be understanding anything you say. Their minds cannot all function at the same speed or level of intelligence. However, Andy knew, to their credit they had to translate into their native tongue. He wondered if Moe was a graduate, or just passed a part of the way through college.

President Muoi drew himself up, obviously about to make his most important pronouncement. "For the Vietnamese State Oil Company, this is a momentous occasion. We are here to discuss a joint venture of drilling in deep offshore Vietnamese waters, where oil has not yet been discovered. We wish to assure you that our government has every intention of carrying out a successful program of exploration, which will determine where such oil reserves exist."

He smiled broadly at the row of visitors, almost daring anyone to dispute that oil did exist.

"Our success is not only important to the commercial interests of World Oil, but absolutely imperative to the future of the Vietnamese economy."

While Andy thought over the previous Viet nearshore oil discoveries, Muoi stopped for a sip of his tea, and motioned for the girl to freshen his cup.

"On the desk in front of each of you is a program schedule, which is to be considered only as a guideline. That series of statements and discussion should fill this entire day."

Everyone shuffled through his copy of the papers.

"Today we will review the geologic possibilities, and tomorrow we may discuss specific areas. Then we will consider proposals for specific block outlines. That will be concluded by the presentation of a summary to Dr. Ho Bac Minh at four in the afternoon. A decision will be made at that time as to what our further course of procedure will be."

Hanby was making short entries in his book, Andy noted, as were some of the accountants. He made a check beside his name on his scheduled presentation.

"Let us now take a few minutes' break to refresh our cups or refill our drinks with ice. Then we will welcome introductory remarks by Dr. William Hanby."

After the boring introductory session, the meeting broke for a welcome retreat. It provided a chance to leave the formality of the stuffy room and get into the fresh air of the adjoining garden. At midmorning, it was already getting uncomfortably warm.

James commented to Andy, "So far, we're heard exactly what we expected—that they want to listen to our offer. Let's hope the rest of the meetings go as close to the schedule as we've predicted."

"I'm sure they won't deviate too much, because it's our money they want to spend," Andy replied.

Bill Hanby and Kelly Johnson strolled up to them, and they were also looking for a place where any slight breeze might be blowing. The conference room was air-conditioned, but not that well, so it was not really comfortable.

"Did you see anyone you recognized from previous meetings other than Moe and our tour guide, Pham Xuan Bach?" asked Kelly, looking toward Andy.

"I'm not sure," replied Andy. "As I said before, Dong Huan Chou still looks familiar. I think he was around the base during the war, but I can't quite place him, even though he has a face that's hard to forget. Of course, he was at the reception in Tokyo."

Most of the other men had also wandered into the garden, and were knotted up in their departmental and ethnic groups. As they continued their musing, Nguyen Muoi and George came toward them, obviously with a purpose.

"Yes, Moe, it's a little warm out here, but the fresh air is good for a break. Your introductory remarks were well received and to the point," Bill Hanby said with a smile, and nodded then toward George.

"We are accustomed to the heat here," replied Nguyen Muoi, "and I came to request a private meeting with you after dinner tonight. Officially, we wish all of you to be our guests at the special dinner we have arranged for eight o'clock this evening. It will be at the Vietnamese restaurant near the Rex, and I have reservations for our group in a private dining room. There we can have entertainment by local musicians." He smiled generously. "I trust that will be satisfactory with everyone?"

"I believe I can speak for the group," replied Bill. "We will be happy to join in a traditional meal. I've often heard about the excellent cuisine of Vietnam." He gave the appropriate slight bow, with a fixed smile and his palms together.

"My secretary, or Pham Xuan, will provide you with the address later," Moe said, as he and George moved away to speak to another group of their technicians.

"It seems they have quite an evening planned for us," Andy said.

He wondered what Moe wanted to say to Bill in private. He probably just wants to feel him out, and see if he can get any edge on the negotiations, which are sure to become very sharp and sticky before we get through tomorrow. There are too many things going on in the background, like their various influence groups within the government. Each person had his own turf to protect, and his own ax to grind.

"They feel obligated to entertain us," Bill replied.

"We'll be fortunate if we come out with any sort of workable agreement, considering their ongoing anti-American sentiment. You can see it in the eyes of some of their people. We know someone in their hierarchy is serious enough about stopping our contract to blast our plane. It can't be the top echelon, or they wouldn't even be talking to us about drilling."

As Andy spoke to the group of friends, he realized that he was just repeating the conversations he and Bill had been through many times during these past weeks.

"We'd better be getting back, if everyone is ready. We have a lot of ground to cover before noon," Bill concluded, and the entire group was edging back toward the meeting room.

The conference room was no cooler than before, but in comparison to the garden, it was refreshing. Bill took the floor, acknowledging the reception, and made a short speech outlining the intentions of the World Oil negotiations group. They were to present the exploration possibilities related to Vietnam, such as the geologic background and the geophysical coverage presently available. Then the exploration personnel would outline areas of interest as determined by the data. The hosts appeared to listen intently.

Bill continued. The summary would be followed by a proposal to explore certain areas geophysically, then select blocks based on early results for further detailed seismic work. That effort would result in contract blocks for exploratory drilling. Reductions in size of the original outlined areas would be made as work progressed. Drilling commitments to earn full rights to the remaining areas would occur as certain time periods and investment expenditure levels passed.

He then turned to Andy, requesting that he present his discussion of the geology and other technical aspects.

For about thirty minutes Andy gave a summary of the general geology and an explanation of how the area around the Vietnamese peninsula related to other known production. Then their regional geologist, Wallace Brooks, took the floor. He was well qualified in the area, for he had been promoted from his job as chief geologist for the Gulf of Thailand, where he worked the South China Sea out of Bangkok.

Wally was an older man, and his hair was beginning to gray around the temples. With his horn-rimmed glasses, he looked very distinguished, and fit everyone's idea of an intellectual college professor. He was particularly impressive to the Orientals, who have great respect for age and for gray hair.

"Nothing is simple geologically in the South China Sea," Wally began his dissertation. "The entire sweep of connected basins have been worked extensively with geophysics, and most parts mapped in great detail. World Oil already owns the data in these areas of the Pacific Rim, starting from the shallows of the rivers south of Bangkok, past the islands of the Thai Gulf, around the horn of the Mekong Delta, and past the producing fields of the Natuna Islands. All of this area has been interpreted by our geophysicists, and covers currently producing areas. We expect to extend the same type of interpretations into the deep waters of Vietnam."

Wally spread a regional map on the table, and identified the important locations.

"Continuing up the east coast of the Indochina Peninsula past the reef banks offshore from the Philippines and northward toward Taiwan, all has been covered by seismic shooting and worked extensively by World Oil. Some of the areas extend into deeper seas, which, as you are aware, require a different monetary scale for development. The cost of exploratory drilling goes almost asymptotically as water depth increases. World Oil will be willing to invest that money in Vietnam if the profit potential is indicated to be commensurate with the risk."

Wally had learned his lessons in technology well. He believed that now, more than ever, the art of finding oil is a science. He had interpreted the geology the world over, from the salt domes offshore of Louisiana and Texas to the oil-saturated reefs of the Libyan Sahara. Since he was a young man, his work had been with companies that had pioneered many of today's exploration advances. He was a real participant in the world's vital search for energy. Together with James Wellman, they could paint precise images of the underground structures that would rank with the world's most valuable pieces of art. Wally was giving a good presentation, which was what Andy had anticipated.

He had been working in the Far East for many years, and his experience was showing. He was an Oklahoma geology graduate, and Andy had recruited him many years ago when he was working in the U.S. Gulf Coast for a competitor. He knew it had been one of Wally's fervent hopes in recent years to explore in that previously war-torn restricted area south of the Mekong Delta. It was a jewel he had viewed from afar during the long years of the war while he was working the adjoining South China Sea areas.

Wally was smiling as he spoke, like a kid with his hand in a candy jar. Here was a brand-new, untested area in which to conduct his dream-like studies, and to create his geologic magic. Andy was happy to see he had caught his own confidence that there was oil to be found in that unexplored basin. All of the conditions were right for the deposition, generation, and accumulation of billion-barrel oil fields.

His final pitch to the rapt listeners was to tell of the active forces of nature that had made this area so complex at depth when it appeared so calm and flat at the surface, where the Mekong River built its delta to meet the South China Sea. Listening to him, one could almost feel the rotation of the earth's plate blocks, and the movements causing the volcanoes surrounding those seas.

By the end of the day, James Wellman's seismic cross sections and Wally Brooks' imaginative geologic map presentations had spurred the entire group to a euphoria of determination that there were a number of gigantic oil fields offshore from the Mekong Delta, awaiting the first drillers brave enough to sink a bit. After their exciting scientific presentations they could almost smell the oil, and it was not going to be difficult to convince their hosts that they should invite World Oil to conduct the first program of exploration.

Their allotted time grew short, and as Andy expected, the data furnished by the local technicians were extremely limited. They gladly relinquished most of their time to their visitors. Tim McAllister gave a short review of possible operating procedures, followed by a discourse on the probable financial arrangements by Ben Brodecki. The meeting was then turned back to the explorationists.

Andy lost no time in presenting the hosts with a proposal for World Oil to contract a large part of their offshore area for rapid development. He did not wish to wait until tomorrow, and allow them to delve into all the reasons oil might not have been trapped there.

He immediately presented them with an outline that World Oil would follow. The contract areas would be covered rapidly with an expensive technically oriented seismic exploration and drilling program. He emphasized that Vietnam would soon be a competitor in the world oil market if its people followed the lead of World Oil's technical staff.

The Vietnamese were all smiles as the meeting adjourned for the day. It looked as if their ideas were going to have an easy reception tomorrow when they got down to the nitty-gritty of their contract proposals with the minister. It would be Ben Brodecki's turn then to dazzle them by his magic balancing act with his calculator and numbers.

They strolled out the main corridor in a group, and Andy caught a glimpse of the pocked face of a short man in a linen suit with dark glasses. It was Dong Huan Chou, and he was headed down the hall into the energy minister's office. Was he going to advise the minister of what had occurred that day in their meeting? It seemed strange that he would be the one to report on the progress of their meeting instead of Moe, whose position it was as president of Vietnam State Oil Company to direct their exploration efforts.

Where information was passed outside of the line of command of an organization, there was a good chance that something was amiss in their internal relationships. Andy knew he must do something to counter Dong's influence, for he could tell from his attitude that something deleterious to their program was being developed in his mind. But for the present, they could not inject themselves into the planning or complexities of the local hierarchy. They must wait and be vigilant.

\*     \*     \*

Hanby had advised their host, Nguyen Muoi, that he was pleased with the way their first day had progressed, and that they were on the threshold of making a mutually profitable agreement with the Vietnamese government. They were intermingled with the local oil men around two great tables of the restaurant's private dining room. The musical entertainment continued after their meal at a low level, which did not interfere with conversation.

Their discussions soon lagged, however, since their topics of mutual interest had largely been covered in the daylong technical discourse. They were all mentally exhausted. This dinner had turned out to be another business gathering, of the same people. The few exceptions were some added Viet staff personnel, but few of the newcomers spoke any English. Andy noted how strange it was that Ho Bac Minh, the energy minister, had not yet made an appearance.

The newcomers were members of the staff of State Oil and the Ministry of Energy. One notable absence was that of the minister's assistant, Dong Huan Chou. It was explained that he lived on his estate in Cu Chi, a long distance from Saigon, and had urgent business at home. None of their local staff appeared to regret his absence, and Moe assured them he would return tomorrow.

The men found they had little in common except to make a business deal to explore for oil, so their conversations were inanimate, and quickly came to an end. They were each thinking in their different native languages, though they more or less understood technical English. They struggled through the egg rolls and rice, using chopsticks.

The music was different, to say the least. They were relieved when a short and proper program of dancing girls climaxed the show in accordance with government planning. At least the restaurant was located conveniently near their hotel. They concluded the meal with dessert and coffee.

While quiet music droned on, they were served with a very good imported brandy. It was Moe's attempt to impress them with their culture, Andy supposed. James was the one who appreciated it most, for he whispered to his fellow explorers that this was the best part of the meal.

They had finished their dinner, which Andy perceived as an uneventfully dull affair served in a mediocre restaurant. Their purpose for the day had been accomplished, which was to make proper introductions of their data to the right people in the government. Now their negotiations could go forward in a more informal way.

Finally, they were dismissed, and all said good night in front of the restaurant with the proper bows, and the visiting World Oil men started strolling in a strung-out group, back toward the Majestic. It was only a short block away. As they went along, Kelly arranged to walk beside Andy.

He said loud enough for the others to hear, "I have a bottle in my room. After we get everyone else to bed, let's continue our discussion." Then Kelly added in a whisper, "Moe brought a message to Hanby about a contact we must make. Wear dark street clothes. I'll come by your room in a few minutes."

Kelly then walked away. Obviously, he did not wish their own people to know they had covert arrangements to explore.

As they arrived back at their hotel, they arranged to meet for breakfast and headed for their rooms. It had been a long day, and tomorrow would be even more demanding. Each had his own part of the World Oil presentations to review. Andy carefully noted the room where Kelly was staying, which was at the end of the hall and across from his own. He wondered if there was any significance to the room Kelly had accepted when they checked in. Since they were on the second floor, there was no need to use the elevator. It probably wouldn't run at night, anyway.

Andy had just changed into a dark pullover and jeans, and was settled under the tiny lamp attempting to read, when there came a very light tapping on his door. When he answered, it was Kelly. He entered without being invited and closed the door quietly. He, too, was dressed for a night in downtown Ho Chi Minh City. He wore dark trousers and a faded T-shirt. Finding a seat beneath the only lamp, Kelly pulled a map out of the light jacket he carried.

"We've had some luck," Kelly began. "Good old Moe came up with some information that he passed on to Hanby for us. That was his reason for their private meeting." He spread the map under the light.

"What word did he have?" Andy asked as he sat on the bed beside the lamp table, overlooking the map.

"He told him the name of a distant cousin of his who has heard some streetwise information about a connection to a robbery that took place about three days after our plane went down. He believes there might be a connection."

"Is that all he knew—just a name?" asked Andy.

"No, there's more. His distant cousin's name is Lam Thang Nguyen, and he used to be a gold merchant here in Saigon. He was wealthy until he was picked up after the war and kept in a reeducation camp. He spent six years up-country at Xuan Loc. His half-brother was finally able to buy his way out, and now he is making a weak attempt to get back into the gold business. He's having little success apparently, because of his poor health. He retains his market connections, however, for they are still his close friends."

"Those camps must be hell from what I've heard. They starve the people while working them to death, and milk their relatives for all they can get if they ever do let them go back home. After all that, they're broken economically as well as physically." Andy shook his head sadly and continued, "Why is Moe willing to help us? Isn't that a little dangerous for him?"

"It's a chance he's willing to take, for he knows the top officials in the government want this deal with World Oil to be a success. Also, he is aware that we are not going to let the accident to our plane just drop. He nosed around his connections, and finally decided he must talk to Hanby about his information."

"Thank God he did. We could look for weeks and not come up with such a lead," Andy replied.

"Here is a map of the city and surrounding area. I got it when I was here last month doing reconnaissance for Bill on how we might get along with the government. I visited Moe at that time. He told me nothing then, but now he seems like a good inside contact. In fact, I was directed to him by our friend, Li Hong Hoe, who is also a distant relative. His wife is Vietnamese, you know, and a part of the Muoi family."

"Then is Lin Jin related to this Lam Thang?" Andy asked.

"I'm not sure I should tell you this, but it turns out that Li Hong Hoe is the one who bought Lam Thang's way out of the reeducation camp. So, yes, he is Lin Jin and Kim's great-uncle on one side. He's their grandfather's half-brother." Kelly watched carefully to see what effect the news had on Andy.

Andy was shocked. He knew Lin Jin's grandfather had connections in Vietnam since he had found his bride and was married here, but he had not expected to meet any direct connections with the family. He wondered if Moe or this "cousin" would know anything more than he had heard about Lin Jin's mother or father. Since she and her brother had escaped to Hong Kong early in the war, their mother had been afraid to come back, even for a visit. It is strange that none of the Hoe family had ever spoken of the father. Lam Thang must have watched over the two children after their mother went to Hong Kong. He realized he was staring at Kelly in openmouthed disbelief.

"Where is this half-brother of Hoe now? Can we find him?" Andy queried, finally finding his voice.

"You bet we can. That's what this map is about." Kelly pointed to the small plat he had laid under the ring of light from the tiny bulb. "I hope you don't mind walking a bit, because we can't arrange transport here without the whole town knowing."

"Do you have a street name, and a number?" asked Andy.

"Yes, I've located it here on the map." Kelly pointed to an area near the old wartime soldiers' stomping ground. "It's across the Rue Catinat from the old Continental Palace Hotel, and down the block a bit. Do you know this area?" he asked.

"Sure, it's right in the heart of town. I've been near there lots of times. What's the number?"

"There's no number where we're going, but I have directions. We'll have to sneak out the back of the hotel to elude some folks. I've already checked out the front, and there's one of our limo-vehicles waiting there with two men inside. I'm sure they're checking to see that we stay put in our hotel, and don't go wandering around town. At least they want to know if anyone goes out. If we have any outside connections here, someone wants to know it."

"We can always use the fire escape," said Andy.

He didn't know if this hotel even had one. Or they could get out a window, but it might be a little tough getting back in.

"Do you know where their kitchen entrance is?"

\*   \*   \*

The French had not been the only taskmasters of the Vietnamese. Their wealthy landowners sometimes exploited the people even more. The sleepy squalid river town of Saigon, forty-five miles from the China Sea, had been developed through rice production in the Mekong Delta country. A beautiful city, with elegant boulevards and handsome flowering trees, had resulted. It was too bad they never learned to bury their electric cables, Andy thought.

Many of the southern inhabitants had been assigned to new "economic zones" outside the city after the war, and most of the ones who were allowed to leave were already gone. Still, during the daylight hours the avenues were filled with bicycles and pedicabs, and a few Hondas that could still be kept running.

It was very dark in the narrow lane behind the main business street where most of the gold traders operated their shops. They had come a half block away from the poorly lit side street providing entrance to the alley, and a few feet into the lane there were no lights to be seen anywhere. Along the sides of the alley there were few windows or doors. And what few there were had heavy shutters, some with bars. Both Andy and Kelly knew that gold merchants in this culture liked to live very close to their merchandise. They could literally feel the closeness of a dense habitation, although they heard no sounds, for it was late. As their eyes became more accustomed to the dark, a sliver of light showed now and then past the shutters.

Kelly found the doorway to which he had been directed, and knocked lightly. A slight sound was heard inside, and it was a full minute before a crack of dim light appeared at the entrance. A lamplight shone on them slightly, and a feeble voice spoke in Vietnamese.

"We are looking for Lam Thang Nguyen," Kelly explained in English.

The crack widened, and the face of an old man appeared. Now he spoke in English. "Who has sent you to me?" he asked.

"Nguyen Muoi sent us," replied Kelly.

"Who are you?" the feeble voice asked.

"We are Kelly Johnson and Andy Cheston with World Oil from Tokyo. We are friends of Li Hong Hoe there. He gave us directions to contact you through Nguyen Muoi." There was a long silence.

"Please wait," said the voice, as the sliver of light disappeared.

Again it was dark and quiet in the alley.

After a few minutes and some slight noises from movements within, for it was obviously the rear of a store fronting on the main thoroughfare, the crack of light reappeared. This time a young round face of a girl appeared.

"Please enter," she said, and the door opened wider.

Kelly and Andy were directed to a back corner of the fair-sized room that obviously was living quarters for an entire family.

"I am Nhung Thi Nguyen," said the girl, who was dressed in a light baba, "and this is Bapak Lam Thang."

She indicated a couch beside the reclining chair in which Lam Thang was resting. He made no effort to rise or to show his hands, which were concealed under a light blanket. After acknowledging the introduction with a bow, Kelly and Andy sat on the ancient seat, not knowing if it would stand the weight of two westerners at once.

"I have been expecting you," said the feeble voice of the ancient Lam Thang.'

It was clear that his years in the reeducation camps had ruined his health.

"What is the purpose of your visit?"

He seemed very abrupt, but then he knew his life was probably getting short, so he had little time for niceties with strangers. Kelly explained about themselves and about what their connection was with Li Hong Hoe in Tokyo. Then he told him about the company plane disaster, and how Moe had directed them to the present abode.

Then Kelly said, "We are hoping that you can furnish us information as to certain connections between those here with the government who would want to sabotage any effort of World Oil to obtain an exploration contract for work in Vietnam."

The young girl Nhung Thi was busying herself in the corner of the room used for a kitchen, boiling water to prepare tea.

"I am sorry that I can be of no service to you, for my family has only recently obtained my release from the reeducation camp. I do not wish to jeopardize my freedom to conduct the little business left to me by having wrong associations, and especially not by being suspected of passing information."

The ancient man closed his eyes as though in deep thought.

"I understand your position, and we'd not want to cause you or your family any trouble with the bodoi," Kelly said.

At the sound of the word "bodoi," the old man's eyes opened, as though a terrible memory had passed through his brain. He looked to his granddaughter, who was taking off the boiling pot.

"It is surprising that you, an American, know the word for such persons as those who tried so hard to end my existence in the dreaded camps," he mumbled quietly. "Were you here in the war?"

"No, I was not in the forces," Kelly replied.

"Yes," replied Andy, speaking for the first time. "I was stationed near Saigon for a long time, in the Army."

It appeared their request for information had met with utter defeat, for the broken old man could not be asked to go beyond his mental capabilities. Tea was served, and they drank it almost in silence. Only polite references to their travel to Saigon, their hotel accommodations, and meetings with Muoi at the State Oil Company were made. They were being treated with respect only because of Li Hong Hoe.

When the tea was finished, Andy decided he must speak out for the first time. There was nothing to lose now.

Addressing Lam Thang, he said, "I must tell you how beautiful your cousin's daughter, Lin Jin, has become. She is the pride of her grandfather, and the hit of our social group in Tokyo. I have taken her to dinner and to the theater many times, and very much enjoy our long talks over the hibachi at her grandfather's estate."

It was as if someone had turned on a spigot, for at once the young girl, Nhung Thi, joined them from her kitchen corner. She spoke with a firm and excited voice. There was a quick series of questions uttered in rapid succession.

"You must know Lin Jin well to have visited their home. How is she? Did she finish her schooling in Hong Kong? Is she beautiful, as ever? How well do you know her? Please tell me everything!" She rattled out the questions in spite of the old man's obvious frowns.

Andy did his best to answer her questions, but it took a long time. She kept interrupting with more probing queries. It was a subject he loved to remember, therefore, many details of their meetings were described— many more than would normally have been imparted to strangers. Nhung Thi soon realized his meetings with Lin Jin were really dates, and she developed a warm liking for this handsome American who had kept returning to visit her cousin. Their discourse went on for half an hour, with Nhung Thi delving in depth into how Lin Jin dressed and wore her hair, what she did with her time, and if she worked anywhere. Kelly remained quietly on the sideline.

All of that time, the old man listened intently as Andy's relationship with their family was unfolded by the questioning of Nhung Thi. She and Lin Jin had lived as one family before they escaped to Hong Kong, and she was the same age as Lin's brother, Kim. They had attended the catholic school together. She could not hear enough about the two of them.

Finally the old man spoke, very slowly, as if it were a pronouncement.

"I am old, and I do not wish to bring more dishonor to my family by putting them at odds with the present Communist government. But some things are wrong, and wrongs must someday be brought to right. We must be very careful, but I will tell you the tales that have generally come to be known by the gold traders on the back streets of Saigon. There is little information that goes unknown to them."

"We will be thankful for any information you can give us, for we have a debt to repay for the loss of our true friends," Andy said.

Nhung Thi refilled their teacups, and the elder Lam Thang went on with his studied statements.

"It is rumored that on the date you gave of the aircraft's disaster, a series of events began. There was a robbery with much shooting in the compound of the assistant to the minister of energy, Dong Huan Chou, at Cu Chi. This is a considerable distance from Saigon, and beyond the airport. A van, which belonged to a maintenance organization operating at the Tan Son Nhat International Airport, was later found in a klong far away, next to the Mekong River, both burned and filled with many bullet holes."

"Why was he robbed?" asked Kelly.

"It is rumored along the street that Dong Huan Chou, known to be an agent of the National Liberation Front, had made a stop at the gold depository and drew two kilos of gold from the NLF's store as he was heading for home that night. It must have been the payoff for the terrorists."

The old man stirred uneasily in his chair, as though each movement caused him great pain. He continued.

"That robbery occurred a few nights after your aircraft was destroyed as it left Hong Kong. Three men of the maintenance group failed to return to work at the airport on the following day. The police investigated, but found they had nothing to do with a robbery, and nothing concerning it was reported officially. Such investigations may not mean a great deal, however, for if there is no money to be gained by them, the police actions are notably lax. In this case, though, they seem to be correct, as I have heard from other sources. The van was not at the Cu Chi compound for the motive of robbery."

This was discouraging news, for it appeared a good lead was telling them nothing concrete on which they could follow up. Andy frowned, but Kelly pursued the story, for he knew it was their only lead.

He asked, "Was there anything else you heard about the maintenance group?"

"Yes, there is much more," said Lam Thang. "The group that visited the home of Dong has connections with a similar maintenance company that services private planes in Hong Kong. Only three of their local men were missing after that night. It has been relayed to me by a source inside Dong Huan Chou's house that there were four men who came to the compound, but only one went inside to visit Dong."

"Then where did the fourth man come from, and what was the reason for their visit?" asked Kelly eagerly.

"There was one plane that arrived that day from Hong Kong, and one passenger came with a return reservation for the following day. That reservation was never used," Lam Thang seemed to be sagging, as his health would not permit him to speak much longer.

"That could be our man," Kelly said excitedly. "Do you think he was at Cu Chi to collect for his work?" he asked.

"Apparently so," replied Lam Thang. "But his collection of a two-kilo gold ingot probably did him no good, for it brought only bullets. Four bodies were later found in the klong a few kilometers from the burned van. There was a man reported missing in Hong Kong who worked for the same company." He stopped to rest and sip his tea.

"It must be the same man," Andy said.

"No doubt about that," Kelly added.

Lam Thang rested a minute before he continued, for his health was not up to the strain of so much talking.

"The reason the van was burned and riddled with bullets was that an armored six-by-six intercepted them as they left the compound, and robbed them of their collection. There was much automatic-weapon fire everywhere around the entire area. Relatives say that two guards of Dong Huan Chou were buried the next day because of an 'accident.' At least that is one possibility."

"What else could have happened?" Andy asked.

Lam Thang continued, "The other possibility is that the collection never took place, and the robbery was a cover-up to make the National Liberation Front believe a huge sum of gold had actually been paid. Someone went to a lot of trouble to kill six men, so there must have been a large amount of gold involved. The rumor from the bank about two kilos would fit well." Lam Thang lay back as Nhung Thi rearranged his pillows. He had talked too long.

"I don't understand," said Andy. "Why would the robbery be staged so carefully, and then the six-by-six leave without the gold unless Dong was planning to keep it? They would have found it in the van. But Dong would then have had more payoffs to deal with. So, I don't think he staged the robbery of his own compound."

"It was dark," replied Kelly. "There was a lot of shooting from burp guns going on, and gasoline burning, with a tank about to explode. Maybe they thought they had the gold and didn't, or looked for it and couldn't find it in the dark. They could have gotten scared and ran. They would have been in a big rush to leave before other guards recovered their sense of duty. By that time, the gold could have been squirreled away by Dong."

"I cannot answer that now," said Lam Thang. "Someday we may know, if my contacts remain alive. Those who know such things are sometimes in great peril. You are now aware that you have our lives in your hands, for the information given you is worth our destruction to the NLF. Please guard it well, and use it wisely." It was as if the old gentleman were speaking his epitaph.

They had stayed well over an hour, and it was time to end the meeting. Lam Thang and Nhung Thi were humbly thanked for their trust and for providing the information. Both Andy and Kelly assured them they would make every effort to safeguard the confidences imparted. They left as quietly and even more carefully than they had come.

Andy and Kelly had little to say to each other as they made their way along the deserted streets to the rear of their hotel. The kitchen access was open, as they had left it. Both men were deep in thought about the implications of the information that Lam Thang had furnished. Now it was apparent that Dong Huan Chou was the NLF representative who had passed on the order attempting to block World Oil's exploration efforts. But was he the one responsible for making the decision that such an action was necessary and desirable, or was he just a hireling carrying out orders?

A restless night followed, as Andy was trying to decipher the implications of all they had heard. That would make tomorrow a long day. All of his days would be long ones until he took care of the man who gave the order to kill his friends. He dreamed of Lin Jin, and of her school days in Saigon. Theirs was a complex family, having been battered by a war of senseless people who weren't sure to which side even their closest relatives owed allegiance.

# Nine

Andy and his exploration team, James Wellman and Wally Brooks, had arrived in Houston with their Far East Director, William Hanby, eager to present their Vietnamese agreement to World Oil management for their vote of approval. They had just returned from their successful selling visit in Ho Chi Minh City, and were greatly enthused with the success of the contract they had been able to negotiate with the Vietnamese. Now they were going through the company process of committee approvals, up the corporate ladder within World Oil, to finally present their recommendation before the chairman of the board, Gilbert Eason.

"I can't believe that Phil Harrison took so many exceptions to our proposed agreement with the Vietnamese State Oil Company. He all but said his President's Committee would recommend we turn down any contract with them. We've worked like hell to give them just what they wanted, and now we get this bullshit thrown at us," Andy said in a huff.

Andrew Cheston was upset, and was showing it. His exploration staff had worked hard to come up with an agreement on the Mekong Delta areas for large offshore blocks with a reasonable expenditure and time frame for drilling. Now it looked like their own company's upper echelon was going to turn them down. If they did, it'd mean starting all over with a renegotiation in Vietnam.

It had been a long day in their Houston home office, waiting for their turn at a committee, going through the long presentation of their big project, then repeating the process. Tomorrow they would see the big boss in the official Board Committee. Final rejection or approval of their proposed contract would depend on the decision there.

For now, they were trying to relax after an all-day session in the conference rooms of their home office, in the bar at the Regency. The Tokyo visitors, including their boss, Hanby, were accompanied by a pair of the young geologists who could advise them of the proper protocol acceptable in the local office. They were the bright young men who showed promise of future promotion in the ranks of the corporation who had been assigned to aid them in their preparations. Andy had been one once.

Now he was speaking for all of his men, but he had addressed his remarks directly to his boss, Hanby. He was aware that he was expressing the way they felt after a long stint of night and weekend work, which might come to nothing if their recommendation was not approved.

"Now, now," teased Bill Hanby with a sly, knowing grin.

"He's right, you know," chimed in Wally. "We've worked too hard and too long on this proposal to let them turn it down without some positive action."

"Don't be too worried just yet," Bill replied, trying to inject a note of calmness to soothe their rancor. "The president didn't get where he is by agreeing with every idea an explorationist presents before his committee. Also, you must remember that if he agrees with everything you say, you might as well have all stayed in Tokyo and mailed your package to him."

"That may well be true, but at least you'd think he'd give us a little encouragement along the line," Andy stated vehemently.

"His way is a little different. If he opposes your ideas, he knows you'll stress the strongest points to support them. Then, when he answers to his boss, Chairman Eason, he'll have the best answers possible for answering his boss. Otherwise the project won't fly," Hanby replied quietly. As he sat back, relaxed, and sipped his drink, he added, "We probably won't ever hear that private conversation, but you can be sure they'll have one."

"His questions about the structures on blocks D and F were certainly to the point," James said. "We're going to have to spend some time this evening recontouring our data to match his suggestions. Then maybe he'll be more supportive, especially if we have a chance to show him our new work before tomorrow's meeting."

"We can have some drafting help available tonight, if that will help. And the reproduction machines will be left on," one of the young geologists injected eagerly. These "map boys" for the board were sharp, and willing to help.

"This is to be a full-fledged board meeting tomorrow," Hanby said. "You'll have to be sure everything is ready for a first-class presentation. Are all of your slides in order?"

"Yes, sir; that is, all we have made to date. We'll try to get the changes incorporated as slides before noon tomorrow. Can you handle that by mid-morning, James?" Andy asked.

"I believe so, if Wally can give me a hand with the contouring. We'll be ready to go back to Harrison by ten," answered James. "It'll be too bad we can't have everything on slides by then. I think the wheels are spoiled, getting everything done up in ribbon; but they must know best."

"Don't cut it too close," Hanby cut in. "It'll be better to have good paper maps to show than a whole fistful of slopped-together slides. Don't show anything with any mistakes or bad copy."

"Yes, sir, I understand," James answered. "We'll prepare the maps first, and then photograph 'em if time permits."

Bill Hanby rose, and said, "If you gentlemen will excuse me, I have an invitation to meet with Phil Harrison and his wife at the Petroleum Club for dinner. I'd better go and get dressed. I'll meet you all for breakfast tomorrow at about seven. Good luck on your maps."

Andy and his exploration group stayed a few minutes longer to finish their drinks, and complete their short period of relaxation before returning to their night's work in the company's nearby office.

"We'd better grab a bite to eat," he said to his exploration staff. "It may turn into a long night's work when we get back to our drafting."

\* \* \*

"I want to congratulate you and your staff personally on an excellent review and presentation of the massive amount of data in the Mekong Delta area. Obviously, everyone on the committee thinks you have spent your time in preparation of this project very effectively. Chairman Eason told me he was pleased to see the fine and explicit display data you were able to assemble, digest, and organize in so few months."

Bill Hanby was discussing the day's activity with his sales team on their arrival back in the lobby of the Regency Hotel. They were on their way back to their rooms after an exhausting night and day of reworking maps and slides. The long session had culminated with their formal presentation to the Board of Directors.

They were not a happy group, for a decision on their project was still in limbo. Their boss, Hanby, was trying to give them some reason to hope their efforts had not been in vain. When their presentation had ended, the chairman dismissed them without ever taking a vote of the committee on their proposals. It was like receiving a limp handshake.

President Phil Harrison had invited them for a gala evening at a formal Petroleum Club dinner party in recognition of their many months of hard work, and in appreciation of their outstanding efforts. It would be a dull inconclusive evening, though, not knowing if their work had resulted in any kind of success.

"Thanks, Bill, everyone has done his best. There wasn't too much BS of the pasture included, we hope. We tried to stick to the most reasonable interpretations," Andy replied.

"Yes, Harrison hardly even sniffed when you showed him the new slides. You'll notice that when the chips got down on the table, he was supportive of our position," Hanby answered, smiling. "He had asked the tough questions in his own committee so he'd already know the answers."

"His ideas were good ones, and it always helps to have an old head put in his criticisms early, especially when there's time to include changes," James Wellman stated.

"We were lucky we had time to alter our slides. It is a shame, though, that they didn't approve our recommendation right up front, so we'd really have something to celebrate tonight," Andy said.

"Don't be too sure they won't," Hanby replied. "The big committee usually does that sort of deferral when they're considering big-money projects. Then they get together in the back of their offices over coffee, and kick it around privately where they can say exactly what they think without pulling any punches, away from the presenters. The decision has already been made, but they want to bounce it off of everyone privately before they tell the secretary what to type into the official minutes."

"I still wish they'd have said 'yes' while we were all there to hear them," Andy said. "It has left us with an empty-gut feeling, so we don't quite know what to think."

"Now that they've had a few hours since our meeting to mull over their intentions, we may even get some indication of their final decision tonight. Just be sure you all behave yourselves, and don't ask too many pointed questions of the big brass. We don't want them to think we have any doubt about our structural arguments."

Hanby didn't normally give such instructions to his men, so Andy knew he must be a bit nervous himself.

"We'll try not to spill wine on Mrs. Eason's gown," Andy replied. "What are your plans for the weekend, Bill?"

"I think I'll stay around here until Wednesday. There are some things Phil Harrison wants to discuss. Also, I have questions about other areas that need answers. What are your travel plans?"

"We all need to get back to Tokyo. There's too much going on, and I want to check in with our travelers who have been conducting their surveys in Saigon," Andy answered. "First, though, James and I are traveling to San Francisco in the morning. I promised my sister, Beth, that we'd come by for a visit. She immediately planned a big party for Saturday night. We should be back in Tokyo by Tuesday night, their time."

"So you're leaving on Monday at noon?" Bill asked.

"Yes, we follow the sun, and lose a day en route," Andy replied. "We made up for it, though, on our way coming over. We worked the day in Tokyo, then overnight to Houston, and then worked the same calendar day here. It's a good thing we sleep well on planes."

"You jet-setters are all alike," Bill said. "Never satisfied unless you're traveling first class. Be sure you don't let Elizabeth detain you too long in Sausalito, or Lin Jin might get upset." Bill Hanby smiled broadly, for he and Jill had more than a suspicion about Andy's feelings for the Oriental beauty.

"No danger, because our schedule is set, and the reservations are already made," Andy answered.

Hanby stood, and turned toward the main exit.

"We'd better be getting ourselves dressed and on over to the Petroleum Club. We don't want to keep our president waiting, especially if he is just bursting to tell us they have accepted the most expensive deal in our company's history. I'll meet you all here at seven, and we can ride over together."

\* \* \*

"It's party time!" Elizabeth stated enthusiastically.

"We're glad your plane was on time. Did the chauffeur have any trouble finding you?"

Andy and James were climbing out of the back seat of the huge white Cadillac. "No trouble at all," Andy answered. "He was right there waiting to collect our luggage." They had been driven straight through San Francisco and across the Golden Gate to the north end of Sausalito. They arrived at the Halstead estate while the sun was still high.

Elizabeth was soon hugging her twin tightly and giving him polite kisses on both cheeks, as he returned her eager embrace. She then turned her attention to James, and gave him a miniature version of the same greeting.

"James, it's good to see you again. It's been over a year since you were here. But I assure you that Leslie Bicknell, whom you were chasing after last year, is still available. Remember her red hair?"

"How could I forget such a wonderful weekend, Beth? You're a great hostess, and arrange beautiful company for your guests," James answered.

"In fact, she is here now. I've invited her and another friend to stay over for the weekend, so they'll be right on hand for the party tonight. Leslie has been speaking of no one else, and is thrilled you came. She's waiting for you, so you'd better watch out."

"That's no problem," James countered. "If she isn't careful, she may catch me. Then she'll really be in trouble. Actually, we already have our plane reservations back to Tokyo, so there's little danger she'd even want to keep me for so short a visit."

Andy put in, as he held onto Beth's hand, "Our mother used to say that her children would never have any trouble with kidnappers, because when daylight came, they'd be sure to let us go." Elizabeth smiled. "I never was quite sure just what she meant by that. Were you, Beth?"

"I think I got the idea, at least by the time I was sixteen. Come on, you two, and let me show you where to hang out. Jeffries will bring the luggage, but right now let's get you two into swim trunks, and hit the pool. It's heated, and still clean, I hope. We use a carload of chlorine and algaecide, it seems."

"That's OK," Andy replied. "How else do you think I keep my curls so blond?"

It was shaping up to be a happy weekend, and Elizabeth led the pair toward the entry hall.

"Go suit up you two. There are some people by the pool who are looking forward to seeing you again. Andy, I've invited Valarie Rogers to stay over, too. Remember the luscious blond you impressed so strongly at the airport the last time you were through here? She wanted to meet you again, and begged to be asked."

That's Beth, Andy thought. Always looking out after my friendly interests.

"Thanks a lot," Andy answered sarcastically, as he gave a boyish grin to his twin. "She probably thinks I sleep all the time. Do you really think I deserve female company of her caliber?"

"Yes, I do," Beth replied. "I don't want you to get too entangled with those Oriental girls. You two both need to meet some nice American females once in a while, so you'll remember what the home culture is like. Besides, it'll be good for your social attitude, because she thinks you'd be a great catch. Don't say I didn't warn you to beware of her net, Andy dear. You could do a lot worse, but you'd need a lot of money, unless you could get some of hers. Now get in there, and we'll wait for you at the pool with a nice Napa Valley champagne."

"Oh ho," said Andy. "Has Hillary upgraded to champagne these days? He must use white grapes, because your feet aren't blue—anymore."

"They've always kept some 'perking in the bodega,' mostly just for our personal use. His big thing is mass-produced Cabernet Sauvignons. He'll be in from the 'ranch' in an hour or so to join us. Then you men can discuss Pacific Rim economics and the production of colored liquids. He wants to ask you about the sake market. Now hurry up and change; the girls are waiting. They may mean business, but they don't want to talk it."

Elizabeth had a nice smile, and an even nicer laugh.

James and Andy made their way to the top of the staircase as directed, and found their rooms with extra swimsuits, terry robes, and towels all set out with neat little folds at the sleeves. One of Beth's tricks, Andy assumed.

"How long has it been since you corresponded with Leslie?" Andy asked.

"Oh, I didn't ever write to her. After that last pass through here, I didn't suppose she wanted to see or hear from me again. She sure has a lot of honey-red hair." James was off in a dream world of the past.

"Well, it looks like they intend for you to make up for some lost time. Obviously, she is not as forgetful as you supposed," Andy said.

"She is a beautiful and personable girl, and I didn't think she'd still be available. It was nice of Elizabeth to arrange for her to be around. A man needs a little female company sometimes, after he's been working hard." James clearly had some pleasant memories of the last visit.

"I'll have to get you to tell me more about that last visit with her sometime."

"How about you? Your last trip through here at the airport must have been an impressive one. Valarie Rogers, is it? I think she and Beth have something lined up for you, or Valarie has a hell of a memory for travelers."

"Oh, she's a nice girl, and has beautiful blond hair—and money. But we met only that once, and had a couple of drinks together. Most of that time Beth and I talked about family. She was probably just accidentally available, and came along to keep Beth company."

Andy knew James wasn't buying it. Also he knew Beth had this weekend arrangement in mind all along, even when they had discussed going to Tokyo for a visit.

"OK," James called from across the hall. "I'm all set, are you? Let's go on down and take the plunge. We'll see just who's got more grapes to stomp."

As they descended the staircase, they met the chauffeur, Jeffries, carrying their suitcases to their rooms. Actually, they traveled very light, as experienced world travelers often do.

They each nodded, and Andy said, "Thanks, Jeffries; just set them in our rooms and we'll unpack what we need later."

"If you wish to wear tuxedos this evening, gentlemen, please allow me to unpack and press your suits," he replied in his best formal manner.

"Thanks very much. I'm sure Elizabeth and her guests would appreciate it," Andy replied.

He and James passed on through the entry into the sitting room and found the double French doors standing open onto the veranda. It was occupied, as they had been led to believe, by three beautiful ladies on lounges, taking the afternoon sun.

"Bikinis must be in style this year," Andy spoke out.

They strolled on over to the lounges, and Andy took the hand extended to him by Valarie Rogers. Obviously, something more than a verbal greeting was expected, so he graciously bent down and kissed her hand.

"Hello, Andy darling; it's nice to see you after so long. Welcome to the vineyards." Valarie sat up on her lounge.

"It's good to see you again, Valarie. This is a much nicer surrounding than the airport," he said, indicating the beautiful pool setting.

"Yes," she replied. "I've been wondering when you'd make it back to Sausalito for a visit. You must get very tired of seeing so few American faces over there in Tokyo." Then she turned her gaze to James. "And you must be James Wellman."

"Yes; Valarie, this is James Wellman; and James, Valarie Rogers." Beth made the introductions.

"We heard about you at the airport on Andy's last trip through San Francisco," Valarie began.

"Thank you. Andy spoke of meeting you when he returned from that company duty assignment. Apparently, his airport stopover was the only happy part of that duty trip, because when he got back he was exhausted."

"He was overly tired when he left us, but we tried hard to keep him awake," Valarie stated.

"He tells me you may be coming to Tokyo for a visit sometime. It's a nice city to roam around in, especially if you know someone there. You'll have to come over and bring Elizabeth."

James turned to the lounge on the other side of the group and said, "And you are looking great, Leslie. It has been a long time since Andy and I were here—a couple of summers, I guess." He walked around the little tables and lounges and, following Andy's lead, took Leslie's hand and kissed it also.

Leslie was clearly flattered, and she began to blush and turn about the color of her hair. Obviously, Elizabeth knew more about her former relationship with James than she admitted to any of her other friends.

"James, it's good to see you again, but I'm very mad at you. You never did write, and after all of your promises." She smiled sweetly as she swung a pigtail to one side.

Andy took in the byplay, for he had guessed as much about their short romance, just as Beth had. He could easily tell that Leslie had been looking forward to meeting James again.

They all found seats on the lounges, and soon were deeply into the discussions of old times. The maid brought the champagne, and James did the honors with a flourish.

"Geophysicists are supposed to be good at opening up the secrets of the earth, and I hereby declare champagne to be one of the earth's best."

"Let the ceremonies begin," Leslie replied.

When the serving was completed, they all drank to that, with giggles accompanying the bubbles all around.

By the time Beth's husband, Hillary, arrived they were all swimming in the pool and trying to drown one another. After a quick greeting of welcome to all, he donned his suit and joined in the water games. It turned out that Leslie couldn't swim, so James immediately volunteered to give her a lesson. He carefully explained that it was easier for beginners to learn to do the sidestroke rather than the breaststroke, but in her case he'd make an exception. He steered her into the deep water, where he could help hold her up more easily.

To that, Hillary remarked, "Here, here; we'll have none of that foolery here. If you persist, I shall call the maid to join the chauffeur to act as our chaperons." That got a laugh from everyone, and the party went on from there.

When the sun disappeared behind the hills, it cooled off in a hurry, so Elizabeth declared an end to the swimming.

"We'd better go in, before we all freeze, and get dressed for the party. Valarie and Leslie, you two show the boys to their rooms. They're in your wing. We'll all meet at the bar at about eight for a snack before the other guests arrive, if you like. The orchestra is to come at nine. Hillary and I can go into our bedroom through the side door here, so we'll see you whenever. Ta ta!"

Leslie grabbed James by the arm and hustled him off up the stairs. Andy and Valarie were left to trail along behind. The last he heard was Leslie saying, "You'll really like this vintage. I've been saving it for a long time." He left Valarie at her door, much to her apparent regret, with just a kiss on the cheek.

When Andy arrived in his room, the phone was ringing. It was Bill Hanby, calling him from Houston.

"Greetings, Andy, sorry to interrupt your party," he said cheerfully. "I've got some news you'll be interested in." Then he paused.

"Nice to hear from you. You're right, the party is getting started well. What's the good word?" Andy asked expectantly.

"It's not all good, but some of it is. Phil Harrison told me that Gil Eason had agreed to the commitment of World Oil to the deal in Vietnam, basically in the same outline as our proposal. He signed the minutes to our meeting, showing their approval. The problem comes in that he received a communiqué from the Vietnamese, saying they want to change some of our previous agreements on which we based our request for approval of the board. They want us to meet with them ASAP in Ho Chi Minh City."

"What do they want to change?" Andy asked, suddenly serious.

"There are suddenly several other players in the game. Some companies have contacted them, and want to open bidding for all of the blocks. That'll slow everything down to a snail's pace. It's bad enough to have to negotiate with an inexperienced government, but to try to get several companies in line with them will be sheer hell!" Obviously Bill Hanby was terribly angry.

"That's not good. Once they start changing the contract parameters we've already agreed on, the whole deal may fall apart. Also, they'll have eight guys trying to get in their pocket ahead of us."

"I'm afraid so. You and I will have to go to Saigon, and get with them quickly to see that things don't change too drastically," Bill answered.

"We have our reservations back to Japan, so we'll be there by midweek," Andy replied weakly.

He was beginning to worry seriously. It was just as he expected. Dong had stirred up a nest of resistance and doubt within their government circles. Not only that, but he had invited other oil companies, who knew how to operate, to talk to them on the inside. Now they'd have to bend their backs and make their previous agreement stick.

"I'll send you copies of everything we received to Tokyo by fax, so you can get right on with making the necessary arrangements. Tell Kelly Johnson I want him to accompany us to Saigon. Try to enjoy the day of vacation tomorrow, for it'll be your last for a while. My regards to Elizabeth. I'll see you on Thursday; we should be seeing the Viets by Monday, so see if you can't arrange the meeting; and we can travel in the company jet. Ciao!" Hanby broke the connection.

The weekend was a huge success from Elizabeth, Leslie, and Valarie's points of view. James and Leslie made it to the party a little late, and Valarie insisted that Andy join her in a late swim. She, too, had a bottle of champagne iced beside the pool, and when they awoke, the sun was shining on their faces. They were still on the lounge.

# Ten

"Hello, is Lin Jin Hoe there, please?" Andy politely asked, as he phoned the Hoe estate from his office in the downtown district of Tokyo. One of the servants had answered, and replied in a quick spiel of Japanese, which he didn't understand. When there was a pause, he repeated, "Lin Jin Hoe, please," in a calm voice.

He heard the female voice say, "Chotto matte," and the phone being laid down, for obviously the servant girl had recognized Andy's voice. He realized it must have been Josan.

After a long half minute, Lin's melodic voice came on the line. "Konnichi wa, my dear Andy-san. Josan knew who you were, and I am so happy to hear from you. Welcome home! How was your trip?" Lin Jin was thrilled, he could tell from her tone.

Andy was happy to hear Lin's voice, too, for it always was so reserved, and quietly euphonious. It gave him a warm feeling inside, and made him want to listen for hours. He said, "Greetings, Lin Jin. It seems such a long time since I left."

"Yes, it was like ages, ne?"

"We had a good meeting in Houston, and everything is working out—sort of. How have you been?" He wanted to ask, Did you miss me? but thought the better of it.

"I am well, and have tried to stay busy with the duties of the household. I am almost ready to look for an outside job. Perhaps Papa-san Li Hong will let me spend more time with him in his office. I think I could be of some assistance there."

"I'm sure you could, with your office management background. I'm sure he thought of that long ago."

"He wished to give me time to get settled into their family life without the burden of a steady job. I'm sure he has reserved a place for me there in his plans," Lin Jin replied. "When can I see you, Andy-san? I have missed you."

"I've had a lot of office work to clear up since James and I returned late yesterday. My desk is piled high."

"I was told that by Chisai. I talked with her recently."

"Bill Hanby and I must make another trip to Saigon next week. I want to see you sometime this weekend, like Friday evening, if you are available."

"I'll check my date book," she replied with a giggle.

"We could have dinner at the American Club and then take in the cabaret at Shangri-la afterward. How does that sound?"

He was hoping she would know he'd be back in town, and would reserve this weekend for him. He wondered if she thought of him as often as he did of her. Somehow his "date" with Valarie Rogers embarrassed him, and seemed to be out of place. He was feeling very guilty, but not guilty enough that he'd admit to Lin Jin that anything had occurred.

"Andy, I'm so delighted you asked. I've been hoping that you'd call this week. I have missed so much hearing your voice." Her speech had a tingle to it. He couldn't help but wonder if she was serious, or if her happy words were just the normal Japanese Oriental way of turning the phrase in the direction that would make a person happy.

"That's wonderful. How would it be, then, if I picked you up at seven on Friday?" He knew if he saw himself in a mirror, he'd see a big grin. He was suddenly as happy as a chicken with a june bug.

"No; I think it would be better if I were to meet you," Lin Jin answered. "I have some shopping to do in the Ginza, and was planning to go into town Friday, anyway. May I meet you somewhere, say, at about six?"

Lin Jin was hesitant, and appeared not too sure if this was an appropriate arrangement for a "date."

"That will be just fine," Andy replied. "Would you like to come to the office, or to the American Club? Or perhaps I could meet you at a department store." Andy realized this could get complicated, but it would save their chauffeur, Jimmy-san, a long drive to the suburbs and back, and give him a couple of hours more in his office.

"If you don't mind carrying packages, you may meet me at the Onsen Tearoom. Do you know where that is, Andy-san, just off the Ginza?"

Andy felt a tingle at being called by the familiar name.

"Yes, Lin Jin, I know the Onsen. But I don't plan to have a massage," Andy joked.

"No, don't look for me upstairs. The tearoom will be the ichi ban place to meet where I can sit, in case you are delayed."

"I'll not be late, I hope. I'll see you there at six on Friday. Take good care of yourself, and regards to your family. Ciao, Lin-san."

Too late, he realized the society greeting word had slipped out. Just as he hung up the phone, James Wellman walked into the office with an armload of maps, accompanied by Kelly Johnson. Kelly carried his "swim pouch" by its strap. They were busily discussing the latest political activities in Ho Chi Minh City, from which Kelly had just returned.

"Greetings, gentlemen," Andy said. "How are your contract plans coming, James? Do you have some crews lined up to bid on the seismic coverage yet?"

"No, they haven't yet started presenting their packages, but they are all sniffing at the bait. Actually, there are only three companies that could qualify within our time restraints. We can't wait for anyone to bring boats across the Pacific, or around the cape."

James knew his job well, and carried out his work in a professional manner. He piled his maps on the table.

"And a welcome back to you too, Kelly. How was your trip to Saigon?"

Andy turned to shake the auditor's hand, since they had not met for two weeks.

"It was as hectic as you might imagine," Kelly replied. "I hear you are having some trouble getting the Vietnamese to stick with their original agreement. That seems to be about par for the course for them. I guess it was not to be unexpected."

"Did you hear anything about it while you were there?"

"I didn't talk to the people who'd be knowing about that, but I heard some rumors. Are they serious?"

"Yes, they've decided they want to discuss our contract again before going any further, which would delay our operation far into the future, especially if we have to renegotiate the entire deal. Then we'll end up splitting up the whole pie, and one piece of it may not be worth going after," Andy explained.

"Dennis Dugan of GCAI, the geophysical company, told me he heard some information from the grapevine after talking with the geophysical contractors. They had been told by other oil companies that there were going to be bids opened by the Viets for various blocks."

"When did you find that out?" Andy asked.

"I heard the rumors before you left for Houston, but they were just rumors. I did some checking in Singapore on my way around from Saigon. I asked the right people, and they were happy to tell me that several major companies had been advised by some high authority, which they refused to name, in the Viet government that they should make the proper advances and see if they couldn't get a piece of the offshore action. They had been told that World Oil didn't have the area sewed up," Kelly explained.

"That would throw a wrench in all of our planning, and at least delay us for several months," Andy said.

"Yes, and apparently it has done so. I did some more checking, and heard they are requesting further conversations before signing a contract. Would you care to guess just who that person was who advised the other companies they were being bypassed?" Kelly asked.

"I could easily guess," replied Andy. "But you'd better tell me what you found out."

"It was none other than our pock-faced Dong Huan Chou. He had the audacity to call some acquaintances of his who are geologists in Jakarta, and advised them the time was ripe to put in a bid and undercut World Oil."

Kelly was speaking calmly, but his face was turning red and he was clutching the swim bag tightly.

"That bastard!" Andy said vehemently. He rarely swore. "Those companies can't afford this big a project, in the first place. The stakes are much too high for them to bid on. Second, they don't have the exploration background to design such an extensive a program as this requires. If other companies get included, it will cause a year's delay in the signing of contracts. Also, they'll want to use World Oil's expertise and data to plan the seismic shooting, and then tie the final bidding to our mapped interpretations."

"We can't just let them hog-tie us like this," James injected. "Especially not when we have a good year's lead on the rest of the industry in that area."

"I doubt if Dong really intended for any other companies to actually get that far into the act. He probably realized that any proposal along a bureaucratic line would foul up their government's operations, and then he could get them to try to handle it themselves, without outside assistance. That little trick can work two ways. In a setup such as their Energy Ministry, if they run into enough red tape, they just might be persuaded to get out the big scissors and clear a path. Let's hope we can get them to do that, and stay oriented in our direction." Andy's face was almost as red as Kelly's.

"It looks like Mr. Dong now has two strikes against him. We may have to go looking for him in a dark alley some night," Kelly stated vehemently.

"No," Andy replied. "That wouldn't be the way. We'll catch him all right, but first we must be sure he's the one who ordered the dirty work. He can be back-alleyed anytime. We must keep him thinking he's getting away with his dirty tricks, until we can prove who is the origin of their directives.

Perhaps his boss, the minister, is only using him as a cover to protect himself from his higher-ups. Or it may also be possible that the leaders in the NLF stay in the background and dictate their specific acts of terrorism."

"That's true," Kelly replied. "We really don't know he is the instigator. He may only be the henchman."

"We don't want to pass up the man manipulating the strings just because there's a puppet out front. If that turns out to be the case, we'll want to even the score with them both."

\* \* \*

When Jimmy-san eased the auto to the curb on the street just off the Ginza, Andy could see Lin Jin through the window, seated alone at a small table near the center of the Onsen Tearoom. It was within walking distance of the Ginza department stores, and he assumed she had taxied into town or had come down with her grandfather earlier in the day. There were several bags and packages arranged on the chair beside her, and she looked as though she were relaxing, having a cup of tea after a hard afternoon of shopping. He stepped out of the car at the curb and instructed Jimmy-san to circle the block, while he went in and helped Lin Jin carry out her purchases.

Walking quickly to Lin Jin's table he gave her a warm smile, and did not hesitate to lean down to give her a gentle hug. He kissed her lightly on each cheek.

"It's great to see you again, Lin-san. My trip lasted much too long."

Returning his mini-embrace, Lin Jin's hand trailed down his shoulder until she caught his elbow.

"Andy-san, your travels have stretched my patience. I have missed our dinners together, and our long walks in the garden at Papa-san's." She was obviously sincere in her statement. They had become more than just good friends since Bill and Jill's promotion party at the Okura Hotel. In spite of Andy's travels away from Tokyo, they had managed to meet on several occasions.

"Jimmy-san will be outside soon with the car, and we can go on to the American Club," Andy said, without offering to take a seat.

"Yes, let us go. My tea is finished."

He motioned for the waiter with a check, and left some yen on the table as he collected her packages.

"He couldn't find a parking place, so he is in orbit until we come out."

They made their way through the small tables to the entry.

"I have been so looking forward to seeing you, Andy-san, and I want to hear all about your trip to the States. Also about your stop to visit your twin sister, Elizabeth, in Sausalito."

Andy helped her arrange her packages and deposit them in the front seat of the auto. All the while, he was wondering who had told her about the stop in California. And he wondered what else she knew. This Oriental had lines of communications that apparently extend all the way to California. Talk about a grapevine! Then he remembered her friendship with the secretary, Chisai. Or had it been Jill?

When they had the packages stowed and were comfortably arranged in the big back seat of the Crown, Andy spoke to the driver, "Let's go to the American Club, Jimmy-san."

"Oh, please," Lin Jin interjected. "Could we possibly go by your apartment? I have a new dress; I want to wear it tonight, especially for you to see, and since we are going out for dinner and to the cabaret. I've been in this thing all day, so I need to change." She was referring to her white winged collar blouse and long, slit black skirt.

"Whatever you wish," he replied, and he relayed the instructions to their driver.

"I hope you won't mind terribly if I borrow your apartment to change into something more presentable. After all that shopping, I need to freshen up."

"No, of course I won't mind. I don't know if James will be at home. He mentioned some plans for tonight, but I don't know what time he'll be leaving. If you'd care to take that chance, we'll go by. or we could just throw him out!" Andy said this with a big boyish grin, wondering what this new twist to Lin Jin's character meant.

"Please invite him to stay, for you may need company. I sometimes dress very slowly," replied Lin Jin, with an equally impish grin. "But I will hurry this night, not to keep you waiting. I want to look especially nice for you when we go to the American Club."

The traffic was as bad as could be expected in the early evening of a Friday night, and the Toyota wound its way slowly through the clogged lanes. Andy and Lin Jin were soon holding hands, and he realized how much he had been missing their weekly rendezvous and classic discussions over the hibachi in her grandfather's parlor. His arm found its way around her shoulder, and she relaxed until her head was against his cheek.

"I have missed you, Andy-san," she said simply.

"And the same with me. I would have called you, but there was always some crisis, some new dragon to be fought and subdued."

"We can make up for the time we have lost now," Lin Jin stated quietly.

Nothing more was said until they pulled up in front of the apartment. As Jimmy-san held the door, Andy helped Lin Jin step down.

"We'll leave the packages here, Jimmy-san, and you can put them in the boot. Do you have what you need, Lin Jin?"

"Yes, this box and my bag."

Turning back to the driver, Andy said, "We're going to walk over to the American Club for a long, quiet dinner, and you can drive us to the cabaret later. Meet us here at about midnight, please, Jimmy-san."

The driver nodded with a knowing smile.

Andy escorted Lin Jin to the elevator, and kissed her lightly on the lips as they reached their floor.

"Now let's see if we need to dispossess Mr. Wellman from his bath," he said.

Lin Jin entered the apartment with her package and handbag, asking, "Would you like to make an inspection and see if there's a room I can use?"

"There's no need," Andy said. "James always leaves the lights on if he's here, so he has already gone on his date."

"Then I'll just be a few minutes," Lin Jin said sweetly, as she turned to look for the bathroom, not wishing to let go of Andy's hand.

"Could I interest you in a drink here before we go?" Andy asked. "I make a great martini, and I have the keys to the bar."

"Do you think I can be trusted to start drinking before we get to the club?" She was speaking quietly, almost as if to herself. "Yes. I believe I'll join you. I can change my outfit later, before we leave. She deposited her purchased box and handbag on the entry table.

Andy met Lin Jin in the living room with a tray and the two martinis, complete with giant stuffed olives. Soon they were comfortably seated on the divan.

"I brought the olives from the States," he commented.

Lin Jin said, "I hope you will bear with me, for I am a very slow martini sipper. They go to my head so quickly."

"Never fear, young lady; Andy Cheston will see you home before morning. And besides, we don't have to drive."

"And now, Mr. Jet-setter, tell me all about your weekend in Sausalito. I want to hear everything. Who was there besides James and your sister and her husband? Were there lots of girls? Did you swim and drink a lot of champagne? I want to hear all of the things a little birdie told me about."

"Let's see . . . James was there, but he wouldn't rat on me. Your connection must be through the boss' wife, Jill Hanby. She must be the gossip-monger." Andy knew Jill well enough to know she wouldn't have relayed any "tales" out of school that he would have preferred be kept between them. So Lin Jin must just be fishing.

"You know your boss' wife pretty well, so I guess I may as well admit that we talked on the phone early in the week. She told me Bill had heard from you in California, and told me where you and James had been visiting," she admitted with a sly smile.

He had been teasing her, so it was only fair that she should not tell him everything she knew.

It took him some time to explain all that had gone on during the weekend, carefully describing the magnificent formal party with an orchestra and the sit-down dinner. One thing led to another, and they talked on into the evening until it seemed there was nothing more of importance to say. She leaned closer and closer to him, as she felt his protective arms around her.

Finally she broke the silence in a wee voice.

"Andy-san, I don't think I need to go to the club for dinner this night. I'd much rather stay here and . . . " She stopped with a little gasp, unable to complete the sentence.

"I know, I feel the same, but I didn't want to rush you, Lin-san," Andy replied, as he fumbled with her buttons. "Let me see if I can find a threshold to carry you across."

She melted against him, and a tear rolled down her cheek as she nestled snugly into his arms. He picked her up carefully and slowly found their way to his room. She looked so innocent there with her long black hair against the soft pillow. He saw her lip quivering, and then he felt it as they kissed. Finally, the shaking stopped as she relaxed.

"Andy-san, I love you."

They never did finish their third martini.

\* \* \*

"We can catch the early morning bullet train to Osaka, and attend the Saturday afternoon session of the opera at Takarazuka. Would you like that?" Andy asked, as he gently stroked her bronzed shoulders.

She had long since lost the top to his pajamas, which she had found under a pillow. Lin Jin smiled luxuriantly now and lay utterly and completely relaxed, resting against his bare shoulder.

"I'll only go if you go," she replied. "I love the opera, and strolling across the bridge over the tumbling mountain stream, and seeing the zoo. Takarazuka is one of my favorite places to visit. Papa-san took me there to see it when I first arrived in Japan." Then she suddenly sat up. "But I have no clothes to go to the mountains. I'd have to return home first."

"I don't know if I can let you go by your home now. Your grandparents might not allow you to leave again, and with me."

He grinned, but he was not sure it wasn't a legitimate question.

"Do not worry, Andy-san, my love. I will tell them I arranged a job for myself to work all night in the cabaret."

She smiled. He would never believe such a ridiculous statement.

"We'll have to come back Sunday, for I have a busy week set up, traveling to Saigon with Bill Hanby and Kelly."

"It will be a heavenly weekend, Andy-san, and I may not care if Monday never comes. Two more days with you will give me a lifetime of joy!" She had closed her eyes and left him for her own little dream world.

Andy suddenly remembered his arrangement with Jimmy-san, and said, "If we don't go soon, we'll miss your ride home, and I won't get back in time to pick you up for the train in the morning." He began to help her pick up her things, and escorted her to the bath.

"I'll get the car around, and will come back for you in a few minutes."

Their late cruise to the suburbs through the quiet Tokyo streets reminded Andy of their first ride to her home together, when he had escorted her from Jill Hanby's Okura Hotel dinner party. That was when Andy had first felt the silky luxuriance of her long, firm legs against his, and experienced the urgent desire of her eager kisses. And now he knew that this lithe, golden slip of a girl was what had been missing from his life. He had come to the firm realization that he loved her.

Lin-san fit so well into the international scene, and would make a wonderful addition to the worldwide family of his employer. But how could he ever reconcile her background with that of his sister, Elizabeth, or his with her Japanese and Vietnamese ties? He still had some convincing to do, if his family future was ever to be calm.

# Eleven

"I don't know why you wanted a geophysicist along on this trip, unless we plan to start our local recon." James Wellman polished his aviator-style glasses as he spoke, jokingly. He was directing his comment to William Hanby, their boss. "I feel like a fifth wheel at this meeting. Discussing changes in contract arrangements is very far afield from doing seismic interpretation."

The five of them were gathered in the bar-lounge of the Saigon Majestic Hotel, and were recovering from their daylong trip to Ho Chi Minh City from Tokyo. The ride in from the airport was the toughest part for Andy, because he needed his sleep after a long weekend out of town.

"You can never tell what information we may need when we get into renegotiations with this State Oil group," replied Bill Hanby. "They obviously want to change things, and seismic programs are where we'll spend our first big money. Therefore, they are the first on our agenda; so we will probably want to discuss seismic acquisition costs."

"I brought along my 'soroban' in case we need to recalculate the payout after they get through butchering our original offer," injected Ben Brodecki, whose briefcase was bulging with the economic details of the previous agreement.

"I hope they won't get into rearranging our basic tender, but we'd better be prepared for anything they throw at us," said Hanby.

Kelly Johnson replied, "We already know there is one in their group who will be certain to put a monkey wrench into the works, somewhere along the line. I hope we can short-circuit his efforts. It may be a matter of how high we can go in their organization to override that SOB's interference. We know somewhere up there somebody wants us to come and work in his country, or we wouldn't have gotten this far."

He spoke from FBI experience, for he knew something about how the dark side of organizations like the NLF worked. Andy had been relaxing and listening to the conversation, while he thoughtfully sipped his gin and tonic.

Straightening up in his seat, he said, "You'd think they would learn to put more ice in these drinks. What time is our meeting scheduled for tomorrow morning, Bill? And do you want everyone to go along, or just the two of us?"

"It's for ten o'clock. I think just you and me for the first meeting. We don't want them to think we attach too much importance to this sudden request for a contract review," Hanby replied.

"Should we set up other meetings with their departments then, and meet back here afterward for lunch? We could decide then if further afternoon contacts are necessary," Brodecki stated.

He did talk a little like a calculator, Andy thought. But he always had all the data together to come out with a correct answer. Brodecki was a jewel that made the financial clock of World Oil tick true.

"They may have our schedule all mapped out, so let's not make any plans on our own for now," Hanby said. "Just stay close, where we can be in contact if the need arises."

"James, why don't you see if you can arrange a meeting with some of their exploration staff for the afternoon —which, in a way, will be justification for your coming here. You need to go over schedules anyway, especially if we can get by without making major changes in our original program." Andy was thinking ahead to make the most of their visit. "And take Kelly along with you, Brodecki doesn't need him to count his contracts until tomorrow morning. He may be able to pick up some background on geophysical field operations that will be helpful in the future."

"Here comes Pham Xuan Bach," said Hanby. "George probably wants to make us welcome, and take us to dinner. I hope it's a better place than the one next door."

"Kelly, if I don't see you before, could we meet back here after dinner?" Andy asked. "There are some things we might need to go over."

"Sure, let's get together then and go out for some air. These are the smokingest people on earth. They start as soon as they can walk, and never give it up until their lungs give out. Their offices and restaurants are real dens of nicotine." Kelly grinned at his uncharacteristic remark. One thing for certain, he didn't carry cigarettes in his swim pouch. The entire group groaned at the unexpected pun, for Kelly was normally the serious type. They all stood to give George a proper greeting.

\*   \*   \*

The alley behind the gold shops of Ho Chi Minh City was as dark as the first time they had stumbled their way through the rubbish. Under all the electric wires strung above the streets, they felt like they were plodding through a spider web. When they passed the shuttered windows and arrived at the back door to Lam Thang Nguyen's inconspicuous well-shuttered abode, Andy stood aside and let Kelly give a gentle rap on the door. There was a noise of someone peering through the peephole, and then a crack of light appeared as the door swung open an inch. Kelly was bathed in the light.

"Konban wa," Kelly said. "Is Papa Nguyen at home?" He didn't know who was behind the door, for he saw only the light.

As the door opened a few inches, the light shined on the two of them, and they could then see that it was the granddaughter, Nhung Thi, who had answered their rap, and she carried a kerosene lamp. Recognizing them, she quickly swung wide the door and invited them to enter. As on their previous visit, her Bapak was sitting in the corner of the room, working on his ledgers. He had a cup of tea on the tiny table at his side.

"Please to come in," said Nhung Thi. "Bapak has been speaking of you, and speculating on when you might return." She had a quiet voice, not at all unlike her cousin Lin Jin's.

"Greetings, my American friends," said Lam Thang. "You have returned to Saigon sooner than expected. Your drilling efforts must be progressing satisfactorily." He rearranged himself in his chair, putting the ledgers aside.

"It is good to visit you again, Lam Thang," Andy said, as he and Kelly pulled benches a few inches closer to the old man's chair. "I have brought you a little gift from Japan. I hope it meets with your approval." As he spoke, he laid two boxes on the stool in front of him.

"You are not expected to come bearing gifts," replied the old man. "Please allow me to savor their pleasure at a later time."

"Very well," replied Andy. "And here also is a gift for you, Nhung Thi." He handed her the second box, similar in size to the first.

"Oh, thank you," she replied. "May I, Bapak?" She turned and asked eagerly, before making any effort to untie the red ribbon.

"Of course, my dear," he replied to her in Vietnamese. "These are our friends."

Nhung Thi wasted no time in getting her box open. When she found the blue jeans and T-shirt inside, she was ecstatic. Then, when the shoes fell out of the package, her joy knew no bounds. She gave both Kelly and Andy a hug, and a kiss on each cheek. There were tears running down her face, she was so overcome with elation.

"Oh, thank you, thank you," she continued, as she draped the jeans to her side. "With the extra-long bottoms, I can make a pair of shorts."

"I hope the sizes are correct," said Andy. "Lin Jin asked me to tell everything about you. From my descriptions, she did the shopping for these. She assured me they would fit well."

"When did you see Lin Jin last? Did she go with you to buy these? Did they come from the Ginza? Are they imported from America?" Nhung Thi anxiously asked all of her questions at once.

"I saw Lin Jin all of last weekend," Andy answered. "In fact, we went to Takarazuka to the opera, and visited the zoo, and walked in the park. Later we stopped at the Nijyo Castle, but we ran out of time. She promised to take me back there for a real visit. It was a wonderful outing."

"I've heard how wondrous the scenery of Japan is, and have always wanted to see it for myself. Someday Bapak and I will be able to leave this place, and then we can visit the world," she added dreamily.

The old man, Lam Thang, smiled almost imperceptibly, as he understood the deeper significance of what Andy had told them. He shrewdly refrained from mentioning this obvious close relationship between Andy and Lin Jin directly. Instead, he added thoughtfully, "You must have enjoyed the long train ride. Does the bullet connect to the Takarazuka local at Osaka, or is there a long layover?"

"Yes, there's a good connection," Andy answered. Then, thinking more of an explanation was expected, he continued, "We stayed overnight on the mountain at Takarazaka in a small inn next to the river. We walked across the 'Sayonara' Bridge of movie fame, and strolled through the gardens and the zoo. Our stop in Kyoto as we returned was short, but the weekend was a welcome break from tedious office duties. Just being with Lin Jin made it wonderfully relaxing."

"It would appear that you have the blessing of Li Hong Hoe," said Lam Thang without a change of expression. "There is a message I would ask you to relay personally to my half-brother in Tokyo."

"We will be happy to do so," Andy answered.

"Please express to him how much our family and I thank him for his assistance in getting my release from the reeducation camps. I know he had influence beyond what we are able to see, as well as the donation of the required funds. Express to him my eternal gratitude."

"Papa-san Li Hong would never admit he had arranged such a connection, but I will be glad to relay your message personally," Andy replied.

"I have also to request what news you have of my niece, Thi Lan, in Hong Kong. I am sure Lin Jin keeps in close contact with her as well as her brother, Kim Jin. It has been long since we have had any contact with them."

It was obvious to Andy that the old man had been harboring these questions since their last visit. At that time, he probably believed he did not know them well enough to ask. Now that he had been told of Andy's closer relation with Lin Jin, he felt such a request would be in order.

He then told the two rapt listeners all he had heard from Lin Jin of her family in Hong Kong, and her plans for the future. He apologized for not knowing more about Thi Lan.

There was a lull in the conversation while Nhung Thi served tea to their guests. She had settled down from the excitement created by the opening of her gifts. Kelly was waiting to join the conversation, and bring up the reason for their visit.

"Have you been able to acquire any other information on the events that occurred after the robbery at Cu Chi? We are eager to know if there is any more direct connection between the Ministry of Energy or the NLF," Kelly asked eagerly.

"No, there is little else I have been able to learn," said Lam Thang. "I have, however, been able to reestablish some old contacts. You may wish to know that I have been in contact with a distant cousin who is a servant and private bookkeeper at the estate of Dong Huan Chou. His name is Tan Tran, and I believe he was a nguy (traitor). He was the NLF contact with whom my release from the reeducation camp was arranged. Therefore, I am sure he can be bought."

There was a touch of vengeance detectable in the old man's voice.

"That is important information," replied Kelly. "Is there any way we could make a reconnaissance of Cu Chi without drawing too much attention from our watchers?"

"Ways can be arranged; however, 'without notice' may be more difficult. Let me think of what can be done for a moment. Nhung Thi, replenish our guests' tea, and if you will excuse me, I will return in a short time." The old man struggled to his feet and laboriously made his way through a curtained doorway. He could be heard slowly climbing step by step up the stairs to another portion of their apartment.

It was an enjoyable fifteen minutes of discussion between Nhung Thi and Andy about her cousin's activities. They really had been close during their early lives. Finally, the curtain parted again, and Lam Thang feebly returned. His face gave no sign that he had accomplished his mission; however, in his hand he was carrying a map. On it, certain roads were carefully highlighted, with newly drawn red markings.

Pointing to a place that was circled, he said, "There is the location of the estate house of Dong Huan Chou. It was a division control point for the Cong during the war, and was suspected of being undermined with tunnels. Dong must be making some use of the location, since he seems to be well connected with the energy ministry as well as the NLF."

Andy recognized the map immediately, as they had copies like it in their own files. "How would we go about getting to and from that place to have a look? Is it possible to rent a car and drive there?" Andy asked.

"No, that would not be wise," replied Lam Thang. "It would be best if you allow me to arrange a different type of transport." Lam Thang carefully eased back into his chair. "Can either of you manipulate a motorcycle?" he asked.

"Yes, I can handle one. In fact; I used to have one of my own in college, and almost killed myself," Andy replied.

"I've had some experience, too," Kelly added. "How would we go about getting the use of a cycle?"

"That I have already arranged," said the old man. "On the back of that map I have written an address. If you go there, well after dark tomorrow night, knock on the rear door. Tell them you are looking for 'Chu Tu.' They will recognize you, and will know why you have come. Payment will already have been made."

"Are you sure this will not get you into more trouble with the government?" Andy asked.

"No, I have already had my trouble. Just ask for the use of their cycle, and proper arrangements will be made. Return it after your use, and no officials will ever be the wiser," Lam Thang said a bit sadly.

"We thank you for helping us. We will do what we can to see that our enemies are punished. Your friends can depend on us to return the cycle sometime during the night," Andy replied.

Kelly zipped open his swim bag and handed Lam Thang a sheaf of folded paper bills. "This should cover their costs. It's best if you arrange proper payment."

Lam Thang protested, but finally accepted the money, stating, "I will make you an account."

Both Andy and Kelly waved his offer away.

At that moment, there was a quiet ringing of a bell somewhere in the depths of the apartment. It moved Nhung Thi to shuffle into her clogs quickly, and go out through the beaded doorway. They sat quietly sipping their tea, and Andy wondered what significance the bell might have. It would be strange if a man in such desperate straits would be furnished with a telephone. Very soon Nhung Thi returned, and knelt on both knees beside Bapak.

"The message was from our friends," she said. "We have an internal communication system," she explained looking to Kelly and Andy. "There is a black Mercedes parked a hundred meters away in the alley, and it has been there for some time. Two men are in the car. Apparently you were followed here, and your activities are being watched."

"That means they suspect you are arranging something to their disadvantage, and will watch you until they are sure of your intentions," said the elderly Lam Thang as he stared into space from his glazed eyes. "Tomorrow you must be extremely careful that you are not followed when you go after the cycle. It would be unfortunate if our friends were found to be assisting the enemies of a high government official."

\* \* \*

On the following night Kelly walked close behind Andy as they paced single file down a narrow street, still a long way from their intended destination. They were on their way to pick up the motorcycle for an inspection tour of the countryside. It was after midnight, and very dark out. They had been walking rapidly for some time, with many changes of direction. There was a black Mercedes following discreetly at a great distance, but apparently no one else accompanying it.

"We'd better figure out something to do to get rid of that car, such as splitting up," suggested Andy.

"Andy, if we are to get proof of who actually instigated the airplane bombing, we're going to have to find something that connects directly to the activity leading to the terrorists. Whoever collected the gold had to furnish some sort of proof, and that's what we need to find." Kelly was speaking quietly as they walked down a dark back street of Saigon.

"That may be very hard for us to come by, since we're the wrong color," Andy replied. "Somehow we must get a look inside their organization. Then we can search for actual proof of guilt—or make someone admit it."

"Criminals are not usually easy to convince that they should admit anything. It has been my experience that they just go along inventing bigger lies to cover up their former indiscretions."

Kelly's FBI background was coming out. "Let's find a spot in the next block to stay a few minutes, to see who is scouting ahead of the car. I've seen some suspicious shadows, so whoever is with the auto can walk as fast as we can."

"If anyone is watching us, it must be someone on foot, for there haven't been any likely bicycles around. It's so late in the evening that any lone cycle would be a bit too obvious," Andy said as he looked cautiously up an alley they were passing.

"How did your session go today? I got back to the hotel rather late myself."

"It was most remarkable. We skimmed right past the roadblock that had been set up, after some relatively short discussion. Perhaps it was because Dong Huan Chou was nowhere around. Some higher-up must have put the squelch on his objections to our immediate signing of the contract. Our firm signature date is all set for next week. I'm glad we don't have to come back for that."

"Don't count on that. Hanby may want your helping hand, and the two of us may also need to be around."

"I certainly hope not, because Wellman and I need to be getting down to Hong Kong to get some geophysical contracts into operation. Hanby didn't seem to miss Dong at the meeting today, and he's a lot happier now. He can call Houston and clue them in with a smile."

"Yeah, it'll be a happy call for a change. Dong was probably off in a snit somewhere, planning some other mischief."

They had covered several blocks along the dark streets, and only a few bicycles had passed them—late workers apparently intent on speeding their trip home.

"Step in here a moment, Andy." They stood in an alley and watched the dark street, seeing no motion.

"I think you are right. There's no car, or they left it parked. You go on ahead and pick up the cycle, and I'll stay here and watch. Make two rounds to lose anyone who might be following, then pass me by here once. If I am facing you, pick me up the second time you pass. Anyone following on foot or bicycle will soon be left far behind." Kelly smiled.

"Right," Andy answered. "If you're facing me, I'll stop."

"And we'll give him some good exercise to make him sleep well. We must have a look at where the action occurred. Then we'll plan some way to get into their dirty little organization."

It was a good half hour before Andy returned. Apparently, Kelly had seen no one who looked suspicious, because he remained a step back in the alley. On the second pass, he stepped out into the edge of the street facing the oncoming cycle. It scarcely slowed down as he swung his leg over the saddle behind Andy. He was better than an amateur rider, and he had adapted to the strange cycle very quickly. As they sped away, a quick look back showed no quickly moving figure following them.

After turns to establish false directions, Andy made for the river road in the direction of Cu Chi. He had no idea what he expected to find there, but he wanted to get a look at the establishment without alerting those who lived there. He needed to confirm that there was a new gate replacing the one that had burned, for it was all he had to go on as a direct connection to the loss of their plane.

Seeing evidence of that fire and firefight would confirm the location connected to the terrorist's payoff, and would add credence to the information furnished by Lam Thang. Andy knew that without his inside connections within the gold industry, they would be completely in the dark as to what events had taken place that night. Now he must see that place for himself, for it was the source of a motive for the terrorist.

They had ridden for a good half hour at top speed, and both were needing a rest, since they were unaccustomed to the steady beating on the unmaintained and pitted laterite roads. Andy pulled the bike off onto a small side trail and doused the lights. It was a great relief to stretch, and then just to stand quietly and breathe in some fresh humid night air.

Soon they saw the lights of a vehicle rapidly approaching along the main road, so they ducked deeper into the foliage. As it passed only a few feet away from their hidden cycle, they saw that two men were in the front seat of the dark Mercedes. Although it looked like Dong's car, it couldn't be him, for he would be riding in the back.

Andy lost no time getting the cycle back on the road to follow the car, but this time without lights. That made their ride difficult, since the road was so rough. Gradually, the Mercedes left them behind as it sped on toward Cu Chi. He didn't have a very good idea of how much farther it might be, but calculated it was only a few kilometers.

Just as he was becoming discouraged about being able to keep the Mercedes in sight, the car slowed, and the lights passed the front wall with its two Spirit Houses; then it disappeared into a lane along the far wall of the estate. The driver was taking the car to store it in some garage at the rear, which must be outside the main walls.

Andy parked the cycle quickly, then he and Kelly made their way along the rough siding of the road. There was some cover of bushes, and soon they found a track leading to the nearest Spirit House. If it was occupied by a guard, he must be asleep, for he didn't show himself.

Andy crept close enough to see the outline of the main gate, with Kelly at his heels. He could hear someone approaching in the lane on the far side, apparently returning to the main entry from the garage. He was thankful it was a dark night, and there were no lights on anywhere around the compound. The figure passed the Spirit House at the far corner, and approached the main gate. After a quiet knock and a few words in Vietnamese, a light appeared shining above the wall. Soon he could hear someone fumbling with the latch and bar across the entrance.

When the gate swung open, a small man was framed in the slit of light, dressed in a white linen baba. Andy knew immediately it was Dong's handyman, Tan Tran. He had been well described by Lam Thang. He had known of him in the past from his connections with the NLF payoff for reeducation. Dong must have stayed at home this night in the company of some bedroom confidant, while he nursed his pique over the failure to stop the contract signing. Or had the energy minister himself been directed by the prime minister to continue with the contract?

Tan Tran did not seem pleased as he conducted a short discussion with the guard who opened the gate. It gave Andy a chance to see that the entire frame of the gate, as well as the massive doors, had been newly rebuilt. It must have been quite a fire, thought Andy. However, there on the framed sides, along both sides of the gate, was the telltale evidence of charred wood. They had not yet covered the black with whitewash, although the many bullet pockmarks showing in the cement block fence had been plastered over. This was the place where the truck had been burned, and where the visitors to Dong's lair had been murdered.

The heavy bar made a rasping sound as it was slid into place. Then there was complete silence, and the darkness returned. Tan Tran must live inside the estate house, and not with the servants to the rear.

There seemed to be no reason for Dong to keep guards occupying the Spirit Houses, and Tan Tran had apparently gone inside to report to his master. What had been the mission that Dong considered so important that he should send his right hand into Saigon for the evening? Surely it must have been something that worried Dong a great deal. Was it possible he suspected the NLF did not believe his story about the hijacking of the payoff gold for their terrorist act?

Dong knew only too well their method of repayment of a traitor for insubordination. He would have to cover his tracks absolutely, so there would be no one to question his actions. Andy wondered if the yeoman, Tan Tran, knew the entire story. And if so, did he realize the danger he was living under? Would it be possible they might exploit this chink in Dong's armor? Was Tan Tran as trusted a servant as Dong believed, or could he be bribed for information? Lam Thang had been bought out of reeducation through him.

The bushes were adequate cover near the Spirit House as Andy and Kelly waited for several minutes, listening for any sound that might indicate activity within the compound. There was none, so they cautiously climbed the hillock along one side of the house and moved along the elevated ground beside the outer wall. Since there appeared to be no light in the interior, they continued their sneaking appraisal around to the rear, where the garage and several shacks stood 100 meters beyond the block fence. Obviously, this area of wattled huts was the servants' quarters, and there, in the back wall, was a small, heavy door. It was their entryway into the main compound.

Through its cracks, Andy could see a light from the interior of the house. The generator was still running far to the rear, but the light in the servants' quarters was only provided by a lone candle. Soon, even that was snuffed out. All was quiet, except for the chirp of the crickets.

Andy and Kelly watched for several minutes from their place in the darkness, and finally the interior light disappeared as the sound of the generator faded. Apparently Tan Tran had finished giving his report on his evening's activities, and had gone to bed. It must have been a difficult statement, for he had failed in his assignment to follow the movements of the World Oil visitors. Now Dong would have to worry about where they had gone and to whom they had spread their questions about his actions. Dong's alert watchfulness indicated he was seriously concerned that someone was getting closer to the truth of his treachery. After several minutes of cramped waiting, Andy and Kelly were becoming stiff from their positions, hunkered down in the cover of the small bushes. The evidence of the robbery was clear, and it was time for them to move.

"Go on back to the cycle, and I'll follow in a few minutes. I want to see around the other side of the compound if I can," Kelly whispered.

"OK. I'll stop by this side and listen a while en route, and then meet you there," Andy answered.

He had been back at the roadside hiding place of the motorcycle for several minutes, and all had remained as quiet as before. Then he heard the slight sound of a door slam, as though it had accidentally slipped. In a few minutes, he saw a dark figure scurrying past the far Spirit House and hurrying along the lane to a spot where there was a bush growing close to the trail. The figure hid there just as another figure, more visible in a white baba, rounded the corner.

As the second figure passed the concealing bush, there was a quick commotion followed by the sickening sound of a heavy thud. Someone would have a big headache in the morning, and he trusted it would not be Kelly. Then a body pitched headlong into the trail. For a few minutes, there was complete silence. Andy held his breath to see if the commotion had attracted any attention from the compound or Spirit Towers, and who would emerge. Finally, there was an onrush of a darkly clothed man toward Andy's hiding place.

He was greatly relieved to see that it was Kelly, and no time was lost extricating the cycle from its hiding place. He ran silently down the road, being helped by Kelly to push the vehicle to where the sound of their motor could not be heard.

"How did you know a guard was following you?" Andy asked, as they rode toward Saigon.

"He must have seen me from his hut. Fortunately, I heard a door close, and waited for him. He'll have a good story to tell tomorrow. If he's smart, he'll just forget it, because he didn't get a look at me, and his guarding ineffectiveness would be hard to explain to his master."

"I hope that doesn't make them more alert in the future," Andy commented.

Now Andy and Kelly knew where Dong and his henchmen kept their secrets and planned their treachery, but they were also aware that he may have been alerted to their investigations. Dong would know that he was no longer safe from their prying efforts, just because he was away from the bright lights of Ho Chi Minh City. It meant Dong must somehow come after them. Andy knew someday he would confront this adversary in his hiding place to obtain the proof of their plane's bombing secreted there, and to reward him with his just desserts. He was only too aware that possession of such knowledge made Saigon an unsafe place for friends of World Oil.

# Twelve

"James, when is the offshore seismic shooting scheduled to commence?" Andy asked, as he watched Wellman and his geophysicist helper align the cross sections on the wall. They were carefully sticking them to the cork wallboard with the big lead-headed pins.

"They're already at work, Andy. They left port yesterday, and started testing their instruments this morning," James replied. "We'll get the first results in off the boat by next weekend. They'll fly it ashore on a helicopter and connect by plane to Hong Kong. I'll meet them with Dennis Dugan there, and we'll take it to their processing office in Singapore."

James Wellman's geophysical office of World Oil in Tokyo was buzzing with activity. Their big hurdle had been accomplished, and the contract with the Vietnamese had been signed. Now the fieldwork had commenced, and it was their responsibility to see that it went forward without delay. The first operation would be conducted by the seismic crew, which was contracted through Wellman's Geophysical Department by Dennis Dugan's company, GCAI. They would navigate their ship along carefully programmed lines, making their tape recordings of the sound echoes that reverberated from the subterranean depths.

"You guys have it easy, now that everything is on tape and digitized. Remember the good old days when we didn't get to massage the data and stack it to get rid of the noise? I used to have a boss who reminded me every day, 'Crap plus crap equals crap.' It was his way of saying you gotta see reflection alignments before you can pick 'em. The strange part is, if you stack enough reflections, even though they're weak, the noise cancels out and the real data comes through. If you stack up noise, you still just get noise." Andy had discussed this with James many times.

"Let's just hope the signals stay stronger than the noise," James replied "These modern-day operations are a far cry from the old prospectors' guesses made with a 'witching stick' as they prowled across those red Oklahoma hills on foot."

"We've got to keep this work going quickly now, James. There's a lot to figure out before we can locate our first drill sight. As the head of Idimitsu quoted the Japanese emperor, 'First stop grumbling. Second, take a new look at the three thousand year history of Japan. Third, start reconstruction immediately.' They read this edict morning and evening to all their men. Perhaps some such regimen would remind us of our goals every day."

"Does this mean we should take time out for sweaty calisthenics?" James asked, with a grin. The remark drew quick laughs from their explorationist cohorts.

They worked on together for an hour, comparing the newest information with what they had already studied. It was an unending process. Andy knew that regardless of the seismic data available, they still required a skilled human interface in the equation if the data were to lead to oil production. The interpretations, whose end result is the spending of millions of dollars for drilling, posed a heavy responsibility. Andy had confidence in the ability of James and his other interpreters to acquire the best possible data for locating their drilling sites.

"Are you coming with me to Hong Kong to see the first seismic results?" James asked. He was surrounded by two large tables, on which lay several cross sections of seismic data. His small desk looked lost in the ell formed by the tables' large working spaces. It looked like a busy, unorganized clutter, but actually James knew where every section fit in relation to its program-line neighbor.

"Yes, I'll go along, but I'll probably not stay with you for your entire visit. I wouldn't understand your velocity analysis software programs, and all of those noise-reduction transforms. Someday you can explain a Nyquist Frequency to me again."

"I've trained you well, it seems." James grinned as he went on with the colored pencil, marking his studied interpretation on the sections.

"I want to see the crew's results as soon as you've had a chance to digest the information, and can give your opinion about how its quality stacks up. Also, I have to look into some other activities we must get started there." Andy was leaning back in the visitor's chair, trying to adjust his line of sight along a direction that James continued to mark with his pencil and some gaudy colored tapes.

James often told Andy that a working office should be no bigger than the walls and tables one could reach from a highly mobile chair. His seat was on casters, and he scooted easily along the hard floor to positions where he could plot the alignments of faults and subterranean mounds. He was literally seeing down into the earth, and he had trained his mind to look at a scene in three dimensions.

"By next week, they should have some of their data into the temporary office in Kowloon. I'll be staying at the Mandarin there. How does that suit you?" James asked.

"It's handy, and that'll suit my purposes as well as being out on the island. I have to look for office space—both for a temporary location and for something that can be expanded if our operations progress as we hope they will. I'll probably ask Tim McAllister to go along and help with that project. He knows all about renting space. I was happy to hear that Hanby was able to convince the Viets we couldn't operate out of their ports for exploration purposes. It gives us a little more freedom to control our destiny without being under their thumb." Andy grinned. "And, too, I like the hotels in Hong Kong better."

"I'll only be staying in Hong Kong for a few days," said James. "Then it's back to Singapore to watch over the data processing. It's important for me to be there in the beginning of the processing to be sure they're using the right data transforms for our area."

"Yes, you'd better oversee them carefully. We don't want anyone cutting any corners just to save a few bucks. No use being penny-wise. We'll need the best answers we can get, especially since this is virgin coverage." Andy rose to leave, and shoved his chair back under the corner of a table.

"And speaking of virgin coverage, do you have a date yet for the Hanby's Saturday night celebration?" He gave a sly grin. "I guess he's pretty happy to reach this stage in our new venture. It's been a long, drawn-out effort just to get started." The grin wouldn't go away.

"Yes, I have a date, but I can't tell you about the virgin part." James smiled from ear to ear, as though they knew he wasn't telling the whole story. "I'm bringing Chisai; she's almost big enough to qualify as a date."

"Ah ha! So you're moving up in the world. And you dare to date the boss' secretary, eh?" Andy knew that Chisai was more than just a secretary. She was an executive secretary, which carried a connotation of company stature.

She often handled Hanby's social arrangements, as well as the secretarial staff. In another era, she could have been considered a geisha. Everyone around the office agreed she conducted herself in a princess-like manner, and she was highly respected by locals and expats alike.

"All that's required is that you ask, and she says 'yes.' Besides, Jill Hanby likes her, I've noted." That was an important point, for James had first met Chisai socially at the Hanby's promotion party, and therefore Jill accepted her as a social equal.

"Yes, you're right," Andy answered. "We're all ready for a little partying after the work we've accomplished in the past weeks. Soon we'll be able to get our work away from the contractors and get down to finding oil."

"How about you? Do you have your date lined up yet?"

"Yes, as a matter of fact, this may be a replay of the party the Hanbys gave for my promotion. Except this time I'm going to pick up Lin Jin on the way. I haven't seen much of her lately, but I've talked to her often, as you know." The thought of her made Andy smile. "I'll have to leave to get her a bit earlier, so you'd better arrange other transportation. Or, I could send Jimmy-san back for you after we arrive. You'd only be a little late."

"No thanks, Andy. I'll need to pick up Chisai on time, so I'll need a car. I'll check one out of the pool."

James was aware that the company drivers were always happy to make a few extra yen by working overtime.

"That'll probably be better. That way we won't get in each other's way."

"Oh, by the way, did I ever tell you that Jill Hanby called for you on Sunday a couple of weeks ago? She wanted to tell you something about Bill's travel arrangements. I told her you were gone to Takarazuka."

At that remark, the whole geophysical staff smiled.

"Thanks a whole bunch. I really wanted her to know that." Andy grinned, because he knew that keeping such a trek a secret might be attempted, but those with sources, such as Jill Hanby, were bound to find out. So why hide it, since he didn't intend for it to be a one-nighter. He didn't care that the staff knew how he felt about Lin Jin.

"I knew you'd want to know," James shot back with a grin.

"We can make our travel arrangements for Hong Kong later then, and I must be off to discuss numbers with Ben Brodecki. We don't want to be over our budget from the beginning." Andy raised his hand in salute as he left. "See you for lunch. If you bring Wally Brooks, we'll talk about how the other structures look to graybeards through horn-rims."

\* \* \*

The Crown Toyota nosed its way into the driveway through the open wrought iron gate of the great stone entry, and paused in front of the portico. It reminded Andy of the stonework around the moat of the Imperial Palace. Although it was just dusk, the lantern above the entrance was already lit. His light tap on the door brought an immediate response. It was the servant girl, Josan, who ushered him into the entry hall.

Almost immediately, Lin Jin appeared through the rice-paper panels from the living area. She was a breath of loveliness in her white metal-flecked sheath. As tight as it was, it still seemed to offer no resistance to her smooth movement across the polished stone floor. Her long black hair was held at the back by a clip, but managed to flow over her shoulder, and almost to her slender waist. Lin Jin knew how to make the most of her walk, even in geta. She slipped into her high heels, which brought her eyes to the level of Andy's chin. She lost no time in greeting him with arms outstretched.

"Konban wa, Andy-san. It has been much too long. I have counted the days for all of this week, anxiously awaiting this night." She did not hesitate to put both arms around his broad shoulders, and pulled him closer so she could kiss him on each cheek.

"It is a relief for my mind to view your lovely face again, Lin-san."

He smiled at his imitation of the flowery Japanese language style.

"I've had a long week of waiting, too. Phone calls just don't seem to give me the pleasure the sight of you does."

Andy knew it was not the kind of a speech he was good at giving.

He also knew he was stammering a little as he added, "You look lovely again this evening, as ever. Here is an orchid I found on the way out."

She took the flower and held it tenderly in her hands as she removed it from the box, and sent Josan away with the wrappings.

"It is beautiful, Andy-san! And what a delicate hue. I must show Ibu and Bapak. And Li Hong wishes to talk to you. Come; they are in the living area."

Taking Andy's arm, she waited while they slipped off their shoes and into geta; then she pulled him along through the intermediate rooms and presented him to her grandmother and grandfather. Andy already knew them well, not only from his previous visits, but from the constant reminders of their granddaughter. He suspected Lin Jin spoke of him all too often to satisfy their Oriental beliefs.

He hoped they were perhaps both understanding of the situation better than Lin Jin, because they knew she was in love, and therefore could be excused. Anything they said that might indicate their feelings could possibly be misinterpreted, either by Lin Jin or by himself. So Andy was happy they said nothing at all that could be construed as being judgmental or impolite. They were perfect hosts.

Andy had long since realized that Bapak and Ibu were only interested in seeing what the feelings of this young American were toward their ward. Did he have the attitude of so many of the servicemen they had seen as visitors to their world? Did he have a bias against the yellow races that so many of his cohorts exhibited? It did not appear so at the moment, but only time would tell. He respected them for recognizing his forthright attitude and direct manner of speaking, and for their realization that Lin Jin had a mind and life of her own.

When the conversational niceties had been exchanged, Li Hong drew Andrew to one side, and addressed him personally. "I have heard from Saigon indirectly. My brother's friend has advised me to relay a message to you. He says that he is watching for any new information, but that none of importance has developed. He continues to observe."

"Thank you very much," Andy replied. "There are many things occurring there that we need to know."

He understood very well that the friends he was referring to were Lam Thang Nguyen and his daughter, Nhung Thi. It was obviously much safer for them to omit names.

"We have mutual frlends who will appreciate knowing that someone is keeping watch over our Saigon interests."

"There was another message that I did not understand, but I am sure you will," said Li Hong. "You are invited to go riding any time you wish. The meaning is obscure to me, but the intent sounded friendly."

"Yes, our friends there are most accommodating."

Andy did not wish to explain. They need not become any more involved, and they had already furnished a contact that had been most useful.

He was happy to see Ibu express her obvious pleasure upon seeing the orchid, and with the colors of the flower. He then spoke briefly to Li Hong Hoe about their progress in oil production of various South China Sea related fields, and about their drilling expectations. Then he asked about how his shiphuilding activities progressed. After he helped Lin Jin attach the orchid to the shoulder strap of her dress, and holding her light wrap to drape around her bare, golden shoulders, they bade the elder Hoes a good night.

He noted that Lin did not speak to them of when she would return, and he wondered if he should mention their plans. Finally he thought the better of making any time commitment, remembering they had said nothing of their weekend disappearance to Takarazuka. He merely turned as they left and, in the Japanese fashion, bowed deeply from the waist.

They were dismissed with bows and a nod of the head by both Bapak and Ibu.

The ride back to the Hanbys' apartment was a pleasant one, for they had much to discuss. They had not had an opportunity to talk, except by phone, since the big office push to sign the Vietnamese contract began. Except for a few meetings for lunch in the Ginza and a Sunday afternoon stroll in a park followed by an early dinner, Andy had stayed very close to his desk. The responsibilities that had been heaped on him by World Oil weighed heavily.

"Andy-san, I have missed you terribly." Lin Jin snuggled as close to him as the orchid and her wrap would permit. "When can we go to Takarazuka again?" She was joking, Andy knew, for he had no time now for such a long, pleasant weekend outing. How he wished he could find time for such a trek, but duty called.

"Maybe we can go there after the party tonight," he joked.

As much as he wanted to take this golden flower and keep her by his side always, he knew where his immediate responsibilities lay. For now, he was married to World Oil.

"I guess not," Lin Jin replied. "I didn't bring my overnight bag."

She looked into his eyes and smiled her lovely smile.

"If I could get away, that wouldn't stop us. It didn't before. We could buy you a toothbrush." Andy had a very serious look, for he realized that he needed Lin Jin to keep him happy if ever his life were to be complete. Man does not live by geology and contracts alone, he reminded himself.

"Or if we didn't get out too much, I might even borrow one. . . . " She leaned even closer. "Andy, I love you. I just want to be where you are. It bothers me greatly when that is not possible."

For both of them it was a sentimental moment, and he didn't want her to cry and spoil her makeup before the party. But she could not stop the single tear that rolled down her fair cheek and onto Andy's lapel.

"There now, this is not the time for such serious discussions. We may want a topic to occupy our thoughts after tonight's dancing is finished. Do you think we might find a way to send James off on some mission? He's a very understanding friend, as you know."

"Will he be at the party?" Lin Jin asked.

"Yes, it's for the entire office staff, and he's bringing your friend, Chisai."

"She's so nice, but so small a girl. James is a big man. He'll smash her." Lin Jin made a pretty grin, for their mood had changed.

"No, I don't think he has anything like that in mind. James is not the rushing type."

"Nor is Chisai, so I believe James will be coming home early this night. Chisai is not going to jeopardize her position with the company without proper justification, ne?"

The conversation evaporated, apparently because there had been no solution to their thoughts and planning.

"Here's the Hanbys' apartment. I'll come around to your side; wait a moment." Then, turning to the driver, Andy said, "Jimmy-san, we'll meet you back here after eleven or eleven-thirty, so get yourself something to eat, and then wait for us here."

While Andy went around the car, Lin Jin straightened her dress and her wrap.

On their way into the elevator bank, she said, "Andy-san, I don't wish to complicate your life with your friend, James. Please don't upset your apartment relationship by asking him to stay away. There will be another day, although I will find it difficult to wait, for I have missed you so."

Andy smiled at her as he composed his reply.

"Lin-san, honey, I'll see what can be done. It's true. There will be another day, but tonight is here and now. And I've missed you, too. These weeks have been very long ones for both of us."

Jill Hanby was at the door at the first ring of the bell, and Bill came just behind her. They each received a hug from Jill, complete with a kiss on each cheek. Lin Jin only received a kiss on one cheek from Bill. That warm reception, and the music in the background, told them that the party was already well under way.

The room was crowded, and Andy could see that everyone who wasn't dancing was holding a glass. It was to be a time to let down their hair and recover from their hard work at the office in accomplishing their first goal—signing the contractual obligation for the offshore of the Mekong Delta. Jill held on to his arm and led him to the bar just off the spacious living room. The furniture had been pushed back, and the music was furnished by a three-man combo.

There was a bartender, resplendent in his white jacket, who held glasses with ice at the ready.

"And what would you like to drink tonight?" asked Jill.

"We should start out with something light," answered Andy. "I see this is to be a first-class party, because you have out the scotch. All scotch here is expensive enough, but this brand you should save for our directors."

"It's for directors, Andy, future directors, and for our very special friends," replied Jill. Turning to Lin Jin who had arrived on Bill's arm, she asked, "What would you like, Lin-san, dear?"

"A small sake will be fine for me," she replied. While the bartender did his work, she turned back to Jill and said, "You have such a lovely apartment; it is always a great pleasure to come here and see what you have done with the decor. You keep changing everything, almost like the seasons. You always have everything arranged in such good taste."

"It's just what comes up," replied Jill. "It looks different tonight because we removed some of the furniture so there would be room for everyone who wants to dance. Almost all the couples from the office will be here, and no outsiders were invited, so everyone can let down his guard and enjoy a relaxing evening. Our people have earned a party."

"Thanks for inviting me," Lin Jin replied. "Parties at your house are always fun."

"The pleasure is always ours when you come, and besides, we wanted Andy to come. Without you he'd have gone off somewhere, like Takarazuka," answered Jill with a sly wink. "The food is on the table in the dining room, and just help yourselves to the bar when you like. And get to dancing. World Oil sprung for the combo, so we have to make the most of it."

Andy led Lin Jin out of the bar and toward the crowded room where couples were starting to dance. First they spoke to Tim McAllister and his prim wife, Pamela. It surprised Andy to meet them on the dance floor, for they were usually seen at a corner table observing the activity of others. There also were Ben Brodecki and Teri, who loved to dance, and they did it nicely together. They were a well-matched pair, just like aces.

Soon they met Wallace Brooks, who was guiding his wife, Beatrice, around the room to meet his coworkers. Her hair was much whiter than his, and it looked very nice, as though she had just stepped out from the hairdresser. But she wore no glasses to match his horn-rims. In the corner, Kelly Johnson had found a pair of visiting auditors. Apparently they had not yet become acquainted with the single girls who worked in the office. The secretaries were speaking Japanese among themselves in a quiet corner.

Andy and Lin Jin slowly made their way toward the group around James Wellman with his date, Chisai. She was always popular with those who worked with her at the office. She was the undesignated mama-san of the staff. Her quiet directions made the work of the secretaries easy.

Chisai and Lin Jin greeted one another with a light hug, which was much more informal that most Japanese feminine greetings. But they both lived in a different world from the normal Tokyo population. James also gave Lin Jin a kiss on the cheek, but Andy omitted that type of salutation for Chisai. Instead, he kissed her hand lightly as he gave her a warm smile after a deep bow.

"Chisai, we are happy to be having a night out, away from the office. It will be a relief for everyone."

As the combo struck up a new tune, they all decided it was time to dance, and the party was off to a good start. Both the music and the company were extremely pleasant, and the supply of food seemed to be unending. Jill's trick was that she had her cook busy in the kitchen, continually baking the delightful and exotic dishes the two of them had been preparing all afternoon.

The party lasted later than anyone had intended, for they were having a great time. The conversation and dancing rose to a pleasant uproarious level. Finally, when it was obvious the booze would not run out, no matter how much they drank, people began to think of going home.

People began to drift toward the door at the end of the delightful fellowship, which had become a somewhat raucous evening. Kelly and his friends decided to sing, and James motioned Andy to one side.

"Kelly and the boys are going to meet at his apartment for a short poker session, and they need a fifth player. I'll go by and try my luck. Since Kelly has an extra bed, I'll just stay there for the rest of the evening," James explained.

"Lin Jin gave me specific instructions not to put you out."

"I'll see you at mass at about eleven tomorrow, then. And try to keep it down; we'll do the same," James said, ending their conversation.

Andy was sure then that James must be dreaming. He'd never be up before noon tomorrow. They came to the Hanbys' front door, and Bill held Lin Jin and Andy aside so they were to be the last couple out.

Jill took Andy's arm and said, "Bill and I are too tired to clean up tonight, and too keyed up to go to bed. Come on over here, and we'll sit and talk over a brandy before you two leave."

It was not so much a request as a command, coming from the boss' wife.

Andy gave a glance at Lin Jin, and, noting her acceptance, said jokingly, "Why not—we've had almost nothing to drink all evening."

After they were seated, he continued, "It might be a good thing if we sit a while and rest. Then we'll be sure we can make it all the way home. Lin-san just about danced my shoes off after somebody turned down the lights, and after we convinced the combo to slow their tempo a bit."

The four of them all relaxed, and discussed the small talk that had come out at the party. Hanby showed he was pleased that the people in their office seemed to be a happy lot, and all worked cooperatively together. These informal company parties were worth the time and effort, if they are held at a time that indicates company approval of work well done.

"We'll have to make a habit of doing this occasionally, Andy. It shows the staff we appreciate them on a personal basis, and not just the fact that they show up on Monday mornings."

"I think everyone enjoyed the chance to talk. The families all live so far apart that they seldom see one another. It was nice that the various ethnic groups of our staff are so well integrated socially. The Japanese men didn't corner the Japanese secretaries and ignore everyone else. We need more of that interaction, because it shows we are learning to think alike. I was even able to get Lin-san back to dance with me once in a while."

Andy was speaking with a grin, but in the back of his mind he was wondering if the conversation was reminding Lin Jin of their racial difference. It was a subject they had not broached directly. He was afraid that once mentioned, he could not adequately define his position. His sister's opinions were still too sharp in his mind.

"Yes, we all enjoyed the evening. And we have a day to rest up before we get back to work on Monday. I need to talk to you, Andy, about your trip before you go to Hong Kong. There are some things I want you to look into while you are there. Come by when you get into the office."

"Lin Jin's grandfather had a message for me this evening. Her uncle's friend, Lam Thang, has no new information, but is watching everything that happens as related to the energy minister's activities. Also, I have been advised that the motorcycle can be at my disposal there at any time it is needed. That will undoubtedly be important to supply us with mobility, which we'll need one day."

Andy did not hesitate to speak of the confidential information in front of Lin Jin and Jill.

"That's good to know. It sounds as if you have made an excellent contact for some unofficial assistance there. It's almost impossible for foreigners to move about unobserved in Saigon, if anyone really wants to keep track of us. Lin Jin, we are indebted deeply to your relatives." Hanby was speaking seriously now.

"I'm sure they have reason to do all they can to help," Lin Jin replied quietly.

"It's late, and it's time we get on our way," said Andy.

"Thank you for a most enjoyable evening, and please do not fail to invite us to attend your wonderful parties in the future," Lin Jin added.

Andy and Lin Jin's warm smiles were an assurance there would be many other such invitations forthcoming. But Bill was not ready for them to leave.

"One other word with you, Andy. Come with me to the kitchen so I can show you the label on a bottle I've been saving," Bill directed his order to his assistant.

Once they were safely out of earshot from the ladies, he said, "I think we need some more assistance from your friends in Saigon. Could you ask Li Hong Hoe to arrange for you to pick up some sort of weapon at the house of Nguyen? I don't think it's a good idea for you to wander around near the estate of Dong Huan Chou without some emergency protection. And you certainly can't carry a weapon in and out through customs there."

"I'll see what he can arrange for me, and for Kelly Johnson. On our first visit to meet him, I'm sure he had a gun under his blanket. That was before he knew us and decided to help. I suppose we have some money in the till to cover any such expenses?"

"Yes, I'll approve whatever you need. Just call it something else and tell me later it's a scotch bribe. I'm sure your judgment will be adequate."

Back at the front door, the ladies finished their conversation and said good night. They departed with the formal hugs and kisses, as well as smiles of the remembrance of a happy evening.

When the chauffeur stopped in front of Andy's apartment building, he was told, "Jimmy-san, you can pick us up here at noon tomorrow. We'll be going to the Hoes' estate then."

As they approached the elevators, Lin Jin said regretfully, "Andy-san, I don't have pajamas or a toothbrush with me."

"That's all right," he replied sympathetically. "I made a special purchase for you, just today. But I'm not sleepy, all of a sudden."

# Thirteen

Andy was deep in thought when Bill Hanby's secretary entered his office on the twenty-third floor of their Tokyo office building.

"Good morning, Doctor Cheston," Chisai said cheerfully, as she placed a fresh cup of coffee on his desk.

It was not a duty she performed normally, for there was another person assigned to the task. Coffee was not the drink of choice for nationals in a Japanese office, and was usually served only to World Oil's expatriates.

Andy had been leaning back in his chair, mentally calculating how much data had been received by their office, available for interpretation, and how long it would take James Wellman's geophysicists to make a first general interpretation. Early analysis of such information was essential if they were to select locations and drill exploratory wells within their budgeted timetable.

The field crew had been shooting steadily for over two months now. The weather had held up well, for no typhoons had tracked across the area. They could cover up to 900 kilometers of the ocean each day, using the combination of triple streamers and firing their multiple energy sources. Wellman had insisted on this type of seismic coverage, using the latest technology, for he wanted to ensure the best possible data for interpretation. He was happy with the quality of their early results.

Another thing Andy was feeling good about was his love life. He was serene in his contemplation of the time he spent with his Oriental beauty, Lin Jin. He had never been in love before, and he was aware of how happy she had made his life. He was pleased, too, with her new habit of spending each weekend at his apartment. This manner of living was true contentment for Andy, for it left his week free to concentrate on his job responsibilities, and yet provided him a well-earned weekly break.

Fortunately for the domestic arrangements at their shared apartment, James was spending most of his time in Singapore, supervising the data processing by GCAI's giant computers. He had provided a steady stream of new cross sections for Andy to study with the staff here in Tokyo.

"Greetings, Chisai, how are your com-skills today?" Andy replied jokingly, pushing the mop of hair off his forehead as he relaxed in his big leather chair.

She smiled pleasantly, then placed a sheet from the fax machine before him.

"*Ichi ban*, Doctor Cheston, for things are going well with Doctor Hanby's office. I thought you might like to read this, as it is addressed to you."

"What have we here?" he asked.

He picked up the perforated paper, and glanced rapidly over the page. It was from his sister, Elizabeth, he noted.

"It just arrived, and I thought you would not wish to wait for office mail distribution," the secretary added.

"Thank you very much. I'll get back to you when I digest this. Thanks," he said, as the tiny Chisai bowed her way out of his office.

The message came as a surprise, for he had not had time to think much about his twin sister since his return from San Francisco three months before. He had been too preoccupied with his new job, and with his Oriental lovely, Lin Jin. Now he was jolted back to the realization that he must soon face the realities of the life he was living, and with his family associations.

The message read:

Dearest Andrew:
Am arriving in Tokyo Friday for one week visit accompanying Jacob Rogers and daughter Valarie. Will call on arrival. Transportation and hotels have been arranged. Will expect to see you Saturday for tour by limo if possible and later for party already arranged by Rogers at Okura Hotel. Rogers' business connections know Bill Hanby, so they have been contacted for party. Please include others if you wish. Can't wait to see you. Advise phone numbers for contact Friday and Saturday.

All my love,<br>Elizabeth Halstead

Andy shook his head. It was a shock to suddenly realize that his sister would be coming here to Tokyo. He felt a quick rush of sentimental feeling, and a tightening in his stomach. It was a true gut reaction. He missed his twin very much, and he was sorry their lifestyles had caused them to grow so far apart, and in different worlds.

Now she was coming with Valarie Rogers for an explicit reason. He was being paired up. Beth would expect him to entertain that forward young lady well, and personally. Who knew what more she expected? This would take some careful consideration, for he knew that he could not avoid meeting with Valarie Rogers. He knew how pushy she could be, and how she would inject herself into his personal life. He was still embarrassed by the thought of that night by the pool at the Halsteads', and regretted it very much. He had been trapped.

The worst part of it was that Beth would be going right along with Valarie's program. If that weren't the case, she wouldn't make this trip with Valarie and her father. If Beth only wanted to see Japan, she could have come alone, or with Hillary. Now what could he do? There was no way he could avoid insulting the Rogers and still maintain his close family relationship with Beth. Worst of all, it was important to him to avoid upsetting his relationship with Lin Jin.

Sooner or later, he'd have to tell Beth he was in love with his Oriental beauty, and then all hell would break loose. He sipped his fresh coffee, but it made him ill. He picked up the phone and called James Wellman.

"Jamie, get up here, I need some assistance of a personal nature," he told him abruptly.

"What's the problem? Are your colored pencils mixed up with your tapes, or are your cross sections entangled?" James asked jokingly.

"No, it's not business. It's a personal problem, so come up as soon as you're free. But no rush—anytime in the next five minutes," he returned the joke.

"I can break away, so I'll be right up," came the more serious reply.

When James arrived, he had a bundle of sections and maps under his arm.

"I just thought I'd show you these while I'm here, if you have time for a quick look."

"OK," replied Andy, "but first things first. Read this fax, and you'll see what my problems are."

James took the paper, and carefully read through the entire message. Gradually a frown came over his face.

"Wow! Now you can expect a very busy weekend. And it isn't even the Fourth of July."

He recognized the significance of the fireworks which could be expected.

"You may be right, because this situation is explosive. When I don't act like a puppet on a string for Beth and for Valarie Rogers, they are likely to be very upset. And Mr. Rogers will be along to record it all." He began spreading the maps on his huge desk. "And if Lin Jin is not included in the activities, she'll figure that I think she's not good enough for my family, and there goes my Tokyo tranquility for the future. Her grandfather won't be happy, either." Andy was frowning.

"I believe I see the problem all right. What can I do to help with a solution?"

"I'm not sure. First of all, I'd like for you to join us at their party. I may need a second there to take notes, or perhaps to hold the pistols."

"Maybe I could spirit Valarie away with me to Hong Kong or Singapore," mused James with a wry smile.

"That's a thought, but you don't like her pushy attitude any more than I do. Besides, she already has you lined up for redheaded Leslie Bicknell back in San Francisco. After our weekend there, Beth and Valarie may not be much interested in being more than barely polite to you, unless you're issuing wedding invitations," Andy quipped.

"Oh, Valarie and I get along. But I don't think I could take her on as a date. If Beth and Mr. Rogers are going to get the drift of how things operate in the international business world, we might as well tell them we are bringing dates to their party. We'll stress the importance of international fraternity. What do you think?"

"I think it's going to be a difficult confrontation," Andy said, frowning seriously.

"Mr. Rogers is certainly having Japanese guests at his gathering, and they'll soon find out that it is not a bad thing to fraternize across the Oriental color line. In fact, it greatly eases the tensions for most business dealings. Maybe we can arrange some tall, dark, and handsome samurai for Valarie, and that would get her off your back."

"It'd be hard to come up with one on such short notice, and he'd have to have proper family connections, like a crown prince," Andy answered. "Perhaps we could invite someone from the office to join us. Do you have any eligible young explorers who'd fill the bill?"

"I have some youngsters who'd like to try, but I'd rather not have them press their luck with as experienced a jet-setter as Valarie Rogers."

"Yes, they need to earn their stripes in a lesser league before getting into her arena. There is one company man who might fill the bill though, at least as a dinner partner. It's Kelly Johnson. He's been around in the world, and he can fit in at almost any social gathering, I've found."

"I guess that would be up to Valarie to decide. It depends on how upset she gets with the other dating arrangements you make. Are you going to bring Lin Jin to their party?"

James had asked the basic question that went right to the heart of their discussion. He watched Andy carefully.

"I haven't decided yet," Andy replied. "If I do, it will certainly upset Beth, as well as Valarie. But sooner or later, they are going to find out the world is not all monochrome. I suppose it may as well be sooner." He thought for a few moments. "I guess I will, for there's no way to avoid it." Andy knew the die was cast.

"I think you're in for a shocking weekend, sir," James reminded him with a smile.

"There's no doubt about that, but 'what will be, will be,' I suppose." There was a long pause, but wheels were turning. "Will you bring a date, like Chisai? She's really pretty, all decked out in her kimono and obi."

"Only if you're bringing Lin Jin. I don't want to be the only one there with my hand in a hornet's nest!" James replied.

"OK, I'll ask her. Let's look at these maps later, like this afternoon. I must have a serious talk with Bill Hanby," Andy answered. "I'll see you at lunch."

As Andy entered Hanby's office, he found him restoking his pipe, and poring over a stack of reports.

"Greetings, Bill. I wanted to check with you before I reply to the message I received from Beth this morning. It seems I am about to have visiting socialites," he said, waving the paper.

"Good morning, Andy. Yes, I know. I've read your fax, and I also heard from Jacob Rogers. I've known him in a business way for several years, and he's invited me to his Saturday night gathering at the Okura, too. We have some possible future business connections, since he is a big export broker."

"I knew you were acquainted with Rogers, and I wanted to check with you before replying with the information Beth requested."

"We'd better each reply. You take care of numbers and the guests you think appropriate, and I'll reply to Rogers, telling him I want to invite Li Hong Hoe. There are some business relationships I'd like for them to develop. I suppose you are going to bring his granddaughter."

It was more of a statement than a question. Andy realized that Bill had intentionally made it easy for him to admit he was going to confront his sister with his Oriental girlfriend. Jill Hanby and Bill knew very well about his relations with Lin Jin, and had always accepted her as one of their own level in society. What the Hanbys weren't so aware of was that Beth had intentionally lined up Valarie Rogers as a mate for her brother. Severe complications were certain to erupt when they met.

"I'll advise them that I'm inviting James Wellman, and that he and I will be accompanied by dates. James is going to ask Chisai, assuming that's OK with you, and they will both be dressed in Japanese style. That should make it more interesting for the Rogers. Also, I think we should ask Kelly Johnson, and introduce him to Valarie Rogers. That will make the numbers come out even, and she'll need someone for company who speaks jet-set English."

"That's fine, go ahead. It sounds like you have things well in hand. I hope everything works out well with your plans."

He knocked out his pipe in the big round glass ashtray.

"Please remind Elizabeth that Jill and I will be happy to assist her in any way we can during her visit. Tell her to just give Jill a call. She can arrange a tea for her and Valarie with some of the company wives, such as Teri Brodecki and Pamela McAllister. The wives are always looking for a good excuse to be social."

"Thank you, sir. I'm sure she'll be pleased to know they have someone to call on here in a strange city."

\*     \*     \*

It was ten-thirty when the taxi pulled into the parking square of the front entryway to the Okura Hotel, and Andy had already been by the office and checked his morning messages. James and Wally Brooks had their explorationists hard at work, and the daily reports from the division offices were on his desk. Thank goodness things were going normally. No testing or fishing jobs, so he'd be free for the rest of the day.

He checked at the hotel's desk to contact Beth, and was directed to meet the visitors in the garden room for brunch. Beth had called his apartment when they arrived, and told him they were exhausted from their long flight. It would be better, she had explained, to his relief, if they all met for a late brunch, and then continued with their visit and their sight-seeing tour.

After securing a table for four, he selected a seat for himself where he could watch the entryhall. Very soon he was rewarded with the sight of his statuesque twin, Elizabeth, confidently making her way into the dining room. She was already at the table before he could disentangle himself from his chair, but he got to his feet and met her in time to give her a brotherly hug and a kiss on both cheeks. Then he held a chair for her next to his. It was nice that she had arrived ahead of their other guests, for he wanted to welcome her in a family manner, and as a twin should. They had family activities to review, and ESP to polish. He could never be very distant from her.

"Andy, dearest, how have you been?" she looked him over as she continued, "You're so white! I haven't heard from you very often during these past months. What have you been up to that you care to tell?"

"World Oil has kept me pretty busy, with all the trips to Vietnam and such. Our exploration efforts are in full swing, and take a lot of my time." Andy felt a bit guilty that he did not mention the trip to Takarazuka and the time taken up by his fully scheduled weekends with Lin Jin.

"Hillary sends his regards, and says to tell you he wants to come over and have a hot bath and massage in the Ginza sometime soon." Beth laughed her nice little giggle.

There is an old saying about those who move overseas. If you stay out of the States for five years, on your return the only things that are familiar are your own house and your immediate family. Everything else has changed. So their conversation, though personal, was restricted to their closest relations. He realized their personal interests, even as twins, had begun to go in separate ways. She was married to Hillary and the Sausalito wine-producing society, and he was married to World Oil of the Pacific Rim.

When the Rogers arrived, Andy was introduced to Jacob Rogers, who gave him an extended handshake like he was judging a prize bull at a county fair.

"Just call me Jacob," he was quick to say.

Valarie Rogers was all bubbles, and gave him what he thought was an overly friendly caress for a greeting in front of her father.

"Andy, how good to see you again, and here on your working turf. We've been looking forward to your showing us the city." She found a seat next to Andy.

It soon became apparent that he had made a mistake in assuming that Mrs. Rogers was not accompanying them on the trip. Jacob explained that his wife had been delayed in their room, and would join them shortly for brunch. She had not traveled well, and was trying to get herself "oriented" after her first date-line crossing.

Andy called the waiter, and asked him to arrange another place setting, as he scooted himself to a corner near Beth. Valarie immediately moved her setup near his, and left room for her mother beside her father. He did not fail to notice the subtle brush of their legs as she shifted into the new position.

"I had a fax from Bill Hanby telling me they and the Li Hong Hoes would be joining us at the dinner this evening." Jacob Rogers fingered the menu as he spoke. "That's good, for I've been looking forward to meeting the head of Hoe Shipping. His business is related to the exporters who'll be attending tonight, so I'm sure we will have many interests in common. They should already know one another, and may even set up some future contacts."

"Probably so, for Li Hong Hoe has been in business here most of his life. He is a fine gentleman," stated Andy.

"And I must congratulate you, Andy, for being in such a responsible position for World Oil at your young age. But you have had a lot of experience and have conducted a lot of international operations, especially in the Far East and around the Pacific Rim. This is the most important developmental area of the world from a business standpoint." Rogers was obviously experienced in circles of international trade.

"Thank you," Andy replied. "I just happened to be in the right place at the right time, I suppose."

"Let's order," Valarie stated. "I'm starved. That food on the plane was atrocious. Now I'm going to make up for two skipped meals. We can go ahead and order for Mother." She directed her speech to her father. "She should be here soon, for she was just finishing her makeup."

"Yes I'm hungry, too," Elizabeth added. "But we can wait for Mrs. Rogers if you'd like."

"No, that won't be necessary," Jacob said. "I know what she'd like. By the time it gets served, she'll be here. What would you girls like? I hear their fruits are good. Could you recommend for us, Andy?"

"Everything here is always good," he replied. "If you're really hungry, they have good omelettes and sausage. Or their waffles are nice, even if they're not from Belgium. They can be served with real strawberries and cream."

"The waffles sound good to me," Elizabeth said.

"Me too," Valarie chimed in, "with sausage."

They had just finished ordering when Mrs. Rogers arrived, and was dutifully introduced to Andy.

"Just call me Vivian," she said, smiling.

Andy stood until she was settled, which took some time, for she was directing a good part of her attention to surveying Andy's appearance. He knew he was being measured for a wedding suit; and again as they were seated, he felt the brush of Valarie's leg close by his.

Mrs. Rogers was a very pleasant lady, and not nearly so forward as her daughter. Andy felt a little sympathy for her, as he believed she was a non-traveler who had been dragged along on this trip against her wishes.

"I've heard a great deal about you, Andy, from Beth and from Valarie. How do you like living over here in the Orient, away from friends and family?" she asked, as their food arrived.

That was representative of a typical mistake most first-time visitors overseas made. They thought those who live outside the United States must be lonely, and did not make friends in their new world, wherever they were.

"I'm much too busy here with exploring for oil, Mrs. Rogers—Vivian—to miss any former associations from the States, except family, of course."

Andy was uncomfortable trying to ease their thinking about his personal life in Tokyo.

"We in the company family of World Oil form a relationship much like that of families elsewhere. And occasionally we get care packages from home." He smiled his boyish grin toward Beth.

The brunch progressed smoothly, and when all were finished, they continued their chatting over the delicate porcelain cups. Andy missed a real man-sized mug, which he preferred. Coffee is quickly cold in these. He soon lost interest in the trivial travel matters being discussed by the ladies. Anything to do with customs agents and luggage inspections or a passport was always news to them.

"Excuse me, I'm going to check on the arrangements for tonight," Jacob Rogers said. "You all finish your coffee, and I'll be back when the limousine is ready."

Obviously, Jacob Rogers was an experienced traveler, and knew how to operate a business arrangement. When their party was called, they found the limousine was already pulled up to the back street entrance as they exited the grand lobby.

They seated themselves comfortably, for the broad back seat easily held three people. Mrs. Rogers entered first and took a back corner seat, followed by Elizabeth, who sat in one of the jump seats. Then Valarie sat next to her mother, and Mr. Rogers took the other jump seat facing the rear. That left one seat in the back beside Valarie for Andy. He got the implication. She was warm against him, as she sat almost too close, with their elbows and legs often touching—unnecessarily, he thought.

Their tour took them around the Imperial Palace, where the emperor had ruled since 1868. Mr. Rogers had even arranged a special entry permit into the grounds. Then they continued their tour through the shopping area of the Ginza. Fortunately, there was no time to allow the ladies to enter the stores. That would be arranged for several other days.

They saw only a small part of the great urban sprawl, of which Tokyo is the heart. It is known as the Greater Metropolitan Area, with a population of 12,000,000 people—and traffic to match. Seeing the masses of people was intriguing to the visitors, but boring to Andy. They had never before realized that such a civilization existed here on the other side of the Pacific. Just imagine—noise indicators on the streets.

Elizabeth insisted that they stop by and visit Andy's apartment, to the gleeful agreement of Valarie. She explained that they wanted to see how a bachelor lived in a far-off city. Andy suspected they really wanted to see if he was sharing an all-male establishment with James.

It had been a trying day for Andy, keeping up with all the carefully contrived implications of conversation between Valarie and her parents. All of their references were pointedly directed at finding out his plans for the future. He was glad James was home when they arrived at his place. Their discussion with him brought out again that they would be bringing dates to the dinner party that evening. He knew they were already aware of his plans from his faxed reply to Beth, but they politely avoided asking who their dates would be for the evening.

Their conversations became a bit strained, and the guests suddenly found that they were running late in their preparations for the evening's dinner party. Their departure was mercifully swift, and they left the bachelors to make their own preparations for an extended evening of dining and socializing. Andy hadn't even hinted that their dates were Orientals.

*May the gods of the Japanese occupation protect me through this night*, Andy prayed.

# Fourteen

It was a long, quiet ride through the late Saturday afternoon traffic on his way to pick up Lin Jin. Andy was deep in thought about the intentional deceptions during the afternoon's contacts, and also worried about the impending crisis. He didn't find it necessary to carry on a discourse with Jimmy-san, who drove the company's Crown Toyota expertly through the conglomerated mass of weekend traffic. He was glad to be able to sit quietly and contemplate the disaster that was going to occur later that evening. He needed rest.

His twin, Beth, would suddenly realize this night that he was serious about this striking Asian beauty, Lin Jin Hoe, whom he was about to introduce to her American society friends. He had never realized until now how bigoted both she and her friends were. Not only would he shock his sister, but he would come very close to insulting her friends, the Rogers.

Andy was well aware it would be offensive to all of his visitors because they did not consider it acceptable in their polite American society for a family member to date a lady of the Far East, no matter what her family rank. It did not occur to those in the San Francisco country clubs that there could be an Oriental society equivalent to their own. Their beliefs were going to be in for a shocking confrontation this night.

He had phoned Lin Jin as soon as he could after the visitors left his apartment, and assured her that he would escort her personally to the dinner. Grandfather Hoe would have been happy to bring Lin Jin with him and his wife, had Andy asked, but something kept telling him he must have this last long, private ride into the center of Tokyo alone with the lady he loved. It would be a pleasant time to talk quietly together as they rode through the dim twilight and mist of the bustling Saturday night traffic. He must talk to her for one more hour, and try to explain what was about to happen, for he knew that after she and Beth met, their future could never be the same.

On arrival at the Hoe estate, he was met at the door by the servant girl, Josan, who dutifully helped him deposit his shoes. He donned his geta, and was escorted from the polished stone engawa into the soft tatami-matted interior reception room. There he was left alone with his thoughts, which was not the normal reception for him at the Hoe household. The rest of the family must also be dressing, and he had assured Josan that he did not desire a drink. He waited quietly, trying in vain to control his thoughts while studying the collection of wood-block prints and painted scrolls displayed there. He invented a game of trying to decide which of the rice-paper panels were really entryways.

The minutes passed slowly until Lin Jin was escorted, almost silently, into the room by her maid. She was a vision of Oriental beauty in her kimono, obi and obi-dome, and her movements were the short-step, choppy imitation of a feudal princess. There was a faint scent of perfume as she came near. Her brocade silk gown was undoubtedly priceless, and had been perfectly arranged for the occasion by her Josan. Andy knew she was playing a part, for he had requested the Oriental attire for the evening as a display of local culture for Elizabeth and the Rogers.

Andy realized that most of those attending would be Japanese business leaders with their escorted ladies. Lin Jin would have been much more comfortable in a golden sheath from the designers of Hong Kong or Paris, but she and Chisai had gone along with his and James' request to dress as the Japanese ladies would for such a gala occasion.

He rose and met her, but they did not touch, for he was afraid he would spoil the elaborate facial makeup.

Instead, he said, "Lin-san, you are more beautiful than ever!" He only dared to blow her a kiss.

Her costume left no place for the flowers he brought, so she took them in one hand then she reached up to feel his face tenderly with the other.

"*Konban wa*, Andy-san; thank you for coming for me, although it was not necessary. I could have ridden with Pak and Bu."

"I wanted especially to see you, and talk to you for this hour of travel," Andy answered.

Her smile was not natural because of the heavy white caked makeup.

"I am glad, though, for we can talk privately on the way to the Okura. Tell me all about your meeting with your sister, Elizabeth. Do you think she will like me?"

Andy noticed the serious question, and also he noted that she had not said "accept me." That was the hurdle that he must clear, and it would not be easy. Beth was traveling as a guest of the Rogers, and their entire party was all about to be shocked by the action of his unexpected invitation of a date.

During their ride into the city, their conversation was stilted and unnatural. It was partly because her attire was so confining, and she did not wish the kimono and obi to be disarranged. Also, her makeup was like a mask, and severely restricted her facial expressions. He was also aware that his own mental strain was being reflected in her attitude.

Lin Jin's few comments during their ride were to ask more questions about his guests. Most of the time he spent just explaining what had happened during their day's tour of Tokyo, and how the visitors had reacted to what they had seen. Andy longed to take his black-haired beauty in his arms and explain to her what he felt, in spite of the reintroduction and influence of his American culture. But this was not the proper time, and Andy was well aware that words alone would not express his heartfelt intentions.

They had been driven to the front entrance of the Okura, and found the huge lobby to be bustling with people. About half of the ladies were dressed in kimonos, which represented a lot of expensive brocade. While Lin Jin excused herself and proceeded to the ladies lounge to refresh her attire, Andy made a fast tour of the lobby. There on the hotel's program of activities was a notice:

Jacob Rogers' Dinner Party—Goshikihama Room—Second Floor.

He knew the room was one of the smaller dining halls, and had been named for an island on the west coast, known for its beautiful seaside scenery. Surely it would be appropriately decorated with white sand scenes and deep-green pine trees to match that locale.

The timing of their arrival had been good, for while he waited, James Wellman entered the lobby, escorting the tiny secretary, Chisai. She also wore brocade, and quickly departed to find Lin Jin before their entry into the second-floor saloon.

Had he not known that it was Chisai with James, Andy was sure he would not have recognized her in Oriental dress. The world is made up of pretenses. As they waited, Andy wondered which of the well-dressed couples making their way past James and him were going to their party, and how soon Pak and Bu Hoe would arrive.

Lin Jin and Chisai apparently knew when the appropriate time for them to make their entrance would be. When they appeared, Andy and James accompanied them, making their short-stepped progress across the lobby to the long, narrow escalator. It was strange how the Japanese preferred those to elevators.

When they entered the Goshikihama Room, they were astonished by the brightness of the decor. It was truly a beautiful seaside scene, and the deep green of the pine trees was startling in front of the white sand seascapes of the walls. There were flowers everywhere, which completely surrounded the small band. They played from a low stand at one end of the hall, although no one was dancing as of yet.

Only one table was arranged for dinner across the far end of the room. As they entered near the room's center, they found themselves in a short line of couples being greeted by Vivian and Jacob Rogers. Andy noted that the long table was set for about forty people, and there were place cards. It was to be a most exclusive group. Of the dozen or so people on the dance floor, he recognized only Beth and Valarie, who were talking to a Japanese gentleman and a lady in a kimono. Beth saw them enter, and raised a hand tentatively. He smiled back rather grimly while he awaited their turn to greet their host and hostess.

The introductions went smoothly, and Jacob Rogers only did a slight double take when Andy presented Lin Jin Hoe. He quickly introduced her to Vivian Rogers, and conducted the conversation among the four of them.

"And you must be the lovely granddaughter of my friend, Li Hong Hoe. He told me you would be here, although I had no idea you would not be in his company. Is your grandfather coming?" Rogers asked with a glance into the entryway. He saw only James and the kimono-bedecked Chisai.

"Yes, Mr. Rogers. He and my grandmother are coming by separate conveyance. I am sure they will be here shortly."

Her voice was pitched somewhat lower than most Orientals, and Andy was proud of the impression she made. She was not one to be put down by a direct question.

"You look very nice this evening, Andy, so formally attired," Vivian Rogers interrupted. "And here is James. Good evening, James. I hope we gave you boys sufficient time to get ready for our little party. We didn't mean to take up your entire afternoon."

"It's all right, Mrs. Rogers," James replied. "We don't spend a lot of time cleaning up our apartment anyway, as you may have noticed. Let me introduce Miss Chisai Matsur," he said to their host, who was nearest.

James smiled at her as she extended her hand to Mr. Rogers. Then he moved to take their hostess' hand.

"How do you do, Miss Matsur. Our friend, Bill Hanby, told me you would be joining us. I'm happy you could come. This is my wife, Mrs. Rogers."

"Good evening, Madam," she replied in perfect American. "It is my great pleasure to meet you both, and please call me Chisai," she continued in a clearly American-accented voice. "It is very nice to meet you after our many letters of correspondence. Mrs. Rogers, I am Mr. Hanby's private secretary, and see most of his communications."

Andy noticed that the Rogers were clearly shocked to see these two kimono-clad ladies speaking such perfect English. They could not easily comprehend that persons dressed in such a strange fashion could think and speak the same as someone would in their own California society.

The four of them excused themselves, and Lin Jin led them to the more crowded portion of the dance floor, as other guests were arriving in the entryway and waited to make their introductions to the Rogers.

They had barely received a glass of champagne when Beth and Valarie made their way over to their group. Beth took Andy by both arms, and gave him a sisterly hug and a light kiss on the cheek. She was quickly followed by Valarie, whose kiss was on his cheek, but not quite so light. Andy thought she was like a bitch dog, trying to mark her territory.

Introductions followed in a very formal way, during which Beth carefully explained to Valarie that Lin Jin was the granddaughter of Mr. Hoe, and that Chisai was the private secretary of World Oil's Tokyo director, Doctor William Hanby.

After a welcoming toast among the group, there seemed to be very little they could say. The two ladies in their Japanese kimonos were not displaying their ability to speak in English.

Finally Andy asked of Beth and Valarie, "What are your plans while you are in Tokyo?"

He knew it sounded like a very flat conversational gambit, but what were they supposed to discuss—geology? This was not a World Oil gathering. He was sorry, now, that Kelly Johnson had been out of town, because he could always stir up a diverting conversation and simultaneously keep an eye on the goings-on.

"We were hoping you'd be able to take some time off and escort us on a tour of the Inland Sea, like Himeji Castle and Kyoto. Valarie wants to see the Omogokei Gorge, and some of the mountains. Is the opera playing at Takarazuka?" Beth asked, obviously having done her homework.

"I believe it is, but I'm afraid I'll have to beg off, for we have meetings scheduled here and in Ho Chi Minh City that can't be changed. Also, James has an appointment Monday in Singapore with the geophysicists."

Andy wasn't lying entirely, but there was no way he was going to make himself available as their tour director. Also, he knew Bill Hanby would be upset if he took any days off now, during their most critical exploration effort.

"And what do you do with your time?" Valarie asked, turning to Lin Jin. "Are you working, too?"

Andy wondered if Lin Jin recognized that as a sharp little dig, since none of Valarie's friends ever worked at a real job. They were only employed as volunteers on charity committees.

"Yes, Miss Rogers. I am a personal consultant in the office of my grandfather, Mr. Hoe." Lin Jin smiled as sweetly as she could through the makeup. "I make every effort to arrange his affairs with his overseas offices in Hong Kong and Singapore—sometimes Saigon, too."

"You must look very different when you dress for the office," Elizabeth said, as she turned to Chisai. "Do you always wear the *kimono* and *obi* for formal occasions?"

"No, not often," replied Chisai. "We only dress in our national dress for special events. Tonight we wore these at James and Andy's request, in order not to be different from the wives of the Japanese gentlemen. Such things are important in our culture."

Andy wondered, Was that a return dig? It wouldn't be recognized as such by their visitors.

"Personally, I am more comfortable in Dockers, but I'm afraid Pak Hoe would disown me if he ever saw me at his office in them," Lin Jin said in her best American accent, and with a light laugh.

Beth laughed at the thought of Lin Jin in sport clothes, but Valarie only stared off into space, as though she were trying to visualize this painted Oriental doll in jeans.

"Here is Mr. Hanby and your grandfather now," said Chisai as she glanced at the knot of people around Mr. and Mrs. Rogers. "We must introduce you to them, as I'm sure they will be most interested in your opinions of Tokyo."

"That I doubt," said Elizabeth, "but I'm sure we have friends in common with the Hanbys. And your grandfather, Lin Jin, seems to be of serious business interest to my father. I'm glad they have finally arranged to meet."

Andy was proud of the way his sister looked, for she and Valarie were decked out in their lowest-cut, Paris best, and made quite a fashion statement to the Japanese businessmen present. But their poise and decor was no match for the centuries of preparation behind the formal dress of the Orientals. They were the perfection of aloofness, personified.

There was a general mixing of people as Bill and Jill Hanby led their friends, the Hoes, to meet with Elizabeth and Andy, and their group. In a swirl of introductions and expressions of admiration and gratitude for having been invited to meet those who meant so much to their friends, the party gradually simmered down into a low and healthy drone—doubtless promoted substantially by the steady flow of champagne. Those who were interested in business found those who sold things, and those who were interested in clothes and shopping were happy to discuss the dress markets of the world, which they knew very well.

The two young American explorers had stayed beside their dates, so there would be no misunderstanding of their commitments for the evening. When Elizabeth had a chance, she whispered to Andy that they had arranged the seating so the "younger set" could be together at the far end of the table, away from her father's business and commerce discussions. When the sound of the deep resonant gong signified they were to find their way to the dining table, Valarie led the small group toward their seats.

Andy found that Valarie and Elizabeth were seated opposite one another at the end of the table. Next to them, he was between Valarie and Lin Jin, and James was placed next to Elizabeth and Chisai. That was as sociable an arrangement as he could have hoped for, since the rest of the guests at the table were generally speaking in Japanese. He wondered how the Hanbys were getting along. Very well, he assumed, since they were near the head of the table and could share translations of the talk with the Rogers.

After a short formal welcome by Jacob Rogers, and a toast to the future success of the Pacific Rim business ventures, dinner was served. It was completely in keeping with the naming of the Goshikihama Room, with its seaside scenery. Andy had never seen such beautiful prawns, and the Kobe beef that followed had obviously been hand-massaged to perfection. As an American touch, Baked Alaska was the dessert. Such food, together with the excellent wines for some, and sake for others, made them a talkative group. He knew, however, that very little business was actually discussed. That would be arranged later by letter or fax.

The younger English-speaking set were busy trying to find out why their paths had crossed so directly. Andy knew the cross-examination was coming, and he wondered how well he would handle it. He realized that Valarie was wondering if she was going to be able to have a real date with him at all, after she came so far across the wide Pacific for that apparent purpose. She had assumed too much.

Elizabeth, he knew, was still trying to determine just what relationship her twin had with this Oriental intruder. Andy could see right into her mind—a sort of ESP. She was thinking, surely he knew better than to date Lin Jin steadily, even if she was the granddaughter of a big commercial wheel. She would be reasoning that he probably had to see her to keep his boss happy. Andy spent a mentally disturbing hour over their giant feast, fielding the probing questions of the visitors.

When the dinner ended, it was time for dancing. The music was a bit sedate, for the crowd was mostly older people, and women in kimonos, which do not promote long gliding steps. The evening was wearing on, and Elizabeth came around the table and asked her twin to dance with her. It was obvious she had something on her mind to discuss.

On the dance floor she asked "Andy, what's going on between you and that Vietnamese girl? I think you are treating Valarie terribly, and she is extremely upset. Is it worth it to ruin our social relations just to show that Oriental a good time?"

Obviously, Beth had worked herself into a mad state.

"I must tell you something, Beth," Andy began.

"I'm not sure I want to hear anything from you, unless it's an apology for the Rogers and an arrangement to take Valarie out tomorrow," she said in a huffy voice.

"Sis—Beth—I should have told you before. Lin Jin is my serious girl-friend. She is really a lovely person, and I have been seeing her for a long time. You are meeting her under the wrong circumstances. She is not the painted doll she appears to be here tonight. Normally, she dresses and acts just as down-to-earth as you and me. She is really a kind, intelligent, and well-educated person." There was a long pause as they danced a few slow steps. "I . . . I guess I love her," Andy stated quietly.

Suddenly Elizabeth's face began to turn red, and she had to gasp for a breath.

"How could you love that yellow little gold-digging bitch?" Elizabeth stopped in midstep, then she quickly turned, left the dance floor, and stormed off to her seat. Andy obediently followed, torn by his conflicting emotions of simultaneous deep inner sadness and of great relief.

They faced each other silently. They were the only ones sitting down at their end of the table, for the music was continuing. Suddenly Elizabeth took her tiny handbag and stormed off toward the ladies powder room, still silent.

As soon as the music stopped, Lin Jin was returned to the table by a gentleman; she noticed Jill Hanby and some of the ladies were going to powder their noses, so she excused herself and joined Jill. Soon Valarie was also returned to the table, followed by James and Chisai, who took their seats.

Then it was the boys' turn. Andy and James excused themselves, and headed off to talk to Jacob Rogers and Bill Hanby. There hadn't been much man talk this evening. That left Chisai and Valarie together for a rather strained discourse. They had very little in common, and as he walked away, Andy wondered what they would find to discuss. Little did he know, it was him.

\* \* \*

Chisai dreaded the thought of this private talk with Valarie Rogers, for she realized that her visit to Tokyo with Andy's sister was for one reason only—to date Andy. It would be hard for her to be civil to her, since she knew and liked Lin Jin so well.

"How long have Andy and Lin Jin Hoe been dating?" was a simple enough opening question for Valarie.

"Quite some time, I believe. They met at the World Oil organizational banquet a year ago, and have been seeing each other ever since," replied Chisai honestly, but she debated with herself as to how much she should tell this intruder into their Oriental world.

"You mean he dates her regularly?"

"I suppose you would consider it regular. I have never seen him with anyone else at any company function, but he is away from Tokyo much of the time," Chisai answered.

"Is he required to have a date at every gathering? Do Bill and Jill Hanby know about her?" Valarie demanded.

"They are the ones who were responsible for their introduction," Chisai replied meekly. "Jill Hanby and Lin Jin Hoe are the best of friends."

"But how could a company like World Oil promote such frater—?" Valarie stopped short of using the word "fraternization" when she realized to whom she was speaking.

Chisai had already recognized the type, and she was coming to a boil inside. How dare this woman come to her country and criticize a man for liking their Oriental women. The reason American men got along so well here was because they were treated like real men, and not like babies. Chisai was proud of her heritage. She was about to explode—but this was the daughter of her host, so she must be polite. Her politeness did not extend to the necessity for lying. She determined she would tell Valarie only the truth.

"Lin Jin is a very sweet person, and she has a great respect for Doctor Cheston. She visits him quite often when he is in town," said tiny Chisai quietly, knowing well that the inquisitive Valarie would lunge at the bait.

"By 'visits him,' what do you mean? Does she stop by his apartment?" Valarie asked eagerly.

"Why yes, I suppose she does. I believe she spends most weekends there when James is out of town on business." She thrust the needle deep. "That seems to be most of the time, recently." She gave it a twist.

There, thought Chisai. She has been allowed to worm it out of me, and I am glad.

Valarie was suddenly flushed. Then she turned red.

"That bitch!" she said in a rather muffled voice. She grabbed up her purse as she left, stalking off toward the powder room.

Chisai was right on her heels when Valarie arrived in the ladies room. There, a quiet ladylike scene was being played out. Elizabeth, Jill, and Lin Jin were seated in a row facing the huge mirror, doing what women do to retouch their makeup. Their conversation must have been a bit strained, Chisai realized, for Elizabeth would have nothing to say to Lin Jin, and Jill would be attempting to keep a conversation going with both.

Chisai wished she had arrived here first, in order to explain to Lin Jin what she had told Valarie. Instead, now Lin Jin was completely unaware of her position and she could see that Elizabeth was upset after her sudden departure from Andy at their table. Jill, too, was completely in the dark, but Elizabeth was trying to explain something to her. Chisai could see the two worlds in separate orbit, but about to collide.

As Valarie stormed over to one end of the room, she called Elizabeth to join her privately. There was a long whispered conversation between the two, and Elizabeth's face was becoming redder and redder as their whispers became louder and more rude. Chisai went directly over to sit beside Lin Jin, and she began to explain what she had done. Their conversation was very short, for Elizabeth suddenly and unsteadily walked up to the seated Lin Jin.

The slap was a direct hit, and a loud one. There had been little warning. Chisai felt the rush of air, for she was seated close beside Lin Jin. She saw the white face paint come off on Elizabeth's hand in an oily smear.

"You yellow-bellied bitch!" she screamed. "You've been sleeping with my brother! I hate you! I hate you!"

Elizabeth was livid with rage, and could no longer control her temper.

Lin Jin was shoved over forcibly, landing among the powders and lotions of the dressing table. Chisai could see that she was more surprised than hurt, except for the red welt rapidly appearing through the powder of her cheek.

She helped Lin Jin sit back into her chair, and began to straighten up the bottles on the table. Nobody spoke, and Chisai could see that both Valarie and Jill were paralyzed in shock. Lin Jin was beyond any ability to reply.

"What are you doing?" Chisai shouted at Elizabeth.

How could a civilized American girl of a good family act like this? And she was their good friend Andy's sister. Such actions fed the image foreigners conjure up of ugly Americans, which most expatriates try so hard to overcome.

It was a most difficult situation, but one over which Chisai had no control. Andy would be deeply affected one way or another. She knew Jill must tell Bill, even though this was not really a World Oil affair. But it affected their operations, so her boss must know. She was glad she would not have to be the one to tell him.

Elizabeth stormed out of the powder room without another word, and she was followed quickly by Valarie. They did not return to the dining hall, but apparently went straight to their rooms. Chisai attempted to console Lin Jin, and help her rearrange herself.

Then no one spoke in the powder room. After minutes of silence, Lin Jin arose slowly and wiped the tears away as they streamed down the white-painted cheeks. She gathered herself together.

"Good night, Jill and Chisai. Please tell Andy that I have gone home with Pak and Bu Hoe."

She selected a pack of tissues, and continued to wipe her cheeks as she departed; she left Jill and Chisai to stare at each other in wonder.

\* \* \*

Andy was frantic. He had seen all of the ladies depart almost simultaneously for the powder room, but he had no idea what had happened there. And there was no one who could tell him at that moment. All he knew was that Beth and Valarie had very soon rushed out of the room, with no apparent intention of returning. Then Lin Jin had walked sedately through the entry without so much as a glance around to see where her friends and family might be.

He did not know what to think. Soon Jill and Chisai returned to their table, and together they explained to him what had happened. Chisai admitted to Andy, then, that she had let slip to Valarie that he and Lin Jin were more than casual friends, and she had gone straight to Elizabeth with the information. That is what had caused the eruption in the powder room.

"I am extremely sorry that I told her the honest answers to her questions, Doctor Cheston," Chisai said, almost in tears herself.

"It's all right, Chisai. I should have explained the situation to Beth before they came to Tokyo," Andy said. "I had just told Beth of my relationship with Lin Jin on the dance floor. That's why she was gone from the table."

By then James had joined their group, and Jill was departing to find her husband. She had seen a messenger cross the room with a note for Li Hong Hoe. He and Bu quickly said their thanks and goodbyes, and departed.

As soon as Andy realized what had happened to Lin Jin, he left for the escalator as quickly as he could without seeming to be rude. As soon as he was outside the room, he ran down the escalator and headed for the entrance. Just as he arrived, he could see the Hoe limousine pull away, and Lin Jin was in a rear seat with her head down. Andy could not forgive himself for allowing this to happen. He knew he must see Lin Jin, and explain to her that it did not matter.

\* \* \*

It was early on Sunday morning when Andy awoke. He dressed and went to the office to check on communications. He was sure the Jacob Rogers dinner party had been a great success, as far as Rogers was concerned, for he had cemented many of his business relationships. But that did not take into consideration the feelings of his daughter, Valarie, and Elizabeth, her traveling companion. Their plans were totally mutilated. Now there would be no family tours or trips to the mountains or to the opera, and sister Elizabeth was incensed. She had never before been so mad at him. How could he have allowed such a social disaster to occur?

Andy was having no luck with his communications, for he could not get through to talk to anyone at the Hoe residence. He had tried to talk to Beth, but she was not answering, either. James had left early for Singapore, and he'd be ashamed to call the Hanbys. His entire social world had disintegrated.

He sent flowers to Lin Jin and to his sister, but received no reply from either. He spent the day moping around and later went to mass alone.

On Monday morning he buried himself in the office paperwork. There was plenty for him to do, even though his heart wasn't in it. With James already gone, he was alone. All he could do was pitch in and get his office work in order, to be ready to depart for Saigon. Kelly Johnson was there already; he said he had things to check on. He could probably help him when he arrived there. Anyway, he just wanted to get away.

During a long and serious discussion with Bill Hanby, he was told that Jill had explained everything that had occurred in the ladies room, and Bill was sympathetic to Andy's feelings of remorse. He assured Andy that time heals all wounds so long as you are in the right. And he happened to think that slight differences of skin color were not the basis of great social conflicts. Bill assured Andy that sooner or later his sister and her society would come to recognize that we live in one world, and we must communicate with all its people if we are to survive into the future.

This was small consolation for Andy, for he continued to feel terrible and alone, and it went on for days. He kept trying to contact Lin Jin, but without success. By the end of the week, he found out through the reception desk at the Okura, that his sister had left on a tour of the Inland Sea with the Rogers, and would not be returning to their hotel before leaving for San Francisco. He had really been cut off from all communications.

It was Saturday morning again when Andy sat moping in his office, still alone. He was wondering how he would arrange his work in Saigon in the coming week, when Chisai entered, bringing him a cup of coffee.

"Good day, Doctor Cheston. I have brought you coffee, and some information," she stated simply.

"What is the latest?" Andy asked, expecting some communiqué from a drilling well in the South China Sea or word of a typhoon in the Philippines.

"It is information from the grandmother of Lin Jin. I was able to reach her on the telephone, and she has told me about her."

"What did she say? Was Lin Jin there?" Andy asked excitedly.

"No, I was not able to talk to Lin Jin. Her grandmother told me that she has gone away from Tokyo—for good."

"Gone away? Where did she go? She left without so much as a word for me?"

Andy was on his feet.

"Yes, apparently so. She departed on Wednesday for Hong Kong. She has moved there to live with her mother, Thi Lan, and brother, Kim Jin, and is to work there for one of her grandfather's shipyards." Chisai was speaking very quietly, with an apologetic voice. "I am sorry, Doctor Cheston, for I know how greatly she will be missed. She was my good friend as well."

"You have done your best, Chisai. Thanks. As Hanby said, time will help heal the wounds. But I won't be happy until Lin Jin and I are together again. I will find her, even hidden away in Hong Kong."

# Fifteen

The zip and sparkle had all gone out of Andy's life. He no longer had Lin Jin near to elate his dreams, and share his weekends. He plunged with all his mental abilities into engineering the success of World Oil's dream. He wanted to be the one who established the presence of huge producing oil fields offshore from Vietnam. It was his only remaining reason for existence. Now he tried with all his strength to concentrate 100 percent on being an explorationist.

He came to realize more and more what everybody knows. It was what all work and no play did to Jack. He was feeling duller by the day, but he tried to forget about the lovely Lin Jin, and to think only of his work and how he could track down the dastardly terrorists. Someday, perhaps, she would accept a message from him again.

As soon as he could clear up his paperwork and make the necessary travel arrangements, he left Tokyo for Ho Chi Minh City. Kelly Johnson was in Saigon already, awaiting his arrival there. Meetings to develop further coordination with the Vietnam State Oil Company had been set up with their contact, George. Andy was glad to be able to do his negotiating with Moe and George of the State Oil Company instead of the energy minister's office. He couldn't decide who in that office he could trust, but he knew there was someone there who was tracking them like hounds after a fox.

Even if Dong had some friends in high places, he was not to be trusted. His boss, the minister, didn't trust him either, apparently. Did he have to put up with him for political reasons? Or was it the other way around? Dong had seemed to try to subvert their efforts at every turn, from his part in the payoff of the terrorists who blew up their plane to his continual placement of obstacles in the way of their contract agreements. But who was the NLF decision maker? Someone's day of reckoning for his part in the death of Harold Blanton and the others on that company plane was long overdue.

The NLF must be afraid they are going to lose control of the income that big oil production would create for their country, or they wouldn't indulge in such desperate measures. That must be their reason for going so far in their attempt to take control of the exploration and production. Andy knew that inexperienced and unqualified operators would never find and develop a major oil discovery without foreign help, and their contracted Russians wouldn't be able to help them do it, either.

Bill Hanby had given him and Kelly Johnson full rein to do whatever was necessary to trace the NLF's activities and come up with the evidence to prove their involvement in the crime. Once the solid facts were in his hands, he knew what the punishment would be—even if it had to be of his own invention. The Viet government could not be trusted to mete out international justice. The crime had not occurred in their country, so they would logically say they were not responsible.

Andy had spent months carefully considering his position, and he had come to his conclusion as to what the repayment would have to be. He knew he could not live with himself otherwise. It must be "an eye for an eye," and he must see to the payoff himself, for there was no other justice in this part of the world. Now all he needed was some solid proof—like a smoking gun. The terrorists must have been required to provide some evidence of their work, or they wouldn't have been paid the gold. He must keep digging until he found that evidence.

Already the inquiries of Kelly Johnson had determined enough solid information about the placement of the bomb. The man who installed it was dead, along with his cohorts. His and Kelly's fortunate introduction and meeting with Lam Thang Nguyen had been a stroke of luck. Had he not been reeducated, he would never have been willing to help them. He had reason for holding a grudge against the NLF and all of their bodoi.

Andy and Kelly had seen the rebuilt gate and the burned fence with its bullet-marked walls. Now he was set to press onward with his search for the real culprit—the decision maker. They owed that knowledge to Lin Jin's family, and he hoped their political position was not being jeopardized. Lam Thang would never have relayed such information had Lin Jin's young cousin, Nhung Thi, not realized Andy's true relationship and feelings for her childhood friend. But now he must not think of Lin Jin, for he had important objectives to pursue.

There was no Vietnamese delegation at the airport to meet him, but customs gave him no trouble. He had a multiple-reentry permit in his visa. In this case, that was as good as being a diplomat, for the name of World Oil was already locally famous. There was no airport crowd, since he had arrived in the company private jet. The car that their new office administrator had sent was easy for him to find, for the driver was waiting for him with his name on a sign bearing the World Oil logo.

It was the usual wild and depressing ride into town, and Kelly was waiting for him in the bar at the Majestic Hotel. It was much easier for them to get around in Ho Chi Minh City now, since they had a company communications center established. Kelly had arranged to rent a small office and hire a local office manager and a secretary who could type and translate. Now, they could make arrangements for contacts, and handle other operational necessities. They did not plan to expand the location into a fully active exploration office yet, but at least they had a fax machine and a room with lockers where they could store some papers and maps. One large inner office would serve as a conference room, where they could hold meetings in private.

"Hi there, Kelly," Andy greeted Johnson as he swung into a seat across the small table. "How is your auditing coming?"

"Greetings, Doctor Ches," Kelly replied. "I hope everything is coming along fine. I see your driver found you. Since we had no exact arrival time, I just had him wait. How are things going with you?"

He used the title as a joke, for company men did not normally use titles—they were a waste of time—especially "doctor."

"It is going, I guess. What are you accomplishing here?" Andy asked.

"There is really very little I can do here except visit the seismic boat on its supply stops, and the local finance office of the Viet Oilers, to tell their director of finance, Binh Tri Quynh, that we are spending huge sums of money."

"I guess it's something they must know. They have to convince themselves we are being active, in accordance with our contract. I'll bet it upsets them that the money payments don't go through their hands so they can get their cut."

"That's one thing we made sure of when the contract was being rewritten. That SOB, Dong, tried to sneak in a clause that made us pay every bill through their office, and you know what kind of a markup that would cause," Kelly said.

"I know, because I helped Hanby argue them out of it," Andy replied. "He really had to bow his neck on that one."

"When the seismic boat made a stop at Ba Dong yesterday, I was down there to check on payment and working hours of the conservation agent we agreed could ride along to see that we don't kill all the sharks. He was unhappy, of course."

"What was his problem?" Andy asked. "His pay is clearly stated, and he gets paid full-time."

"He was claiming overtime for working on Friday and at night." Kelly was grinning. "I've seen all of those claims before, so I just told him we'd get another agent if he didn't like the pay. He got back on the boat, fast."

"I'm sure he didn't want to take a chance on losing such a soft, well-paying job. Most of their people are happy just to work a couple of days a week."

"I brought in some tapes and shipped them off to Singapore this morning. The rest of their supplies seemed to be arriving on schedule, but they're bitchin' about the meat. It's a contract the local suppliers can't afford to lose, I guess," Kelly mused.

"Was there any other contact with local authorities there?" Andy asked.

"Yes, there was a Viet Navy rep nosing around. He was asking the captain of the boat a lot of questions about where they were shooting and how long it would take to finish the job. The data had been furnished officially already, but all departments have to get their nose in."

"Perhaps the conservation man isn't smart enough to file his reports," Andy quipped.

"I thought their conservation boat riders would have convinced them by now that we really are operating in their area offshore, since they claim everything in the South China Sea all the way to Borneo. Maybe they follow our recording ship with their PT boats. I hope they don't get their mines tangled up in the cables," Kelly joked.

"Have our boys seen anything of their Navy at sea, or of anything suspected of being a pirate boat yet? I understand they aren't bashful about boarding anything that isn't pretty well armed."

"No, they've had no direct approaches, but they have had some boats that get in the way of the cables. They don't understand that a mile of cable being towed can't be turned or stopped easily, once they're under way."

"We're going to show their geologists some real evidence of our coverage tomorrow. James is supposed to be meeting me here with his latest seismic sections, and we'll show those to George. He'll want to show them to his boss, Nguyen Muoi, in his own office. That'll be about Friday."

Andy ordered a double scotch and soda with a lot of ice from the split-skirted barmaid as she sashayed past.

"Then what'll be the result of that meeting?"

"If we have indications of drillable structures, we can start talking about which blocks we wish to select, in accordance with our contract."

"That will mean a meeting with their big boss, the energy minister, won't it?"

"Yes, and for that, Bill Hanby will have to be called to come over. Big bosses like to talk directly to the head man."

"I've been studying the contract," Kelly said. "It states that they get the original seismic tapes before the assignment of blocks can be agreed upon. How can we give them originals when the tapes are needed in Singapore for processing?"

"I'm not sure," replied Andy. "It's one of those things most companies and governments take on faith. You just assume that as soon as it is possible, you will comply with the agreement, and overlook the p's and q's of the written contract. How that will work with guys like Ho Bac Minh and Dong, I don't know. If they really insist on getting the originals, it will shut our work down."

"It'd work OK if George were running their operation," Kelly stated.

"That's true, but he has a lot of pressure from the upper echelon, I expect."

Andy was keeping an eye out to the entrance of the bar, wondering when James and his contractor coordinator would arrive from Singapore.

"Are you worried about their insistence that we comply to the letter with the agreement?"

"Yes, I've been thinking about how to handle it."

"If they insist, it will set our field operations back at least a month, which would put us into the bad weather." Kelly was always thinking ahead.

"One other little problem not covered in the contract is the cost of reproduction of original tapes. There are about twenty-eight thousand of them; at twenty-eight dollars each, that's over seventy-eight thousand dollars." Andy did a quick calculation. "They'll expect us to absorb that—or perhaps we can get them to sell them to any new companies who wish to process the data for themselves."

"Would you pay it if the data had already been worked up? Our Viet friends will want to pocket any profit from tape sales if it can be made available by simply pointing to the contract."

"That is exactly what I'm worried about." Andy sat up closer to the table. "Our 'friend' Dong, or his boss, is certain to latch onto that technicality to delay us. We'll have to take our case past them, and sell someone on the need for expedience in conducting our scheduled operations. They've already dragged their feet to delay the contract signing. They can't be allowed to slow our operations any further."

\* \* \*

"George, welcome to our tiny new office!" Andy had risen and gone to the door to greet Pham Xuan Bach. It was a good thing he had an American alias. Andy took his elbow and led him into the inner room that contained their conference table. The furniture was sparse. With so large a table on which to display maps, and walls covered with pin-up boards that needed to be accessible, there was no need for many chairs.

George was a pleasant sort, and he had brought his director of exploration, Doctor Bien Giap, and his assistant, Thieu Long, with him to observe and to take notes. Overseas government companies are padded with people with titles. They eagerly shook every hand in greeting, and settled into the available seats.

James conducted the presentation. "We have some good news," he began. "While our processors, represented by Mr. Dennis Dugan here, of GCAI, have been turning out our stacked data sections, my staff and I have been interpreting some preliminary maps. To our delight, they show some valid structures."

This brought smiles to their visitors' faces. It was what they had been waiting to hear, so they watched eagerly.

James continued, "Provided our further efforts justify these beliefs, we should have no problem selecting areas for further seismic detail study. That would result in the pinpointing of specific drilling locations in the future."

The next two hours were spent in the detailed examination of the cross sections and maps as they were shown by James Wellman. Each man stretched out the rolls of sections in front of him, and peered down the alignments of colored markings with critical eyes. They did not wish to appear inexperienced in front of these foreigners. After sections were all examined, and the sketched maps studied, tea and sodas were brought in for a break. It was time to discuss their future plans.

"I believe you have discovered significant structures in the offshore area of the Mekong Delta," George proudly stated. "It is time now for me to make this information known to President Nguyen Muoi."

"That will be fine," Andy replied. "Could we have a meeting with him and make our presentation?"

"That would be best. I will have to check with his secretary," George answered. "Normally, for something as pressing as this, he will rearrange his schedule. He is most interested in the rapid initiation of a drilling program. Let us try to arrange for Friday morning. Could you have your data in order by that time?"

"Yes; we can be ready for a preliminary presentation. Please make everyone aware that this information is in the early stages of interpretation. We will need several months more for final mapping, but we will show Nguyen Muoi what is now available."

Andy did not want his explorationists to be rushed into final presentations without fully considering all of the available data.

Their meeting broke up with no mention of ownership of the data tapes. There would be time to talk of such money problems later.

\* \* \*

The exploration group of World Oil who accompanied Doctor Andy Cheston were escorted into the large conference room of the president of the Vietnam State Oil Company by Pham Xuan Bach. George indicated their seats, and Andy was to the right of the head of the table with James and Kelly. Across from him was George, then came Doctor Bien Giap and his staff, Thieu Long, Tri Mang and Mguyen Mu. At the far end of the table were their legal representative, Kong Van Dieu, and their director of finance, Binh Tri Quynh. Andy was struggling to remember all of their strange names.

When everybody had greeted one another, and was seated, they all patiently awaited their boss, the president of the Vietnam State Oil Company. When Nguyen Muoi arrived, they all stood, and introductions were acknowledged. Then they again found their seats. It was almost a ritual.

George began with a presentation of the facts he knew, which were that the representatives of World Oil had data to present which looked promising for future oil development offshore in the area of the Mekong Delta. He delivered his introductory remarks in one long breath in English, which fortunately everyone present understood.

After a short introduction of the status of their seismic coverage, Andy asked James to present the significance of their seismic cross sections and what they had been able to map. He showed them many long regional seismic sections, representing hundreds of kilometers of ocean coverage. Then he showed mapped areas where it was possible to contour closures of structures to be considered possible future drill sights.

Following an hour of discussion, George requested a recess for refreshment. Andy noted that he and his leader, Nguyen Muoi, left the room with their heads together in rapt conversation. They were gone for over a quarter of an hour, and on their return, they were accompanied by Dong Huan Chou.

When their meeting reconvened, Dong took a stance beside the chair of Nguyen Muoi. No effort was made to introduce him to their visitors, nor did he give any indication that he recognized the World Oil representatives. He stood glaring at the maps through his dark glasses, listening intently as the Viet Oil president summarized the significance of their findings.

Nguyen Muoi concluded by saying, "I believe we have sufficient data to present to Minister Ho Bac Minh. He wishes to stay abreast of developments in order to set up a schedule for further contract negotiations. He believes that the many companies who are daily requesting information on obtaining development blocks should be given early access to data in order that they may start their own reviews and interpretations. In that manner, they will not be very far behind World Oil in their exploration efforts." He was looking directly at Andy.

"When would he be able to conduct this meeting?" Andy asked, fully expecting that Dong was there to instigate a delay.

"Immediately. It was by his request. He advised me that if the information you have is of sufficient interest, we should review it this afternoon. He has scheduled a conference for three o'clock. If you agree, I'll advise him we will be there."

"That will be fine," Andy answered with relief. "I hope to convince him with the data we now have available. We can draw up our selection of blocks for detail exploration while the seismic crew is still on location and available. That would save money and expedite our exploration, for we wouldn't have to remobilize a seismic crew for detail work on the drillable structures."

All the while during the meeting, Dong had stared in disbelief at the mapped structures. It was obvious that he was not aware the Americans could progress so rapidly to a state of readiness to select drill sights. Andy could see his wheels turning, trying desperately to think of some tactic for an extended delay.

\* \* \*

The afternoon meeting was smaller, being attended only by the department heads. It was conducted in the director's conference room.

Andy realized that it was probably the former office of the American ambassador.

Ho Bac Minh entered from his office at the same time Andy and James carried in their armload of maps and sections. They were followed by Moe (Nguyen Muoi) and George. The assistant to the minister, Dong Huan Chou, and their legal representative, Kong Van Dieu, were already seated at the large table.

Their greetings were rather formal, with Andy and James leaving their papers at their seats and going to the head of the table to shake hands with the minister of energy.

The Viet Oil president, Nguyen Muoi, made the necessary introductory remarks, and from there the meeting proceeded very much in the same order as their morning session had gone. The energy minister seemed to be pleased, and when their presentation was complete, he thanked them for coming to him with their early interpretations.

"Minister Minh, we would like to arrange a meeting with your staff for sometime early in the month after next to present our selection of the blocks we will choose for exploration in accordance with the contract," Andy began. "By that time, World Oil will have our basic interpretations complete. We can then furnish you with copies of our maps at all pertinent levels, for your staff's review."

"Is such a meeting in agreement with our contractual obligations?" the minister asked as he turned to their legal representative, Kong Van Dieu.

"I will have to review, but from what I have read and recall, I believe that it could be," the lawyer replied with some hesitancy.

"There is one other great difficulty that has not been considered," Dong stood and interrupted.

It was the first time he had spoken.

"What problem is that?" Minister Minh asked.

"There is a matter of the contractor, World Oil, who is to furnish us with original tapes for those who wish to consider their own bids on the available blocks. We have requests for such data from fifteen companies, and would need to give them time to make their own reviews before any such blocks could be considered for assignment." Dong was speaking brusquely. He had played his trump card, and the ace, if recognized by Minh, would cause a great delay.

"How long would such an arrangement take?" asked the minister.

"That is a problem for World Oil to comply with," Dong stated harshly, gritting his teeth.

Turning to Andy, Minister Minh asked, "What would be the time frame for your furnishing such tapes?"

"That is a difficult question to answer," Andy replied. "First, I do not believe it is in Vietnam and World Oil's interest to wait for the reinterpretation of this large amount of coverage by many groups before proceeding with our drilling of exploratory wells."

"What does the contract say?" the minister asked.

"It clearly states that World Oil will be assigned blocks first to expedite early development, which has always been our intent. The contract reads that on completion of the reconnaissance program and its interpretation by World Oil, eight blocks will be assigned to us immediately for detail seismic coverage in preparation for drilling. Only then are the tapes the property of the Vietnamese government."

Dong was staring directly at Andy, and looked menacing even behind his dark glasses. He stood, a sheaf of papers in his hand.

Andy continued after a pause, since no one else spoke.

"There are about twenty-eight hundred original field tapes. To copy these and furnish the originals would cost over seventy-eight thousand dollars. To do that for fifteen companies would cost around a million dollars, just for the tape copies. If the stacked tapes are used as the basic originals, there are about six hundred of them. To furnish copies of them would cost much less—about fifteen thousand per company."

"And where would such copying be carried out, and at whose expense?" the minister inquired.

"According to our contract, the original tapes belong to Vietnam on the assignment of the first set of blocks, and any Singapore copying of the tapes would be for your expense. Of course, any company who wished to buy the tapes from you could be asked to pay a fee to cover the cost of such reproduction. It is not a cheap process."

"But would such companies need the use of only the six hundred stacked tapes?" asked Nguyen Muoi.

"Yes, if they are smart. That is what World Oil would do if they were buying into an operation whose tape stacking and processing had been properly supervised and executed. A duplication of the stacking would be unnecessary. Then each company interested would have to put up the fifteen thousand, plus the expense and time of processing their own data. You may wish to sell the stacked tapes, and also sell them copies of the original processed cross sections developed by World Oil. They could then do their own interpretation."

"But all of that would take many months of work for each company's interpretive groups," the minister responded, with a perplexed look at his assistant, Dong.

"That is very true," Andy replied. "That is why we have come to you as soon as possible with our preliminary interpretations. You can see what a bulk of paperwork our only copy of the interpreted data has become. It will be carried back to Singapore to be integrated with newer processing when Doctor Wellman returns in a few days. In the interim, he will work on it here, as we wish to expedite the process of assignment of the quota of exploration blocks in accordance with our contract. We intend to go ahead with our drilling program as expeditiously as possible."

"You may be sure that the government of Vietnam wishes also to go ahead with such exploratory drilling at the earliest possible date," Minh stated. "Our postwar finances will receive a great boost when oil is discovered, and that is vital to our future economy."

"Early drilling is a relative term," Dong retorted, still standing. "We cannot allow World Oil to push us into allowing them to pick the plums off the tree without giving other qualified companies an equal opportunity to bid for the best blocks. Those bids are worth much money to us. We must select proper areas for our own exploratory drilling as well."

Dong was vehement, and almost shouting. Were it not for the dark glasses, Andy was sure that sparks would have covered the maps.

"Please realize that World Oil has developed the project to this point entirely at our own expense." Andy spoke directly to the minister. "We have paid for all of the seismic coverage and processing, as well as the other agreed-upon prepayment fees to place our company in this preferred position. Now, according to our agreement, we may select blocks based on the information developed and proceed with our structural detailing and proceed to the drilling phase."

Everyone was following his comments carefully, but none cared to interrupt. Andy continued.

"We have paid dearly for this first-choice option. Other companies will not delay to offer substantial sums to be allowed to explore in adjoining areas, for who knows which of the blocks will result in oil production. There are no guarantees that the best-appearing structure on the maps will yield the most hydrocarbons. The world average is only one producer for ten exploratory wells."

"You have a valid point. If we wait for others to make their bids, many months will pass." Ho Bac Minh looked very serious. "Dong, review this with Kong Van Dieu, and if you cannot come up with a more valid reason for delay, set up a meeting as they have requested. We must press on with our country's development of natural resources as rapidly as possible. I want no more unnecessary delays."

Minh was extremely curt as he stared at Dong Huan Chou, almost to the point of being ill-mannered.

"Leave your maps and sections with us for tonight, and we will make our own further review," Dong stated, as a firm directive.

Not on your life, James wanted to reply. Instead, he said, "These are my personal interpretations, and I plan to work on them in our office tonight. Sorry, but they're my only copy."

At this, Dong erupted in a lengthy tirade in Vietnamese, but was eventually silenced by the upraised hand of his minister.

When the World Oil exploration group had returned to their new small office building, Andy placed a call to Bill Hanby in Tokyo. He explained that Hanby would soon be receiving notification of a meeting, to present their final request for drilling blocks. The meeting would take place in the minister's office, sometime within the next two months. Hanby was pleased with the results of their meeting, and encouraged Andy to proceed in haste to complete their mapping so they could select the eight areas with proper geophysical and geological justification.

"Bill, I think I'll take the company plane to Singapore with James and Dugan, to review the latest data. From there, I'd better touch base in Jakarta with our operations, and then return through Bangkok. I should be back in Tokyo in about a week."

It was going to be a busy period of travel for Andy.

"That will be fine, and Wally Brooks can hold down things here until your return. Getting the final data in hand and interpreted is our main priority now."

"I'll bring James back to Tokyo with me when I come, with all the data available."

"There's one more thing, Andy. Perhaps you should return through Hong Kong. Some discussions with Mr. Hoe have indicated that we may have difficulty in setting up an office for our drilling operations from there. You'd better go by and talk to his office people first. Then you should talk to the British government officials, and start some arrangements. I think both they and the Chinese will be happy for us to operate out of Hong Kong instead of using Vietnamese ports."

"That will take me a few more days than I had planned."

"That's OK, take whatever time you need, and the group can handle things here. They need time to work, anyway, and we must get our feet on the ground in Hong Kong. I'll have Pug Cox, who'll be our drilling superintendent, meet you there and attend your meetings. Just give me a date and a hotel."

"Very well, I'll fax you from Jakarta when my schedule is firm, and I'll try to keep the NLF out of our hair."

Andy hung up the phone, and the entire group gathered around to hear what Hanby's response had been to their news. He addressed them quietly.

"Bill was pleased, and directed us to continue what we're doing—only faster. He wants to see maps as soon as possible, James. He will probably want to take them to show Gilbert Eason in Houston and get his blessing before making any commitment with the Viets."

"Did I hear you mention going to Singapore with James?" Kelly asked.

"Yes, but you can stay here, and meet me in Hong Kong later if you have any ends to round up. Anyway, I want you to be in on our government contacts there."

"It sounds like we'll have a busy month, and an even busier week," James stated. "We'd better get at it, boys. Help me round up these maps and sections, and we'll get on with our work early in the morning."

"Have you made your departure plans?" Andy asked. "It's pretty hard to get reservations out of here."

"We have tickets out on the airline the day after tomorrow," James replied.

"It'd be better if you all came with me in the company jet, since I'm going that way tomorrow, and there'll be room," Andy stated.

"We don't really have space to work in this office, so going with you will be much better." James thought a moment. "Let's round up all of the data, Denny, and take it back to the hotel with us. Then we can leave directly from there in the morning. We'll call the airline and cancel our reservations from the hotel later tonight."

"Did you leave anything in the way of maps or sections with George? Dong wanted them to keep, didn't he?" Andy reminded them.

"No. I told them these were our originals, so we must keep them all in our hands to continue our interpretations. It was a little white lie, but the fact that they think these are the only originals won't hurt them. We'll keep the copies at the processing center in Singapore well hidden." James displayed his boyish grin.

"It's better they don't know," Andy replied. "Kelly, you and I should go for another little stroll tonight, after dinner. There's a visit we need to make before we leave Saigon, and I have some gifts to deliver."

"I'll get an early bite to eat and work on the data in my room," James told them. "With all our maps here, someone needs to stay with them, just in case."

"No, don't do that," broke in the contractor, Dennis Dugan. "I'm tired from all this traveling, and I can baby-sit the maps while all of you find a restaurant. I'll eat later."

Dugan normally said very little, and spoke only when spoken to, but it was a kind gesture on his part.

"Thanks very much," James answered. "Someone really should guard our data. We could lock all of it up here in the office and pick it up in the morning, but coming past here in the early traffic would delay us a lot."

"No, let's take it with us. And I really don't mind eating later," Dugan persisted.

He appreciated World Oil's business, and he also knew that if he went along, he'd have to pick up the check. There was a contractor's method in his madness.

"You work it out, and we'll see you gentlemen later," Andy said. "I'll treat you to dinner somewhere if you'd like. We deserve a mini celebration for getting the ball rolling today. Meet us at the Majestic bar in an hour."

# Sixteen

After dinner, Andy led his former FBI agent friend, Kelly, on a long walk away from the Saigon Majestic Hotel and around the dimly lit back streets of Ho Chi Minh City. They made many turns and detours to see if they could observe anyone showing an interest in their activities. As far as they could tell, nobody was watching them, or cared where they went. They were in need of the long walk, anyway, for their dinner party had lasted much longer than the many courses of food and dessert required. The restaurateur had found an old bottle of port wine, which the group of them finished over a plate of mild cheese. It was a very civilized way to end a fine meal, Andy thought.

It was late in the evening, but there were a surprising number of people who were still stirring about the streets. Perhaps it was because it was the only tolerably cool part of the day, and yet the humidity was still oppressive. The alley behind the gold market was now a familiar place to the World Oil explorers, and they didn't need a map to show them the way, even in the dark.

When they finally made their way to the door of the gold merchant, Lam Thang Nguyen, all the lights in the lane were out. They knocked lightly and waited. No response was heard, and they waited two minutes before they knocked again lightly. At last a crack appeared, and the girl, Nhung Thi, peered out to see who was coming calling so late at night.

As soon as she realized who they were, she opened the door immediately and whispered, "Come in and have a seat. I will return in a few minutes."

She set the lamp on a table beside the papa-san chair, and left hurriedly, adjusting her light robe around her.

When she returned a few minutes later, she was accompanied by Lam Thang, and they both greeted them like honored visitors whom they had not seen in too long a time.

"Please excuse me for keeping you waiting so long, but papa-san was asleep already," Nhung Thi said.

"Welcome to our humble house. My apologies for not being dressed."

Lam Thang spoke weakly, as he carefully felt his way into the room. "This day I am having more trouble with my walking," he said, as he lowered himself into his chair.

"It is we who should give regrets, both for coming unannounced, and for arriving so late. Unfortunately, our schedule is not always predictable," Andy stated.

He was pleased that they welcomed him as though he were still in the good graces of their beloved Lin Jin. Perhaps the word of her move to Hong Kong had not reached them.

"How is the progress of World Oil's drilling for oil offshore from the Mekong?" asked Lam Thang. His arthritis was apparently much worse, for his entry had been extremely slow and he made his way quickly to his chair.

"We are doing everything according to schedule, thus far. That is the reason for our visit to Saigon. We have been presenting our data to Ho Bac Minh, the energy minister, and are attempting to arrange for the assignment of specific blocks in which we will do our first exploratory drilling."

"It seems to take much time to make all of the arrangements for your work. Everything progresses slowly, as the mills of the gods. But then," he reflected slowly, "time does not mean as much to me now that I have been reeducated by the NLF. Nothing does. Life is only a succession of hardships and disappointments to be overcome, or to be endured."

Andy was sorry he had reminded the old man of the difficult times he had spent in the grievous torture camps. The girl, Nhung Thi, was busy bustling around, picking up things and getting the kettle brewing. Obviously, she intended for them to have tea.

"I have brought you some packets." Andy fished in his pockets. Both he and Kelly produced paper-wrapped bags from their pockets. "Here is some tea from Japan, and a bag of sugar as well."

Kelly stepped into the circle of light near the great chair, and spoke for the first time.

"Nhung Thi, you do not need to give us refreshments tonight. We have had a large dinner, and it is late. We only wanted to bring our greetings and, check with you. Is there any new information on the NLF activities?"

"All that I have found is that there have been no more late-evening withdrawals from the bank, but there was a large deposit of gold in an account sometimes used by the NLF to pay smugglers and pirates. My friends keep a tab on such activities. Someday, Dong Huan Chou will have to expose his personal accounts, unless he is keeping his fortune buried in the tunnels. That, however, is not at all unlikely."

"How far does his tunnel extend?" Kelly asked.

"I do not know this, but you may be sure his tunnel is well sealed to prevent intruders from below. My information comes indirectly from his yeoman, Tan Tran, by way of the girl, Vu Thi. She is well known to many locals, who are friends of Nhung Thi."

The girl smiled. "I only know them slightly from schools, not from work," she injected quickly, as though trying to indicate something about her morals, which were in conflict with the lifestyle of Vu Thi.

"Please keep us informed if you receive any new information, and someday in the future we will be able to prove whether or not Dong was the instigator of the terrorist activities," Andy said.

"I am sure he was," replied the old man. "But proof of such an action will be difficult to find. His pride is great, however, and it may cause him to retain evidence that would have been better off destroyed. I will encourage my friends to remain alert."

"Thanks to you, we have learned as much as we have of his actions. Next week I am going to Hong Kong, and the company will set up a temporary office there to direct the Mekong drilling. I'm going to visit Lin Jin, if she will see me. I don't know if she will speak to me, since she was insulted by my sister; they had a terrible confrontation. I must explain to her that my feelings are not like those of some bigoted Americans."

"I have heard that Lin Jin was in Hong Kong working at the shipyard of Li Hong Hoe." Nhung Thi spoke rather sadly as she turned off the fire under the kettle.

"She left because she did not wish to jeopardize my family relations after she was confronted in Tokyo by my sister, Elizabeth. It was not her fault, but she was highly insulted, and left without speaking to me," Andy explained woefully, for he knew he owed them that information.

"I did not know why she had left Tokyo so suddenly. Please tell her of our regards, and I hope your future will work out amicably for both of you."

Lam Thang spoke slowly, "You must be very careful in all your activities, for the NLF has demonstrated that they will stop at nothing to prevent you from achieving your goal of drilling in Vietnamese waters. They are desperate to reserve all profitable oil enterprises for the NLF. You are wise not to announce your travel plans, and to arrange your security carefully. They are all devils."

"We have thought carefully about that, and how to avoid contact by our necessary negotiations here. It is one reason we will operate from Hong Kong. When visiting here, we guard our company plane carefully and do not announce our departures. Our pilots take turns sleeping there. Even our hotel has extra security."

Andy turned to Kelly, and continued.

"When you are finished next week in Hong Kong, you'll be returning here. If Mr. Nguyen has new information, he can send a message to you at our local office, or at the Majestic Hotel."

"The care you are taking is wise. Please relay my regards to Li Hong, and to her mother, Thi Lan. If you would, we have a few letters for you to deliver. Otherwise our communications are not reliable."

They left then as quickly and as quietly as possible, for they felt bad about disrupting the rest of one who so obviously needed his sleep. As they exited the alley, there was the black Mercedes parked on the main street, just as they had encountered on their previous visit. Apparently, the care they had taken before their arrival had been for naught. Pretending not to notice the two men in the auto, they walked toward their hotel. The car moved away. Why would anyone want to know where they went for their exercise?

\*     \*     \*

It was four o'clock in the morning when Andy's phone rang. He was dead asleep, for their evening of excesses and the late visit to Lam Thang's had been difficult for him, on top of their daylong meetings. It was the hotel desk clerk, who fumbled with a phone connection. Finally, a man speaking excitedly came on the line.

"Doctor Cheston, is that you?" asked a voice.

He assured the caller that he was Andy Cheston, and then the high-pitched, fast message went on.

"Andy Cheston, this is Pham Xuan Bach—George, with the State Oil Company."

"Yes, George, what is the trouble?" Andy asked, still half asleep.

"I was called by the minister, and he directed me to contact you. He was alerted tonight by the fire department. There has been a great fire that destroyed everything. It raged hotly through your office. All was burned."

"What? A fire in our office?" Andy bounced out of bed.

"Yes, all was burned. It raged for a long period."

George was still excited, and was not speaking clearly.

"You mean our company office here in Saigon?" Andy's knuckles were white on the phone.

"Yes, your World Oil office, where we met to study your data only yesterday."

"Are you sure it was in our office?"

"The minister seemed very certain, for he wanted me to inform you immediately. He said you could call him if you wished."

"That won't be necessary. But there was nothing there to start a fire. Surely it couldn't have been a bad heater, as we have none."

"It was not from a heater, Doctor Cheston. The fire was started by an arsonist. A man was seen running away to a black Mercedes by a neighbor, just as the flames grew big. And there was the smell like napalm," George went on breathlessly.

"Did they get a number from the car? Will the police be able to do anything?" Andy asked.

"It is not likely they will help. These things happen here, it seems. The police will make a report, but likely nothing will be solved, for there is no pay in it for them," he stated honestly.

"How badly was the building burned? Did they save anything—like our files?"

"No, Doctor Cheston, they said nothing remained. It was a complete job of arson. There was the smell of gasoline. It all burned to the ground."

"Then I'm afraid there is nothing to be done now by me. I'll check with you in the morning. Thanks for calling me, although there are some things one would rather not know. Good night, George," Andy said, as he hung up the phone.

He was already thinking the Mercedes must have been the one he and Kelly had seen near the alley. Also, he remembered telling the Viets in their meeting that their only copy of the data would be stored in their office this night. How fortunate it was that James had taken the trouble to arrange an early start for tomorrow.

There was no way to contact World Oil's local office keeper, and there was nothing he could do, anyway. He'd find out soon enough in the morning. Also, there was no reason to awaken his staff here, for they also needed their rest. Andy tried to go back to sleep, but he kept seeing the black Mercedes slowly easing along the dark street.

\* \* \*

When the staff met for breakfast, Andy told them of his interrupted night's sleep, and explained all he knew about the fire. They then hurriedly collected their gear and departed. On their way to the airport, they took the time to have their driver cruise past the company office.

It was as George had said. The building was completely burned to the ground. Only smoldering ashes remained. Their office keeper and the secretary stood forlornly in the nearby street, making no attempt to keep passersby from probing through the ashes for anything worth keeping.

"It's a good thing you decided to leave directly from the Majestic this morning, and carried all the data with you last night, James," Andy said. "You really had a good idea to stay and guard the maps and sections instead of going out to eat."

"I guess it was some kind of premonition," James answered.

"In the good old days, such care was only necessary in the domestic oil market, where each company had its own scouts watching. Everything is so tied up by contract in international operations that security is usually not considered a problem."

"Yes, Andy. Dennis made a worthwhile sacrifice. We do appreciate it, Denny," said James, now unable to grin. "Otherwise we'd have to get a whole new set of colored pencils, and start our interpretation from scratch."

"And guess who thought they knew the maps and sections were there, and could not be easily replaced? That's what you said yesterday in the meeting. Did you intentionally plant that information, Andy?" Kelly asked.

"No," he replied, "but it didn't hurt not to let them know all of our business. I'm sure this arson must be Dong's doings. In the meeting, we led them to believe that the sections and maps were originals, and not replaceable. Now we know why the black Mercedes was following us last night."

"Yes, we are lucky everything didn't burn and set us back by a couple of months of hard work." James was thinking aloud.

"Well, there's nothing more we can do here, so let's get on to the airport and wake up the pilots. We can be in Singapore by midday. I'll call George from there before we fly, but I won't tell him they didn't burn the sections and maps. Somebody is sure to be surprised when we come up with our block selection next month, and right on schedule."

"Yes, our work hasn't been affected, but they don't know that," James replied.

"I'll have a quick word with our office man here, and then we can be on our way. He'd better find us a new place to hang our hat while in town. Maybe we should just rent a room in the hotel."

Andy was thinking about their disaster, and how they might avoid a continuation of such delaying confrontations. Somehow the NLF must be convinced that World Oil would not be deterred from their drilling plans or from the contracted obligations.

Also, he was thinking far ahead, about the week after next, when he'd be in Hong Kong. Would Lin Jin see him if he called? He certainly would try. He knew he must see her personally, and tell her what she really meant to him. He wanted to find out why she had left Tokyo without letting him explain his feelings for her. Then he remembered—he had told Beth at the party that he loved Lin Jin. He realized too late that he should have been telling Lin Jin.

# Seventeen

On their arrival in Singapore, Andy and James took a taxi directly to the New Raffles Hotel to claim their reservations, while Dennis called his office to have someone send a car. Andy really preferred the old hotel, with its long bar and its tall Singapore Slings, for there he had spent many pleasant business visits. He enjoyed sitting quietly in the Palm Court garden, and could readily see why so many English writers had spent their days working there during the colonial era. It was a restful setting, close to the gin and tonics, which were good for malaria.

The next two days Andy and James spent working hard in the digital processing office, going over data with the geophysicists. Then Andy hurried back to his hotel to get his communications with the various company offices in order. Two nights later, he and James went to dinner at the Troica Russian Restaurant, high atop the "Wall Street" of the Far East, overlooking the anchorage of ships. Kelly met them there to go over their plans. In Andy's serious mood, he hardly noticed the magnificent view of the cable car passing above them en route to Sentosa Island. Business came first, and they wasted no time in acting the tourists or discussing sights such as Tiger Balm Garden. They had seen them before. This meeting was to plan their future activities, and how they could make their recommendations come alive with action.

Before continuing his travels to visit other company offices, Andy made one excursion for personal shopping at the Singapore Handicraft Center. There they have shops from each of the Far East countries, displaying and offering their specialties for sale. He knew a gem merchant in one of the shops from Thailand whom he could trust, so he made his way there for a visit. His selection for purchase was a beautiful sapphire ring, with earrings to match. There might come a time soon when he'd see Lin Jin again, and need such a gift.

As an afterthought, he stopped in a Japanese shop nearby and picked up a double strand of pearls for Beth. He must somehow get back in her good graces, although pearls may not be the way. The women of his life were tearing his formerly well organized business career apart.

Andy's trip by commercial plane to Jakarta was longer than he had planned, for he encountered personnel problems that demanded he stay for an extra day. He found that he resented this interruption of his work on the Vietnamese project, for it demanded all of his concentration.

The stayover in Jakarta delayed his arrival in their office in Thailand a day, but fortunately, the World Oil manager there had everything in order, and their production was developing nicely. The only problem for the moment was getting around by car, for all of the downtown streets were nearly underwater, and taxis were stalled everywhere. He hoped the rainy season didn't leave Saigon in the same condition, for that might disrupt their planned meetings.

He appreciated the way the people in Bangkok lived. Their manager certainly knew how to entertain. His wife must spend all of her time teaching the servants to serve "at table." It would be nice to live like that someday, but what if Lin Jin would never see him again? Andy constantly carried his worries about the Oriental lovely with him.

It was too bad he could not stay in Bangkok long enough to accept their invitation to get in a round of golf, although he knew there were much better courses in Japan than those in Thailand. His visits to Siam were always too short, and he regretted having to take the long ride to the airport. It was sad to have to leave such a beautiful land and its happy people. It seemed duty always was calling.

Andy hadn't traveled anywhere alone for quite a while, and it gave him time to think—and remember. It was rather nice, though, for on this leg of his trip he'd fly over Saigon without stopping, and he could catch up on his dreams. Soon he remembered, however, it was important that he get to Hong Kong to meet their production manager. He must meet Kelly there as well and get their office arrangements organized, in case they achieved their goal to start drilling an exploratory well.

Hong Kong was one of his favorite places to visit, but he had never had a working connection here. It was a proper destination for vacationing and shopping, where one could buy suits hand tailored from British fabric at a fourth of the price charged elsewhere. And they could deliver them, hand tailored, in a day. Someone was always asking him to bring back a '43L' shirt, or some slacks. One had to look quickly at its sights and try to remember them, for they would tear down a mountain, dump it into the sea, and build a new office complex on the spot before you knew what had happened. Hong Kong was expanding rapidly.

Andy had loved the smell of the old city, but now it had outgrown the rickshaws. He used to wander in the alleys and watch the people, who were all making something with their hands. The Star Ferry connecting to Kowloon was no longer a nickel, yet it was still reasonable enough to command use by the majority of the pedestrian traffic. The new tunnel linking the island to the mainland was a long way around, and not nearly as quick. He wondered which side of the great harbor their office should be on. That decision would soon have to be made.

Hong Kong really is the crossroads of the Orient. It seemed that every time he went to visit a company office in the Far East, he had to stop over there. It coexists with a giant who could take it over anytime it wished, but the Chinese apparently consider it more advantageous to wait for the British contract to expire. He knew its shield would not fall so long as it is supported by the British lion on one side, and the Chinese dragon on the other.

The refugees and the moneyed bankers who flooded into the island from Shanghai after the Communists came to power in 1949 are both uneasily awaiting that expiration. They will see if the shield remains standing with the dragon alone. Until that time, Andy knew that all business negotiations continue in a state of flux. He wondered how World Oil would handle such things as borrowing needed money and local cash payments. Brodecki would be certain to have a firm grip on the banking when the time came.

Andy felt as if he had been running on a treadmill. Just showing his face at their various company offices was a tiresome, tedious job. Fortunately, Wally Brooks had kept their normal operations moving by communications from their Tokyo office, and so long as there were no big problems that required major money expenditures or decisions, he ran everything quite well. If there was trouble, he would contact him, or if that was not possible, he'd bother their boss, Bill Hanby. Andy had welcomed being relieved of the daily grind of communications between their operating offices. He could spend his time more profitably planning what to do about the future of their Vietnam blocks.

Andy knew he had been daydreaming, but he had come to a decision. He knew now, after his visit to the offices that reported to him, that they were in good hands. He was no longer desperately needed as their supervisor, for now he had a more important job handling Vietnam, which usurped all of his time. He would be happy in the future not to be required to run all of the Far East operations for World Oil. If they asked him, he'd like to be the manager of one operation for which he had total responsibility, and run that well. But now was not the time to rock the corporate boat.

\*   \*   \*

Andy awoke just in time to see the apartment houses on the side of the mountain flash by close under the wingtip, and he knew they were still a couple of minutes from touchdown. By the time the big jet landed on the runway, which ran into the bay at Hong Kong, he had completed a good sleep, for he had been so exhausted by his travels.

The airport terminal and facilities were really crowded with the apartment complexes growing ever higher onto the mountain, and into the sea. The flight pattern for big planes approached very close to the contour of the mountains, and their roll out on the single runway was directly into the bay. Only water showed itself through each side window. If one hadn't done it many times before and didn't know better, it was, indeed, scary. He'd better get himself awake and ready to meet his drilling supervisor, Pug Cox.

There was only one way to describe Pug. He was just a great big man. Andy had worked with him many times in his years of well-sitting and supervising the exploration operations of World Oil in various Far East locations, since Pug had often been his drilling superintendent. They liked one another and worked well together, but they looked like they were from two different worlds.

How he had obtained his college degree over in Baton Rouge, Louisiana, was not clear. He was plenty smart enough, but he just didn't look the part of a college man. He reminded Andy of the advertisement, "Tough, but oh, so gentle." He had always treated Andy with the great respect that field personnel normally show for an educated boss. Pug's big, square jaw always appeared to be in need of a shave. And yes, his neck was more than a little red—from the time he had spent on the drilling floor of oil rigs around the world.

Andy was aware that Pug would make no effort to handle him with kid gloves, because he had shown him many times that he could handle himself when push came to shove. He had also noted, though, that Pug was always around on the derrick floor to see that the roughnecks treated him with the respect due a friend instead of a boss. Wherever they went together, it was as though no one dared think of crossing their path. Just the threat of a swat by Pug Cox would clear almost any barstool.

Pug was easy to spot as he stood waiting when Andy came out of the customs line, for he was a head taller than the crowd.

"Welcome to Hong Kong, Andy," he commenced. "Have a good trip?"

"Yeah, a sleeping one, and I needed it."

"I got here late yesterday afternoon from Manila. I hope you like the transport I arranged."

They hustled Andy's luggage into a waiting limousine and tried to leave the congestion behind.

"Yeah, it looks fine. We have to do some visiting around town, so some wheels will be needed. How were things in the Philippines?"

"Oh, they're fine. I think the boys should be able to handle things down there for a few days, provided they don't have too many volcanoes erupting or typhoons showing up."

"It's always something in the China Sea. We can handle the natural calamities sometimes a lot easier than the political ones," Andy answered thoughtfully. "How have the typhoons treated your drilling operations lately?"

"Not too bad. We haven't had to move any rigs off location this year, so far." Pug kept close tabs on his field operations.

"Have you met Kelly Johnson yet? Is he at the same hotel you're in?" Andy asked.

"Yes, he was out running his traps. He had a meeting with someone this afternoon about a rental property. I told him I'd meet you and get you to the hotel."

"Thanks, I hope he does some good."

"If he's successful, there'll be some office space reserved for your approval tomorrow. Personally, I hope it is close to the airport, for I'm going to have to be in and out of here several times a week."

"That'll suit everybody just fine if it is. We also need to have access to drill supplies and air transport, especially a heliport. There's no need to be close to government offices or banks, or other oil companies here. We're just going to use this as a base for your drilling operations. The more convenient for you and for our communications, the better."

"Besides office space, we need to find a good administrator here to handle the office, because I'll be out on the drillship most of the time. I want someone I can trust to make supplies move out on schedule."

"Communications may be a deciding reason for placing the office near such facilities. We'll need to be where the radios can be installed, and heard a few hundred miles away."

"Maybe we'll have to get on top of Victoria Peak." Pug was showing his teeth in a broad grin. "Then we could ride up to work by cog tramway."

"That's not likely. Is there a chance of going international from a helipad from atop the island? We might get away from the airport traffic."

"I'll have to check on that. I'll let you know tomorrow." Pug was all serious again, and the limo rocked as he turned to watch the traffic.

\*   \*   \*

They were staying at the Mandarin Hotel on the mainland of Kowloon, and a few blocks inland from the Star Ferry slip. As soon as Andy could get in touch with Kelly Johnson, he was brought up to date on what had been accomplished in his search for an office, and other necessary arrangements for shipping and communications.

"I have a couple of office possibilities lined up, but I'm not sure you'll like either of them. One is too far into the banking district and the other is too far out in the boondocks. That's a good Tagalog word Pug could have brought from Manila. I hope you brought a sack full of money with you, for this property comes dear."

"I'll be happy to have a look, but let's not go overboard on expenditures; we just need a communications office. We're not trying to impress anybody."

"The ones I've seen that we can afford certainly won't do that," Kelly replied.

Apparently, Kelly had been hard at work, but was not too pleased with the outcome thus far.

"We'd better take Pug along tomorrow morning and touch base with the Hoe organization. I assume you've already talked to them," Andy stated.

It was a subject Andy hated to bring up, for he knew if Kelly had seen Lin Jin, or had any contact with her at their office, he'd have an idea about how she would react to his presence in Hong Kong. He wondered if she would see him.

"Yes," Kelly answered. "I have set up an appointment with their manager and his administrator for ten in the morning. After lunch, we can go have a look at the office spaces, if that's OK."

He had not mentioned Lin Jin, and Andy hesitated to ask the direct question.

"That sounds fine to me, and that'll be a good start. Did they have any recommendations as to where we could find an office manager who would honestly fill our requirements here?"

"I don't think that's a problem here. They did name a couple. You can just pick your color and height in this job market, but they all are expensive. We need one with recommendations. Do you want an Englishman, or a Chinese person?"

"We may be influenced by the Viet State Oilers to pick up a man from Vietnam, and keep him on the payroll. The local governments usually have a lot to say about hiring their own people to work on their projects. They want the money to come back home. We may end up with George's cousin working for Pug here."

"That'll be the day. But perhaps you're right. Moe's nephew is already on the seismic boat as a conservation agent."

\*   \*   \*

The Hoe shipyard was on the outskirts of Kowloon, and just getting there through the bicycles, pedestrians, and taxis was quite a feat, even without considering the stench at some intersections. When they finally arrived, they were only a few minutes late, and the three World Oil men were ushered in like executives. They were brought into the one room that was adorned with drapes and leather-covered chairs around a small glass ring stained conference table. This was obviously not their home office.

Their manager was named Ian Hakka, doubtless from one of the families who tilled the New Territories hillsides. He wore a tie that was a little worse for wear, for he apparently spent most of his time in the shops. Around the walls were pictures of small ships under construction, and models of half-hulls as are normally displayed in shipyards. His assistant wore a loose-fitting white shirt, and was obviously accustomed to working without air-conditioning. There was no upwind side, and the office was cooled with only one fan.

"We thank you for taking time to see us and to help in the arrangements we will need to get an office established," Andy began.

"It is no problem," replied Hakka. "We received a message from Li Hong Hoe in Tokyo. Our offices are at your service, Doctor Cheston."

Soon he and Kelly were talking to Ian about the necessities such as telephones, working permits, and postal addresses. Pug had cornered the administrator. He was asking him how they came by their supplies, such as steel tubing and plate. He wanted to get contacts and prices and a million other things that would allow them to operate in a strange new location. Pug had done this several times before in locales strange to him, so he knew what questions to ask.

After a half hour of discussion, during which Andy relayed the best wishes of Li Hong Hoe from Tokyo and Lan Thang Nguyen from Saigon, they were taken for a quick tour of the company's construction yard. It was interesting, but not as large as Andy had expected. He knew they had other yards in other countries, but was surprised when Ian explained they had laid the keel on a larger vessel for a seismic exploration company in their other local yard, for it had heavier cranes. That was of great interest to Pug, and he made a date to meet Ian and review that location later.

When it was noon, Andy asked, "Is there a place nearby where we could invite the two of you to join us for lunch?"

"No, I am sorry," Hakka answered. "We bring food and do not leave during the day, for we must get back to our tasks."

Andy had looked about carefully, but he saw no evidence of Lin Jin working there, nor any office he would want to see her occupy.

"Would it be possible to speak to the granddaughter of Li Hong Hoe? I expected to see her while I am here," Andy finally mustered the courage to ask.

"Miss Hoe has taken the week off to help her mother move to a new apartment. I think she will be back in the main office on Monday." Ian Hakka had a knowing look in his eyes.

"Would it be possible to get her address? I'd like to call her, or visit while I am here."

"I have the address and phone of her mother's old apartment, but they have not yet given me a new contact. I expect she will give those when she returns to the office next week."

"I'll do the best I can with the old number, then and thank you. Perhaps they left a forwarding address."

The trio made their way back to their limousine, thanking Ian for his trouble on the way, and particularly for his help in locating office space. Andy knew that the most worthwhile space was only obtained by recommendation of friends. It was the Oriental custom.

As they were about to depart, Andy saw a man arrive in a pedicab, and recognized him with a start. It was Kim Jin Hoe. What was the brother of Lin Jin doing here? He knew he had graduated from the college, but he thought he was living in Tokyo.

He called out to him, "Hello there, Kim! What are you doing in Hong Kong?"

That gained his attention, but it took a few moments for Kim's face to register that he recognized his friend.

"Hello, Doctor Cheston," he finally replied. "I live here now with my mother, and they are trying to find a place for me to work in the shipyard."

"I didn't know you were trained to be a shipbuilder," Andy replied in jest.

"I'm not. I graduated in business management, but there are few openings at the top these days," Kim answered, returning a smile. "What has brought you to Hong Kong?"

"World Oil is trying to get themselves established here in preparation for drilling off Vietnam. I thought you would have known."

"I've heard something about it. Lin Jin keeps a close eye on your operations. Are you going to call her?"

"I'd like to do more than just call, if she'll see me." Andy felt a little guilty, speaking so personally in front of everyone. "Do you both live with your mother? And could you give me your new address?"

Kim Hoe hesitated a moment, obviously embarrassed.

"I would if I could remember it; but, I'm sorry, I can't. We just moved into the place. I can find my way there, but the numbers have not yet settled into my brain. Could I call you later, or ask Lin Jin if she will? Where are you staying?"

"We're at the Mandarin Hotel in Kowloon, and we'll be back there by late afternoon. Please call me there, and I'll see if I can contact Lin Jin this evening."

Andy was not too pleased with the arrangement, but it was all he could do. Now he would be on pins until he heard from either Lin Jin or Kim. He only hoped the day of insults in Tokyo was far enough behind her that she would consider speaking to him again.

The ride back to the center of Kowloon was even slower than their trip out, so they had the driver deliver them to a restaurant as soon as he found one that was suitable.

Over a sandwich and a beer they discussed the information they had gained during the morning. Kelly had learned some things about setting up communications, and Pug was anxious to see their larger shipyard. It might be of use to them in setting up their supplies for delivery to the drillship.

"Was this the first time either of you had met Kim Jin Hoe?" Andy asked.

"Yes," replied Kelly. "I hadn't seen him before, but, then, he and I both move around a lot."

"He doesn't travel in Manila circles, I guess," said Pug. "Before I got there he was probably in school. He seems like a nice young fellow, with his head on straight. At least he knows he needs a job that fits his skills, and that he won't get to start at the top. Most of those kids educated by money don't even know where to look. Either that, or they take a good education and start out welding, then never get away from it."

"I was thinking, Pug, Kim might be of use to you here. Could he become your local gopher? He has the education for it, and knows his way around Hong Kong. He just might make a good office manager, and we know he comes from an honest family. Also, the Viets couldn't say he wasn't a native hire."

"He seems to be a nice enough kid, but I'd have to see how he approaches real work. Would it be possible to try him for few weeks on odd jobs and contacts until we decide if he can be trusted not to sell the diamond bits?"

"That sounds like a reasonable idea. That way, we wouldn't be committed in case his work doesn't pan out. When you go visiting Hakka, ask him how they'd feel about us using Kim. I'm sure they don't have a spot for him right now, or he'd already be in it."

"I'll talk to him when we go out tomorrow. I'd like another beer—I'm used to the bigger bottles."

Pug had rapped on the table with his big fist and obtained the waiter's immediate attention.

"No more for me," said Andy, and Kelly joined in. He continued, "If I get a chance tonight, I'll sound him out to see if he's interested, but it'd be better if you hired him, Pug."

Andy was sincerely hoping he'd have a message before this evening, telling him where he could contact Lin Jin. He had missed her more than he had been able to admit, even to himself.

\*   \*   \*

The trio had returned to their hotel and taken time to go to their rooms and clean up. They had arranged to meet later in the lounge, to exchange ideas and decide what to do for the evening. Andy was hoping he would not be available, and when he arrived in his room he saw the message light was winking at him from the phone. His heart took a leap.

It took the operator forever to find his information, and when she returned, it was a fax from Bill Hanby advising him they were having Houston company visitors in Tokyo early next week, and that his presence was desirable. Their president, Phillip Harrison, and an entourage of exploration types were coming to review their status.

They wanted to know exactly what their progress was toward Vietnamese drilling. He was right up-to-date on it, and could easily explain to them where they stood at the moment. The real crunch would come when they tried to sell their selection of blocks to the Viets and get their name on the dotted line.

He had a quick shower, and put on a fresh shirt. He wore a tie, and carried his linen jacket. As an old friend had once told him, "Always carry a sugar cube in your pocket; you can never tell when you might meet a horse." In this case, the sugar cubes were sapphires. Dejectedly, Andy closed the door to his room, and barely heard the ring of the phone as he turned to leave. Excitedly, he fumbled with his key-card, and rushed to catch the phone before it stopped ringing. It was Kim.

"Hi, Doctor Cheston. I'm glad I caught you. I just got home, and now have that address and phone number you requested," said Kim. "My sister was not sure you would want to know where she was, or she would have contacted you herself."

"Is she there? May I speak with her?" Andy was suddenly weak. It had been months since he had heard her voice.

"Yes, she is here. One moment, sir." The phone was muffled, as though the speaker had been covered by his hand.

After a time and some extended conversation, he heard a swishing transfer.

"Hello, is that you, Andy-san?" came the sweet voice of Lin Jin.

How he had missed hearing her.

"Yes, Lin Jin, it's me. How I have missed you these past months. Why did you run away from me without a word? I've tried everywhere to contact you, but my letters kept coming back, and I didn't have your phone number."

"Oh, Andy-san, I've missed you, too. I did not think you would be interested in talking to me, after your sister was so upset. To tell the truth, I could not face you."

"What happened that night in Tokyo between you and Beth has nothing to do with the two of us. My sister doesn't think for me. You and I know how we feel about one another. No matter what our families think, we know we are made for each other."

"Oh, Andy—Andy-san," Lin Jin stammered. "It's so good to hear you, and to know you still think well of me. These past months have been a living hell for me. I am aware that it is important what your family thinks of me, or you and I could never have a proper respect for each other. Your twin sister is a part of you. For us to ever be one, she must completely accept me as well." Lin Jin was beginning to cry.

"I'll always think well of you, Lin-san. How can I see you? I have a car. Do you live far away? I'll come after you right away." Andy was breathless.

"Oh, you can't possibly see my family like this. We've just moved into this apartment, and everything is such a mess. Kim and I are sharing the place with Mother Thi Lan. I do want you to meet her, Andy-san, and soon; but she would not receive you this way."

"But I must see you, right away, tonight. I'm leaving for Tokyo in two days—I'm supposed to be there Sunday. Hanby is expecting me for a meeting, so I can't delay my departure. Please, let me pick you up now, and we can talk. I have to see you soon, Lin Jin, or my brain will simply burst. I've done nothing but think of you for these past months." Andy realized he was too excited to think straight now, knowing Lin Jin would see him. It was good he didn't have to drive.

"All right then, Andy-san. I can meet you in front, and we'll reserve the family introductions for later."

"Give me the directions then, carefully, for I'm not really all here at the moment. And give me your phone number in case I get the address wrong."

He made his excuses to Kelly and Pug in the reception lounge, and explained that he would need to use the car for the evening, provided they could manage with taxis. He didn't even wait with them long enough to have a drink—for he was already drunk enough with excitement at the thought of seeing Lin Jin. Office space discussions must wait until tomorrow.

The limousine had barely stopped in front of the apartment complex, when Andy was out and hurrying to the entry doors. He was looking for a bell to ring, when suddenly, there she was. Lin Jin stepped out, and they literally fell into each other's arms. She was the vision of Oriental beauty of which he had been dreaming. Her straight black hair was held by the same gold clip, and hung down to her waist; it was even longer than he remembered.

He could not stop talking, for he was trying to answer the hundred questions she asked. The ride back to the Mandarin was not long enough for them, as they were held tightly in their lovers' grasp. Andy apologized again and again for his sister's actions, and promised he would never let such a thing happen again. Lin Jin explained that her feelings had been so hurt and that she could not believe he would still want her.

She carefully explained that she only knew her lover's sister had insulted her, and that they could never again have the respect for one another required if they were to spend a lifetime together. In an Oriental society, family objections would have ended the relationship with finality.

Andy was happy their ride to the Mandarin Hotel was an hour of confessions, and a time for making up. In the end, they could talk quite civilly, and by the time the limousine pulled up the steep incline in the driveway of the main entrance to the hotel, they were again two lovers on their way out for the evening.

Andy escorted Lin Jin to the elevator, and past the reception lounge where he had left his friends, Kelly and Pug. They apparently had already gone on to dinner elsewhere. At his room, he permitted Lin Jin to rearrange her makeup while he called to make reservations at the best hotel dining room. There would be much champagne drunk this night. He had let the limo and driver go, telling him to return in the morning.

When Lin Jin came back into the room, he held her tightly, being careful of the makeup, and said simply, "My dearest Lin-san, I have missed you so, for I love you. I'll never let you leave me again."

She replied, "Andy-san, I, too, love you—so much. Before we can be happy together, though, I must convince your sister that I am worthy of you and of your family."

# Eighteen

It was a festive relief, in a way, for Andy to be back in Tokyo and working in their office where their routine went ahead with a certain expected sequence. Things were going ahead on schedule and with a pattern. Their Vietnam exploration also was marching ahead. What pleased him most, however, was that his relations had been renewed with Lin Jin. Although all was not a bed of roses, at least she was speaking to him and he could look forward to visits in Hong Kong.

The trip had been a tedious one, with all its setbacks and successes. Now they had their Vietnamese contract promised, an office in Hong Kong, and he had met his lady love's mother, Thi Lan Hoe. He knew that Bill Hanby was relieved to see his exploration group back in Tokyo, and in such an agreeable mood. He confided in Andy that the past few months had been hell around the office, for all anyone wanted to talk about was exploration contracts in Vietnam, and how they were going to repay the terrorists who wiped out their friends. It was upsetting as well as depressing.

Andy now felt that he could smile once in a while, and would talk about something besides structures and contracts with James and his seismic explorers. He even gathered his staff together after work one afternoon for a few beers at the Tokyo Onsen, and answered a few questions about his meeting in Hong Kong with Lin Jin's mother, Thi Lan.

At an informal dinner party at the Hanbys' apartment one evening, Andy at last felt he could open up to his friends and tell them about how his less intimate private affairs went in Hong Kong. He was relieved to be able to of speak openly about Lin Jin, after so many months of everything being bottled up within himself. Only the McAllisters, serious Alan and prim, mousy Pamela, and Bill and Jill were there. He explained that he had met Mother Thi Lan Hoe at their new apartment, and learned something about her early life in Vietnam.

"I'll bet that was a traumatic meeting, for you as well as her mother," Jill said, jumping right into the topic.

"Yes, it was," Andy replied. "But she is every bit Lin Jin's mother, so you might suspect how she would act. She was all tact, and evidently is willing to accept her daughter's attitude toward me without reservation."

"Did she give you a big hug?" asked Pamela bashfully.

"As a matter of fact, she didn't. She showed nothing but respect, not to wear her feelings on her sleeve. I only kissed her hand when she offered it."

"How is her English? Is it as good as Lin Jin's?" Jill asked.

"Yes; she has a little accent, but just enough to be interesting. She definitely thinks in English, if not in American."

"Did she tell you all about her family, and about her children growing up in Saigon?" Jill asked.

She wanted to know the full story of Lin Jin's childhood, for they were close friends, and yet she had never talked about her early days. Jill was sharp, and must have known there was a story hidden there somewhere.

"She told me what she wanted me to know, I guess. When the French were driven out, she had lived in a Saigon suburb with her babies, Lin Jin and Kim Jin. She had a rough time because her husband had been killed while fighting in the war."

"That must have been terrible," Pamela sympathized.

"Her family helped her, and they struggled along until the Americans came. Finally, when she could put up with the terror no longer, she escaped to Hong Kong with her children and Nhung Thi, whose parents had both been killed in the war."

"How horrible!" Pamela added, her voice, filled with grief.

"There they established their right to British citizenship. With the aid of Li Hong Hoe, she found herself a job, and created an independent life for herself."

"Then how did the children get educated back in the Catholic School in Saigon?" McAllister asked, as he was intently taking in the dialogue.

"Thi Lan soon found that she couldn't afford to keep the children in a school of quality in Hong Kong, so she sent them back to Vietnam, to be watched over by the nuns and their half-great-uncle, Lam Thang Nguyen. For some reason, she could not bring herself to return. It was a complex family tree, but they were a unit, and they took care of one another when it was necessary."

"She must have trusted Lam Thang a lot to let him rear her two children along with his granddaughter, Nhung Thi," Jill said. "I'd have gone along if they were mine. She must have had a very good reason for not returning."

"It appeared that she had a great fear of living in Saigon, even with a well-positioned family for protection. As it turned out, when the war ended it was well that she had stayed away, for her part of the family was very much anti-Communist. She would have ended up in the reeducation camps. Maybe that's what she feared."

"She has had a hard life, and I'm glad I didn't have to walk in her shoes," Jill stated, shaking her head sadly.

"While in school there, Lin Jin and her second cousin, Nhung Thi, grew to be great friends. She still regrets that she was not able to get her out when she and Kim escaped, but she made a choice and elected to stay with her grandfather."

Everyone was deeply pondering the Hoe family problems. It was too sad a story, so Andy changed the subject.

"What do you have planned for entertainment for our visiting dignitaries, Jill? Are you going to hire geishas and take them to the cabarets in the Ginza?"

Andy was teasing her, as he often did, about getting a massage in the bath houses.

"You just mind your own business, young man, until you get invited yourself—then you'll know," Jill replied with her motherly smile.

After dinner, Bill invited the two gentlemen rather formally into his study for a brandy, obviously with the intention of discussing important company business. Andy suddenly realized this was the reason for this carefully orchestrated private dinner meeting. He wished to talk with his two managers, and away from his official Tokyo World Oil office.

They settled into the deep leather chairs placed around the hibachi, and Bill served brandy in the great thin crystal snifters. The VSOP was more to be enjoyed for the bouquet than to be tasted, for a sip evaporated in the throat without ever reaching a warmed interior. It was "the good stuff," normally reserved for important visitors.

Bill commenced by saying, "I asked you both here tonight to relay some information that is not to be spread around to our local personnel, as yet. When Phil Harrison was here last week, he told me that the U.S. government has informed World Oil management that the trade embargo prohibiting American companies from doing business in Vietnam is going to be strictly enforced."

"Uh-oh, that sounds disastrous," Tim stated.

Andy began to turn the startling revelation over in his mind, for they had been led to believe some exemption would be granted.

"It could be a real stopper. Our request to the U.S. government for relief of that requirement is going to be turned down, and the ban affecting our operations is expected to become effective in the very near future. It means, simply put, that the conduct of our operations in the offshore Mekong Delta will have to cease, or undergo a drastic change, somehow."

Both Andy and Tim were shocked. It had been assumed that the government wanted World Oil to get into business in Vietnam very badly, even though it was officially against current policy. The belief within their top management had been that the embargo would be overlooked in the interest of expanding better American relations with all of the countries in Indochina.

"That would take quite a reorganization," Tim replied, already thinking ahead to replacing World Oil with some other company organization in their Vietnam contract.

"How can they change their minds about this at such a late date?" Andy demanded. "We've already invested upward of fifty million dollars there, just getting our feet wet. And we haven't even started drilling."

"They are the government, and can do whatever they wish, so long as it can't be proven illegal," Bill replied.

"We have been operating on the assumption that they wanted us to start working there worse than they wanted to continue the sanctions," Tim injected again.

"Is there any way we could avoid their interpretation of the restrictions?" Andy asked. "Perhaps we could get a special dispensation—like, from the President."

"That's not too likely, but it is the route we are exploring now through our legal department in Houston. They have already sent a delegation to Washington. They aren't very hopeful, however."

"Is there any way we could force them to give us permission, like suing to tie them up in court for years while we go on operating?" Tim had a legal background.

"No; that wouldn't be considered wise, for we have too many other interests around the world, and it could backfire. If we finally lost the suit, we'd owe them a lot of back pay, as well as lose whatever current position we'd hold at that time."

"So what can we do?" Andy asked. "We can't just sit by and let them give our exploration investment to Viet State Oil. They'd just turn all the data we've gathered over to the Russians, to Vietsovpetro, to operate. What a boon that would be for them. They'd love it. Does the NLF have an inside connection to our State Department?"

"No, I don't believe that could be the case. But Harrison and I discussed ways to keep that very thing from happening," Bill said. "Vietsovpetro has claimed they already have production of a hundred thousand barrels a day from the old Mobil discovery at Bach Ho. Theirs is the only oil production presently active in the country, and they would be the big gainers. We can talk to our government quite civilly about it though, because they really don't want that to happen. They just don't know how to avoid it."

"Surely we can avoid just giving everything away. Can we stay in the game somehow? Couldn't we form our own non-U.S. company? We'd need a lot of financial support to get started, and a lot of drilling luck to obtain production early and remain on the profit side." Andy was thinking very hard.

"There is a slim possibility that we'll get the dispensation from the U.S. government, since we went into the operation with the blessing of the State Department—at least they didn't say 'no' when we asked," Bill continued.

"So what do we do? Just sit and wait?" Tim asked.

"No, we must begin to explore other options, such as the one you suggested, Andy. We must consider forming a non-U.S. company. Harrison and I talked about such a possibility in Houston. That is, a company wholly owned by funds from outside of the United States. World Oil has some income from totally foreign sources that could be diverted to use overseas by a Board of Directors of a new company. It would be one set up as a foreign corporation. How does that sound to the two of you?"

"It sounds like it would be very difficult to find the necessary backing from the money markets unless the new company were originally completely funded by World Oil's foreign capital. If they did that, it wouldn't legally be a new company," Tim stated, trying to think like a lawyer. "Or would it?"

"It would be a rough step for anyone to take from a professional standpoint," Andy added. "If the new company falls flat on its face, say if their first attempt were a dry hole, World Oil might not want to hire a loser back into the home organization. Also, they may later wish to take back control of the company if the venture were successful. And assuming, too, that someday working in Vietnam would no longer be banned by the United States."

Andy was thinking ahead, for he already realized why Bill Hanby was discussing this with him and with Tim McAllister. World Oil always planned far ahead, and they had already selected the new company's Board of Directors. This little dinner party was an evening for setting the future.

"You both have valid questions, but Phil Harrison has already reassured me on those points. World Oil can provide enough 'free money' to make the new company solvent. That is, they would have enough capital to back whatever loans would be required to cover the expense of drilling, as well as maintaining a staff. Also, he assured me that anyone who left World Oil to become a director of the new company would receive stock options as a bonus payment of considerable size—enough to make it worth the risk of leaving World Oil. Then he wouldn't have to worry about being hired back if their exploration in the Mekong Delta fails."

"It sounds like this has gone beyond the discussion stage," said Tim, swirling his glass and inhaling the brandy.

"It has, I'll have to admit," Bill answered. "We were waiting on the U.S. government decision before discussing it here, but we're not sitting on our hands. We have already decided that our company will be named VietAmer Oil Corporation, and their headquarters will be in Hong Kong."

"It sounds like a logical location, at least for the next few years," Andy answered. "And the name goes along with the area to be worked."

"Gilbert Eason and Phillip Harrison have authorized me to discuss the possibility of such an organization with the two of you. Together, the three of us would form the Board of Directors of the new company, VietAmer Oil." Bill was looking back and forth from Andy to Tim to see what reactions that disclosure created.

Finally, after a lengthy silence, Tim replied, "I don't see that it would be too difficult for Pamela and me. Living in Hong Kong would not be bad, if we could find an adequate school for the kids. And if it didn't work out, we'd have to make some other arrangement. In the meantime, I suppose a director gets a better salary than an office manager."

"How about you, Andy? You'd be the president in charge of the new company, VietAmer."

"I'm still reeling. That would be a big step up if we can make the area produce oil," Andy answered seriously.

"That it is, and World Oil's confidence in the integrity of the three of us is the reason why they're willing to back such a venture, outside of their direct control. Our only connection to World Oil would be our promise to return the profits to the company; otherwise, it wouldn't be legal." Bill laid the fact right on the line.

"I like the idea of living in Hong Kong, too, at this time," Andy replied. "I'm still hoping to convince Lin Jin that my family will accept her, even though she still has serious doubts—serious enough that she only admits to our friendship part-time."

"Jill and I have thought about her. If you lived there, things might work out for you and Lin Jin much easier. How would you like to operate a full-fledged office from Hong Kong?"

"It would be tough going to operate a new area without the support of the World Oil staff," Andy replied. "There'd be no James and no Wally—and no Ben to call on. If we had a discovery under our belt, it would be different. Starting out with just a jingle in your jeans to buy your way into a dog-eat-dog industry, and in a strange, hostile country, will be very rough."

Andy was thinking seriously, and took time to push the mop of hair back off his forehead. It was a nervous reaction, and such a venture as indicated by the name "VietAmer Oil" was a lot to consider on such short notice. Andy had never worked overseas for anyone other than World Oil.

"Also, I don't think it would be too easy to find an equivalent position to exploration manager with a failure in one's pocket. Here, our efforts are assigned to the entire group's decisions, but with VietAmer Oil, all guilt or innocence would belong to one person—the exploration chief."

Andy wondered if he should dare accept such a serious step, and at his young age. Was World Oil going to push them out, or did they have any real choice? No—the decision had already been made by World Oil's top brass. They knew the two of them could not turn down such a plum.

"I see your point," replied Bill. "You'd just have to weigh the costs. If the operation were a success, you'd find yourself the part-owner of a great deal of production money. I guess you understand they are thinking the three of us would form the Board."

"What would be the interest assigned to each of us?" Tim asked.

"That will have to be decided later by Houston; Phil mentioned forty-forty-twenty for percentages of ownership control, but with differing World Oil stock options. Sorry, Tim, but exploration gets the lion's share."

"I can accept that, for they get the blame if everything is dry," Tim replied thoughtfully. "I'd still be better off salary-wise, and would have a shot at ownership in the future."

"This will require some deep consideration," Andy said. "It has been a long time since I've worked for anyone other than World Oil. My father always told me to consider carefully before I became a 'job-shopper,' and I haven't worked for myself since my paper route. Dad was one of the old school, who stayed with assignments until they were finished."

"OK, now you have the facts. We won't know in which direction to move for a few weeks yet. Think it over, and I'll call you both if the State

Department sends us any new information. I want you each to be up-to-date. Please keep this information a secret among ourselves, because I wouldn't want this to get out before we're ready. I'll let Eason know you are both interested, and we'll draw up the details as we go."

There was a resonant ring to the brandy snifters as the three of them clinked carefully together.

\* \* \*

The meeting in Vietnam for proposing block assignments was being held in the energy minister's large conference room, formerly the American Embassy of Saigon. All of the important parties were in attendance. Dong, still in his dark glasses, sat beside the minister. Down the row were Nguyen Muoi of the State Oil Company, with his assistant, George; next to him was Dr. Bien Giap; then their legal rep, Kong Van Dieu.

On Bill Hanby's side of the huge table for World Oil were Andy and his map handler, James; then their office manager, Tim McAllister, with the "legal beagle" from the Houston office, Eric Goff. Everyone came prepared with notes and maps, ready to do battle to achieve the most advantageous segmentation of the offshore blocks. They wanted to lay a claim on those blocks that World Oil thought would be most productive.

After the introductory remarks and a presentation of the intended agenda by Ho Bac Minh and Nguyen Muoi, the meeting was turned over to World Oil. Bill Hanby first presented a quick review of the fieldwork that had been accomplished, and the amount of money they had spent. Then Andy stepped up with their proposals.

He first showed the maps and presented a discourse about the structures that they had contoured. Then he displayed the selection of the eight blocks World Oil wished to retain as their exclusive right to explore by drilling.

The meeting went well, and by eleven o'clock the table was completely covered by displays of all the areas. The ones that World Oil expected to claim by contract were outlined in a broad colored stipple. Andy had made certain that everyone understood the intentions of their future operational planning. They hoped to conclude the meeting by agreeing on these as the outline of their final contract for exploration and development drilling. Then arrangements would be made to hold a formal contract signing.

It was then that the assistant minister, chunky little pock-faced Dong, appeared to come awake from his set, staring position. He stood up, and walked briskly to the head of the table.

"It is requested that we adjourn for a private review and discussion of this information before we continue. We may return to discuss our position at two this afternoon."

It was an abrupt statement, and it was presumptuous of Dong to supersede his boss, the minister, in advising of the temporary adjournment.

The schedule alteration was meekly agreed upon by Ho Bac Minh. As they departed together, Bill invited Tim McAllister and Andy to accompany him to take Moe and George to lunch. It appeared that the energy minister had been hurried away by Dong Huan Chou for their own private discussion, to the insulting exclusion of their oil company president. Who knew what monkey wrench Dong was cooking up to brighten their afternoon? Something would be sure to slow their agreement. Andy wondered if the move by Dong had been arranged by his boss, who might be using him as a pawn to cover his own directions. That could explain Dong's abrupt and unexpected action.

They had a pleasant luncheon in a nearby restaurant. Moe indicated that he was pleased with the work they had accomplished, and he would recommend they make only minor changes to the blocks that they had requested. He wished to keep some of the selected areas for bidding by other companies, who would be buying their seismic coverage, as well as for Viet Oil's own future drilling.

This had been expected, and Andy had agreed with Bill Hanby earlier that any one company could adequately explore only a few areas at a time. Therefore, if they could hang on to four of the requested eight blocks, their efforts could be considered a success. They had brought back a broad authority for such selections from their Houston management.

When their meeting resumed, Andy made a quick review of the map presentation. He then requested the Vietnamese agreement with the World Oil recommendations.

Dong was on his feet again quickly, and stalked back to the head of the table immediately.

"We do not agree with the selections that you have outlined. You have obviously selected only the areas where oil is expected to be found, leaving the 'pasture' for us to try to sell to the many other companies who are daily knocking at our door with offers to spend large sums for an opportunity to press on with their own exploration." Dong raised his voice, for he was speaking with vehemence.

"We are making the selections in accordance with the agreements outlined in our contract," replied Andy. "Our expenditure of money has already earned us the right to make these selections." Andy tried to keep his voice low.

Dong pounded the table with his fist while holding his glasses on with the other hand.

"The contract says that you will accept blocks selected after the preliminary work is completed. Not that you will try to take only the parts of interest to you, leaving us with the dregs."

Dong made no pretense to hold his voice in check, and his actions had caused him to perspire excessively.

"If we are not to select areas based on the results of our studies, there would have been no reason for our large expenditures in doing the surveys," Andy replied quietly.

"But you are leaving us nothing to sell to other bidders! You intend to get all of the production and leave the remainder of the pasture for us to try to sell, with no carrot to put on our stick!" Dong's voice was still at a high level, and he was beginning to pace the floor.

"That is not yet known to be the case," Andy replied. "It is well known in the oil industry that maps made from first seismic coverage are often misleading, because their data are not tied directly to geology, or to wells drilled in the immediate area. That early drilling leads to step-outs in the directions that geological interpretations show will find oil in subsequent wells."

"When, and if, you drill in these blocks, you will not give other companies the information from such well logs," Dong stated.

"That is very true, for we'll spend many millions of dollars getting that information. We cannot be expected to give it away for free. Later, however, we reserve the right to trade the data with others for information on wells that they have drilled. Such exchanges will be of assistance to both our interpretations. We are required to furnish all data to the Vietnamese State Oil Company, but it would be most unethical for them to pass it on to our competitors," Andy reminded him.

Dong then carefully dug into his silvery aluminum briefcase and brought out a small block map, which he laid out on the table. It had obviously been quickly marked by hand, and probably was the result of his lunch-break meeting with the minister, or some phone call to the NLF leaders who certainly were his mentors. It showed outlines of four blocks, none of which coincided with the selections of World Oil.

"Here is our recommendation for blocks to be accepted by World Oil for drilling development, in accordance with our contract." Dong stated his position with finality as he flung the map into the center of the table.

Andy wondered what his authority was to speak for the government. He noted that the minister said nothing at Dong's presentation.

"That selection is yours alone, and is not in accordance with our contract," Andy stated.

He looked to Bill Hanby and to their legal representative, Eric Goff.

"We are entitled to eight blocks by our contract, not four. We have the right to select the blocks in which we will continue the expenditure of money for drilling exploration," Andy answered with some force, still trying not to raise his voice an octave.

Dong turned to Kong Van Dieu, their legal representative, and said, "Explain the contract to them, Kong!" His voice had turned nasty with venom.

"Wait!" interrupted the minister. "I'm sure they have their interpretation of the signed agreement. Let us see if some compromise is not in order."

There was a deathly silence in the room. It had suddenly become apparent that Dong did not speak for all of the government, for Ho Bac Minh still held the power.

"What compromise would you suggest?" Bill Hanby stepped into the conversation, since it was the minister speaking.

"Perhaps we could agree to cut the number of blocks to six," said Ho Bac Minh. "They are all fairly large areas, and would each give room to locate many structures."

"One moment please, Minister." Bill drew Andy aside for a private discussion.

"Do you think that's the best we can do, Andy?" Bill asked.

"Yes, I think that was the minister's fallback position. Now we see who really has been instigating the objections to our operations. It's that little fat bastard, Dong. Ho Bac Minh has just had to put up with him."

"I agree. OK then, I'll accept his proposal."

They returned to the table.

"Very well, Minister Minh. If you allow us to select the six blocks, that would be agreeable," answered Hanby. Andy nodded his assent.

"I think it would be more fair to all concerned if you selected three for yourselves, and we selected three for you from those remaining within your original eight," the minister stated. "That would give you six blocks, three of which were your own picks. We would then be left with something we have selected, which we would be able to sell to other oil companies for their exploration."

The minister obviously intended that to be the final word.

"Very well," Hanby replied. "Let the minutes of this meeting show that we will present you with our selected three blocks, and you will follow by awarding us those three blocks plus three that you select, all to be from the eight that we originally outlined on these maps."

It was a cumbersome statement, but it got all the facts together. There was relief in the air, as James and Andy gathered and folded their maps to fit into their cases. All the while, Dong sat absolutely still, staring toward Andy. He was obviously brooding about his loss of control over the blocks, and his loss of face before the group. His grip over the minister of energy had been severely tested, and he had lost.

When the table was cleared of maps, everyone settled back into his chair, seeming to realize there were orders of business that were not quite complete. A hush fell over the group.

"There is one other point I wish to bring up," stated the minister in a quiet voice. "We are still hopeful that your government will come to their senses, and cancel their illegal embargo against American firms operating in Vietnam. We would welcome other American company investments. There are only a few more months remaining until we no longer will reserve areas on which American companies can bid for exploration."

He surveyed the table, looking from Hanby to the legalists, Dieu and Goff.

"Have you considered how you will proceed if the requested dispensation of your government is not awarded?"

There had been no love developed for Americans by his government since the war. Many of their ministers had been summarily fired just for showing inclinations to attempt to deal directly and honestly with Americans, or even for showing too much friendship. Their country's need for commerce and development of trade, however, was too great to ignore.

"They will have to give up their data!" responded Dong quickly, seeing another chance to get control of the areas for themselves.

The minister silenced Dong with a small wave of his hand. He had come right to the point of World Oil's problem. Andy noted that Dong almost smiled; he was so delighted with the thought of all the data having to be turned over to them without any cost. He knew as well that Dong must deeply regret that the original data on the tapes would be safely stored away in their air-conditioned vaults in Singapore until the contract was officially signed. Only then would they be accessible to their government. World Oil's control of those tapes was a critical point.

"We have carefully considered what to do in case such a dispensation is not forthcoming," Hanby replied. "Our contingency plan is that, in accordance with our agreements, we would form a separate non-American corporation, not a part of World Oil, but owned by foreign money belonging to World Oil. The new company would be an independent international corporation, not under the control of World Oil. Such an arrangement is within our right by contract. World Oil has specifically retained the right to assign this contract to whomever we wish."

As he spoke, he looked to the legal rep, Eric Goff, who was nodding his firm agreement.

"And where would you get personnel to run such a corporation?" asked the minister.

"It would have a new name, and its Board of Directors would be former employees of World Oil. I would be the chairman of its Board, and Doctor Cheston would be the president of the company. Mr. Tim McAllister would be the director in charge of financial and office management. The name would be the 'VietAmer Oil Corporation,' with its principal office in Hong Kong.

Dong Huan Chou scraped the floor with his chair as he rose and stalked noisily out of the room, carrying his silvery case with him.

# Nineteen

"Come along, Hillary," Beth called. "Let's sample some of the wine they're serving for breakfast here in the garden wing restaurant of this famed Shangri-la Hotel."

This trip was strictly a vacation for Hillary Halstead, for he had never visited in Singapore before, nor anywhere in the Far East. Elizabeth Halstead had been so impressed by the Oriental scenery and mystique on her excursion through Tokyo with the Rogers that she had influenced her husband to take time off from his grape cultivation and wine making, and tour the South China Sea countries.

Beth had arranged their schedule, and she planned to make Singapore their base. Then they would fly out to Bali for a weekend, and up to Bangkok for a restful stay in the resort town of Pattaya Beach. She wanted Hillary to see and enjoy the scenic hotel there, overlooking the Gulf of Thailand.

"Don't rush me," Hillary answered. "I haven't gotten over the jet lag yet. I feel like I need to sleep some more, but I guess I can do it by the pool later. The trouble is, I'm awake all night."

They were content in their garden-wing suite at the hotel off Orchard Road. They could step out of their suite directly into a lovely Japanese-style garden, and cross an arched bridge over the lily pond with its gorgeous golden carp. Then they'd stroll into the covered patio restaurant beside the giant swimming pool.

Beth was starved, as it had been a long flight and she never did like airline food, even in first class. Breakfast was a range of choices. They could have wonderful fruits, such as fresh, ripe pineapple and golden papaya, or luscious pink mangoes with waffles or eggs, while lounging luxuriously amid the exotic flowers. It was all too heavenly and restful, hence the fitting name.

She knew the other scenery was appreciated by Hillary, for the huge swimming pool was surrounded by umbrella-covered deck and lounge chairs, all occupied by lovely brown-skinned ladies. Husbands are a sorry lot, she remembered Dagwood saying. Apparently, most of the Oriental men stayed out of the sun, but the women loved it. The other thing she noticed was the number of small children chasing their beach balls amid the recliners.

"The ladies are much taller and less round-faced here than I've been led to believe. Education is a great equalizer," Hillary stated.

"Who knows what they've been educated in?" Beth replied.

"Have all of these women had their eyes doctored?" he asked. "I don't see many with the slants I'd expected. Do the Chinese eyes slant up and the Japanese eyes slant down?" he asked jokingly.

"Hmmmm!" Beth replied, looking away. She really didn't want to talk about Oriental women. In the back of her own mind, she was still trying to decide why she had insisted on this trip. Did she need to get close to Andy again? Maybe her mind wouldn't let her be at ease until she had made peace with his lady love. She could still vividly remember the sting of her hand and the white residue from when she slapped her. ESP between twins is a strong emotion.

"Someday you'll have to tell me what you have against yellow-skinned beauties," Hillary remarked. "Some of them really are quite beautiful—and besides, they're not yellow; they're just tanned," he continued.

"It all depends on your point of view, I suppose. I have learned if we stay with our own class of people, then you won't be hurt by snide remarks behind your back about the company you keep. So there." She was mentally torturing herself.

"You wouldn't call yourself a bigot, would you? Don't forget—over half the people on earth live in areas where yellow skin is very acceptable. Besides, everyone else here has it; and I'll bet they refer to us Yankees as 'whities,' " Hillary said, as he tried to avoid an obvious craning of his neck to watch the two browned lovelies as they strolled past their table.

Beth replied, "I must admit, I gained a much healthier respect for some of their ladies after my tour of the Far East with the Rogers. They are much more reserved than the people we meet at home. You have to give them credit; they're a lot more selective of their company than we could ever be, even in our restricted clubs. Theirs are all one color, and only visitors are crossing their color lines. They pay more strict attention to family ties, where we have to have laws to keep our color lines open."

"That's true, I suppose," Hillary answered. "Their society is more reserved than ours, all by custom. We meet their ladies only through introductions by their family men. The exceptions are the ones we see in movies, and on which we form our opinions. We have heard nasty things about their women all our lives, like the stories about the girlfriends of occupation soldiers, whom they thought were geishas; and accounts from the Korean veterans who took R and R where the girls were pretty loose."

"That's all we had to go on, but perhaps we were too gullible," Beth said.

"They all had stories to tell about the 'geishas,' which have turned out to be 'tales about tails.' One fellow I knew came back telling all the boys in the locker room that, where our streetcars run 'north and south,' theirs all run 'east and west.' "

"Shame on you, Hil, for bringing that barn talk home." Beth was teasing him, for she was no prude. "Nobody'd really believe such a thing."

"Nobody with any intelligence, but that doesn't include half of the world's people. Really, a geisha is a companion and entertainer, and not always a bedroom decoration. Our education along Oriental lines has been sadly missing, caused by our lack of communication. But they are the ones who didn't want to get involved with us. Admiral Perry changed all that back in the 1850s when he sailed into Tokyo Bay and presented the emperor with a treaty."

"Did he accept?"

"Not immediately. He had to return the following year to get the agreement in writing. After then, we started speaking to each other, but only from afar. The men who work in our shops and vineyards at home are a good class of people, and they have the same ancestors as these folks." Hillary rambled on, "I think I could learn to like the way they live here, for their higher class have a respect for one another not seen among people in the U. S. of A."

He was gazing out across the colorful parasol umbrellas around the pool.

"And there's just something about those little brown bodies that is intriguing," Hillary added.

"Stop it!" Beth was smiling. "I may have to take you straight to the room and put soap in your eyes."

"Remember what I've told you. One of my eyes never did get married."

Hillary grinned, and went on with his brunch.

"You never did tell me what happened between you and Andy when you were visiting in Tokyo with the Rogers. Didn't he and Valarie get along? They sure seemed to be OK in Sausalito, but I guess that was mostly her doing."

"I suppose I might as well tell you, although I've been too ashamed of myself since then to bring it out in the open." Beth was looking sad.

"Do tell me all. It's high time I took your confession, and then you'll feel better—or I'll feel worse. I've always imagined that a priest who hears confessions all day must take on the problems of his parishioners. If he did, though, he'd never be able to carry the load."

"I was made so mad one night at a fancy-dress party in Tokyo that I actually slapped Andy's Oriental lady friend hard. She was my own twin brother's date!"

Beth stopped, turned red, and didn't move, waiting to see what her husband would say. When he only stared, open-mouthed, she went on.

"There, I've told you. It's finally said, and now I feel more like talking about it. I'm sorry I still feel the same way about their relationship, I guess, but maybe not so strongly. At that time, I had decided to arrange Andy's life for him, and I thought Valarie would make the ideal mate for an oil executive. She and her family thought so, too, but I'm beginning to realize now that both of us failed to consult Andy about it."

"Why would you do a thing like that?" Hillary finally asked, disbelief showing on his face. "I know you'd never act that way normally. You've never even slapped me."

"Because I was so mad. We were at an important party in the Okura in Tokyo. It was a gathering of Jacob Rogers' business associates, and instead of coming with us as Valarie's date, Andy and his friend, James, brought their Oriental girlfriends in their fancy, dress-up kimonos. At first I thought they came along in native dress just as a special effect, and to impress the American visitors."

"Didn't they?"

"They certainly didn't. I found out at the party that was not even close. The Japanese private secretary of Andy's boss, Chisai, told Valarie when they were alone at the table that this girl was living with Andy every weekend when his roommate was away—which was often."

"But how did you find that out?" Hillary was having trouble keeping all the characters, none of whom he knew, straight. He needed a program.

"Valarie rushed straight into the ladies' room where I was talking to Jill Hanby. Jill was sitting next to Lin Jin Hoe, Andy's girlfriend. She came right to me and blurted it all out. When she told me, I just saw red. It was more than I could take, so I just stood up and slapped her, and it was not a gentle tap, because I really meant it. It sent her right across the dressing table in front of Jill Hanby."

"Did she slap you back?"

"No; she remained very ladylike, and did nothing. I suppose she was too shocked. That's not what I'd have done under the circumstances, but then she must really be a lady. Then I stormed out, immediately, and Valarie followed. We went to my room, where I cried for hours. We never did see Andy again on that trip. He probably will never speak to me, because I've heard that his girlfriend, Lin Jin, left the party and went home with her grandfather. To make it all worse, a week later she left Tokyo, still without seeing Andy, and moved in with her mother in Hong Kong."

"You seem to know a lot about what happened later. How'd you find out?"

"I got the information by writing a letter of apology to Jill Hanby, and she is a good friend to Andy. She wrote back, attempting to soothe the waters."

"I can see why Andy might be a little upset with you. Has he gotten back together with the girl?"

"I don't know any more than I've told you. But now that I can talk about it, the time is right that I make an attempt to see Andy again. Now you know why I insisted we fly directly to Singapore, and not stop in Tokyo. I couldn't face him, or Jill Hanby."

"It's time you got over that, it's true. Perhaps you should make an apology to him. Have you thought of that?"

"I'd be awfully embarrassed, but I suppose. . . . I know you're right. I did write to him, and halfway offered for us to get back in contact with each other. After all, he is my twin brother. When we get inside, Hillary, I'll try to call him in Tokyo. I just wish he'd let me do his social calendar for him. I wouldn't get it as screwed up as he has. Of course, he may have more fun doing it for himself."

"He has been a big boy for quite a long time. Perhaps he likes to pick out his own streetcar line." Hillary grinned.

Beth did not reply, but after a few moments' consideration, she did give in to a sly little smile.

"How'd my best girl like to go out to dinner this evening for some real American food? We might even find a good French wine, although I'm sure it won't compare with our bodega. I know where there is a place in the Mandarin Hotel on Orchard Road where you can get good steaks. A friend told me to be sure and try it while were here. It's the Saint George's Grill, up on their third floor. If you go there often enough and run up big enough tabs, they'll put your own plate up in the foyer, with your name imprinted in gold. How about it?"

"That sounds good to me. First, let's go for a little tour out to see Sentosa Island. We can ride the cable car out, and come back in time to get in a little sun before the cocktail hour. After all, we're on vacation."

\* \* \*

"Just look at that shopping center, Hillary. It must be ten stories high!" said Beth. "We'll have to get down here tomorrow and go all through it, provided my feet can stand the walking."

They were cruising down the one-way Orchard Road, en route to dinner.

"It's handy here to the Mandarin," said Hillary, as their taxi was pulling into the driveway. "We're a little early for our reservation, but I want to show you something. The top floor here is a bar and lounge, and it goes around once an hour so you can have a moving view of all of Singapore."

"That sounds like fun. I should have brought the camera."

"A friend back in San Francisco showed me a picture he made here, all taped together. He set the camera on the table and snapped it every five minutes for an hour. The results were truly spectacular."

"Could you see all the way to Malaysia?" asked Beth.

"Well, you could see where Malaysia is. But we can see for ourselves. We got here in short order, since it's one-way in the right direction. It'll take longer going back if there isn't a similar road returning, and I hear there isn't. You can't get there from here," Hillary said, his directions a bit confused by all the curved streets.

They were escorted through the glass doors by the sharply uniformed Indian Gurka Guard, and soon found themselves exiting the elevator into a dimly lit cocktail lounge, twenty-six floors up. The bar was set up only two tables deep, which seemed to continue forever. It did, when you realized you were looking at the side of a giant circle, with window glass on one side and reflecting mirrors on the other. They were escorted to a table by the window, and were warned by the waitress that Beth should not put her purse on the window side of the booth, or it would slowly drift away as their booth turned.

Their drinks were ordered, and they were busy trying to recognize where their own hotel was situated, and what else they might see from this height that would be familiar to them. The scene was fantastic. It was just like a fairyland, with all the lights coming on at dusk. There was the old airport, and the old Raffles, and all the ships at anchor.

Suddenly there came a voice from the center hall of the circle.

"Elizabeth! Hillary Halstead! What are you doing here in Singapore?"

It was James Wellman, and he was coming out of the elevator with another gentleman.

They stepped off the stable central platform and came straight to their table. He gave Beth a hug and a kiss on both cheeks, and then shook Hillary's hand firmly. Then he turned and introduced his friend.

"Beth and Hillary Halstead, this is Dennis Dugan, Eastern Geophysical's Singapore processing manager. We just finished our day's work on the Vietnam data, and came up here to rest our weary bones and regain our sanity. It is quite a surprise to meet you two here in Singapore. We're all a long way from home—except for Dennis. He lives here."

"We're here on vacation, and just came up to view the scenery," Hillary said. "We'd heard it is spectacular, and we're not disappointed."

"Are you staying here?" asked James. "My room's over in the other wing, and I've been here a week."

"No; we got into town yesterday, and came to try their food, since it had a good recommendation. We're staying in the Shangri-la," Hillary answered.

"That's really first class," Dennis Dugan said. "We put our directors there when they come to visit."

"It's really quite nice," said Beth. "We have a place in the garden wing, so we don't have to wait for the elevators."

"What brings you to Singapore? Are you going to be here long?" James asked.

"No, we will finish Beth's shopping and my money, then we're off to Bali for the weekend," replied Hillary, smiling.

"That'll be a great trip. Bali is always a lot of fun, and so interesting to Americans. You'll have never seen anything like it." The conversations came to an abrupt halt. They were each waiting to see who would mention Andy first.

"I met your brother in Saigon a couple of months ago," said Dennis, stepping into the breach where angels fear.

"Oh, I didn't know if you knew him. He's my twin, you know," said Elizabeth.

"Yes, James told me he was a twin. It must be nice, having someone closely in touch with your most intimate thoughts. At least, that's what I've heard. Have you seen him on this trip?"

It was the thousand-dollar question everyone else had avoided.

"No. We didn't come through Tokyo," Hillary answered.

He stepped into the conversation because he could tell that Beth was busy thinking.

"He's spending most of his time in Hong Kong and Saigon now, isn't he, James?" Dennis did not know he was acting the Devil's advocate, but his comment was welcomed by all.

"We still have our apartment in Tokyo, but we are both away now most of the time," James replied.

"That's probably why I couldn't reach him this afternoon there. I put through a call, and got no answer from his office, nor from your apartment," said Elizabeth, letting James know she really had tried hard to contact him.

"You could probably reach him at our new office in Hong Kong. He spends most of his time between there and Saigon. I'll give you the phone number, and his hotel phone number there as well. Then you'll have a better chance of contacting him."

She knew James was trying to make it easy for her. He must know they had not been in touch since the Tokyo incident. It was not natural for twins to be mad for so long a period. Perhaps Jill Hanby had told him about her letter. They continued discussing the company's efforts in the area, carefully avoiding any reference to Tokyo.

Beth finally poked Hillary with an elbow and quietly urged him to invite the men to join them for dinner downstairs. She knew after working together all day they would enjoy some fresh company, and she knew also that it would be good for her and Hillary to have someone different to talk to. He had now already heard all of her intimate stories.

James and Dennis were delighted to accept their invitation for dinner at the Saint George down on the lower floor, and Hillary enjoyed one of the best steaks he'd had since Sausalito. Elizabeth surprised even herself by ordering the steak tartare. That you do only in a restaurant where you trust the chef, and this one had impressed her. She was not disappointed.

After thanking James for Andy's phone numbers, and receiving their gratitude for the excellent dinner, they left the two men, and went for a long walk. Back at their hotel, she convinced Hillary to take her into the Shangri-la's local disco. It was on the main floor, and the music almost reached out into the lobby and pulled people in. The dancing was just what she had expected, but their mode of dress was entirely different. It was really flashy, and mostly cowboy—just like at the Houston clubs.

She almost asked Hillary to take her back to their room so she could change into something slim, slinky, and split to the thigh. But after all, she was a married woman, out on the town with her own man. She didn't have to impress anyone, but all of those Oriental girls really did impress her. Were they just imitating Westerners, or were they going them one better? Sausalito had some things to learn, even if here they did love imported American country-western music. It was a little startling to see round faces and slanting eyes under cowboy hats, and with fancy boots showing under their jeans.

When they returned to their room, it was a little after midnight. Now, thought Beth, would be a good time to contact Andy. Surely he would be in his room by this hour. She prepared herself for bed, and tried to compose her thoughts. Really she must talk to him, for she knew what she had done was wrong. She must admit her error, and apologize. It would be hard for her to do, but easier on the phone than face to face. Also, she had an excuse to call, since they were in the area and had just met James—and were only a couple of hours away by jet.

After placing the call, she could hear the phone ringing. It took forever before anyone answered.

"Hello," said the sleepy-sounding voice. "Who is calling?"

"Andy, is that you? It's Beth. Did I awaken you?"

"Beth! Is it really you? Are you at home? Is anything wrong?"

Suddenly Andy was alert and sitting up in his bed.

"Yes, it's me, and no, I'm not at home. Everything is fine. I just saw some friends of yours. Hillary and I had dinner with James and Dennis Dugan at the Mandarin in Singapore, so I wanted to call."

She got it all out in one sentence.

"It's so good to hear your voice, Beth. Have you been all right? I've tried to write you, but somehow I've been awfully busy. What are you doing in Singapore?" Andy spoke excitedly, no longer sounding sleepy.

"I know just how it is, Andy. Me too."

There was an awkward silence.

"Really, Andy, dear, I called to tell you how sorry I am about what happened in Tokyo. I didn't mean to mess up your life. I was just too dead set on making arrangements that made sense to me, but I hadn't stopped to consider your wishes."

Great tears ran down Beth's cheeks.

"I guess we'll live through it, and I've tried to contact you, but you've been in hiding," Andy replied sadly.

"Can you forgive me? I didn't trust myself to talk to you before. I haven't had the nerve to call you until today, and that's because I finally explained to Hillary what really happened. He made me see how wrong I've been. I'm so sorry, Andy dear."

It was a very nice apology, and one that Andy could tell she meant from her heart. It was one he had longed to hear.

"Beth, I could never be mad at you for very long. I have been feeling awful about this situation. It wouldn't have bothered me had my intentions toward Lin Jin not been serious, as I told you that night."

"Has she been in touch with you yet?"

"Yes, in fact, we have met, and she is speaking to me again—now and then—but she still is not too happy. She blames herself for coming between you and me, and with her ethical views, that's not acceptable. I've seen her a few times, and I met her mother, with whom she and Kim are living here in Hong Kong."

"I want to see you, Andy, and her. I owe her my deepest apology, which must be made in person. I hope someday she will see me—but it may take a while for me to get the nerve."

"I think I'd wait a while, but I'll tell her. The mills of the gods, you know. It will make her very happy just to know you want to talk to her, I think."

"Please do tell her. Do you spend a lot of time in Saigon now?"

"Yes, everything is coming to a head at once. I have really been awfully busy. I don't know if you've heard that our government denied World Oil permission to operate as a U.S. corporation in Vietnam. Our only recourse has been to form a new private corporation, using money not controlled in the United States."

"How can you do that? What is the new company?"

"The name is VietAmer Oil Corporation, and Hanby is the Chairman of the Board. I'm the president, and am presently setting up an office here in Hong Kong."

"Andy, that's wonderful—I think! But don't you work for World Oil anymore?"

"I'm not sure. We have a sort of gentlemen's agreement. They loan us the money to operate, and we report to them if we make any return on their investment. It's a rather loose arrangement for the moment. But we definitely are not a U.S. company. We can prove we don't work for World Oil too, so we're on our own in spite of our close ties. We lease out a lot of their technicians to do our fieldwork."

"I don't know if I like that or not. Do you still have a U.S. passport?" Beth ask in a worried voice.

"This has nothing to do with citizenship. It only refers to business contracts."

"When do you start drilling for oil? Isn't that what it's all about? You've been working on this project for over a year now."

"That's the point, exactly. We are getting the drillship in position now, which takes a lot of surveying. We still have some paperwork to iron out with the Viets as well. They're a little difficult to deal with, since some of them don't like Americans too well. We dropped too many bombs on them. I spend half of my time there putting out paper fire, and most of the other half in Tokyo getting Hanby's signature on documents."

"Andy, I want to see you. Also, I'd like to tell Lin Jin Hoe that I am sorry I slapped her. I didn't understand how much she meant to you at the time. Is she there?"

Beth realized too late that she might get a surprising answer, should Lin Jin really be right there. She had only meant in Hong Kong.

"Lin Jin lives here with her mother and her brother, Kim, who works in our office. She is in town, I suppose, and she works full-time in her grandfather's local shipbuilding office. Lin Jin is speaking to me, but not too happily. She still worries a lot about family ties, and does not wish to come between you and me. Such relationships mean a lot to Orientals."

"Can you make it to Singapore during the next two weeks? Hillary and I want to see you. Our plans are set to go to Bali for the weekend, then to Bangkok and Pattaya Beach. We'll see you at the airport in Hong Kong if nothing else. Otherwise, our reservations are all set. We'll be through there on the Singapore Air flight to Tokyo at mid-afternoon."

Beth was thinking how they could change their schedules.

"I'm afraid that would be impossible for me, because there are too many meetings already arranged that can't be changed. I may even be on the drillship then. I'll have to take a rain check, but I'll try to kiss you at the airport as you pass through Hong Kong. Look for me, and if at all possible, I'll be there."

"Bring Lin Jin if you can. I won't rest easily until I've talked directly to her."

"I'll try. Convince Hillary that you both must come back to visit me in my new home office here in a few months, after we get all this paperwork put to rest. I'd love to have you stay with me, and maybe by then we can get our personal affairs straightened out."

"We'll look for you. And Andy, I love you—twin."

Andy hesitated, but the twin ESP was working.

"There is still some personal business I must attend to, related to Harold Blanton's death. When that's done, I plan to take some time off for myself," he explained to Beth, without saying exactly what he was planning.

It was the first time he had mentioned his intentions related to Blanton's demise to anyone, especially to Beth. He thought she should at least have an idea that he had certain obligations that must be fulfilled if he was ever to live with himself afterward. One never knew what the outcome of such an adventure might be, so he wanted to be at peace in his mind with the person closest to him in this life. In his own mind, he knew what he had to do.

"All right, darling. You do what you have to do, but don't be foolish, please. And be extremely careful if you have to do anything dangerous. We'll look for you at the airport as we pass through, and will try to return soon on a visit to Hong Kong. Please tell Lin Jin I want to meet with her, and perhaps then things will be different. We love you, and I'm sorry to get you up so late. Bye!"

"Good-bye, dear Beth. I'll look for you if I can, but will see you when you come to visit VietAmer in Hong Kong."

When Beth hung up the phone, her tears had run down into the mouthpiece.

Hillary rolled over and smiled, and said, "Good girl!"

# Twenty

Andy had thought twice before he invited Pug Cox to accompany him to Vietnam. He just might be too tough and, oh, not so gentle to the Vietnamese when they got there. He had not been to Ho Chi Minh City before, and had asked to be taken along so he could meet the "chinks" who ran the office there of the Vietnam State Oil Company. He said he wanted to get to know some of the people he was supposed to be working with.

Andy realized when you spend your life drilling offshore, you associate mainly with your own office and with the drillship's crew, so he deserved an introduction to the shore operation. It was a chance to wash some of the salt out of his hair, and to know a new part of the world he worked in. After all, he had cut his teeth in Korea.

Pug had spent enough days at sea living with their multinational crews and with World Oil's own company geologists. All he'd been shown about the nationals who worked for exploration was that they were busy examining the washed-up samples pushed out by the drill bit. Aboard ship, the individual crews were a tightly knit group who worked like well-oiled machines. Every shift of the twenty-four-hour, round-the-clock operation had its job to do, and nobody was allowed to shirk his duties.

The drilling superintendent doesn't usually get to meet the people who actually own the rights to the property being explored. Andy wanted Pug to have a chance to see some of those people, for drilling off the Mekong Delta was just like drilling in the Gulf of Mexico, once the helicopter lands you on the drillship's helipad. All ocean water looks alike, most of the time. It was just wet, sometimes more wavy than others and not to be used for drinking.

It would be a challenge for Andy to keep the worldly-wise drilling superintendent from insulting the local oilers, for tact was not his strong suit. He thought it best to also bring along their office man, Kim Hoe. He could smooth their way by speaking the language with the Viets, and it would also keep them from talking behind their backs.

Pug was still single, and had lived a life overseas for the last twenty years, always on expenses. His bank account must be beautiful, for he never had to pay for anything on his own account, except vacations and to buy his one suit for weddings and funerals. His paychecks were sent straight to his bank in Corpus Christi, uncashed. The other side of the coin was that he had no place to call his home, and few family members to visit when he left the drilling rig for a leave between wells. He was a travel agent's dream. Andy was beginning to feel sorry for such people.

Fortunately, Pug was an amiable fellow with those he liked, and the company's expatriate families often invited him to dinner when he came ashore. He enjoyed playing with their kids on his days off, and kept them amused with his inept magic tricks. Pug liked girls in pictures, but he was deathly afraid of live ones—unless they were others' wives. Then he felt safe, and they got along just fine, for while ashore he was a friend to everyone.

When out with his men, though, he was different. It was as if he changed his stripes like a chameleon when he left the office and family groups. On the rig, he barged headfirst into the land of the deckhands and roustabouts. To him, the tough seamen lived in the real world. When he visited the working locations there, Andy appreciated having him along.

The employees of VietAmer Oil no longer had the privilege of calling for the use of the company-owned jet. They either had to arrange their schedules according to the airlines, or charter a plane. Andy regarded renting a plane as the more dangerous of their choices, because he couldn't control their operations closely enough, and guard their safety as he'd like. That lack of safety control could be too dangerous when you had enemies in high places, as had been proven too clearly.

He had arranged through Kelly Johnson, already on the scene for a week checking out information, to have a car and driver waiting for them when they arrived at the airport. Getting through customs proved to be no big problem, after they finally were able to sort out their luggage. The sullen customs officers did have a second look at Kim's British passport, but since he was with VietAmer Oil it was like being a diplomat, and they passed him without a serious review.

Andy would get along with only a carry-on bag as Pug and Kim had done, except that he needed proper clothing to make a presidential appearance at their meetings. He had to carry his briefcase and a tube of maps in hand. Those he would not let out of his sight, for they were not so easily replaced as were his shirts and shorts. His locker in their office was beginning to contain changes of clothing he had left on previous visits.

It was late afternoon by the time the trio arrived at the Majestic Hotel. There they met Kelly in the bar as planned, and spent the evening going over the presentations for the following day. It was to be a morning gathering of explorationists at the office of President Nguyen Muoi of Vietnam State Oil, and the afternoon would be spent at the energy minister's conference.

Maps showing where they were locating the drillship had already been forwarded to them, and now VietAmer Oil simply wished to review the data and explain their reasons for selecting this particular location for their initial drilling site. It was important to everyone concerned that they discover significant hydrocarbons early in their exploration venture. For Andy, they had to justify their expenditures to their bankers, and for the Viets, they needed to sell the adjacent blocks to other companies.

George was at the door when they arrived, just on schedule, at 9 A.M. in their conference room. After the introductions of the newcomers, Pug and Kim, to George and his director of exploration, Dr. Bien Giap, and geologist Thieu Long, the group had found their seats informally, leaving the head of the table vacant for Nguyen Muoi, or Moe, as he requested to be called.

Andy and George remained quietly seated while Kim and Pug talked to the staff about their recently concluded efforts of securing supplies and properly surveying the sea bottom location for the drillship's positioning at their first location. They had already been in communication by fax to obtain the necessary onshore benchmark coordinates for proper surveying reference, and to check out their ties to the satellite references. Nothing was ever simple in such an expensive and exacting operation.

When President Nguyen Muoi entered, there was a flurry of greetings and introductions before the meeting came to a kind of informal order. Andy presented his maps and sections with a serious demeanor, showing where their seismic surveys had indicated the drillship should be located. He briefly explained why they thought this would be the best site for a first exploratory well, for it was on a structure that had an excellent possibility of containing oil. He expressed their sincere hope to start their operations out with a discovery.

Kelly continued the presentation with a description of their arrangements to get the sea-bottom surveys completed; the information furnished the ship's captain with information to achieve the proper positioning of his vessel over the desired wellsite.

Pug Cox took over then, and explained how the anchors would be placed, and how the moorings would keep the ship at the proper location above the stationary sea-bottom wellhead. He explained the safety precautions built into the operation, such as blowout preventers also located on the sea bottom, and quick-release mechanisms in case there was a disaster such as a typhoon, and the ship needed to escape.

He spent some time going through the simple laws of physics that dictated ships float on water. As long as their computers kept the correct tension on the anchor cables, the ship would remain directly above the sea-bottom wellhead. Then drilling could proceed.

Pug went on to explain that when troubles occur, such as a gas blowout, they must be able to shut off the blowout preventers on the sea bottom in time, or a disaster of major proportions would occur. He then cited several examples of blowouts that had actually happened, and he was there!

He continued to explain that the problems resulted from the fact that when gas escapes into the water on which the drillship is floating, its specific gravity changes until suddenly it will no longer support the ship. With nothing holding it up, the ship falls in on the drillstem, down toward the wellhead hundreds of feet below the level of the sea. The ship is much heavier than the gas bubbles, which quickly replace the water. Men don't breathe water or escaping gas, either—and live. Andy noted his little example had made a stark impression on his audience.

It was a sinister and gruesome picture Pug painted, and he sounded like he knew from experience that it could happen very easily to any drillship-mounted rig, and especially possible in an untested structural basin. There was no previous experience to indicate when such a gas blowout might be encountered. That's why the control of operations was always in the hands of alert drillers and geologists who constantly watched for indications of increasing pressure.

Pug spent some time going over the safety aspects of such drilling. He was a specialist at this, because he had personally been through the experiences of almost everything bad that could happen to a rig on a drillship at sea, and survived. His discussion was mostly directed toward their stock of safety equipment aboard the ship as they prepared in advance for such disasters, and how blowouts could then be controlled.

When their technical discussions were over, having talked about the geology and the plans for drilling, Kim Hoe explained the communications setup by which they planned to keep their office informed of the progress. Directions for continuation of the operations, day or night, would be relayed directly to the drillship by monitoring their radios. In that way, it was not always necessary for their entire geological staff to live aboard the ship in order to keep abreast of drilling developments.

That is when Muoi spoke up for the first time.

"The office of the energy minister had advised me that all such instructions relating to the drilling operations will be required to be relayed through his office. No communications will be allowed to go directly to the ship without prior clearance. Our communications officer will relay all message data to them as you wish, but no direct transmissions will be permitted."

It was a positive statement that obviously had been prepared in advance, and there was apparently no room for discussion. The Viet officials had definitely decided.

After his pronouncement, the meeting continued for a short time as they talked about how such information could be sent by radio or fax. Andy knew it was useless to object. They broke up amiably to go to lunch, and Andy invited the group to accompany them to a nearby restaurant. There they could have a large table, and order plenty of rice dishes. It was unusual, but President Muoi, also, accepted Andy's invitation to eat with his staff. Usually their men of position steered clear of any gathering that could be considered fraternizing with Americans. It could be political suicide for them.

Andy counted—there were eight of them, so he would order eight different dishes, and then pass them around to everyone, as their custom had developed. He'd probably better order an extra fried rice and prawns, because that's what he and Kelly liked best.

Pug ignored the little hot cup of tea that was served, and, after a glance at Andy, personally ordered beer for the entire group. It came as a surprise to Andy that Pug was able to handle his chopsticks like a veteran. He had already demonstrated his own ability while dining with Kelly on their many previous trips to this same big table. It was difficult to dine out alone in Saigon. Their food lent itself to group meals, and Saigon had not seemed to have retained a source of hamburgers, French fries, and pizza.

Their afternoon meeting was much more formal, and they were seated around the energy minister's large conference table. Again there were introductions on their arrival, and the only people different at the table from the morning conference were the minister himself, Ho Bac Minh, and his chubby, pock-faced assistant, Dong. He was still wearing his dark glasses, like a security blanket, for he was never seen without them, day or night. And his acne was acting up as usual.

Before their presentation began, Dong called a page girl over to his side and whispered an instruction to her. After a short delay, a small man entered the room dressed in a baba, and found a chair at the far end of the table. He looked embarrassed, and was then introduced as Tri Mang. It became clear later that he was to be the chief of communications.

Their presentation continued much the same as it had gone that morning. Andy pronounced his introductory remarks, and made the display of the maps showing the wellsite selection. Kelly followed by describing the sea-bottom surveys, and then Pug Cox showed them how the anchors would be positioned.

At that point, Nguyen Muoi broke in, and requested that Pug Cox repeat the science lesson he had given them that morning. He wanted the energy minister to hear his description of what could occur in the event of a serious blowout with escaping gas. The word-picture Pug had created of the drillship and men sinking to the bottom, even though sea level was hundreds of feet above, had greatly impressed him. Ho Bac Minh and Dong Huan Chou listened intently to the same tales of possible disaster, and seemed deeply impressed by Cox's harrowing experiences.

When Kim rose to tell them about the ship-to-shore communications, the minister interrupted for the first time.

"You are Kim Jin Hoe. Aren't you the grandson of Li Hong Hoe, the shipbuilder?"

He had spoken in Vietnamese.

"Yes sir; my mother is his daughter by a previous marriage. He left Vietnam during the French occupation after my grandmother died, and began to build ships in Japan. He is now married to a Japanese lady, and lives in Tokyo," Kim stated.

For his reply, Kim had also slipped into his native tongue without realizing he had done so.

"He has prospered well there. His Japanese connections are well known, as are his shipyards throughout Indochina and elsewhere. Where were you born?"

It was a simple question, but in this state of police control, one of great importance.

"I was born in this country, sir," Kim replied uncertainly. "My mother left Saigon with my sister and me before the war and established our British citizenship in Hong Kong."

Kim did not mention that he had returned to attend the Catholic School, and he seemed to be clearly worried about such direct questioning by one in authority. Andy did not understand the words, but he realized their significance from reading Kim's face. He was beginning to wonder if he had been wise in bringing Kim back to the country of his birth.

Andy broke in, "We are using Kim as our communications specialist because of his education and his language ability. We need Vietnamese nationals in our office organization who speak your language fluently, for in the future we must hire many of your personnel in our field development and training programs."

"That is true," Minh replied thoughtfully.

"It makes our operations run smoothly, and we thereby have a much better feeling for the coordination of our joint efforts."

He could think of no other pertinent remarks that would divert the minister's attention from Kim's ancestry.

"There is a problem with the manner in which you have set up your lines of communication for operations. Dong Huan Chou has advised me that it is in our interest to examine all directives to the control of your offshore drillship. In that manner, we will be certain that your company is complying with all of our contracted requirements."

It was the same kind of statement that Muoi had pronounced this morning. Apparently, there was no choice but to obey their edict.

"That will be satisfactory," replied Andy, "if we can be assured our orders will be passed accurately and promptly. We must ask for your assurance that there will be no changes, corrections, or delays in communications, for often the loss of even a little time is important, from a safety standpoint as well as concerning added expense."

"I can agree to that," Minh said.

"Then our legal representatives will draw up an agreement reflecting this expansion of the meaning of our contract, and submit it for your signature."

Andy wanted to make his position clear, and in writing, so they would have no later misunderstanding.

"We do not need to alter the contract, for we already have the authority to monitor your activities," Dong retorted brashly, breaking into the conversation.

"Such a clarification may not be necessary, but it may be in order. Send the document to our legal representative, Kong Van Dieu," said Minister Ho Bac Minh.

Again he had cut his assistant short in front of foreigners. Was he playing with fire? Dong had proven himself to be a mean enemy, and again he had lost face. Now Andy was sure that Dong was the NLF's watchdog over the minister's office, and over the VietAmer operations.

What devilment would he arrange next to stop their drilling progress? Andy knew they must be prepared for anything.

# Twenty-one

"I'm getting tired of this café, Kim. Perhaps you can tell them something to get them to spice up their menu," Andy said to Kim as they found their seats around their preferred table at the Vietnamese restaurant near their office in the Majestic Hotel.

"Please let me order today, and perhaps you will enjoy a different entrée," Kim replied.

"I can go for that," Kelly added. "Be my guest."

"Just bring on the beer and the fried rice, and I'll be happy," Pug told him.

The visiting VietAmer explorers had returned to their office after the meeting, then had gone nearby to eat. They were completing another dinner with chopsticks in their handy restaurant when the president's assistant, George, and his director of exploration, Dr. Bien Giap, entered the restaurant. Obviously looking for the explorers, they headed directly for their table. It was a shock for Andy, because fraternization was not the usual Vietnamese cup of tea.

In fact, he was well aware that it may not even be safe for the technicians to initiate such informal associations. The least that could happen would be the loss of their jobs. Therefore, they must feel secure in their reasons to initiate such a visit. They must have been directed by some higher authority, or they would be risking reeducation.

George led his fellow explorer directly to the big round table, and immediately Andy invited them to sit down and join them in finishing the wine. They were delighted to do so, as unaccustomed as they were to imported French wines, and all Vietnamese, except the very rich, look like they need a good meal. Unfortunately, it was true.

"I was greatly interested in the drilling technology you described, Mr. Cox," he began. "Doctor Giap and I would appreciate hearing more about the operations of a drillship, and how it is kept on location so close to the exact spot above the wellhead at the sea bottom to keep from breaking the drillstem—or, as you called it, the marine riser. It surely is not easy while floating in a running sea, hundreds of feet above."

Now it was becoming clearer to Andy. They had come to learn more about how such technical operations were conducted. Where better to find out the details of the drilling technology than from an expert who had been duly recognized by their energy minister. It must have been their assignment for the evening. They had to strike while they had knowledgeable people available, and could corner them for questioning, privately. They had few such opportunities to speak to engineers with Pug's experience. Certainly, it would do them no good to ask anything from the Russians of the Vietsovpetro company.

"Just call me Pug, I'll be happy to tell you all I can about offshore drilling," Cox replied.

Well, thought Andy, Pug Cox is an authority, and he can fill them in on all the war stories of the entire South China Sea, but it'll take more than one session.

Their conversations ran on for two hours, and Pug fielded a steady stream of questions from the two Vietnamese geologists. They had some understanding of offshore operations, but just enough to get themselves into trouble. Still, they knew basic facts to stimulate a lot of intelligent discourse. Pug's drilling stories were of great interest to them, and they loved to hear his colorfully descriptive anecdotes. They seemed to understand his roughly worded field language better than book learning. Finally, the restaurant was closing and they had emptied another wine bottle, so it was time for the group to leave.

As they said their good-byes to the two visitors, Pug Cox drew George aside and invited him and Giap to go with him to a nearby club for a nightcap. It was again a surprise to Andy when they readily accepted. Apparently, they had not had enough of the drilling tales. The rest of the VietAmer group turned and walked off toward the Majestic.

Kelly spoke to Andy when they were out of the hearing range of the visitors.

"I've been having some interesting conversations this week with Lan Thang Nguyen. He also has possession of the gift for you, which was surreptitiously arranged by his half-brother, Li Hong Hoe."

"Since we are leaving Saigon soon, we'd better go and see them now. Would they expect us this late at night?"

"Yes, I told Lan Thang that you would be here to confer with the energy minister, and that we'd be coming to visit them and to discuss what he had heard from his gold-market sources, as soon as your schedule would permit."

"This would be good timing then. Kim, how would you like to accompany us to visit your great-uncle, and your cousin, Nhung Thi?"

"That would be good, Doctor Cheston," Kim answered with boyish enthusiasm. "I haven't seen my cousin since we attended the same school with Lin-san, and left Saigon when I was a child. I was hoping there would be a chance for me to visit their home on this trip, but I did not want to interfere with company business. Just in case, I brought along a gift for her and for my uncle. But I left them in the hotel," Kim stated apologetically, for he was a conscientious worker.

"Let's pass by the hotel first, then," Andy decided. "I want to pick up some presents I brought for Nhung Thi also."

Fifteen minutes later, Kelly was guiding Andy and Kim down several back streets on a circuitous route toward the gold market. It was late enough for the streets to be nearly deserted, and only an occasional scooter passed them. The mist had settled in, making the sparse streetlamps glisten in their aura. The steel lampposts held up a netting of telephone wires, creating an eerie, web-like canopy for them to walk under. Most of the windows along the narrow alley-like streets were shuttered tightly, with only an occasional crack of dim light showing.

When they arrived at the Nguyen's door, they again performed what had become almost a ritual—the tapping and the waiting. Their window was shuttered tightly too, and soon a thin crack of light showed there. This time, the wait was not so long, for apparently they were expected. Nhung Thi did not have to leave and get dressed, for she soon opened the door a crack. Andy saw her peer through the slit, and she quickly ushered them inside. Lam Thang was already seated in his chair across the floor from the shuttered window, and had apparently been sleeping, arms folded, in the dark.

The room was now dimly lit by a single shaded bulb. The old gentleman sat up, rustling his paper that lay across his lap, now dark, but beneath an ancient gooseneck lamp. His magnifying glass had fallen to the floor. When the three of them were ushered into the room by Nhung Thi, she suddenly screamed. She had recognized her long-lost cousin.

"Kim-san!" she cried. "How did you get here?"

"Thanks to Doctor Cheston, he brought me."

She clasped him tightly around the neck in a loving embrace.

"I didn't believe we would ever be able to see you again. How you have grown since you were a little lad."

Great tears were streaming down colorless cheeks from her almond eyes, as she was overjoyed.

"Nhung Thi, it is so good to see you. It has been many years, but I remember you well."

"You look wonderful—I still can't believe it." Nhung Thi was trembling, almost unable to speak from her surprise.

"We used to have great times playing and studying together with Lin Jin. And I bring greetings from her, and from my mother, Thi Lan. She, too, would like to visit here someday, if it becomes possible."

Kim's eyes were filled with tears as well, and it was plain that he was deeply moved.

"How are you able to come here? Are you not afraid, even with your passport?" she asked, holding her hands tightly around his arms.

"No, it should be no problem for me. I am in the employ of the VietAmer Oil Corporation, and now I am working in their office in Hong Kong," Kim replied with a great grin.

"You work for Angi-san?" Nhung Thi asked, pronouncing Andy's name with a lisp.

"Yes, it is a good arrangement for me. I help with their communications, and watch after Doctor Cheston's office interests and management, especially the Vietnamese translations."

"Are you living with Auntie Thi Lan? And where is Lin Jin?"

The questions flowed in a steady stream.

Kim released his embrace of his cousin, finally, and crossed the small room to shake the trembling hands of Lam Thang Nguyen. He was unable to get up easily, and had remained seated in his big chair, reveling in the joy expressed by his children. It made it difficult for Kim to embrace him, but he leaned down and gently kissed his old great-uncle on both cheeks.

"I have brought regards to you from Mother Thi Lan, and from Lin Jin," he said gently.

The men engaged in a short conversation to bring Andy up to date on rumors and facts that were available concerning the activities of the terrorist, Dong. They were told of the NLF's apparent connection with pirate vessels, and how some of their boat raids had been successful in the recent era. Nhung Thi busied herself with lighting a small stove to heat water for the little cups of strong tea.

The visitors then each produced packages of sugar and other comestibles that they had carried past the customs on their persons, without detection. It was a common practice, and overlooked by the officials if they could find a few packets of cigarettes purposefully left for them to confiscate.

"Since our office was burned, we have moved our local communications center to a rented room on the top of the hotel, where we have applied for a radio permit. If that ever comes through, we will be able to operate more efficiently. For now, we are required to send our messages by commercial means, or by private courier," Andy explained to Lam Thang.

"I heard rumors about the fire in your former office, and how it was intended to stop your progress. Also, I have been told who actually set it. Such information would be ignored by the police. It was a deed by the NLF, intended to burn your original maps, and thereby slow your progress."

"We were fortunate to have had our data in the hotel with us. For once we outguessed those ba . . . rascals," Andy stated.

"You were fortunate not to have been there yourselves. I was happy to see that apparently it did not delay your efforts. How did that occur?"

"I'm not sure," replied Andy. "James Wellman had a premonition, I guess, and took the data along so we could leave the hotel and directly head for our company jet at the airport on the next morning. Kelly and I were followed when we left here, I guess. Apparently, it will be impossible to keep an office in Saigon where we can conduct any serious work. Our technicians work better, anyway, where they can live comfortably—and safely."

"No one stays in Saigon now who is able to leave," Lam Thang stated sadly.

"Besides, few people here will rent to us now. We had to coerce the hotel into giving us a permanent room by threatening to move our business elsewhere. Commerce is the root of good works, as well as all evil."

"Yes, and the NLF wishes to retain any oil profits that are developed for themselves, one way or another. If you once get into production and the money flows to the government, they know it will seriously diminish their influence. That worries them greatly. But that is the best hope for our people."

Lam Thang was looking off into space, and dreaming. Then the old man fumbled slowly beneath his paper, and his weak hands reached under his chair.

"I have this package for you, which was arranged by Li Hong Hoe. It is the gun your director, Doctor Hanby, requested be furnished for your use here. It is a thirty-eight, with appropriate ammunition. I would not wish to be in front of it if it were ever used, for it would be nasty."

Apparently, Lam Thang had some experience with weapons.

"Thank you very much, sir. I appreciate your obtaining this for me. Perhaps it will never be needed, but someone thinks we are not welcome here in Vietnam, and we must be prepared to protect our interests."

"Will you leave the weapon here?" Lam Thang asked.

"I don't think that would be wise. If you were caught with a gun, they would send you back to a reeducation camp, never to be released. We will not allow that to happen."

Andy was vehement in his pronouncement.

"It is best. Where will you keep it?"

"I'll store the pistol in my personal gear in our office at the hotel, and our local agent can see that no one tampers with my locker there, unless it is needed."

When the quiet whistle began to blow, Nhung Thi handled the boiling pot, and tea was served. A general family discussion ensued. Nhung Thi wanted Kim to tell her everything about his mother and about Lin Jin. Finally, she asked Andy when he had last seen her cousin, his lady friend. She knew something had happened between them, or Lin Jin would not have moved away from Tokyo. Andy's later move to Hong Kong must have also affected their associations. She politely did not ask directly if they were seeing one another on dates again.

"You must know," Andy said, "how I feel about Lin Jin."

He felt he owed these people an explanation, for they were risking much in continuing their association.

"She and my twin sister had a confrontation when Beth was visiting in Tokyo. Beth had come with a lady friend from California to be my date, and she did not think it acceptable for me to be escorting Lin Jin. She made it clear to her that my dating an Oriental woman did not allow me to fit into her society in San Francisco. Lin Jin was deeply insulted, and that's why she left Tokyo so suddenly."

This was shocking news to Nhung Thi, who had covered her face with her hands.

"Angi-san, I am sorry. Has your sister had any change of heart toward Lin-san?" she asked quietly, as the pale face reappeared.

"I saw her recently. When she and her husband were vacationing in Singapore, they returned and met me at the Hong Kong airport. She is learning about the people of the Orient, but she has not totally forgiven me as yet. That fact is keeping a cloud between Lin-san and me. We love each other, but she will not come to me freely now because she maintains great respect for my sister's wishes," Andy admitted openly.

He had never spoken so plainly in front of Kim and Kelly before, but he was not embarrassed by the truth.

"Time does not heal all wounds, but many can be put far away. If you wait, the sun always comes again," the old man stated wisely. After a long pause, he continued, "I will keep listening and monitor the rumors of the gold market here in Saigon for news of Dong's activities, but there is probably little more I can learn. The dog has already hidden his bone."

"Don't get yourself involved in dangerous affairs any more deeply, and unnecessarily," cautioned Andy. "The leaders of the NLF already have your name near the top of their bloody records, and if it suits their interest, they will not hesitate to attack you."

"I am no longer afraid. What more can they do to me? We know Dong picked up the gold bar at the bank and paid off his henchmen who were hired in Hong Kong through a maintenance group working at the Saigon airport. When they came to collect for their terrorist deed, they were met when leaving with the gold, and were destroyed in a fire fight by robbers."

"Where was Dong at that moment?" Kelly asked.

"He must have been inside, and ran out when he heard the gunfire. What happened to the gold ingot is not known, but knowledgeable rumor is that it was not finally taken by the robbers, or the gold marketeers here would know. They apparently drove their armed truck away from the scene of the fight and fire without carrying their loot."

"How do we know that?" Kelly asked.

"Because the gold did not appear in the marketplace. If that is true, then the gold must have been retrieved by someone else. Dong and Tan Tran were the closest ones there still alive. Dong has not deposited the gold, nor returned it to the coffers of the NLF! He must be extremely worried, wondering if the NLF set up the robbery just to steal their gold back, in which case he would soon be eliminated. I have not been able to determine if the NLF suspects him," Lam Thang stated.

"Does he have anyone still living at his lair who would know what actually occurred?" Kelly asked.

"If he hid it, then he must have a secret place at his estate. The only one who would know that is his yeoman, Tan Tran. He has many connections outside of his duties with the books of Dong, but he operates quietly and is very secretive. Yet he could not have taken the gold, or Dong would know. The girl, Vu Thi, did not obtain her position there as Dong's personal servant accidentally. She is a distant cousin of Tan, and she learned her trade after the American soldiers came to the streets of Saigon," the ancient stated slowly.

"It seems there are many family relations involved," Andy said.

"Yes, and there is more—much more," replied Lam Thang. "Vu Thi is a past friend of granddaughter Nhung Thi, for they knew one another slightly when both were in school. Vu Thi is more educated than the average street girl of Saigon, and she knows well that her future is better served away from the clubs and off the street."

Turning to Nhung Thi, Andy asked, "Have you been in contact with Vu Thi since the terrorist action?"

"No, Angi-san, I have not," she replied with her Oriental lisp. "I would not know where to find her outside of their compound, and I hear she rarely leaves. But I will try to contact her carefully."

"Have the police found out anything about the arsonist who burned our office?" Andy asked.

"No," Lam Thang replied, "but that is as expected. They have no intention of discovering too much about the despicable deeds perpetrated by the henchmen of the NLF. They like their jobs too well."

"If you have no more words to tell, Papa-san, I wish to show Kim-san my collection of pictures relating to our childhood. They are in my scrapbook, upstairs in my room, if you wouldn't mind climbing the steps. You may come too, Angi-san, if you'd like to see how Lin-san looked as a young girl in school. Even then it was clear she would become a lovely lady." Nhung Thi led the way, and Andy followed with her cousin, Kim.

They left Kelly to keep the old gentleman company, and talk about their possible future contacts. Andy could hear them talking as the trio passed down the narrow upstairs hallway toward the bedroom. Kelly was examining the pistol, and loading it. It was obvious from the clicks, whose echoes carried throughout the dimly lit apartment space.

Andy knew they were discussing the possibilities of getting Dong to admit that he alone had planned the bombing of their plane, and how there must still exist some bit of evidence to tie him directly to the dirty deed. Unfortunately, it all may have sunk with the shreds of the plane. The only other place to look now would have to be at the location where the payoff was made. There had been enough dastardly acts that night to fill a book, but only a new gate and a damaged wall were the visible evidence remaining.

Kim and Andy had been gone several minutes, when suddenly there was a rippling of a shutter and a crash of a window. It was followed by the rattle of a grenade rolling across the floor. There was no time to move as the blinding flash lit up the bedroom, and a giant roaring concussion came up from the room below. Metal fragments bit into the flesh of Lam Thang Nguyen and Kelly Johnson, spreading their blood across the floor. Lam

Thang slumped across the arm of his chair, dying.

Andy and Kim ran downstairs and burst back into the room, followed by a screaming Nhung Thi. He heard two quick shots fired just outside, and then Kelly came staggering back through the front door. They found Lam Thang slumping out of his chair onto the floor. When Andy straightened him back up, it was already apparent that he was beyond any help they could give. Nhung Thi was hugging his head to her breast, and getting blood all over her clothing. She didn't care, for he was her grandfather.

Lam Thang gave a gasp, and made one last desperate effort. He pulled the ear of Nhung Thi close to his mouth, and whispered to her in Vietnamese. The only thing Andy caught were the words "Thi Lan" and "French." Then, sadly, Nhung Thi's principal reason for living was dead.

She kept repeating "I love you Pak" in Vietnamese.

Kim was doing his best to console her, but nothing now would help, for he was beyond reeducation at last. Nhung Thi was sobbing loudly in her grief, and Kim wept silently.

Kelly was luckier than Lam Thang, for he had one piece of metal lodged deeply into his thigh and another in his left shoulder. He told Andy he had heard a squeak at the window and started to investigate. The grenade had come crashing past his head. He had not hesitated, for his training as an investigator told him where their attacker must be. Grasping the pistol in his good hand, he struggled through the door in spite of his wounds. There, scurrying down the alleyway, went a figure dressed in a white baba.

Kelly had raised the pistol and fired. The figure lurched, but kept running. He fired again, but his arm was so tired, and that time he missed entirely. By then the small figure had turned the corner and disappeared from view. Kelly explained that he was in no condition to give chase, so he had turned back into the room to see what destruction the grenade had caused.

It was a horrendous mess. Andy knew it was useless to try to follow the attacker, for he was too long gone. He covered the body of the old man with his quilt, as Kim led Nhung Thi away. Andy helped Kelly lie out flat on the floor, and attempted to stop the flow of blood from his wounds.

"My arm is aching, and I'm losing too much blood—I may pass out," Kelly said weakly.

The burst of exercise to get outside had done him no good, Andy knew. The thigh wound was most serious, for it looked deep, and he found a belt to place a tourniquet on that first. Then he padded the shoulder.

"Just lay quietly, and we'll get some help," Andy told him.

He tucked the gun in his belt and found the extra bullets, which he stowed in his pocket.

"Kim, see if you can take Nhung Thi to find a neighbor, where she can stay safely. Then find a phone and call an ambulance. Kelly must get some treatment right away."

Andy knew there was little use in having anyone call the police. He tended to Kelly's wounds with the tourniquet as best he could, and waited for help to arrive. Kelly could barely speak and was sometimes incoherent, for he had lost a lot of blood.

"I think I hit the baba boy with my first shot," he whispered, as he lay on the floor. "I saw him lurch," Kelly said weakly, during one of his periods of coherence.

"Just be quiet and rest," Andy told him as he tried to prop his head up with a pillow.

"The second shot missed. I couldn't hold the damn gun up. He was around the corner so fast."

Kelly was acting as if he were very tired, but Andy couldn't keep him quiet.

"I'll get you to a hospital soon, and we don't need to worry about moving Lam Thang—he's long gone." Andy was trying to think of some comforting words.

"I figured as much. He was right on top of the explosion." Kelly was talking more and more quietly.

"Don't say anything else; I'll take care of you. Just rest," Andy directed. "When I can find a light of some kind I'll look outside to see if there's any indication of blood on the street. Then we'll know how well the terrorist has been marked for later identification, the bastard."

Kelly groaned, and closed his eyes.

"When we get you in a hospital, I'll charter a plane to take you back to Hong Kong, and get you proper care." Kelly was not hearing him, for he had passed out from the loss of blood. He guessed he'd have a funeral to attend tomorrow, Andy thought. He was glad to have Kim along to carry out the conversations, and to interpret for him, but if he didn't hurry, he might have two funerals. Now what will Nhung Thi do for a place to live? Andy realized he was talking to himself. It's a good thing Pug hadn't come along, for he would have been in the room with them and he'd have both of them to doctor, or probably worse.

\* \* \*

Kim had kept his head and acted calmly. He had deposited his cousin, Nhung Thi, with a neighbor and found a phone. It took a full half hour for an ambulance to arrive, and in the meantime, Kim had called the hotel and found Pug Cox. It took a little time to explain how to get there, but Pug still arrived just before the ambulance. He was puffing, and must have run all the way, and still smelled like a brewery.

It was just as well it took some time, for Andy knew there was nothing he could do except tend to the tourniquet regularly. He kept pressing the padding on Kelly's shoulder wound. By the time the ambulance arrived, Kim had also returned. He explained that he would stay with the old man's body while they accompanied Kelly to the hospital. Andy agreed that was best, for someone needed to stay and keep the house and look after arrangements in the interest of Nhung Thi.

A stretcher was brought in, but Pug lifted Kelly up gingerly, as if he were a feather, and carried him carefully through the door and into the ambulance, to place him on their bed. At the hospital, they were met by a doctor who seemed to know very well how to tend to such wounds. He was an older, gray-haired man, and had obviously had plenty of practice.

Seeing that there was nothing he could do immediately, Andy asked Pug to stay at the hospital while he returned to their office in the hotel to make some arrangements. On arrival there, he put in a call to Hanby's apartment in Tokyo. The connection took forever, but finally the call went through after he assured the operator several times that it was a dire emergency.

"Hello, Bill. It's Andy. I'm happy to catch you at home, and sorry about the hour."

There was no way Andy could break the news to him gently that he had gotten one of the company's trusted friends killed, and one of his employees injured.

"Hi, Andy. It's rather late for a call, so it must be serious. What has happened?"

"We were visiting our friend, Lam Thang Nguyen, and caught a grenade through the window. It killed the old man outright, and injured Kelly pretty bad. We have him at the hospital now, and I don't know how serious it's going to turn out. The doctors are with him, and Pug Cox is watching. They seem to think he will pull through, although he has passed out from the loss of blood. I left Kim at the Nguyen apartment to take care of the family."

"Damn! Those sons of bitches are going to have to be taken care of. Where were you? Are you all right?"

"Yes, I'm fine, and so is Kim. We had just gone upstairs when the grenade went off. I'm in the office now. Pug Cox wasn't with us at the time, fortunately. Nhung Thi had taken her cousin, Kim, and me upstairs to look at her picture album when it happened. Luckily, we'd left the room a minute before, or there'd have been a bunch of us down."

"I'd say you were lucky. It could have killed all of you very easily. They must have really been after you personally, Andy. I've been worried about them following you there."

"I think that's what they intended, for someone certainly followed us there. Also, they could have blown up Lam Thang's room anytime if they'd just wanted him."

"They certainly intended to get you and your crew to delay the location of the drillship. The NLF just won't give up, will they? How'd your meeting with the minister go?"

"Not as well as I would have liked. They insist on us relaying all of our communications with the rig through them. That'll slow us up some, but we can stand it, I guess. Dong was pretty upset in the meeting when his boss reversed his decision and agreed to having our lawyers write up the new agreement covering communications. That may be why he acted tonight. He's lost too much face lately."

"That is certain to make him act brashly."

"Yes, we're going to have to do something. Just attacking him is not enough. We will need to go after proof, and that means a raid of his stronghold."

"You can do that anytime—if you can stay alive long enough. Right now we have too many irons in the fire with the drilling, so it's better if we can wait and see what else develops, and if we can stir up some help from their government."

"Help from them isn't likely, but you're right. Now isn't the best time."

"You seem to have everything in hand. I'm really sorry this has happened. Lam Thang was a real friend of World Oil. Express my deep sympathy to his granddaughter. And we can't afford to lose Kelly, so do all you can to get him back on his feet. Is there anything I can do to help you?" Bill asked thoughtfully.

"Just keeping Kelly alive is my objective right now. Could we borrow your company jet for a couple of days? I'll have a funeral to attend tomorrow, I guess. Then, if Kelly is in any shape to travel, I'd like to transport him to a hospital in Hong Kong. He'd get better care there, I believe, if it wouldn't hurt to move him."

"That'll be no problem from this end. I'll arrange for the plane to be there the day after tomorrow at about midday, and you can schedule it on from there. Maybe all of your operations should be conducted by fax. It'd be safer."

"No thank you, because there are some things I need to be here to take care of. I have some plans that have to be worked out back in the Hong Kong office, but I'm returning to Saigon very soon. I'm going to have a meeting with a certain bastard here, which is long overdue."

# Twenty-two

It was hazy over the South China Sea. The big helicopter had been airborne for about an hour, and the only thing Andy had been able to see was the glare off the water through a few miles of haze. He hadn't seen any boats on the sea since they left the fishermen near the Vietnam shore, and now they were over 100 miles at sea. He felt a little sick to his stomach from the constant roar of the engine and the incessant rocking vibration caused by the rotor. The pilot nudged him, and didn't try to speak above the noise. He just pointed. There it was—the drillship with its anchors set, and the supply ship about a mile away, swinging on its own anchor.

There was no one on the helipad when the big chopper circled, then sat down there, bringing Andy and the replacement well-site geologists to the drillship. It wasn't that they weren't expected. The rule was that, for safety reasons, nobody went on the landing deck unnecessarily when a helicopter was operating.

As soon as the group climbed down the ladder and hustled themselves with their gear into the gangway, they were greeted by the giant drilling superintendent, Pug Cox. His big hands were like hams, and he grasped the hand of each man as he entered. Andy knew enough to grab him firmly, or his fingers could be cut by the ring he wore.

The noise was deafening, and Andy reeled a little as he struggled down the gangway. As soon as they were inside it became obvious that it was not the copter he heard, but the constant roar and the terrible vibration caused by the ship's drilling engines.

As they reached the gangway, Andy tried to speak to Pug and then realized you only spoke aboard ship when communication was absolutely necessary; and then it was at a shout. Pug hustled them all into his office and quickly closed the door. That helped some, but the ever-persistent roar of the engines pervaded everything they did, and everything they tried to say. It was definitely not a place to hold any discussion.

"Did you have any trouble finding the ship?" Pug asked in his abnormally loud voice. "Our location is not exactly marked on the maps. It's kept secret from the pirates, you know." He grinned, hoping he was joking.

"None at all," Andy replied. "The pilot told me visibility is pretty good today, for this area. Besides, you're the only thing out here."

"It's good to see you here on schedule. You must have made a good connection after your jet landed. Some of the boys are getting pretty edgy for their delayed mail. How's Kelly gettin' along with that red-headed nurse?"

Pug had spent a lot of time with Kelly in the hospital in Hong Kong before the drillship was ready to spud this first location.

"He seems to be doing well," Andy answered. "He sends his regards. The doc says he should get out of the hospital in a couple of weeks. He won't be going for any bicycle rides, though. He's lucky just to be alive."

"How's young Kim? Is he gettin' all our messages straight after they go through Saigon? I don't trust those sons of bitches to relay everything straight—especially since we know they stuck their noses in just for spite."

Andy noted that Pug had developed a certain respect for the boy's office capabilities while he worked in Hong Kong before the drillship arrived. Now he depended on him to run his errands ashore, because he wouldn't be going ashore himself and leave his ship until they finished the first well.

"He stays on top of them, it seems. At least they won't be putting any Viet language past him. It's good to have him with us, and I'm glad you broke him in well," Andy replied. "Now tell us about the important things. I heard you got the casing set. How deep are you?"

"Right! It's well cemented, and we're back in the hole, drillin' out." He leaned over his desk to pull out a chart and pored over it. "We're at fifty-eight hundred feet—a few minutes ago."

"That means you've drilled out early. Was it any trouble?"

"Not a bit. We set the surface casing and the blowout preventers with the sea bottom wellhead last week. When we had the first string set, we started back into the hole at two this morning. We've been turnin' to the right like clockwork ever since." Pug grinned, a little proud of their good progress.

"At this rate, you'll be down to a horizon we can recognize any time now. Wally Brooks picked this casing point to be sure we could recognize the marker. Once these offshore operations get started, they sure don't take long."

It was a statement, and not a question.

"No!" Pug replied. "They'd better not, at the rate the company is paying for this rig. We've gotta make every minute count."

"That's so very true," Andy replied. "Let's be sure we don't get delayed from lack of supplies on hand. Do they have the right sizes of casing and bits stored where it's available?"

"They have enough right onboard here, and the rest is stored off there on the supply tender. It's anchored a mile away, and can be brought over if we need anything, like mud or more pipe. Otherwise, the little stuff, like bits and little tools, can be brought over by workboat, provided the seas aren't too high."

"Are your weather reports coming in regularly? This is the season, so we don't want to get shocked by any typhoons sneaking in," Andy reminded him.

"That's no problem. One thing I do wonder about, though, is the visitor we had yesterday."

"What kind of visitor?" Andy quickly asked, for that got his attention.

"It was some type of speedboat. They ran a circle around us and the supply tender," Pug replied.

"Was it a PT boat of the Vietnamese Navy?"

"It was that size and it flew a Viet flag, but it wasn't marked like a Navy ship. In fact, it was pretty dirty. It had a lot of rust, and drums were stacked on the back deck behind the pilothouse. I didn't see any guns."

"Did you hail them?"

"We tried, but they didn't answer—probably didn't speak English."

"What do you think they wanted?"

"I suppose they were just looking us over, but this is pirate territory. Our protection is not really that good if we have to depend on the Viet Navy. I'm sure the U.S. Navy doesn't cruise their territorial waters too closely any more, since Tonkin," Pug mused.

"You wouldn't be too easy for pirates to raid here on the drillship, since you have to come aboard from any boat seventy feet below the deck by using the sling hoist. The supply tender, though, is another matter. They could be boarded by anyone coming alongside. What protection do they have, other than a couple of burp guns?"

Andy was clearly worried about the men on the tender, because he had heard of too many ships being boarded by pirates in the South China Sea's waters. One thing in their favor was that there was little of value to the pirates aboard a tender that they could steal. If they carried off the mud and steel, they'd have to find a market for it to be of any value. They could sure make a mess of the men, though.

"They've operated in the South China Sea before, and they came equipped. They have a twenty-millimeter cannon mounted both fore and aft. That would make any normal pirate boat think twice. The pirates usually just go after easy prey, such as the boat people's gold," Pug stated.

"Let's hope they know that. I'd hate for our contractors to shoot up a Viet patrol boat just coming alongside for a social visit," Andy stated.

"Just in case, I arranged a little surprise for anyone trying anything, short of torpedoes, before the supply tender left Singapore. I had them put a couple of toys onboard, especially for me, and had them labeled 'drill bits.' Then when the supply vessel arrived, I had them brought over here and stowed where they are handy, next to the helipad."

Pug was being very careful about what he admitted to his boss. Andy knew he hadn't received prior approval. Now Pug seemed to be a little ashamed, but he apparently wanted Andy to know what he had done.

"I see you have your old forty-five hangin' there, but that wouldn't do much good against pirates with automatic weapons. Come on now," Andy asked smiling, "what else have you stowed away that would be for the protection of an entire ship?"

"I may not have been in the action in Vietnam, but I did see a lot of service in Korea. I learned to lay down quite a nice fire pattern, just using a bazooka. And these new bazookas are a lot better than the ones I cut my teeth on," Pug stated proudly.

"Where did you get new bazookas? Do you think two of those might deter invaders?" Andy had a worried look, but then, he wasn't the one out here with so little protection. Secretly, he was glad to hear Pug had a backup plan.

"I just ordered them out of the catalog," he lied. "They were called core barrels and fishing jaws."

Pug was serious in telling his secret to Andy, and not yet sure how he had taken the news.

"Those wouldn't deter a warship, but the South China Sea pirates aren't that sophisticated. They operate with speedboats and machine guns. Anything bigger than that can be caught in the Viet Navy's nets, if they're of a mind to." Pug was still shouting, because he wanted Andy to know his actual status.

"You old Marines will try anything," Andy said. "How are you going to get the pirate boats to hold still for you, or let you get close enough to use a bazooka?"

"I haven't worked all of that out yet, but I figure we have a supply boat on station here, tied up down below by the moon pool. If there's any trouble, we'd launch that as a bit of honey to attract any pirate speedboat. Then, when they'd get close enough, we'd pop up and let 'em have it—right in their gas tanks." Pug grinned, knowing he was being a bit dramatic.

"It might work. At least it would be better than just sitting in the radio room and yelling 'SOS.' Be careful you don't shoot yourself in the foot."

Andy wasn't so sure, and he wasn't smiling. He knew, however, that Pug was a responsible supervisor, and he was the one who had to stay out here and deal with whatever came.

"It's too bad we can't keep a real Marine helicopter gunship here on deck."

"I think we'll protect ourselves OK. How long are you going to stay with us? Can I tell the pilot he can go as soon as he's loaded?"

Pug was picking up his phone.

"That depends. When is your next crew change from Saigon arriving?" Andy asked.

"It should be out here tomorrow afternoon. If you'd like to stay, we'll send a crewman on in today, and save you a seat on tomorrow's run."

"Yeah, let's do that. I'd like to take a ride over to the tender and see how that's set up. While I'm hanging around here, you might just drill into something interesting. I want to spend some time looking over the samples, too. Maybe Wally Brooks will teach me something," Andy answered in a yell.

Pug called on the phone and gave the directions for the crew change and for the pilot to continue his flight. Then he called again.

"Ace, tell the supply boat we'd like to make a run over to the tender, and call the tender and see if we need to bring anything more than the mail when we come."

He hung up the phone, and turned to Andy.

"Are you sure you want to get yourself dirty goin' over to that scuzzy supply tender? It really is a filthy mess, because handling all that pipe and mud doesn't encourage very neat housekeeping."

Pug looked with disdain at the sport shirt and freshly pressed slacks Andy was wearing.

"Maybe you can find me a pair of coveralls. Then I can lean on the rails if I need to," he answered.

Andy's borrowed coveralls were too short, but they covered a good part of him. When he had completed his gear with a rain slicker, they left the relative quiet of the cabin, and made their way onto the drill floor. Pug checked the registers to see how drilling was progressing, and noted the pressures the driller was carrying. Then they went down a deck and checked the weight of the mud they were using, and read the clipboard that told of any changes that had occurred during the past shift.

The noise was a roar, and the mud pits were an organized mess of large pipes and chocolate-colored vats. It looked like they were getting ready to bake a giant cake. At the end of their dark-brown, flowing rivulets were chips of samples being washed out on the shale shaker. An hour before, those had been buried 5,000 feet below for the previous 50,000,000 years, at least.

A small round-faced Chinese boy was busily placing the cuttings in small white bags, while a second man was more carefully labeling their exact depths. These were the raw data the geologist would study through microscopes, looking for recognizable paleo bugs that would define the age of the deposition.

Down another deck, and they were just above the waterline a few feet. There was the moon pool. It was a hole through the bottom of the giant drillship, extending all the way up through the substructure to where the drilling floor blocked their upward view. Above the floor was the derrick, and at the top, the crown block holding up the kelly and the drillstem. If they didn't hold up on the thousands of feet of heavy pipe, its weight alone would stick the bit. Then, without circulation of the mud, there could be no drilling.

Down from the drill floor plunged a square kelly attached to the drillstem. It reached through the moon pool and into the dark water for the sea bottom, always "turning to the right" to keep the drilling supervisor happy with their downward progress.

It was a strange, overpowering feeling of tremendous uncontrollable forces at work, and an eerie sight as well. Here was the culmination of effort being expended by the entire mass of machinery whirring above and all around them. Looking downward into the moon pool, instead of seeing the black water, they saw the infiltration of sunlight entering below the sides of the ship. It made the water in the hole a light green. With the drillstem turning there, it could only be described as an exciting and beautiful feeling. Andy had never tired of seeing such a sight.

Back on the upper deck, the supply boat was already alongside, and the hoist was rigged to carry them downward to be deposited on the deck. It turned out to be a fairly large speedboat, for the supplies it hauled often consisted of forty-foot sections of drillstem, and tons of drilling chemicals and mud. The two of them were quickly lifted off the deck, clinging inside a rope-net basket. They were swung out over the sea and set roughly aboard the bobbing craft.

As their supply boat left for the tender, they waved to the pilot of the helicopter as it rose from the upper deck's heliport. It swung away northward into the haze, in the general direction of Saigon.

It was a great relief just to get away from the 120-decibel noise level of the drillship. Andy soon realized Pug was right—it was an unproductive visit to board the supply ship. All such tenders look pretty much alike. They walked to the bow, and back to the stern to have a look at the mounts of the two twenty-millimeter cannons. They, at least, were impressive. No pirate in his right mind would mess with those if he only had machine guns.

Their return trip was a little rougher, for the seas were rising. They tied up alongside; the basket with its ring of netting was lowered again, and lifted them carefully up 100 feet above the sea, and then swung them onto the deck where the overbearing noise greeted them once more. It was an educational trip, but one that used all of Andy's strength. The constant motion keeps the muscles all in tension, for the body automatically fights to keep its equilibrium. He realized how important an exercise regimen was to keep up his muscle tone.

Andy now knew what he had gone to the tender to find out. They were well protected against any pirate boats they could see, and their radar and searchlights would alert them if anyone came near at night.

"When the boss comes out, the cook puts on a spread," Pug stated proudly, when they got back in his quarters. "We're going to have a party tonight. That means a giant steak, and all the apple juice you can drink. Sorry we don't have any alcoholic beverages aboard—unless you declare this a medical emergency." Pug gave Andy his option.

"I don't think this is the time for that; and besides, you might need your emergency supply later," Andy answered.

He knew he was being tested, but Pug could be trusted to keep a sober ship when he was alone. It wasn't like the French seismic boats he'd visited, where wine was their order of the day at meals. All of the American crews he knew were dry.

Andy was pleased to be able to spend several hours later in the evening with Wally Brooks and the other geologists on duty, examining the cuttings that had been dried and placed out for their inspection. He was aware that these men knew the geological section expected at this location very well, for they had studied similar sections from related areas. It is never possible, however, to predict what changes Mother Nature will send up in the cuttings at a wildcat well location.

They had correlated the samples carefully with wells in Brunei, and were confident they knew what beds they were drilling. For the thickness, however, they had to depend on seismic picks. He checked their correlations, and studied the cuttings for hours before finally agreeing they were correct. Drilling more holes was the answer. James had predicted they should be coming to a drilling break right around 6,122 feet.

If that break occurred as expected, they would be well on their way to designing a proper casing program to ensure that when they reached their drilling objectives, they should be able to hold any gas kicks just by increasing the weight of their mud. Pug would see to it that the engineers calculated the mud weight to a balance that would hold the blow, and yet not be sucked back into the formation. It was a juggling act. Andy had faith in the ability of his staff.

The next morning at five, Andy was awakened by Pug, shaking his shoulder.

"Hey, boss, we have a visitor nearby," Pug said loudly with a sharp tone to his voice. "I thought you might like to see him."

"What is it?" Andy shouted back, as he slipped into the coveralls.

"It's an old PT boat of some type, it looks like—the kind the pirates rig up to prey on the local trade."

"What's he doing?" Andy asked, wondering if he should be excited.

"Nothing much, he's just circling and having a look at us. He's passing around the drillship now, and he was there at first light. We watched him come earlier on radar," Pug said. "Let's get up on deck, where we can watch what he does."

From the deck, they could see that he had made one full circle around the drillship, and now he was headed off for the supply tender a mile away.

"There he goes, circling them now. I called the tender earlier when we saw the boat approaching, and alerted them to get those twenties uncovered. I want the pirates to be sure to get a good look at those." Pug seemed calm under the circumstances.

"Do you think they're up to anything right away?" Andy asked, realizing he had a knot in his stomach.

"We'll soon know. Look there! They're turning toward the tender. I'll bet they're going to try to board her." Pug was getting excited.

"They're not too fast. It'll be five or ten minutes before they get close. Should we call on the radio to be sure they're alert over there?" Andy asked.

"No, they're alert, all right. I've talked to them and they're watching. Now let's see what they do," Pug replied.

"I can see through the binocs, that the gun covers are off," Andy stated.

"They'd better be," Pug answered. "They're going to be needing them now any minute."

"There! They are shooting! There's a row of explosions in a neat line right across, in front of the pirate boat."

Just as he was speaking, they heard the bam-bam-bam-bam sound of the guns arrive. That impressed Andy.

Apparently, the guns had impressed the pirate boat also, for they veered away sharply.

"It looks like they got the message. Do you think they'll try it again?" Andy asked, as Pug borrowed the glasses.

"No, it's not likely. They'll go off and sulk a while. Then after they've thought over the damage those twenties could do to them, they'll probably try to forget about stealing supplies from our tender."

"I hope you are right, and it looks like you are. They taking off in the direction of the Mekong Delta," Andy observed.

"Then I guess I'll go back and finish my sleep. Will you do the same?" Pug asked.

"No, I think I'll get some breakfast, and then visit the geologists for another look through their microscopes while I'm here. Call me if he comes back. Otherwise, I'll see you at noon before the copter leaves."

Halfway through Andy's breakfast, he heard a change in the tempo of the drilling engines, so he took his coffee and went up onto the drilling floor to see what was happening. Soon he knew.

They had a drilling break and a little gas kick, so they were holding off the bit to increase the weight of the mud. Half an hour later, they drilled ahead, but much more slowly and cautiously. Knowing it would be a while before the cuttings were washed to the surface, Andy returned to finish his breakfast.

The geologists were in the mess hall by that time. They knew about the drilling break, and wanted to finish their breakfast and be ready to spend a full morning in their lab, as soon as the samples were available for study.

Andy and Wally took a stroll down to the mud pits after they finished their coffee, just to watch. There by the eerie glow of the moon pool light was what they were watching for. There was a scum of black, dirty liquid appearing on the surface of the creamy brown fluid. They had pumped up their first show of oil.

By noon, they had confirmation of the horizon. Now they knew the formations they were drilling positively, and could estimate when to expect to drill into the more prospective horizons. It was getting exciting. This was what they were spending so much of the stockholders' money to see.

Andy watched out over the hazy sea to the west as he flew toward Saigon in the crew-shift helicopter that afternoon. He was looking to see if he could catch a glimpse of the pirate boat. He saw nothing but the hot sun glistening off the empty, shimmering sea below.

Just the same, he'd go to the energy minister when he got to Ho Chi Minh City and request that they keep a watch with their Viet Navy patrol boats. It was the least they could do to help improve their country's future oil productivity.

# Twenty-three

When the helicopter dropped Andy Cheston at the airport northwest of Ho Chi Minh City, he had the driver of his waiting car take him directly to VietAmer's office in the Majestic Hotel. He did not check into his room first, as he usually would, but he was in a hurry. He assumed the office manager would have taken care of that detail. Instead, he went directly to the office on the top floor to use the phone. He was mad, because the Viet government had not furnished the protection that had previously been promised.

His call to the communications center of the energy minister went through immediately. Getting Tri Mang, who happened to be on duty on their radio, he had him send a message to Kim in Hong Kong. It told him that he was in Saigon, and included a coded number indicating their drilling depth and marker horizon. That would excite his office exploration staff.

He then placed a phone call to Nguyen Muoi, the president of Vietnam State Oil. Moe was not immediately available, but after a five-minute delay, his assistant, George, came on the line.

"Hello, Doctor Cheston," he answered cordially.

"Greetings, George. I tried to call your boss, but he wasn't in. We need some immediate help. Can you take an official message and relay it for me, right away?"

Andy was all business.

"Yes, sir. In the absence of President Muoi, I am authorized to react," he stated officiously.

"We have just had an attempted attack on our supply tender by a pirate PT boat, and we want some protection furnished by the Vietnamese Navy, right away. Can you arrange that?" Andy asked pointedly, and with a slightly raised tone.

"You had an attack? When was it, and how did it happen?" George asked, raising his voice to a higher pitch.

"It was today, this morning, early, before I flew back here. The PT boat flew no flag, and after circling the drillship and the tender for an hour or so, it turned to come alongside the tender. We were sure they intended to board her."

"Did they get aboard?" George asked breathlessly.

"No," Andy replied. "They stopped short when a burst from the twenty-millimeter cannons showed them what would happen to their boat if they came any closer."

"You were fortunate to be able to repel their attempt," George stated.

"Yes, we were," Andy answered. "The point is that repelling pirates is not our job. We contracted to drill for oil, not fight a war. We want the Vietnamese Navy to get a boat out there to protect our operation, and right away."

Andy was making his demand as strong as possible.

"I will make the request in official message form and transmit it immediately to the minister of energy. He will make the demand to the Navy, and I am sure they will act by coming to your assistance," George stated with authority.

Andy further informed George that they would send a request in writing, confirming their official demand as soon as possible. That ploy did not impress George, for he explained that tomorrow was Saturday, and their offices would be closed until Monday.

"I certainly will see to it personally on Monday, Doctor Cheston, at the very first hour."

Andy knew it was hopeless to expect any results from their request before Tuesday at the earliest, and who knew what could occur by then. Now he began to appreciate the preparations Pug had taken on his own, to supplement the normal defensive armament arranged for ships operating in those pirate waters. They would have to stand on their own until then, but he went ahead and placed the official request into their communications transmittal file.

It had been over two weeks since the funeral of Lam Thang, and he knew it was important that he check on how their friend, Nhung Thi, was getting along. Her plan was to have a friend move in temporarily, until she could get her life back together. She had no other close relatives she wished to have moved to the gold-district apartment permanently, and probably would not even be able to keep that apartment for long, now that she was alone.

There was only one way he could contact her, and that was by going to the apartment, for there was no phone. He dressed himself in his most inconspicuous clothing—dark trousers and sneakers, with a deep-blue pullover. He had a thin jacket that fit loosely, and he tucked the .38 Magnum into his belt. He did not like the idea of going out alone into the alleys of Saigon without some protection. Too bad Kelly couldn't come with him, he thought.

It was getting dark when he arrived at Nhung Thi's apartment, and he had spent considerable effort to disguise his movements. He had even gone so far as to keep his car and driver in front of the hotel waiting, while he sneaked out a rear entrance and walked away. Kelly had taught him the value of that trick.

He was sure he had not been followed when he arrived at the apartment, and his light tap soon gained him admittance. Nhung Thi was delighted to see him; however, her face showed signs of the strain she had been through.

"Ange-san!" she lisped. "It is good to see a friend again. I feel so alone since Papa-san has gone."

She gave him a prolonged hug, and kissed him on both cheeks.

"Nhung Thi, it is good to see you, too. I came to check on how you are getting along. Is there anything I can do for you, or that you need?" Andy asked sympathetically.

"I think I shall never be well again, Ange-san, for my life is so empty without Papa-san. Only time can help me put the past behind, and I must work to find a new life."

Nhung Thi was an intelligent girl.

"I have an ulterior motive in seeing you, as well. I do not wish to involve you in any further intrigue relating to the NLF, but I have nowhere else to turn," said Andy quietly.

"You know I will do anything to punish those who killed my grandfather. They tried to kill you and Kelly as well. We have a common enemy. I will help in any way I can, even to my death," she replied adamantly.

She still clung to Andy's arm.

"I will try to see that nothing happens to you, but Lam Thang said you knew the girl, Vu Thi. Do you ever see her?"

"One time a month past, I was buying vegetables late one afternoon, and I saw her going into a bar with a small man dressed in a white baba."

"Would she go there every week?" Andy asked.

"I do not think it is a regular habit of hers, for now she is 'employed.' It is the only time I have seen her since many years ago."

"Do you know the servant, the yeoman named Tan Tran?"

"No, Ange-san, I do not. Perhaps it was he who accompanied her."

"Very likely, for Dong would not trust her out alone. Is there any way you could talk to her, privately?"

"It would be difficult, for if I went to her at home while her employer was at work, the world would soon know. It would be best if I try to see her away from Dong's compound," Nhung Thi said as her brow wrinkled.

"Could we visit the bar tonight, and see if, by chance, she might be there? I know it would be a coincidence."

"Perhaps not so rare, for it is the weekend, and old habits are hard to break," Nhung Thi stated. "Now would be a good time. I will prepare, and tell my friend upstairs that I'll be gone for some time—shopping."

When she returned, Andy was shocked. He had never seen Nhung Thi dressed to go out. She had on heels and a short, slit skirt; frankly, she looked like a bar girl. She quickly explained that anything more modest would not be the proper dress, and would call too much attention to them in the club where they intended to go.

They left the apartment alley, and Andy led his friend on a long walk down the back streets, carefully observing every shadow to see if anyone was following. Apparently, no one watched them. Finally, after circling the Cholon market, they arrived in one of the better lit areas where American soldiers used to go to search for girls, beer, and dope. It was still an active location, and no one seemed to pay any attention to them when they entered the bar.

Nhung Thi led the way straight to a back booth as though she knew the surroundings. Andy sat with his back to the crowd, and he'd have to risk letting Nhung Thi be his eyes. He did his best to find some cover, but there was no way he could disguise the fact that he was an American.

He ordered beers, and they tried to talk quietly over the noisy musical din of the saloon. Andy ended up drinking his and hers as well, and they spent the better part of an hour watching. Without straining too much in his chair, he could see one table where a girl with a lot of dark makeup, taller than most Viets, was entertaining three soldiers. She was "undressed to the hilt," and doing her best to keep all three occupied. Occasionally, her eyes caught Andy watching her actions.

Nhung Thi had seen nothing of Vu Thi, or the man who had accompanied her. She told Andy of the many uniformed Vietcong soldiers with girls at nearby tables, but he dared not look. They were all entertaining the men with their most provocative manners and short, slit skirts, obviously ready for any price offered. Coming here had been a shot in the dark, anyway, so Andy called for the check and laid out 200 dong on the table.

There was little chance of seeing Vu Thi. The men at the tables were obviously talking about them, and making insinuating remarks. Nhung Thi told Andy some of what they said, and it wasn't complimentary. One burly soldier seemed more interested in him than the rest, for he kept teasing his girlfriend about him. Andy heard the word "American" occasionally, and he was talking loudly to his friends as he nodded toward their table.

Andy determined they should leave quickly, and as he stood up, the soldier stood also. He walked forward to face Andy, pulling himself up very straight to impress his friends.

"You American!" he began. "You are here during war?"

The soldier did not wait for an answer.

"We whip ass once! What you do here with our women?" He nodded toward Nhung Thi, his lips curled back in a leering grin.

"You're about two decades late, soldier," Andy said, just as the big fist of the stocky Viet skipped off the top of his ducking head. Andy's reflex was to fight, and he couldn't stop himself. His quick right uppercut caught the soldier square on his chin.

It was a trained blow, for it hit just where it had to land to do the damage needed. The soldier landed flat on his back, with both arms up and right at the feet of his cohorts, who were still seated. Now they had a table and beer in their laps.

No one stayed seated for long, for suddenly everyone at the bar was on his feet. Andy anticipated what was about to happen. He pushed Nhung Thi toward the door in one swift motion.

"Wait outside in the nearest left alley," he whispered to her, and quickly turned back toward the belligerent man.

By the time she was gone, the other three soldiers had helped their leader to his feet, and were slowly advancing toward the retreating Andy. It was obvious that there was no way he could win such a fight. Much against his wishes, he felt the gun at his waist. It would have to be his salvation.

Not taking his eyes off the four advancing antagonists, he pulled the .38 from his belt. It gave him a feeling of sudden strength. He was almost back to the door, for his foes were pushing to attack him outside in the street. He raised the gun into their line of sight, and aimed it first at one man and then another. One by one, they stopped as they looked into the steady barrel of the menacing weapon. It was convincing—legal or not. Each suddenly became convinced it was not his fight.

Their hesitation gave him time to get out the door, and he hurried down the street. Finding a niche in a nearby storefront, he backed in and waited to see if anyone had dared to follow. The gun had done its nasty job, much to his relief, and his heartbeat slowly returned to normal.

He waited a few minutes to make sure he was not being chased by the hoodlums. Then he walked as inconspicuously as he could down the alley to look for Nhung Thi. She was waiting half a block away, just as he had planned.

"Ange-san, are you all right? Is your head hurt? How did you get them to leave you alone? There were four."

She hugged Andy in her excitement.

"But there were three of me, Nhung Thi: me, Mr. Smith, and Mr. Wesson. Both of them look very strong, so the cowardly big-talkers were afraid to fight," Andy replied whimsically.

"You mean the gun that Lam Thang provided. He is still doing good deeds, even after death," Nhung Thi said seriously.

As they turned to walk away from the bar and toward a darker alley, a black Mercedes pulled up to the club door, and a thin, young girl stepped out.

"Look, Ange-san!" Nhung Thi whispered as she tugged at his arm.

Andy knew the slender girl in her shapely dress must be Vhu Thi, for the girl on his arm had suddenly gasped. Then behind her, climbing out of the back seat, came the little man in the baba. It was Tan Tran, he was sure. He had once seen him enter the compound. Furthermore, he had one arm in a cast, which was held by a sling. That answered a lot of questions. It is very hard to break an arm keeping books.

"Walk on, Ange-san, quickly," said Nhung Thi. "They did not see us, and they must not see us together now," she spoke, as though short of breath.

They walked rapidly away from the crowded district of eager short-skirted girls and drunken soldiers. When they arrived at a secluded alley, they then walked more slowly and talked quietly. Nhung Thi was not so accustomed to high heels. They were painful on her feet, so she removed them.

"Are you sure that was Vu Thi?" Andy asked. "Those girls sure all look a lot alike."

"Oh, yes; I'd know her anywhere. She has not changed. And the man with her was the same one who accompanied her before, except this time he has an injury."

Andy laughed. "I think it was given to him with this gun, shot by Kelly on the night of your grandfather's death. He must have been the one who threw the grenade." Andy wanted to return to the bar, for he had scores to settle with this Tan Tran, as well as with his master, Dong Huan Chou. But the time was not yet right. He must have patience.

"I must go back into the club and talk to her, Ange-san, alone," Nhung Thi paused. "I will find out what happened inside the compound on the night of the fire."

"No, Nhung Thi, you can't return there, either. If Vu Thi knows you, then she will tell Tan Tran who you are and he will then realize you have connected him to the night when the grenade was thrown. Also, he'll know that you have seen his bandaged arm and know that he was the one who broke the window and threw the bomb into your apartment. It would be unsafe for either of us to return now."

"I am sorry, Ange-san, that I have failed to get you the information you wanted. I have remembered something else I must tell you, however. We were so worried about Kelly Johnson after the funeral that I did not recall everything that happened that night. Now I have had time to think."

"It was a stressful time, and you can be forgiven. What did you wish to tell me?" Andy asked.

"It is about Papa-san's dying words. He whispered to me with his last breath only a few faint words, and they did not make sense to me." She looked as if she were straining to remember that night.

"Did he say that his vengeance wish had not been fulfilled, and that he could not yet close his eyes if he died? I'm sure that's what he was thinking. But tell me, what were his exact words?" Andy asked.

"He said, in Vietnamese, 'Thi Lan—raped by a French soldier.'" She looked perplexed. "I had forgotten he said that until today. Could that be true? What does it mean?" Nhung Thi began to cry, thinking of her closest relation who had died in her arms.

"It could mean many things. Possibly he wanted to get a family secret off his conscience before he died," Andy replied, doing his best to comfort her.

"Also, it could mean either Lin Jin or Kim Jin is actually half French, and thereby only half kin," Nhung Thi stated, as she recovered her composure.

"That would be a rather far-fetched thing to find out after all these years. Their mother would have told them long ago, I would think. What happened to Lin-san and Kim-san's father? No one ever mentions him."

Andy was trying to put together their family tree, and to remember ages and dates.

"Thi Lan's husband was killed. He was a soldier for the Khmer Krom of the Mekong Delta early in the war, and died an honorable soldier's death. Both of the children grew up depending on their grandfather for his support of Thi Lan. She did not wish to leave Saigon, but was finally driven out when the war made it too hard for her to make a living and keep her young ones in school."

"How old were the children at that time?" Andy inquired.

"Lin-san was in lower school, and Kim was younger. They took me, as my parents were dead, and went to Hong Kong and established our residence there. Then life became too expensive for our support, and we three children returned to Catholic School in Saigon. Lin-san and Kim-san later went to Hong Kong for school, aided by money from Li Hong Hoe. It was necessary for me to stay and look after the interests of my grandfather, Lam Thang."

"He was a gold merchant, then?"

"Yes, and he did good business with all the soldiers. Unfortunately, some of his family were closely allied with the Vietcong. They knew too much about his politics. After the Cong took over, they invited him for a few days' 'reeducation.'"

She spoke slowly, and thoughtfully.

"How long was that?"

"It was six years. Li Hong Hoe bought his way out."

"He could arrange that from Japan? He must still have good Viet connections," Andy stated.

"He has some, but he was not strong enough to keep his brother-in-law from the terrible beatings administered regularly by the bodoi in their filthy camps. He was finally returned home, completely a broken man. His renewed struggling gold business was only a token from his friends to support our barest existence."

"Then how can you live now? Did he leave you enough to support an apartment?"

"I will find a job, Ange-san, for I must find a way to eat. I have no close relatives left here—only a few friends," she replied sadly.

"For now, I will leave you some money, because I know what happens to girls who try to live off the street. We must solve your problem of earning a livelihood in the future. Could you reactivate the gold trade in his shop?"

Andy tried to think ahead, but could think of no solution.

"I know those who control that business here, and we are friends. The problem is capital, for it takes much dong to restock a gold market store. That money I cannot raise."

It was a thoughtfully considered reply, for she showed intelligence.

"It appears that many in the government here are bent on destruction of the working people. They don't want anyone to make an honest or decent living."

Andy was mad, and he realized he was gripping the arm of this innocent girl too tightly. What had she ever done to deserve such a life? He watched her hobbling along beside him, with her shoes in one hand and desperately clinging to him with the other. He realized that when his business with the NLF here was completed, it must include some future plan for this girl who had helped them, even after the death of her grandfather.

# Twenty-four

"Kim, haven't we received an answer from our message to the minister, Ho Bac Minh, yet? It's been almost a week now," Andy said, as he peered into Kim's communications station in their Hong Kong office.

"No sir, they haven't said a word. Of course, it was over a weekend, so they're closed down mostly. They are transmitting our messages to and from the ship with only an hour of delay, though," Kim replied.

Andy had returned to his Hong Kong office from the trip to the drillship and to Saigon, and he had renewed his request for a confirmation of receipt of his important message. He wanted to be sure the energy minister had actually gotten his call for assistance, and arranged to send a Navy patrol boat to protect their drillship and supply vessel from the aggressive Vietnamese pirate. It was a pressing matter, he knew, and as yet no answer had been received.

That had been almost a week ago. He wished now that he had stayed in Saigon long enough to make his request directly to Minister Ho Bac Minh, instead of trying to relay it through their communications system. Sometimes channels had a way of being intentionally blocked, especially if there was an assistant in the chain named Dong Huan Chou.

Andy was extremely nervous, pacing back and forth between his office and the message center. The communications being relayed from the ship were coming through OK, but there was always an hour's delay when they passed through Saigon. Why were they sitting on the information? It couldn't help them any. Obviously, they were first translating the data for review in the minister's office.

Later in the day, Kim appeared in the doorway to Andy's office.

"Here is a message from the drillship, that just arrived," Kim stated, as he carried the paper to Andy at his desk.

"It sounds like they have drilled into something good." He studied the lines carefully. "They are getting the mud heavier to control a strong kick. That means they are getting ready to core. I suppose the geologists are busy checking correlations and making estimates of the age of the formation being drilled before they run logs of the hole." He was talking to himself mostly, for he knew Kim didn't understand the reason for their actions.

There are adjoining basins of the South China Sea that produce oil at several age levels. It was a very expensive guessing game, for if they were off in their depth calculations, they could core the wrong beds. That might cause them to screw up the entire operation, like blow the drillstem out of the hole, or stick the bit, or twist off. It was an expensive game.

"Thanks, Kim. Call me if anything new comes in," Andy directed.

VietAmer had borrowed the use of some of the World Oil staff to sit on the well, and several knowledgeable geologists were aboard the drillship. Andy had his friend, Bill Hanby, to thank for that. As they logged the well before running their intermediate string of casing, they'd have to also conduct a velocity survey. That was critical to making their depth calculations. With the exact velocities, they could calculate the depths related to their seismic time sections.

Andy had requested that his former apartment-mate, James Wellman, be loaned to VietAmer from World Oil's Tokyo office to ensure the survey was conducted properly. He missed his friend being here in Hong Kong, for he depended heavily on his interpretations. He was glad he was going to be aboard, being aware that James and Pug Cox had worked together on such surveys on the atolls of the Reed Bank off the Philippines, as well as the Indonesian islands. It would be like old home week for them while James was aboard the drillship.

Time seems like an eternity when you have a drilling well bucking. All Andy could do from Hong Kong was drink coffee and pace the floor. The last fax said they had just seen a blip on the ship's radar showing a boat approaching sixty nautical miles to the northwest. Could that be their pirate coming back to see what mischief he could do? Andy could only speculate, and sincerely hope not. They already had their hands full on the drillship without an added pirate complication. His stomach was a knot as he watched a tablet fizz in the glass. It was upsetting.

"Anything new, Kim?" he asked, as he stalked back into the communications room.

"No sir, not since the radar blip." Kim was thumbing back through his copies of the messages on a clipboard.

"Here's a message that just came in from Tokyo. James Wellman is making the crew-change helicopter connection straight to the ship, and will be there to supervise the velocity survey when the logging is complete," Kim read from the clipboard.

"That's great. I asked for help on that, but I wasn't sure they could spare James. I'll be glad to have him on hand. He'll probably come back through here later to drop off the data and his calculations."

Andy was clearly pleased to hear that he'd be visited by James soon. He had missed his friend and confidant.

"Do you want a copy?" Kim asked.

"No, but you might call and remind Lin Jin that James will be here sometime, and probably would like to say hello. Tell her I want very much to see her when this business is done. I'm going back to my office to make a phone call. If anything new comes in, bring it to me right away."

It was hard not to think of Lin Jin, but with so much activity going on in the office, he resolutely deferred his feelings until he could do them justice—like on a date, if she'd accept.

As Andy walked back down the hall to his office, he was elated to meet Kelly Johnson, who had entered from the receptionist's area.

"Kelly! What are you doing here? You're supposed to be resting. You just got your hospital release from the doc yesterday."

Andy was a little upset, for he knew that Kelly was supposed to stay off his feet for at least a week after the doctors allowed him his freedom. Also, he knew Kelly. If he could walk, he'd be out and about, getting back into his investigative work for World Oil. He was like a bloodhound that simply would not let a trail get cold.

"Oh, I got tired of lying around. Besides, I feel fine, and I want to hear about your latest trip to Saigon. I heard about you using that thirty-eight to get out of trouble. I'm just a little weak from not getting any exercise during the past month. Now I need to be doing something. Action is the best therapy."

"Don't rush into anything you don't feel up to."

"What do you have going on that I can help with?" Kelly was firm in his request.

"There's plenty going on. Maybe you'd better have a seat and go over the recent comm files to get yourself up to date. Are you sure you are up to this?"

Andy looked him over carefully. He seemed fit, but he didn't move quite as fast as he did before the incident with the grenade. The bandaged arm showed, and he knew his chest was still wrapped, under his shirt.

"OK, I'll look into the files. What's happening on the rig? Have they drilled into the pay yet?"

Kelly had been keeping up with their daily activity while he was hospitalized by calling Kim regularly, and having him read the current reports.

"That's why I'm here so late," Andy replied. "The well is bucking, and Pug is trying to hold it down with mud, and get it in shape to run logs. They'll go in with the core barrel next, and see if we can have a look at the formation."

"This is the critical time then," Kelly stated.

"Yeah. That'll tell us if we have a producing well from this level. Right now, all we can do from here is have patience, and hope all goes well on the rig so we can get the answers we need."

"After the trouble Saigon is giving us with our ship communications, that's hard to take," Kelly answered.

"The thing that really worries me is that they had a visit from a pirate vessel that snooped around the drillship and tender last week. They had to drive them away with the twenties. We thought that gave them the message. You'll read about it in the file. But right now, Pug thinks the same boat is coming back. They're watching it on radar with one eye while trying to hold the kicking well down."

"What's the deal with the energy minister getting us the Navy protection you requested? Have you heard anything on that yet?" Kelly asked.

"No, not a word. But I sure wish we had. I think I'll try to phone the minister after a bit, and see what has been done. I really hate to go over the head of Viet Oil's president, but we need answers now. If that really is a pirate boat coming back to do mischief, it's probably already too late for them to help us. They should have done something already," Andy stated in disgust.

"Well, I'll be in the comm office, Andy. Call me if there's anything I can do. I really feel for Pug out there, with all his problems coming at one time. I wish I were there to give him a hand to repay the way he helped me that night in Saigon. I kept coming to and seeing that big grizzly mug of his as he carried me out to the hospital."

"James just arrived aboard ship to do the velocities. Perhaps he'll be of some help—at least hold his hand for moral support," Andy told him, as they walked to the door.

When Andy sat back at his desk, he went over the situation in his mind. He tried for an hour to get a call through to the energy minister, Ho Bac Minh, but with no success. Apparently, someone there was canceling his calls. He had a decision to make. It was agonizing, but he made it. He'd get some more help from Hanby and go to Saigon himself. He was determined to act, as he placed a call to Bill Hanby in Tokyo.

Fortunately, Bill was in his office, although it was already after dark in Tokyo.

"Hello, Bill. It seems I'm always calling you for help," Andy began.

"What can I do for you, Doctor Cheston? It's late here, and you just barely caught me as I was leaving," he joked.

"I'm serious, Bill. Our well is kicking, and Pug is trying to get it in shape to log. So far, our cement jobs are holding OK. I just heard that James made it out to the well to supervise the velocity survey. Thank you for that." Andy got the operational details out of the way.

"That's OK. It was what you asked for, wasn't it?"

Bill knew there must be more, so he waited.

"Yes, as far as it goes. There is a new problem, though. The pirate boat is headed back into their area apparently. Pug picked it up on their radar an hour ago, and they think it's the same one as before. Pug's busy getting all his supplies aboard to hold the well down so they can get the logging tools rigged and into the hole."

"There's no trouble with supplies, is there?"

"No, sir. He'll handle that as well as anyone could. He acts gentle around us and the office, but he's plenty tough in the field. He wasn't a Marine in Korea for nothing. But I think we have another more serious problem."

"What's that, Andy?" Hanby was all alert now, for he realized this was no social call.

"I don't think our request for Navy assistance to Minister Ho Bac Minh ever reached him. There's a block in our line of communications, and you know where that must be. I need to get to Saigon, and go directly to talk to the minister to see if he ever heard of our request. Time is of the essence. If he hasn't gotten the request, he'll be able to figure out who stopped the transmission."

"You're thinking it could be Dong? He wouldn't dare," Bill stated sharply.

"He's just the type who would. This week of delay is giving the NLF time to cook up something with the pirate boat, and I'm sure they're behind whatever those yellow sons of bitches have planned!"

Andy couldn't put it any stronger.

"This certainly seems like a critical time for personnel problems to be causing troubles with our Viet relations. I agree with you, Andy. You should go directly to the minister, and as quickly as possible. When do you want the plane?" Bill asked.

Andy hadn't yet asked for use of the jet again, but that had been the primary purpose of his call.

"Can you get it here by first light? I'll be grateful. They have a night-landing restriction past eleven here because of the apartment complexes along the approach pattern, so there's no need in arriving earlier. I'll be waiting at the airport, and as soon as it's refueled we can leave. We'll be in Ho Chi Minh City by midmorning. Kelly is here now and thinks he's well, so I'll ask him if he's up to going along. He knows how things operate there. We'll try not to get into trouble again, sir," he stated respectfully.

"Yes; you be careful. My grapevine told me about you getting into, and out of, a barroom brawl. I'm glad we were able to be of some help—providing the gun."

"It's a good thing you arranged it, or I'd have ended up in an alley like a wet mop. Thanks very much for the timely assistance," Andy answered.

\* \* \*

"Get that damn mud loaded on the shuttle and started back here! You've got a boat approaching about thirty miles to your west, so you should be in the clear for two hours or so. Our location was put here by geostationary comm satellites that are accurate to five meters, but I'll bet that son of a bitch knows exactly where he's headed to the inch!"

Pug Cox was shouting into the radio from his office on the drillship. There was no doubt in the tender crew's mind about when he wanted the extra mud available on the rig. His coffee was cold, but he gulped it down anyway. What could the pirates have up their sleeves?

He left his cabin suddenly, and went up on the drilling floor. He nervously checked the log and the clipboards as the drillers watched their pressure gauges and manipulated the giant pumps to keep the mud flow steady. No one said a word to him as he prowled the deck like a lion.

For now the well was under control, and he could not fault any of their procedures. But if they were to keep the hole intact, they had to get the well logged and the velocity surveyed. Then they could safely run casing into the hole and cement it. Only when that was set would they be safe. They could drill out then, and go in with a core barrel to find out if this was the producing horizon they had spent two years and fifty million dollars to find.

Pug paced the deck, letting everyone know he was upset and worried. He wanted to get his extra material onboard, and be ready for them when the pirate boat showed up. Ready for what? He could only guess. Surely they knew better than to try to board the rig. That would be impossible. If they tried to board the tender, they'd run into the twenty-millimeter cannons again long before they got close to the ship, and they should know better than that. So what could possibly be their purpose in returning?

An hour later, the supply shuttle arrived back from the tender, and tied up alongside to offload the needed supplies. Things were going on schedule, and Pug began to relax. Suddenly he heard a loud screech and whine of a loose cable. The loading winch had broken a cable. Pug ran to see if anyone had been caught in the recoil.

He quickly took in the scene. The cable had parted when the load was high, and it dumped the mud into the ocean. Quickly he scanned the men on deck. Nobody was down.

"Mate, was anybody hurt?" he shouted.

"No, Super, we just lost a pallet of mud, is all. Everybody's safe," came back the reply.

That was a relief, and probably not so serious a loss. Mud could be replaced.

"OK, let's get that line replaced and finish this job. We only have another thirty minutes before company arrives."

The shuttle boat remained tied up opposite the stern, and there was only one way to get aboard it. That was by using the sling that was operated from a crane on the drillship. No one was going to attack from that direction. And the big steel plates surrounding the moon pool were as good as armor. It'd take a torpedo to get through those, and pirate boats don't carry that kind of armament.

It was well after noon when the crew-change helicopter arrived. Pug was waiting in the passageway below when James came down the ladder. He carried his briefcase and his overnight bag in hand, and didn't look much like a sailor.

"Hello there, Jamie Boy!" Pug shouted. "I didn't think we'd get you way out here this far from the hot baths of the Tokyo Onsen. I hope you had a good massage before you left, 'cause you won't be getting anything out here but exercise and grease," Pug kidded his office-oriented friend.

He was happier now that he had everything onboard, including the new crew.

"I think I can handle those all right, you old goat. Why don't you have 'em clean this rust-bucket up so a fellow won't get his pants dirty sliding down the chutes? How about loaning me some coveralls?" James joked.

"Sure, we'll fix you up. You won't have anything to do for a couple of days probably. If we can get the stem outta the hole, the geologists will be logging this thing for that long. Then you can do your thing. Come on along with me, and I'll bring you up to date on what's going on with our pirate friend."

Pug was shouting to be heard above the roar, and was happy to have his old friend aboard.

Once into the cabin, Pug closed the door and that helped shut out some of the roar, but the vibration was eternal. He handed James the message clipboard, and he read everything that had happened since the last pirate boat visit. Then they discussed the possibilities that might cause the mischief makers to return.

"Do you expect them to attack, or are they just out to see what they can pick up?" James asked.

"They seemed to be impressed by the twenties, so I think they must have been sent back by the NLF with some other devilment in mind," Pug replied.

"I hear Andy is still in Hong Kong. I'll bet he's plenty upset about the drillship not having any Viet Navy protection," James said.

"Yes, and I don't think he'll sit still there any longer. He'll soon go over to talk directly to the minister about it. His messages indicate that he thinks our previous requests weren't relayed at all," Pug stated.

"We should have expected that, with that bastard, Dong, positioned where he is. I wonder when we'll find out which side of that NLF political struggle the minister himself is on."

"I just hope that when we find out, it isn't the hard way," Pug answered. "Get your slicker, Jamie Boy, and let's go out on deck and watch for that yellow feculent buccaneer. See what I learned in college?"

He showed James that tough-but-oh-so-gentle grin.

Another hour passed, and the pirate boat had approached their location as predicted, then slowed. After another hour of keeping watch, the intruder began a slow circle around both the drillship and the tender, staying well out of the twenty millimeter cannon range. Anyway, thus far they were only tourists, and hadn't shot at anybody. Hailing them on their radio, even in Vietnamese, produced no reply. They just cruised on around them, and watched.

By morning, the mud was in shape, and Pug gave the order to start the logging operation. As the drillstem was withdrawn, it was replaced with the proper weight mud. When all was ready, the logging sonde was lowered through the upper casing into the open hole, and recording commenced.

"Are you sure you guys can read these logs after we get them, or are you just guessing?" Pug joked with the geologists, for he got a certain enjoyment out of teasing them about things he wasn't trained to understand.

As the sonde was slowly passed into the hole, at the bottom of its heavy cable, impulses were sent out as feelers into the rocks. The signals, that returned were fed through the cables back to the surface, and duly recorded. Then the logs would later be compared to other areas and interpreted by the geologists as to the formation characteristics. Pug was happy now, for things were moving, and going just the way he had planned.

James stood in the recording shack talking to Pug, when a message came from the comm center in Saigon. Pug read the paper and passed it to James to keep him informed. It stated that Andy and Kelly would arrive there by mid-morning, and Andy wished to keep in direct contact with him, if it were possible. He wondered how Andy had arranged to get there, since there was no scheduled flight. And it would be impossible to charter a flight at night and on short notice from Hong Kong.

James followed Pug to the deck below to get a better view of the "tourists," and they stood on the stern below the heli-deck. They took turns watching the pirate boat through binoculars as it slowly circled their drillship.

"Look," Pug said. "He's making a turn toward the tender. It's at least a mile off, and there's nothing illegal about it coming a lot closer than that, I guess."

Still, it was a provocative action. Pug had a phone connection patched into the radio, and he called the tender.

"If that yellow bastard gets too close, give him a burst from the twenties. We've warned him in three languages that we don't want any company. Maybe he'll understand that kind of a statement better. If he keeps coming, he'll get what he's asking for!" Pug shouted.

He had no gentle grin now; he was all tough.

As if in direct response to his message, the pirate boat pulled directly toward the side-loading platform of the tender. When he was about 200 yards away, the rear twenty-millimeter cannon opened up with a short burst, neatly drawing a single line of water-spouts between the pirate boat and the tender. Pug tried to count the blips in the water, but the delayed arrival of the sound told him it was about ten shots.

"That'll show 'em!" Pug shouted at the top of his voice.

Their reaction was instantaneous. The helm was put over and a clatter of machine gun fire harmlessly raked the heavy shielding around the gun-mount. They had definitely declared their intentions, and Pug assumed now they could only attack and be sunk, or call it a bad day and leave for home. But they did neither. They just started another circle.

A half hour later, Pug had sent messages describing the action to be relayed to their offices in Saigon and Hong Kong. Surely, now the Viet Navy would bring a gunboat of some kind that would chase the pirates away. Their radar showed that no help was on the way.

He watched with binoculars as the pirate boat had taken up a position a couple of miles away, and seemed to be rigging something on their rear deck. He wondered what they could be doing.

There was the usual stack of fuel drums there, but they were working on something else. They had a big draped block they were working on, and another large object. Pug could not imagine what that might be.

"James, look at their stern. What is that rig?"

James took the glasses, and kept watching the pirate boat for a solid half hour. He, too, was puzzled.

Finally he said, "Something about that begins to ring a bell. I've seen a rig like that before—somewhere."

"What do you think it could be?" Pug asked.

Gradually, as they pulled away their tarpaulins, a giant reel began to be exposed.

"Now I know," James said excitedly. "It's an old-fashioned seismic cable reel—the kind they used to use when they shot seismic coverage years ago with a single string of seismometers."

"But what could they possibly be intending to do with a cable? Did they think they could rope a ship? Be serious."

Pug and James discussed the possibilities, and finally decided they must be completely crazy as they worked on another big block. As the pirates slowly uncovered the other object near the stern, suddenly it all made sense to Pug.

"That big block is a mine! I've seen them before, years ago," Pug shouted. "They intended to string out that mine at the end of the long cable, then tow it in such a way as to wrap it around the tender."

"That'd blow it all to hell," James replied. "The supply tender's skin is only a full eighth of an inch thick, and no match for a mine. They're going to sink our supply boat!"

James was suddenly in shock.

Pug knew if they didn't do something, and soon, they were going to be put out of business. Without more mud and supplies, their well would quickly get out of control, and the gas would blow. They might very well cause the drillship to sink into the bubbles as he had described.

It was time for action, but how could they fight off a ship a mile away?

"Now's the time to wish for that helicopter gunship," James stated.

"That ain't gonna happen, so we'll just take care of it ourselves, Jamie. Come with me," Pug shouted, as he stalked away toward the heli-deck. "We're going to go out and meet that bunch of pirates head-on!"

# Twenty-five

"Good morning. This is Doctor Cheston of VietAmer Oil. Do you speak English?" Andy asked the girl who answered the phone of the Ministry of Energy.

"A moment please—a little—we see," came back a very hesitant reply.

"Don't go away. That's good enough. I am Doctor Cheston, president of VietAmer Oil. It is extremely important that I speak directly to Minister Ho Bac Minh, please."

"That impossible, sir. Minister not in office," was her hesitant reply.

"His secretary, then. Please let me speak to his secretary."

"A moment—please, sir."

Andy heard switching and voices in Vietnamese for half a minute until he got another answer.

"Hello. I speak some English. What do you want?" came a voice with a little more assurance of authority.

"This is Doctor Cheston, president of VietAmer Oil. I must speak directly to Minister Ho Bac Minh, as soon as possible. This is an emergency. Is he available?"

"No sir. He is not in. Whom did you say was calling?" asked the silky voice.

After several repeats, Andy finally convinced the person, who was the minister's secretary, that he must talk directly to the minister, and that it was most important. They were able to agree on a time for a private audience at three that afternoon. He was not available to speak by phone before then. It was the best she could arrange.

It was almost noon, and Andy had arrived using the company jet at the VietAmer Saigon office in the Majestic Hotel. Kelly had convinced him he was well enough to travel, so he was along. Their borrowed jet had served them well. The messages awaiting them told about the well logging that was under way, and that everything was proceeding on schedule. The drillhole's sidewalls were standing up in good condition, and they were encountering little resistance to lowering the sonde. That was one worry out of the way, but there were so many others.

What bothered Andy most right now was the information about the pirate ship, and the fact that it had actually attacked the tender with machine gun fire. He knew that machine guns were no match for the twenties mounted on their ship, but he could not understand why they had not been driven away. Surely the pirates knew that their odds of achieving a successful attack were too slight to give any hope of a successful raid. So, by rights, they should have left the scene with their tail between their legs.

Andy contacted Nguyen Muoi by phone, and told him what had been done—after the fact. That obviously did not make the Viet company president very happy, but Andy wanted him to realize how upset he was with their failure to handle their important communications. The snub, administered at the right time, might actually help achieve his purpose.

When he and Kelly approached the big conference room that afternoon, they could hear raised voices. Someone was having a heated discussion, and it was all in Vietnamese. On entering, they saw it was the president of Vietnam State Oil, Moe, already seated there with his assistant, George. The assistant to the energy minister, Dong Huan Chou, was the one making the noise. He was standing, hovered over Muoi, and waving his hand in a threatening manner.

It was obvious that Dong was irate about something. Andy could guess that it was because he had gone behind his back and called directly to the minister, insisting on this meeting. If he had not passed on Andy's request for naval assistance to his boss, Ho Bac Minh would soon know it, and someone would be in deep shit. It'd serve him right, Andy realized, as he saw Kelly's broad grin of appreciation.

There were no introductions or greetings, and they found their way to their seats. Immediately, the minister himself entered. He came around the table to Andy and Kelly and shook their hands.

"Doctor Cheston, I was distressed to hear of the burning of your office. These things happen, and usually at the most inopportune times. I have been told it was the result of faulty wiring. It was most fortunate for your operations that you did not lose your maps and data."

"Yes, we were indeed lucky, for we had taken the maps with us that evening in preparation for an early morning departure," replied Andy. "Perhaps you have not heard of the bombing of the house of our friend, Lam Thang Nguyen. He was killed in the attack, and Kelly Johnson here, who was visiting at the time, was severely injured. He was released from the hospital in Hong Kong only yesterday."

Andy was watching the minister and his assistant, Dong, carefully to see how they would respond to the mention of the catastrophes. He was sure they both were already aware of all the details.

"I am sorry to hear of your troubles. It seems your company is having difficulty operating in our country. Perhaps if you used only Vietnamese nationals to conduct your efforts, things would go more smoothly. But then, I realize, such is not always technically possible. If it were, we would be drilling the wells ourselves."

"You are right," Andy answered. "We must be able to plan and execute our programs reliably and on schedule if we expect to be successful. Great delays in operations cause even greater delays, until finally nothing is ever completed and all of the money we spend is wasted."

"So, you have requested this meeting in an urgent manner. I hear you are logging the well, and that drilling has progressed as planned. It would seem you would be glad. Are you having difficulties?"

The minister had obviously not been reading all of the communications passed through to VietAmer by his staff.

"Yes, sir, we certainly are. As you will note in the recent communications, our ships are being harassed by a PT boat. It has been cruising around our drilling location. We suspect it is a pirate vessel. It has attempted to attack our tender, unsuccessfully, and shots were fired."

Andy paused to see what effect the notice had on the minister. He waited, but the only reply was a serious stare.

"Over a week ago, I requested, through channels, that you provide protection for our operations, such as a Vietnamese Navy gunboat to drive those intruders away. We have not received any such assistance to date. Last night those pirates acted in a menacing and threatening manner. Shots were fired and our ships are currently being attacked."

"Dong, why have these communications not been brought to my attention?" the minister demanded loudly, and in English.

Ho Bac Minh looked directly at his assistant, and appeared to be staring right through his black glasses. It was the first time Andy and Kelly had ever heard him raise his voice. Dong's face was becoming redder by the second, and he busied himself by shuffling papers in his silver case.

"I would like an answer, and immediately!" the minister almost screamed.

Dong recoiled, by half standing and trying to ease out of his chair.

"The communications have all been handled by Tri Mang. He is the one who did not relay the messages, if there has been a problem." When he was standing behind his chair, he went on.

"These inept American operators are now trying to cover up their own inefficiency in not requesting the proper Vietnamese protection for their own contractors. Now they try to blame the government of Vietnam. Americans are not worthy to conduct operations in our country, and the contracts should never have been awarded!" Now Dong was shouting.

"I will decide such issues as contracts!" Ho Bac Minh answered in a scream. "Muoi, have my secretary get Tri Mang into this conference. There are questions I wish to ask him! Get him now."

The minister was obviously highly irritated at the breakdown in communications, since the agreement had been so pointedly made and documented at their last meeting. He continued in an irate voice.

"Dong, he'd better have the right answers to my questions about this matter, or I am going to hold you and your continuing uncooperative attitude toward our VietAmer contract responsible for any problems that have been caused. You had better hope those pirates are just snooping around the drill location, and have no seriously disruptive actions planned."

"You cannot hold me responsible for actions taken by the pirates. They operate by the directions of the NLF. How would I know what their plans might be?" Dong hedged.

Too late, Dong realized he had associated the pirate actions to orders from the NLF. His colored glasses could no longer hide the fact that he knew he was in trouble with his boss, for he had been associated with one too many of a series of disasters.

"You know very well what the NLF plans are for this drilling contract. They are to disrupt the success of the American wells in any way they can, and to indicate the superior performance of the Vietnamese and their hired Russian bumbling explorers in the Vietsovpetro," the minister said, speaking vehemently, directly to Dong.

The minister was enraged, and continued almost screaming. He turned to his secretary who had stepped into the room. "Where is Tri Mang?"

The secretary winced as she quietly replied in Vietnamese, indicating that he was on his way. Her boss had apparently never before raised his voice in a meeting, so Andy knew she was justifiably scared.

Dong was edging toward the door as the communications man, Tri Mang, eased himself hesitantly inside the room. He looked scared, as he might well be.

"Here is Tri Mang. He is responsible for communications and will answer all of your questions," Dong stated nastily.

Then he turned and quickly walked out the door without waiting to be dismissed.

The shy man dressed in a thin white baba stood near the door holding a clipboard, apparently dreading to come all the way into the room.

"Yes, Minister? You sent for me?" he said in Vietnamese, Andy assumed.

"I did! Where are the communications Doctor Cheston sent to me requesting our Navy provide protection from the pirates at their drilling rig?"

He spoke in English, but Tri Mang understood perfectly.

His steely eyes were boring holes into the scared little staff member.

"I have them on file, Minister, just as I was advised to handle them." He spoke very hesitantly.

"What do you mean, you were advised to file them?" stormed Ho Bac Minh. "You were directed to pass all communications through my office. Why did I not receive them?"

"They were passed through your office, Minister. They crossed the desk of Dong Huan Chou. He initialed them, and returned them to be filed," Tri Mang replied weakly.

He took a step back, for he had admitted what he dreaded to tell—the real facts. He was as white as his baba, and trembled violently.

"Why was that request not acted on? He must have had a reason. And knowing his connections, I think now I know what that reason must be. If I am right, Doctor Cheston, you have more to worry about from the pirate vessel than just prying eyes, which are taking notes for Vietsovpetro!"

"Why? What do you think are their intentions?" asked Andy, wondering seriously if it was too late to provide any assistance for the drillship.

"I have always suspected that Dong's interests were those of the NLF. I did not realize to what length they would go to negate any influence of American companies, and any Western efforts to establish economic recovery in Vietnam. You well know that the first step in such a recovery would be the development of our own energy sources. That is why they are so adamant to claim any such success as their own."

"Dong seems to have a lot of support to stay in his position," Andy commented.

"I have been unable to rid myself of him. NLF control over energy would cinch their political control over the entire future of our economy. That is the reason they have gone to great lengths to keep Dong on my staff at a top level."

"What can we do now? He has already sent the pirates to do their worst. Can we call in the Navy on short notice? Do they have access to helicopter gunships?" Andy asked.

"We can, and we will, but it may take some time, even if they use an attack helicopter. Time is something we probably do not have, since the pirates are already at the site. I hope your crews are prepared for whatever attack they have in mind, for they certainly intend to stop your operations completely—even if it requires sinking your vessels," Ho Bac Minh stated.

"Our men will do their best with the defenses they have at hand, which are too few for comfort. My last message from the drillship said they are very busy just keeping the well from blowing out, and getting it in shape for logging," Andy replied.

"Tri Mang, come with me! We will immediately contact our minister of defense. Excuse me, Doctor Cheston. When this is taken care of, I personally will see to it that Dong is made to pay for his intrigue. We will arrest him, and confiscate the records at his estate, for that is surely where he has gone. He will be accused and tried for his actions."

"What will happen to him then?" Andy asked, wondering if they would really attempt to prove anything against the representative of the NLF.

"Dong will be charged with treason against the nation. We will see if the NLF can protect him now. There should be enough evidence there in his personal files for me to rid him of his post as energy assistant forever," the minister said vehemently. "And my apologies to VietAmer Oil for our inefficiency in furnishing support."

"My first concern is the safety of our men aboard the drillship and tender. I hope help does not arrive too late."

"I will first tend to the support request; then I will see that Dong Huan Chou is properly taken care of."

Ho Bac Minh walked rapidly out the door and down the hall, with Tri Mang scurrying along behind him with his clipboard in hand.

\*　　\*　　\*

As they rode in their car back toward the Majestic Hotel, Kelly asked, "Andy, what do you know about the family of Dong Huan Chou? He lives there with his mother and the girl, Vu Thi. Does Tan Tran live in the main house, too?"

"Yes, that must be the arrangement. We saw him go in that night. The servants all come and go through the back entrance, but they all would live in their own quarters. Why?" Andy asked.

"Because there is something about the family I don't understand. I've had a lot of time to think lately, lying in the hospital. It's something Nhung Thi said one night. There's a family connection between Lam Thang Nguyen and Dong somewhere. Have you ever thought about how easily he knew the answers to our questions about their estate?"

"I supposed the info came from his friends with the gold market connections."

"How did he come up with information about the night of the gold robbery there, which most people would find very difficult to obtain? That wasn't gold market information."

"I guess I've been afraid to ask. Probably I considered that Orientals have a way of passing information within their occupational group. But you may be right. It makes more sense that there's a family tie somewhere along the line."

Andy thought a moment.

"But I can't believe that Lin Jin or Kim is related to that bastard, Dong! I'd never believe that."

"Perhaps we should ask someone. Now that Lam Thang is dead, don't you think it's strange that Nhung Thi has no relatives she wants to claim, outside of the Hoes?"

Kelly was always asking questions, and they had a tendency to be the right ones.

"Do you think Nhung Thi could tell us anything more if we pressure her a little?" Andy asked.

"It wouldn't hurt to try, and she lives just a few streets over. Let's go by her place and find out for ourselves."

This time, they didn't have to be sneaky, for they knew who their adversary was, and that he had very likely headed for his compound to get things in order, and to report to his real leaders, the NLF. If their plans worked out, he might soon be a hero to them. At least he wouldn't be following them in the black Mercedes now.

The driver parked in the narrow street, very near the doorway, and Andy noted there was a new shutter over the window. It was the one where Tan Tran had pulled out the cover and thrown in the grenade.

Nhung Thi met them at the door, and immediately opened it wide.

"Come in, Ange-san; it's good to see you are well, and out of the hospital, Kewwy," she lisped.

Her embarrassed girlfriend, who was apparently visiting, quickly took flight from the room, leaving them to talk privately.

"Our offshore drilling may be in trouble, Nhung Thi, so we must speak quickly," Andy began.

He related the story of their difficulties with the pirate ship, and the meeting they had just had with the energy minister.

"Now the minister is convinced that Dong has been spying on his office to cause trouble for VietAmer Oil's operations. It is apparent that the NLF caused our plane crash and burned our office, then killed your grandfather. All of those deeds were done at the direction of Dong, and arranged by his yeoman, Tan Tran. Now he is going in for bigger mischief—he has sent the pirates to try to destroy our drilling operation."

"How could he do such a thing? Since the war, my grandfather has had problems with him. He caused Lam Thang to spend six terrible years in the reeducation camps. I hate him!" Nhung Thi was crying, and great tears rolled down her swollen cheeks.

"What can you tell us of Dong's relations? Do you know his family? We need to know now, for he has gone back to his compound, and will destroy all evidence of his past associations. We need to know about his household. What is his hold over Tan Tran and Vu Thi?" Andy asked as gently, yet as forcefully, as he could.

"Dong is a great shame for our family. I was sworn to secrecy about him when I was a little girl and Grandfather came home from the camps."

"Please tell us everything you can now, Nhung Thi. Your grandfather is gone, and we need all the information we can get to confront Dong's organization," Andy pleaded.

The tears continued, and Nhung Thi sat uncomfortably, going over the past in her mind. She apparently realized these were her only friends left, so she would help them if she could.

"I will tell you all I know, Ange-san, for you are my only true friends. The old woman Dong calls his mother is the sister of Li Hong Hoe's first wife. She is the owner of the estate, and is the aunt of Thi Lan, Lin Jin's mother."

Nhung Thi told the facts nervously.

"Then Lin Jin and Kim are related to Dong?" Andy asked, with sudden realization. It was like a sharp coal in his brain.

"No, not quite," replied Nhung Thi, hesitantly. "He calls her 'Mother,' or Ibu, but she actually is not related to him by blood. He is the son by a previous marriage, and came into the household with her marriage to his father.

She brought the estate as her dowry. When her husband was killed in the war, Dong gradually took over as the director of that estate, although it is only his right because he is strong. He worked the black market, and secretly belonged to the Vietcong. He had been the political enemy of the Hoe branch of the family, even before the war."

"Why did you not tell us this before, Nhung Thi? Is there more?"

"Yes, there is more, probably, but I have said too much. I tell you this now because Lam Thang is gone, and because he whispered to me as he died. I believe he wanted me to tell you something, but I do not know what it was. He only said a few words, and they were so weak; I hardly can believe them." She had stopped crying.

"That can wait. What about Tan Tran and Vu Thi? Are they part of the family?"

"Vu Thi is not. She is a street girl who knows a good position. I am sure Dong considers her expendable. But Tan Tran is different. He is Dong's confidant; and, yes, he is another cousin. He is a cousin on Dong's side of the family, and his loyalty to the Cong is sometimes waning. Only Vu Thi was my friend, but now she secretly trysts with Tan Tran when Dong is away. That is how I knew they would be at the bar last week. Vu Thi and I sometimes met there in secret, and that is how Bapak Lam Thang came by much of his information."

Nhung Thi was gazing blankly into space, apparently glad to have this information off her conscience.

"Now what will happen to the three of them if Dong is arrested by the minister?" Andy asked, as Nhung Thi again began to cry.

*   *   *

It was dark by the time Andy and Kelly arrived back at the communications desk in their Majestic Hotel office. There was a stack of messages, which Andy grabbed up and started to read.

"Look at this! They've had to warn the pirate boat off with their twenty millimeters again."

He was silent for a whole minute as he read.

"Now the pirate boat is standing off, and doing something on their stern deck. You can bet they're up to no good."

"They've got to be staying there for a reason. They're going to try to blow up something, you can be sure. We can't help them from here, though. We've done all we could by alerting the Navy. Let's just hope they get a copter there in time, but that'll take several hours," Kelly summed up the situation.

"And while they're out there doing their worst, Dong is at home, probably burning any evidence of his past associations. I'm going to go after him, and right now, before the NLF realizes how great he is and promotes him to general. You take the pistol. I won't need one for that yellow bastard, if I can find him!"

"We can't go riding out there in a car. He'll see us coming and shoot out all the tires, or worse. We'd better take the motorcycle. It's much easier to hide, and we can get off the roads if necessary." Kelly was already planning ahead.

"Can you take the jolts now?" Andy asked, concerned about Kelly's recent hospitalized condition and his mending stitches.

"Sure I can, when it's for a good reason, and I can't think of any better one. I had some auditors on that plane too," Kelly answered.

"No," Andy decided. "We'll take the car and take our chances. You need springs under you. It'll be faster, too, especially if we leave our driver behind."

# Twenty-six

Pug watched as he and James followed the movement of the pirate boat through their binoculars. They had slowly begun to pay out the cable from the giant old seismic reel mounted on the rear deck of the pirate boat. Pug had noted the big splash when they dumped the mine off the stern, and now they were going to string it out a mile behind them. The pirates could stay out of range of the twenty-millimeter cannons mounted fore and aft on the supply vessel, and still be able to drag the mine through the water until it struck against the hull. They'd blow sky high, and the supply tender would sink in a minute.

It would take them some time to get the mine into position, but the pirates would believe they had all day. The explosion would be very effective, for the outer skin on the supply ship was a standard gauge for an ocean-going ship. It was only an eighth of an inch thick or a quarter, at most. It certainly wouldn't withstand a battle with a mine. They'd sink like a rock.

"It's pretty obvious what they intend to do, and they think their boat can stay safely out of range of those twenty millimeters. How long do you think it will take them to string out that cable, and tow it around into a position where they can drag the mine against the ship?" James asked, as he continued to watch through the binoculars.

Pug was rubbing his chin, and thinking.

"Do you have any idea how long that cable might be?" he asked.

"It could be any length. We used to use a four thousand foot line on a reel that size. That'd be my best guess, but I haven't seen anyone use cables like that in many a year. They must be left over from an antique operation."

"Then I'd say we have about an hour to see what we can do to stop 'em," Pug said. "Stringing the cable will take a half of that if your length estimate is right, and then they'll have to maneuver the mine into position. We've got to come up with something right away, because those twenties will keep the boat at arm's length, but won't stop the mine."

"Did I hear you say you had a couple of bazookas? What could we do with those?" James asked.

"Yes, and I know how to use 'em," Pug stated. "We also have the boat tied up below that we use to transport supplies. It's an old tub, though, and couldn't outrun anything," Pug stated sadly.

"They don't have to be outrun, because towing that mile of cable, they'll just be inching along. They won't be maneuverable while they're towing a long cable," James reminded him. "We could catch them easily."

"The problem is that they also have machine guns aboard. What could we do about them?"

Pug was asking, but he was thinking at the same time. There might be a solution, he decided. If they could rig casing for a shield, that'd be the ticket.

"Remember those fuel barrels stacked on their rear deck? If we could get close enough, and could hit those tanks with a bazooka shot, we could blow 'em out of the water!" James was grinning at the thought.

"I wouldn't ask any of the crew to run our boat up under those pirate machine guns, but that's our best chance of stopping them. I'll go and give it a try. I've never fired a bazooka from a rolling platform before, but now I'm going to give it my best shot. I want to get those sons of bitches. I want to send them all straight to hell! I've never had a ship sunk from under me, and I don't intend to start now."

Pug was red-faced, and getting more riled up by the second.

"You won't have to go alone," James replied. "These are a part of the same group who downed our company plane, and blew up our friend in Saigon. We might even do this for Kelly. If he were here, he'd be on the bow, helping us. If you can aim and shoot, I can steer the boat," James stated loudly.

"I have an idea about some protection from their machine guns. You go have a crew load some casing joints back onto the boat. Be sure they have some of them extend up past the cabin on the left side. The others can protect the same side in the rear cockpit. I'll go and get the bazookas loaded. You sure you can steer a boat?"

Pug was grinning now that they had a plan, and their nervousness from inactive tension was broken.

"You bet," James replied. "In college, I majored in Sunday afternoon canoeing on the local pond. The steering part is what I was best at." James laughed, too, as he marched quickly away to instruct a loading crew.

A half hour later, the supply shuttle boat was loaded. They had done their work on the side away from the pirate boat so they could not be observed, just in case they were also being watched, and they were certain they were.

"Jamie Boy, you did a great job stacking the casing," Pug said as he reviewed the arrangement. It was eight-inch size, so it stacked up neatly along the outer planking, beside the steering cabin. Then it extended on back into the well, toward the stern. A second stack was interlaced with the first, but it extended from the small steering cabin aft, and was stacked up onto the stern transom. The pieces were nicely laced to form a slot near the stern where a bazooka would just fit nicely. It had been a quick but masterful construction of a wheelhouse and a rear cockpit, armored on one side. Pug was pleased, even if it would cause their tub to steer a little one-sided.

Several of the loading crew had volunteered to go along to attack the pirates, for they all had an interest in a successful outcome. Pug immediately vetoed their help, and was joined in his staunch, one-way decision by James. The two of them were enough men to risk on such a questionable and dangerous adventure. If the two of them couldn't do it, there was no sense in risking more lives, Pug decided.

He was pleased to see James accept an automatic rifle handed to him by one of the crew, as the last sling was hoisted away. He had laid it on the seat beside the wheel within easy reach, as Pug found his place to the rear in the cockpit with his bazookas.

"Let 'er go!" Pug shouted, and they quickly warped away from the drillship.

He felt a little lonely as they came out from under the protection of the noisy monster. Now that he could hear himself think, Pug wondered if this trip was really the intelligent thing to attempt. He could think of no alternative, though, to save his ship and Andy's company.

As they rounded the drillship's stern, he could see that the pirate boat had now fully extended the mile of cable, and they were slowly getting under way. They were headed for a point about a mile aft of the supply tender.

"Looks like they intend to line up the cable aft of the ship, and then cut back to wrap the mine around into it. It'll certainly work if we can't stop 'em," Pug shouted from the cockpit, raising his voice above the diesel.

"Let's go around the ship, and meet them on the other side before they can get the cable close enough for the mine to hit," James yelled back.

It was hard to shout over the noise of the slapping waves and the engine. But then, little more needed to be said, for they both knew what their actions must be. Pug fully realized his responsibility for their decision to act, and had sent messages to the supply vessel and to their office via Saigon telling them of their intentions. In case anything happened, he wanted the world to know they had made an attempt to save their operation, and who was responsible for trying to stop their progress toward the success of VietAmer's exploration.

As they cleared their supply ship, they could see the pirate boat slowly moving into position, crossing their bow a mile ahead. The aft twenty-millimeter cannon opened up with a few short bursts, but the pirate vessel was clearly out of their range. They could see the little plumes of water sprinkled around the boat. It would be pure luck if they hit anything from that range, so they were just letting them know they must keep their distance.

As he and Pug had previously agreed, James picked a point where he predicted the pirate boat must make a turn into the supply boat in order to drag the cable and mine into deadly contact. He set a course, and steered the supply shuttle toward the point. The slow shuttle was still a speedboat compared to the pirates' gunboat, with their heavy cable in tow. With an occasional wave of agreement from Pug, James kept adjusting the intended point of intercept. They soon had passed the tender, and the pirate boat was off their starboard bow. Their casing-armor was stacked on their port side.

Pug kept busy arranging his equipment, which was two bazookas and a box of ammunition. It had been a long time since he had used one of those, and he hoped that his aim was still as good as it had been in Korea. Good or bad, it was their only chance to save the vessels, so they had to try. The rolling deck was not going to provide the best of conditions for good aiming. He just trusted that machine guns were their only armament.

What else could they carry on a small boat? Could they have bazookas of their own? Or if not those, they might use grenade launchers. He hoped they wouldn't have to get that close. He was confident his cockpit armor protection against their machine guns was good enough, unless they were awfully lucky. They'd shoot first at James, though, he knew.

"How close do you want me to get?" shouted James.

"Head right for 'em. Then, at about two hundred meters, machine gun range, turn to the inside and put our port casing-armor toward their boat. Then keep your head way down," Pug yelled.

A sea was running, and the constant rolling motion was not going to help his aim.

They were getting much closer, and a lot sooner than Pug had anticipated. The pirate boat seemed almost to stand still, held back by its heavy tow. Somehow they were attempting to increase their speed, in anticipation of the interception. Pug could hear the roar of their engines. Their own diesel was running at full revs, and now they were closing on the pirates rapidly. They must think we are going to try to board them, Pug thought.

They continued on their collision course, and just as James was about to turn to the inside, Pug shouted, "Look out! They're turning."

It was true. The slow-moving boat had swung its bow toward the supply ship, its slower speed making their turn seem faster. Now if James turned inside them, they would come very near. It was too late to do anything else, for they must make their attack now before they could get to the ship. It was now or never!

Pug remembered a line from the old *Bowdich US Navy Manual:* "When a collision appears imminent, turn toward danger."

"Turn it, James. Turn it now!" Pug shouted at the top of his voice.

James had already pulled the rudder over, and a scattering of machine-gun bullets pelted noisily against the unprotected bow of their boat, as he ducked. Several slugs shattered his windscreen, and shards of glass sprayed across the little control house.

Pug watched him as he checked himself over, but found no blood. It was several seconds before the boat responded to its rudder, and that was an eternity, for if they stayed in the line of fire long enough, James was going to get hit, so he just prayed.

As their bow inched around ahead of the pirates, the casing slowly and mercifully became their shield, much to Pug's relief, for he worried about his young friend. The remainder of the glass fell from the windshield. It splattered across James' automatic rifle, and onto the adjoining seat. The din of the ricocheting bullets now sounded different. More of them were finding their boat, but most of them were bouncing off the metal of the casing. Their armor was doing its job.

But they were now passing very close, with the bow of the pirate boat only a scant 100 yards away. Pug could see two men with guns standing on their open bow and firing constantly at them. He'd need to stop that, if he had any chance of completing his job.

He watched as James leaned his knee against the wheel, and grabbed the gun with both hands. He fired as rapidly as he could toward the two men on the bow, but Pug knew it was only a distraction. At least it would give them something to think about and spoil their concentration until his position near the stern became apparent to them.

Suddenly another figure appeared on the pirate boat's bow. It was a little man with a big weapon. He was holding a rifle with an attachment. It was an antitank weapon! Now they were passing right in front of the bow of their boat, and James was left facing the new rifle, which was taking aim directly at him. He was only fifty yards away.

"Duck, James! For God's sake, duck!" Pug heard himself yelling.

James was already firing his burp gun, and doing his best to hit the new target. He'd never know if the burp gun had found a mark.

Pug saw the flash of the grenade launcher out of the corner of his eye, and the sickening streak of the missile coming directly toward their wheelhouse. It was as though everything were switched into slow motion. At the same moment, he pressed the trigger. He also saw a stream of fire heading directly to the forward cabin of the pirate boat. He had gotten off a shot with the bazooka, and it was accurate!

At the moment of the explosion on the front cabin of the pirate boat, the three men there lurched forward into the sea. But it was too late to avoid the damage to their own boat that they had caused. Their missile fell just short of its intended target. Thank God! Pug thought, even though he wasn't a praying man. It hit the wooden side planking of their supply boat just above the water line, and below the casing. It ripped a good-sized hole in the gunnel, and the blast threw James out of his seat and onto the deck.

Pug saw James grab for his left leg as his torn pants began to turn a bright red. He was amazed that James wasn't making any sound. It had just wrenched him sharply around, and some of his pants had been torn away. The blood kept streaming—James' blood. He knew they had a real problem.

At that moment, though, Pug knew they had more serious business to take care of. Their boat was passing on ahead, with the pirate boat crossing their stern. Pug knew the danger. It was like Nelson at Trafalgar. He had "crossed their tee." Now he had to get himself back into a position where he could fire again, and attack the pirates from their side, where he knew they were vulnerable. For the moment their gunfire had stopped.

Pug shouted, "Swing 'er, James, now!"

It was almost quiet now, after the explosions and the steady whine of bullets had ceased. Pug watched and hoped. Slowly, he saw James gather his strength, and then he swung the bow, apparently without thought of his blood-gushing leg. This time it was to his left—turn toward danger. That would put their protected port side and his bazooka in view and range of their gasoline supply.

Soon there were more men with guns, firing from the afterdeck of the pirate boat. It was their boarding party. Pug crouched low behind the stacked casing as their boat swung all too slowly around the disabled pirates. He prayed they hadn't had time to rig another missile launcher.

"Duck, James. Duck!" he heard himself shouting, knowing full well that he wasn't heard over the roar of the engines and the sea and the guns firing at them.

Pug watched as James dropped his weapon on the deck; he was concentrating on slowing their boat so he could get a steady bazooka shot before they were out of his range. Still the bullets found their ship, making the two distinctly different sounds of plugging into the wood siding and ricocheting off the steel casing.

Whoosh! The stream of fire toward the stack of oil drums behind their deckhouse was the most beautiful sight Pug had ever seen. Suddenly the sky was streaked with light, as the great explosion of the gasoline drums lit up the entire center of the pirate boat. It was fortunate they had drifted on past, or they would have been enveloped in the blast. The entire boat was soon aflame, and the men who were previously firing from the stern were nowhere to be seen. Possibly they had been blown into the water.

Pug went forward as they continued to cruise slowly along the old seismic cable, which now was lying slack in the water. James would not remember, for he lost too much blood, and had passed out. Later, when he returned to consciousness, he confided in Pug that in his excitement he had hardly known he was wounded. Pug had ripped the trousers away from his leg, and bound up his wound. He had stopped the bleeding, and was pouring cold water over his brow.

James shook his wet head.

"Hey, what're you doing? he demanded, as he came back to the conscious world.

"Just trying to get you back among the living is all," Pug replied. "You took quite a rip there. Fortunately, it was just a little above your waterline!" he grinned, then helped James back onto the seat in front of the wheel.

"Hey, I'm better now, and I remember seeing that great explosion and fire. Is there anything left of the pirate boat?" James asked unsteadily.

"No; nothing is left. It went down after the fire reached some explosives they had stored below, I guess. It blew a hole you could drive Davy Jones through, so he went in—in about five minutes."

"How long have I been out?" James asked.

"Not too long—about fifteen minutes. Sorry you missed the sinking," Pug answered.

"That's OK by me, just so long as it sank." James peered around the horizon. "Were there any survivors?"

"I don't know yet," replied Pug. "There's some debris floating around over there. When you feel up to steering, we can have a look. But we have another job to complete right now. Do you think you can stay awake long enough to steer this thing?"

"I can sure try. I'm feeling better now, and steering doesn't take much effort. What do you have in mind?"

"We'd better blow up that mine before it drifts into the ship and does the pirates' dirty work for them. Just hold it on this course, and we'll soon be at the end of the cable. We should find a mine attached."

James held the course while Pug returned to the cockpit and prepared his bazooka for yet another shot. This time it should be much easier, just as long as they didn't get too close. Pug acted as their lookout from the bow, and with his direction, James brought their craft around and approached the mine from downwind. They didn't want to chance drifting into it, so they slowed the boat to a crawl.

Pug tried a shot first from long range, for safety's sake; but the missile fell a few feet away from it with no effect, so they moved closer. The second shot did not fail.

There was a gigantic explosion, and a great tower of water rose up to envelop the area. Pug was almost sorry they had not made more attempts to detonate the mine from the greater distance, for their small boat was rocked to the point that they were shipping water. The hole the antitank grenade had left in their side was too near the water line for comfort.

When their boat and the sea had settled down, all that remained of the pirate operation was some flotsam and an old seismic cable. The cable they could ask the Vietnamese Navy to retrieve later, if they wished. For now, they should look to see if there were any pirate survivors, so Pug gathered their guns into what was left of the wheelhouse.

As they pulled nearer the floating wreckage, Pug could see that there actually were three desperate men clinging to the pieces of wooden hull that had escaped the explosion and fire. They were all suffering from burns, and gave no trouble as they helped each other into the stern of their supply boat.

Pug remained beside James in the wheelhouse, with the burp gun aimed toward the pirates. It was really unnecessary, for their burns plus the hour's stay in the water had taken their toll. The fight had all gone out of them.

The crew of the tender cheered loudly as they passed them on their way back to the drillship. When they tied up to their mooring near the stern and below the helipad, the drilling crew were cheering for them, too. First they lowered the basket to retrieve the pirate captives, and then to retrieve

Pug and his wounded steersman. James needed their doctor's immediate attention, but loudly insisted he was going to recover.

Interrogation of the three surviving pirates was a simple matter for Pug. He just looked his sternest, and loudly relayed the simple question to them simultaneously.

"Who hired you to attack our supply ship?"

They all wanted to talk at once, for they sincerely believed their captor was the personification of the American devil, and was as mean as he looked. He spoke only English, but they understood him perfectly in Vietnamese. The drillship crewman who was doing the translating explained that they knew exactly what he was asking.

A long message, explaining all of the events that had occurred during the attack, was duly transmitted to the Vietnamese communications center, and promptly relayed to the VietAmer offices in Ho chi Minh City and Hong Kong. Pug realized that, being so late in the day, there would probably be no one in their Majestic Hotel office to receive the exciting information. He had to tell someone they were safe and that the pirates had admitted they were hired by Dong Huan Chou of the NLF.

Pug did his best to take care of their geophysicist, James, and make him comfortable aboard the drillship until a copter could come to evacuate him. James took exception to that.

"I have a velocity survey to complete," he reminded Pug. "I'm almost sorry we had to leave the quiet of the supply boat with its small diesel engine and the plink of machine gun bullets keeping me awake. Here on the drillship, there's no escaping the roar and the vibration of the drilling engines."

It was several hours later, and very dark when a helicopter gunship of the Viet Navy made two circling passes around their ships, and then tipped its blades. Pug blinked their derrick lights at them. The gunship turned, and headed back for the Mekong Delta. Their work had been done for them.

# Twenty-seven

"Let's go, Kelly. We've got work to do!" Andy said firmly, as he checked his gear in preparation for their departure to find Dong Huan Chou in his compound.

He knew that if they didn't get there soon, Dong would have destroyed any evidence that might exist, and probably would have taken off for the hills to convince the NLF that he was a hero for sending pirates to stop their operation. They must find proof he had given the order to blow up their plane, as well as commanded his henchmen to burn their office and kill Lam Thang. They already had proof he disrupted their communications.

Now was the time for confrontation with this devil, or he would destroy all the evidence and escape. They must get there ahead of the raiders of the energy minister, for they would carry off everything, including the pock-faced Dong in his dark aviator glasses and with his silver briefcase. If that happened, they would never be able to prove his responsibility for the killings. They were only interested in punishing him for treason.

Both men had dressed in navy pullovers, dark trousers, and black shoes. They might have an opportunity to sneak up on their elusive adversary in the dark. Kelly handed Andy a flashlight and tucked his own in his jacket pocket. Andy handed him the .38 pistol.

"Here, you'd better take this. You're more accustomed to using a gun than I am. Besides, I don't feel like I need a gun for what I want to do. I just want to get my fists about six inches deep into that conniving bastard's face."

"Easy, my friend. He's cunning, and didn't get where he is by not being prepared for anything that comes. It's better that we also are ready. Some of the guards in that compound carry Uzis. We'll have to sneak up on them if we expect to get to Dong, and to the treasures he has squirreled away inside," Kelly reminded him.

"I know that getting in will not be easy, but we'll have to find a way. We've simply got to get at him. He burned our office down and he killed our friends. Now he must be repaid, and we're the only ones here to do it. We'll find some way to get him out in the open."

"Do you think his place would burn?" Kelly asked.

"With a little gasoline on the thatched roof, it would go up like a torch. Anyway, let's see if there's some other way first. Remember, the woman he calls 'Ibu' lives there, and she's a Hoe. She is Lin Jin's great-aunt. The girl, Vu Thi, will be there too, probably. I'll bet she can take care of herself, though. Tan Tran I'm not worried about, because he's Dong's torch and grenade man. He'll have to answer for his part in all this, as well as Dong. The police will probably be looking for him as an accessory," Andy answered.

"Are you sure we can get there by car, or should we go by motorcycle?" Kelly asked again.

"There's little reason now to be sneaky about how we get out there. If Ho Bac Minh did what he said he'd do, the police or soldiers should be getting there very soon. We'd be sure to learn a lot more if we arrived there ahead of them, so let's move. If they take Dong into custody, we'll never see him again, and God only knows what influence he can bring to bear on them. He may be in the mountains by morning, hidden forever with his stash of illicit gold.'

Andy thought for a few seconds.

"And I'm sure you don't need a long ride over bumpy roads on a cycle in your condition."

"That's great by me, and we won't need to take the driver. I'm sure you know the way there now, even in the dark. Besides, we won't have time to wait for any language translations," Kelly stated.

"I hear the fax running," said Andy. "Let's check the messages before we go. It might be from Pug Cox and James, and we need to know what happened to their pirates."

\* \* \*

It was much easier to negotiate the pockmarked roads in a car, as Andy sped along them northward toward Cu Chi, to the estate of Dong Huan Chou. There had been no maintenance of the roads in the area since the war, and the potholes that had developed were there to stay. Occasionally there was a small detour around a cave-in or a mud hole, but mostly the road was just a rutted mess, following along the ancient tracks, seeking the high ground.

Andy was in a serious mood, not knowing what troubles might be in their immediate future. They discussed the events of the day at the drillship, and commended Pug Cox and James Wellman for their intention to defend the drilling operation. The message Andy had read told only that they were going off to battle the pirates. There was no time for them to wait and see if their plan was a success.

"If they waited for the Vietnamese Navy for protection, they would have all but lost their supply vessel by now. I sure hope Cox is as good a shot with that bazooka as he says he was in Korea," Kelly commented.

"If he isn't, they may cause us to start over with the drilling. By this time, the drillship, too, could be in serious trouble and about to lose their hole," Andy answered.

They both knew what might happen should the deep-hole gas pressures get out of control. There would be a blowout, and the whole ship could go down. Pug and James were definitely their last line of defense.

"They'll give the pirates a run for their money. I'll bet Pug mounts that bazooka on his living room wall when he retires, if they get out of this," Kelly mused.

"I wish we had them both here. His tough expression could scare Dong right out of his lair," Andy added, smiling.

"I'm glad to see you can smile after all that has happened. By tomorrow, we might really have reason to smile—or maybe not."

That was Kelly, Andy thought. Always the optimist.

"I'm sure the message about the pirates attacking has been relayed to Bill Hanby, and he'll send it on to Houston. They'll want to know the status of their investment in VietAmer Oil. No matter what happens now, Dong'll not be around to get in our hair anymore. We can get on with our exploration, assuming we have a drillship to get on with."

"What's going to happen to Nhung Thi now, without a family and only friends to help her?" Kelly asked.

"I've been worrying about her. We can give her some money, but I don't think that would help for long. She needs a permanent solution, like being set up in a business she can run," Andy replied.

"What she needs is a rich man," Kelly commented with a grin.

"Are you volunteering?" Andy asked, grinning back slyly.

"No, she needs an Oriental man. But a good-looking girl like her won't have any trouble along that line, especially if she had a prosperous business of her own."

"Sorry about all the bumps, Kelly," Andy said, as he rushed the auto along the rough road. "I hope you hold on to your stitches. There's no way to miss all of the potholes, and we need to get there as soon as we can," Andy apologized.

As they neared the compound, they could hear the clatter of the machine-gun fire before they saw the police car blocking the road. It was 100 meters short of the entry to the estate. There were soldiers rushing all around the outer fence of the compound, and they could see that the main gate was completely missing.

Just as they pulled up to an officer standing by a car parked across the road, they heard a giant blast. One of the Spirit Houses came tumbling into the road. Andy pulled the car onto the narrow shoulder of the lane, and both he and Kelly got out. The officer waved them both to move aside, but before they could move, the other Spirit House followed the first into the road. They had apparently been blown away by grenade launchers.

All of the exterior guards were gone, either scared away early or lying dead. When the soldiers and police arrived in force, Dong's little guard contingent had withered, for they didn't amount to any formidable deterrent against such odds.

The officer standing by the blocking car waved them to one side, but they walked up to where the policeman was lighting a cigarette, leaning unconcernedly against his vehicle. He had his burp gun cradled in one arm as he manipulated the lighter with the other. He was making no motion to stop them, but obviously he was there for just that purpose. He assumed his authority was unquestioned.

They made no attempt to walk past the police car, but any foreigner who drove his own vehicle these days in Vietnam deserved some attention. The officer watched them candidly, saying nothing. The rattle of machine-gun fire went on inside.

Andy tried to talk to the officer, but at first his efforts had little result.

"No speak Engliece," was all they could get out of him.

Andy was persistent, however, and he went on talking and trying to repeat words that might mean something in relation to the officer's reason for being called out on this night mission, which was resulting in so much gunfire. At least he had his attention, and he was listening.

"VietAmer Oil Corporation—Doctor Andy Cheston—Kelly Johnson," Andy went on.

Nothing seemed to ring a bell, for the man stood with a languid, deadpan face, telling them to go away in Vietnamese, Andy supposed.

"Minister of energy, Ho Bac Minh."

Bingo! Abruptly, the man stiffened. That name rang a bell. The name of the minister had gotten the attention of the officer immediately, and he stood stiffly erect.

They continued to trade words and names. The officer rattled on in Vietnamese, until it was quite evident that he knew Andy was the head of the American company that Energy Minister Ho Bac Minh had personally called them out to protect. Their job that night was to arrest the traitor, Dong Huan Chou, who had committed crimes against the people by opposing this man's company. His duty became quite clear. Anything Andy wanted, he would arrange immediately.

Andy motioned that they wished to go and see what was happening in the compound, in spite of the continuing rattle of the guns. Immediately, the officer called a soldier over to them, and gave him instructions in Vietnamese. The soldier motioned for them to follow. As they marched down the road behind their guide, the sound of the commotion inside the compound grew louder.

When they arrived at the front gate's former location, it was amply apparent what had happened to it. In the middle of the compound was a large Army truck—one with a machine gun mounted over the cab and a broad reinforced front bumper. The top gun was still manned. All of the gunfire was from the outside, and was directed at the house.

A dozen or more soldiers were running around inside the compound, and they were trying to get their truck close enough to break in the heavy front door.

"Let's get away from here for now," Andy said. "As soon as they break through that door, something's gonna come out, and fast—probably bullets."

Andy led the way as they ran back across the road. Beyond the lane littered with pieces of Spirit House was a steep slope, partially covered with bamboo clumps and an occasional banana tree. They crouched down behind the brush for cover and watched, just as the truck's engine whined and the truck rolled over the border of white rocks and the step. Then it crashed through the heavy barred door into the entry room with a great screeching uproar.

There were a few brief bursts of gunfire, and then all was quiet. When the big truck was backed away, all was quiet inside, and the soldiers formed a semicircle around the destroyed front doors.

Suddenly, a figure appeared. It was Tan Tran, with one arm bandaged and the other holding an Uzi. He swept the ring of soldiers, who quickly melted away. While they sought places of safety in which to hide, he ran for the road.

"Here he comes!" Kelly shouted. Then quietly, he warned, "Here,

Andy, he's coming this way. Take the pistol."

Andy thought a split second, and replied, "No, Kelly. You're the one he hit with the grenade. You can repay him."

Andy was stunned as the big gun went off so close to his ear, but it had been effective. This time, Kelly had not hit him in the arm, which still had its bandage. Tan Tran lay flat in the road. Andy never knew if the shot by Kelly had flattened him, or if it was the barrage of fire from the guns of the soldiers. It no longer mattered.

Tan Tran lay dead in the middle of the road, and the bright red blood was spreading across the white baba as he still clung desperately to the Uzi. He had tried to protect his master's property to the end. Andy saw him as he lay, clutching the tools of his recent trade, and he felt no remorse. This was his richly deserved payment for killing Lin Jin's relative, Lam Thang; for injuring Kelly; and for burning their office. They were both lucky he had not also killed them with the grenade.

Slowly he and Kelly walked back to the gate, leaving the yeoman lying dead in the road. Such dedication to duty was undeserved by such a master as Dong, Andy thought.

"What do you think they are going to do now? They still haven't found Dong," Andy asked, still saddened by the bloodshed.

"I don't know," Kelly replied. "If I were running this show, I'd take a swat team and go in and find him. Of course, they might get shot doing it, so they may have another plan. The officer with the horn must have been calling for Dong to surrender, but apparently he got no response."

"I think they believe Dong may have already escaped. See that soldier over there with the can of gasoline?"

Andy pointed to the corner of the compound.

"Yeah, he looks like he has his instructions."

"I think they are going to burn the place. Look! He's putting a match to the torch. They're going to smoke him out, if he's still inside."

Kelly shook his head.

"They can't do that. Ibu and Vu Thi are in there with him, aren't they? Of course, they could have escaped out the back."

"That's not likely, for with as many soldiers as they have around here, that exit would have been blocked before they ever started their attack," Andy replied.

"There they go," Kelly cried. "They're setting fire to the roof all the way around. Whoever's in there had better come out soon, or they'll end up being a baked Viet!"

"You're right, and it won't take long. There's only one front door, and see how they have it ringed with soldiers. we'll see someone run out soon, or never." Andy was already about to choke on the smoke, so he knew those inside had to leave.

He saw a flash of white at the inner door past the entryway, and a coughing, choking Vu Thi came stumbling out, stepping wearily over the crashed door and into the courtyard. She was grabbed by a soldier, and almost dragged away toward them at the main gate. When the soldier hurried her past, she seemed not to notice the two Americans.

Then she suddenly pulled back, and cried, "Ibu, Ibu!"

She followed by spouting a torrent of Vietnamese, but they understood her message. She wanted them to get Ibu out of the fire.

Then she seemed to relax, for another figure came, coughing, through the door, stumbling as she tried to walk rapidly. Her arthritic limbs prevented her from moving with any speed. She, too, was taken by a soldier, somewhat more gently than the young Vu Thi had been. He led her, half stumbling, toward the gate.

Suddenly, Ibu shouted in Vietnamese, and with a burst of vigor that startled the soldier, she broke away. She actually was able to run screaming, back into the burning building. There was no way the soldier could catch her.

She disappeared into the smoke and flames that were rapidly consuming the entire wooden structure. Ibu would not be deterred from her mission, which must have been terribly important to her.

Vu Thi turned to be led out of the compound by the soldier. When she saw the Americans, she stopped.

"Why did you have to come to Vietnam? You had all the rest of the world to explore. Dong could have done the drilling here. Dong was a great genius. And both Dong and Tan Tran loved me."

She sobbed in great gasps.

"What did Ibu say when she pulled away from the soldier and ran back into the house?" Andy asked her.

When finally she was able to reply, Vu Thi sniffled and said, "She wanted her sealed envelope. It has her personal papers, and she always guarded them well. Dong had taken them to hide them safely for her, but now she wanted them back. You see, they were most important to her."

"But where is Dong? Has he chosen to burn in the fire in preference to arrest?" Andy asked.

"Who knows where Dong has disappeared to. He is like a ghost—he comes and he goes, where no one can see him. He is a phantom. He must have gone early, and he left without me!"

She was crying now, with the first realization of troubles in her future life. She soon was raving loudly, for she had just seen the bloodstained body of Tan Tran. She must have become a little unbalanced from all of the sudden deaths of her only real friends in the world. The soldier led her away more gently, as she had stopped struggling, or stopped caring about anything.

Andy turned to Kelly and said, "Just as we feared, the soldiers got here ahead of us, and if there was any evidence left to find, it has all gone up in smoke by now."

"Do you think there's anything we could find by poking around in the ashes?" Kelly asked.

"I doubt it. Maybe an old toothbrush. But we've got to satisfy ourselves by having a closer look," Andy answered. "After all, the soldiers were only looking for Dong, or they wouldn't have burned the house. When they have determined he is missing, they won't be interested in looking for evidence. It'll be dawn before it's cooled down enough for us to look over the place carefully."

Much sooner than either of them expected, the soldiers finished stirring and sifting through the smoldering ruins, looking for anything of value. Having found very little, they carried away the bodies of Tan Tran, which lay outside the front gate, and Ibu, who was found inside, huddled against the bookcase. Strangely enough, the bookcase was still a recognizable piece of furniture, although it had its doors burned off, and the contents were only a mass of ashes. To one side of the room was the padded sofa, burned to a crisp outside but still smoldering.

The soldiers were readying themselves to leave, for they had been on duty the entire day before. There were a few of Dong's guards on the Spirit Guard Towers to be carried off with the dead, but apparently all of the house servants had fled at the first indication of a police raid.

By the first light of dawn, Andy found that he and Kelly were almost alone, except for one policeman left on guard at the front of the estate, and one at the back watching the garage. The black Mercedes had been driven away when their truck left. Why they needed to leave guards was not clear, for there was nothing of value left unburned.

As Kelly and Andy strolled through the rooms, they looked for clues to Dong's lifestyle, and Andy was trying to make sense out of his actions. His car was driven here, so he had returned home. He didn't leave in it. Why had he returned directly to his home when he was threatened? Surely he knew he would be arrested when the police arrived. Where is he now? Did he have advance notice of the police raid, so he could escape? Very likely, Andy thought.

If Dong was going to escape, would he not have taken Vu Thi with him? Apparently she loved him, in a way. And Tan Tran, his dependable yeoman and henchman—any civil director would not have been left to face the police alone. If Dong were gone, what had he returned for? And if he left, why was Tan Tran still here? What was he protecting? He should have escaped as well. There must be another answer to his disappearance here somewhere.

Andy and Kelly were tired from the long day's efforts, and they found a place to rest and to think, awaiting the new day.

# Twenty-eight

As they picked their way through the charred and burned furnishings, Andy looked at the spot where the body of Ibu was found. Why had she picked this place, in front of Dong's bookcase, to die? Burned shards of paper and remains of the old bindings lay beside where her body had fallen. He picked up a book, half ashes. What volume was it? Surely these burned clumps were not remnants of her important papers, for they looked as if they were sets of large books, fallen from the case. Her papers would have been in some envelope, and would have burned to a crisp. There must be another reason. Suddenly a chill came over Andy, and he felt a tingle of cognition. The solution to the mystery came to him in a flash.

"Kelly, come here!" he shouted. "Look at this bookcase."

"What have you found?"

He pointed to the floor in front of the bookcase.

"See those marks?"

"What about them?" Kelly saw nothing unusual.

"Dong hasn't gone," Andy rushed on excitedly. "He just hid himself in his own hiding spot, right here behind the books."

Kelly looked at him as though he had lost his mind.

"But what are the marks?"

"He has a tunnel entrance right here from his lounging room," Andy explained. "Ibu knew that he would go straight there to retrieve his important papers, the minute he got into trouble. I'll bet he's still hiding in here."

"You may be right. Let's see if we can open it."

Andy shoved against the bookcase.

"It gave a little. Help me scoot this thing forward, and we'll dig him out."

The excitement of the realization surged through Andy. He could hardly contain his emotions. They still had a chance to catch Dong. He had thought all was lost, and destroyed by the soldiers. Now he was positive that Dong's trick had caused them to miss their quarry.

"You must be right," agreed Kelly as he examined the marks on the floor.

"Tunnels don't burn, Kelly. He's still in there. He might be short of air to breathe, but he's still there. The soldiers left him for you and me to deal with, just as we planned," Andy spoke, excitedly.

He turned his flashlight upward and was astonished. The roof of the estate house was completely gone—burned away. It was going to become light soon, so he conserved the flashlight for later study of the interior. Kelly then lit a candle to free their hands.

Together they got a good hold on the charred corners of the case. Then with a great heave, it came forward with a rush, and fell into the middle of the room.

There it was! A squared hole in the outer wall, which extended back into the earthen embankment. At the back of the hole, Andy could barely see the top slat of what appeared to be a crude ladder.

"Dong must be at the other end of that tunnel." Andy's adrenaline was pumping, and he was more than ready to go in after him.

"But he must be expecting company, Andy. Surely he's heard us, and possibly even has seen our light. Perhaps he has a burp gun or grenades for protection," Kelly reasoned warily.

Andy nodded, realizing that discretion must prove to be the better part of valor, so he and Kelly stood back and recounted the possibilities for their attack.

"If Dong went into hiding, either he is down there waiting, or there was another way out of the tunnel," Andy said.

"I doubt if there would be another accessible entry to the tunnel, or Dong would not have considered it to be a safe repository for his treasures. Therefore, if anyone goes in, Dong will still be there waiting," Kelly said.

"That's true," Andy agreed. "We're not equipped for a frontal assault, so we must think of some trick in order not to walk straight into Dong's blazing Uzi. Now he has nothing to lose, so he will fight to the death rather than surrender."

"He'll have a gun, or guns. I only hope he doesn't have any grenades. I wonder what he kept stored there, for he probably didn't have a lot of time to prepare his escape."

"We can only hope he knew a damp tunnel was not the place to store weapons. Also, he knows the layout of the cave."

"One advantage we have is that it's dark down there, and there are two of us," Kelly said. "If we try to take a quick look with flashlights, he'll probably shoot at anything that shows a beam. That'll tell us where he is, at least."

"Going in with a light would be too dangerous, even foolish, so let's find another way." Andy tried to express some logic.

"What other choice do we have?" Kelly asked.

"We have three, I guess. we can wait and let the police blow him out with grenades, or they may talk him out and capture him. Otherwise, we have to go in after him without a light."

"We can't both go in at once. The tunnel's too small," Kelly objected, without even considering the police options.

"I'm going in alone; it's the only way," Andy said with finality. "Besides, you probably aren't physically recovered enough for this sort of climbing job."

He was hoping the tunnel wasn't designed like those on Easter Island. There, you had to start in facing the right direction or your body couldn't make it around the twisting turns, and you'd get stuck.

"You may be right," Kelly gave in reluctantly. "I don't feel much like any physical contests, but don't count me out completely. How are you going to handle it?"

"I saw a chunk of sheet iron outside. I'll try to use that as a shield. If he shoots first, I can shoot back. Then I'll know where he is. If he doesn't shoot, I'll just keep pushing around in the dark until I find him at the end of the tunnel."

"And then what?"

Andy didn't answer for a moment.

"Then I'll have to ask the memory of Harold Blanton to let me know what to do next. If I get that far, my conscience will have to be my guide. Should something happen and I don't come out in a reasonable time, call the guards to get the police. Don't you try to come after me." Andy was explicitly dictatorial.

"OK, if you must go in alone," Kelly agreed. "I'll stay here now and stand guard at the entry."

A half hour later, they were prepared. Andy had doubled a large piece of corrugated iron until it was about two feet high and sixteen inches wide. He made a handle out of an old belt he'd found in the servant's quarters, and tested the makeshift shield to see if he could move it handily. It was heavy, and it wouldn't be easy; but he found he could move about with it hung on his arm. It would be better than nothing.

Taking the .38 from Kelly, he checked it for bullets, and filled a pocket with spares. Then he placed the flashlight in his hip pocket. It might be too dark down there to dare to turn it on, and might possibly be better to just grope in the dark. He had also brought some candles he had found in the servant's supply. He placed a couple and some matches in another pocket.

He was ready. It was now or never.

Andy moved over to the black hole, trying to ignore the clutched feeling in his midsection. He held a fist-sized rock in one hand as he stood beside the black void.

He shouted loudly, "Dong, this is Andy Cheston. We are here with the police, and we know you are down there. Your house has been burned. Tan Tran is dead, so there's no use in your waiting for help. I will count to twenty, and if you don't come out by then, the soldiers will blow you up with grenades!"

He waited a good ten seconds, but there was no sound.

"Shout if you are coming out, and you will be treated as a captive! Otherwise, you'll end up dead! One—two—three . . . "

The count went up to twenty, and there was no response. It was as if Andy were shouting into an empty hole, and all he got back was a faint echo.

"You've had your chance, Dong! Here comes a grenade!"

Andy waited five seconds, with still no response, so he tossed the rock down the hole. He could hear it hit and bounce against a ledge, finally landing on some dirt surface far below.

Without waiting, Andy plunged into the black hole, grabbing the spot where he knew the top step of the ladder must be. Quickly he found his way to the next steps below, until, about fifteen feet down, he found a flat surface.

This was not a time to stop, Andy thought, for with his threat of a grenade, Dong would logically have taken what cover he could. But now, when he realized there was no grenade, he would know the exact location of the entry hole. It was Andy's most defenseless moment, so he had to move, and fast.

He extended his left arm with the shield, and it scraped along a dirt wall. Crouching as low as he could, he moved forward carefully, hoping there was no hole in the floor ahead of him. He came to a corner. Should he turn? Yes, anything to get away from the known point of entry into the tunnel.

Andy moved left around the corner and scooted along for several feet. Then he stopped and listened. The tunnel was deathly quiet, without a sound of any kind. It was hot down there, and smelled of fumes and smoke. There was not a breath of movement in the dirty air, which apparently had been heated by the fire above. The intensity of the darkness was so absolute, and this Andy had not previously been able to imagine. He waited for about two minutes, just listening. There was no sound to echo and tell him how big the tunnel might be.

Then he heard a click and a foot drag on the dirt floor. He guessed it to be thirty feet away. Suddenly a whole covey of Uzi bullets whizzed past him in the entry hallway. A feeling of horror swept through him. They would have obliterated anyone who had been standing in the entrance he had so recently vacated.

Now he knew he and Kelly had been right. Dong was here, and he was armed. Also he knew how ardently each wanted the other dead.

Andy wondered, engulfed in the darkness, is there time to think of my position, or is there only time to act? Reasoning had gotten him safely into the tunnel in a position to attack, so he must continue going slow and easy, outthinking Dong.

Now he knew where Dong was, he thought carefully, or had been. Could Dong move without him hearing something in this humid, deadened silence? Andy remained absolutely still, and listened intently. The dank odor was now mixed with the smoke of gunfire, and the stench was oppressive. He remembered Dong had been sealed up in here for several hours already. He must crave action as well as oxygen.

Dong was not moving. Echoes of the gunfire told Andy something about the size of the cave. Dong, he reasoned, was in a room with space to create an echo, and he was in a narrower side tunnel. Dong had moved out from behind something before he fired the burst. So the bigger room wasn't perfectly square.

Andy tried to move soundlessly. He inched along his protected hallway, feeling his way in the dark. He bumped into something metal. His exploring fingers quickly told him it was a standard office filing cabinet. Inching around it, he deduced that he was in a dead-end area, dug as a wing to the side of the main cave. He worked his way back to the edge of the entry tunnel. Now Dong surely knew where he was hiding, for his burst of gunfire had not hit him. What would he do next? Apparently, Dong had no grenades, or he would have used them by now.

How long could this waiting game go on in the dark? Would Dong get tired of waiting and create a light of some kind so his automatic fire would be effective? Or would he just fire into the void occasionally, in hope of being lucky? Would light help to see Dong? Andy wondered. To whose advantage would it be if I use the flashlight? I need to force him into some action, Andy decided.

He carefully moved into the center of the entry cavern, and got as low behind his shield as possible. With the pistol raised high, he fired one blind shot. As he did, he rolled quickly back to the file cabinet. Dong's response was almost immediate. The burst came from the same location as the first. Dong had not moved back into his hole, and now he knew Andy was armed.

Again deathly silence reigned, but the echoes of the gunfire were still ringing in Andy's ears. The smell of burning powder added to the stench of the humidity. Then he heard a scraping sound and stiffened. Was that a different noise he heard? Yes, it was. It was the sound of dirt moving. Dong was digging! Where did he think he could go?

The noise was definite. The chunk, and then swish of dirt falling was clear. He was trying desperately to dig into something. What could be his purpose? It must be with an intent to escape.

Andy knew if he went forward to attack Dong's position, he would meet the scattered fire of the Uzi. He had no idea how much ammo Dong had, or he might try to keep him shooting blindly to waste it in inaccurate fire. If he was digging, it must mean that he was trying to dig into some other passageway. He must hope to escape, otherwise he would be more aggressive with his shooting. It was safest for now to listen and wait to see what would develop.

A half hour passed, and the digging did not stop, except for an occasional rest period when Dong would fire a burst into the void. Andy threw a rock across the room, and soon he could judge the size of the cave. Each time he tested for the size of the area, the digging would stop, and Dong would fire into the center of the room again. Then he'd return to his digging.

\*   \*   \*

Kelly had found a partially burned bench in the entryway, which he dragged into place near the black hole of the tunnel entrance. He wanted to be able to hear anything that happened below.

He started to stand at the sound of shooting below. Heart hammering, he waited for more shots, then settled back onto the bench. Every few minutes, the scene was repeated at the sound of more shots. The only thing he could make out, though, were the bullets from the Uzi that periodically came whizzing into the black hole fifteen feet below the entrance.

He had deduced from the pattern of shooting that Andy must still be all right. Otherwise, Dong would not still be shooting at him. And, too, he had heard Andy fire the Magnum once. That must have been to advise Dong he couldn't try any rushing tactics.

He glanced above. It was becoming daylight outside very quickly now. Kelly was getting restless just sitting on the bench and staring into the black void. He didn't know what final sounds he would hear that would tell him Andy had cornered his prey, or that he had been attacked with disastrous results. All he could do was wait.

Kelly stood up occasionally, and stretched. His wounds were healing well, but the stitches itched terribly. He walked a few steps around the center of the roofless room, and he came to the low table with a burned, padded rattan divan behind it. It wouldn't hurt to look.

He checked the charred drawers. Nothing. The soldiers had looked there first. Then he turned the cushions forward onto the table. As he did, he heard a clink against the charred wood. Looking down, he saw the handle of Dong's stiletto protruding from the side of a burned cushion.

The ancient knife was beautiful. The handle was gold, and the twelve-inch blade was highly polished steel. The weapon must have been an heirloom, for it looked to be both very old and valuable. Kelly carefully tucked it into his belt, and returned to his seat facing the black hole.

It was daybreak, and he could now hear the guard walking around the compound, just beyond the wrecked front door. Kelly wondered if there was anything he could do to help Andy. Nothing came to mind, so he waited, impatiently, and listened intently in the still morning air.

\* \* \*

An hour must have gone by; and still it was pitch-black in the cave, and the air was more stagnant than ever. The smell of smoke had not helped Andy's breathing any. Suppressing coughs was becoming increasingly difficult.

Normally one's eyes became accustomed to the dark after a few minutes, and one could see shapes and figures. But in total darkness, that didn't happen. There was no light here. Not even a pinhole. Dong had moved a lot of dirt, apparently, so he must be exhausted. Now Andy could hear him scraping against something, like a dirt wall. Then he heard him frantically grunting as he pushed against what sounded like loose dirt. Could he be escaping?

Andy knew he must look to see what Dong was up to. He carefully began scooting the heavy file cabinet out into the open room. He could hide behind it if he could keep it moving. It would be better protection than the little tin shield, for it was probably full of paper files.

Obviously, Dong had heard him moving the cabinet, but instead of gunfire, his grunting and scraping noises increased. Then they slowly quieted, and what sounds there were now came from farther and farther away. Dong must have escaped into another segment of tunnel.

Andy carefully turned on his light and waited for the expected gunfire. Nothing! Slowly he peered out from behind his protection. At the far end of the long tunnel-like room, there was a great pile of fresh earth, and Dong was gone. Above the mound was a narrow hole along the ceiling. So that's what he had been trying to push his body into. More important to Andy, there on the ground at the bottom of the dirt pile was the Uzi. Dong must have forced his way through the narrow hole so fast that he'd forgotten his gun, or he was out of ammo. He had lost his principal protection.

Quickly lighting one of the candles, Andy made his way to the entry ladder.

"Hey, Kelly, are you there? Dong has gone."

"Sure, I'm here. What's more important is that you are there. I heard the Uzi. Were you hit?" Kelly inquired.

"No, I'm OK. I think Dong used up all of his ammo, and dug his way into another tunnel. Anyway, the Uzi is here. By now, he's either long gone, or bottled up in another black space, and without a gun. Do you think you can climb down?" Andy asked.

"I'll give it a try," Kelly replied.

Andy set the candle on the file cabinet near the middle of the hollowed-out room, and returned to the ladder to help Kelly down. He was still too sore from his recent grenade encounter for this kind of operation, even if he was an experienced G-man.

When Kelly was again on his feet, they conducted a joint exploration of the entire cave. It must have been some kind of command center for the Vietcong. At the far end was a second short wing. Obviously, the end where Dong had been hiding was the old connection to the tunnel system. There he had chosen to dig his way out, while he kept Andy at bay with the Uzi.

They carefully aimed their flashlights down the opening. It was at ceiling height, and was part of a collapsed segment of tunnel. Andy hoped they'd find a little "Viet" Dong stuck in the hole, but he could see nothing past a few feet. Apparently it allowed Dong to slither through the caved-in portion and into a continuation of the system. They could only hope that it was not still connected to the outer world.

Most of these old tunnels had long since been abandoned. The groundwater had done its work, and now they were caved in to the point where most of them were no longer connected, or usable.

"Do you think Dong had a chance to look at the papers in his cabinet?" Kelly asked.

"He knew what was there already, and perhaps he had no light with him. We can look at them later," Andy answered.

"I don't suppose he carried much away with him into that tunnel anyway," Kelly stated.

"Ibu certainly thought there was something here worth keeping."

"Are you going to go on in there after Dong, or should we wait for soldiers to ferret him out?" Kelly inquired.

"We've waited long enough. Right now I'm going after Dong, and you can have a look at the files. It's probably all in Vietnamese anyway, and we'll have to get someone to translate for us," Andy said.

"Do you really want to press your luck again by going into that dark hole? If he isn't gone already, he'll be waiting for you around some dark-black corner, ready to knock your head off, or to slice you into little pieces. You'd better be careful." Kelly looked concerned.

"I'll try to take care, but I'm going after him. I won't quit until he has paid his price, and is brought to some kind of justice," Andy stated vehemently.

"OK, it's your dying wish. But be careful, so it won't be just that!"

Kelly reached for the knife tucked in his belt.

"Here, take this with you. It's Dong's stiletto. I found it in the burned-out sofa while you were exploring in the dark. It'll be better than nothing if you lose your gun."

"Thanks, it may help." Andy slipped the long knife into his belt, thinking what justice it would be if he fought Dong with his own stiletto.

He slipped the reloaded .38 in his belt, and placed the flashlight in his pocket. Then he boosted himself into the small hole. With the help of Kelly pushing on his legs, he squeezed through, back into the complete dark.

The old tunnel had been filled with dirt, fallen from the roof. After a dozen feet of squirming along the arch of the fallen roof, the level of earth dropped off about three feet to a floor of sorts. Andy had made it into the old connecting tunnel. It was strange—the air was fresher here than in the entryway. There was not so much odor of smoke. It was cooler, but still as dank, and had the odor of death.

He shivered as he felt for the sides, and discovered the tunnel was only about five feet high, and about four feet wide. Small people could have passed beside each other in it. Andy's neck was stiff from keeping his head down.

Without a light, it was difficult to go forward at any speed, and after fifty feet or so, Andy stopped and listened. He heard no sounds. He knew he could not afford to play the wait and listen game again, for if Dong was running, he would get away clean. There was no way to tell how far the tunnel was open. He must make himself go forward. Also, he knew that he had already made enough noise that if Dong were waiting for him, his presence was too well known. Therefore, he reasoned, he may as well use his light—sparingly. He consoled himself with the thought that Dong had no light, and the realization that this tunnel must be unexplored to him as well. They were on a more even footing.

Andy made one quick sweep with the beam and then took a bearing on the tunnel. Quickly he dropped to the floor, in case Dong was in the habit of throwing things. Nothing came. Besides, if he had a knife, he would more likely hang on to it for another purpose. Knowing his light beam had shown his position, he rose and hurried forward as far as he had seen. Slowly he inched on down the tunnel until he felt a corner of the wall.

He listened and waited a full five minutes. He must make a decision as to direction, but first he must have another look. He switched on the beam and again quickly got his bearings. There was a fork in the tunnel. Straight ahead it seemed to continue, and to the left there was another corner, out about twenty feet. That wing must be a dead end, but he had to know. He could not risk Dong being behind him in the tunnel.

Andy crept halfway down the side cut and turned on his light, rapidly covering the other ten feet to the turn. He shined the beam into the new direction as he aimed the .38. It was a dead end. Immediately he returned to the main tunnel, and waited.

There came a slight sound. It sounded like it was only a few steps down from the tunnel ahead of him. Dong had no light, so he was probably as lost in the tunnel as was Andy. He flashed another quick view of the narrow hole ahead, then rushed as far as he dared in the dark. Again he listened. This time there was no sound. Dong must also be waiting and listening for him.

Andy again used the flashlight to take a bearing on the tunnel ahead. As far as he could see, it was empty and without any side cuts. Turning out the light, he pressed ahead. He still held the gun in his right hand, and cautiously walked forward.

Puff! There was a quick stream of moving air in the dank tunnel. He had heard nothing, but he felt the air move. And then it struck. Suddenly, a great pain exploded in his right arm. The gun went flying, and his arm went limp. It was broken below the elbow. His brain screamed for control of his body.

The pain was excruciating, and Andy found himself hoping he did not pass out. He had been hit by something very heavy, like a post. It had been a lucky stroke, for he was sure Dong had no idea exactly where he was striking. Dong must be desperate, and therefore he knew of no way out of the tunnel. Now Andy knew Dong could not run. He would have to fight. But Andy's arm didn't feel like a fight, as he struggled to subdue his pain. He kept reminding himself of Harold Blanton.

Andy crumpled to the floor of the dirty passageway, and lay up against one wall. He heard no movement, but Dong had to be very near. Where was he? Would he come raging with his cudgel? Did he know he had knocked the gun out of his hand, and that it now lay in the dirt, just as accessible to Dong as it was to Andy? Probably not.

There was no way he could know the damage his swing had done, although he probably had heard the gun fall. Andy was in great pain, but he had to go on. He had to get that yellow bastard, because it might well be the last thing he ever did.

He still held the light in his left hand, but if he turned it on, he might find Dong was closer to the gun. That would be the end of their fight. It would be better if he waited to see if he could control his pain, and what Dong would do next. He then realized why he knew he was near, for he could smell him.

The attack wasn't long in coming. There was a slight swish in the black dark—right in front of his face. Dong had a knife! He was swinging in the dark, hoping to again be as lucky as he had been with the cudgel. Andy placed the flashlight on the ground and felt for the stiletto Kelly had given him.

It was there, OK, but he was in pain, and he had no experience using a knife with his left hand. He'd have to make it work. He must protect himself, or he would be finished, all alone, here in a foreign land in the pitch-black dark with an insane terrorist. He remembered his literature of long ago in another land, and "screwed his courage to the sticking place."

He tried desperately to recall some knife training from his war days. He got to his feet, held the stiletto straight out in front of his body, and started alternating slashes and thrusts from side to side. He had never had to do this before, for real. At least it would keep the yellow son of a bitch from walking all over him.

Suddenly his stiletto struck metal. Eerily, their knives had met in full swing. Andy pressed himself forward quickly—as fast and as hard as his pain would permit—and in a great wave of nausea, he found his upper frame was leaning solidly against the stocky body of his perspiring enemy.

For a split second, he smelled the stale odor of Dong's sweat. His forward press had kept the two knives in contact against their hilts. He could hear the labored grunts of Dong's foul words as he pushed against him, and it made him feel worse. He knew if he slacked off, Dong could swing his knife in a new attack.

Andy kept pressing onward, trying to think of a trick he might use. Both he and Dong were leaning forward, each thinking of the protection of their vital parts from knee kicks. It occurred to Andy that he might use this fear of Dong to his own advantage. He must do something quickly, for his strength was ebbing.

Suddenly he stepped into the stocky Dong, right between his legs. In one motion, he raised his knee and pushed the body he met with all his remaining might. There came a stinking huff of his breath. Dong screamed as he reeled backward.

If Dong landed on his back, he would attack him immediately. Andy gathered his strength for a move.

Dong had been caught off balance, and he could be heard stumbling across the dirt clods as he staggered backward.

Andy's scalp crawled. He heard Dong groan as he fell, stumbling backward. It was a strange sequence of sound for he had not immediately hit the floor of the tunnel. He had kept on falling. When he struck a floor solidly below, there was a bloodcurdling scream, followed by a hideous gurgling and gasping sound as his lungs collapsed.

Slowly the echoes died away, and again all was silent—deathly silent. It was the quiet one could almost touch, in the absolute black, with no movement.

Andy lay for a long moment, and then he realized he must move before his strength gave way to coma. He groped carefully for the flashlight he had dropped, and flipped the switch. Before him was a wall at the end of the tunnel, not fifteen feet away. Then he looked down. The tunnel was changing levels, and there were crude, ladder-like steps almost straight down for ten feet. He edged up to the pit and peered down.

There on the floor of the lower cave was the body of Dong, face down! In the dim light, he could see the tip of a knife protruding through his back. A ring of blood was spreading as he watched, and it was obvious that Dong had created his own last act. He had fallen on his knife.

\*   \*   \*

Andy found the pistol, and with the aid of the flashlight he struggled back to the cave-in where he had, so long ago, crawled through the narrow hole at the roof. Now he was eager to wedge his way back out, but it was a struggle, with only one good arm. He tried to grip his belt with his right hand to hold the arm steady, but the pain was too much. It was better to let it drag.

He was concentrating to keep from passing out, for he knew Kelly could not come in after him in his wounded condition. At last, he made it into the hole that Dong had dug so frantically.

"Hello, Kelly. Are you there?" Andy shouted.

"Right here. How are you?" Kelly asked.

"I'm hurt—broken right arm. But that yellow bastard is very dead back there in the tunnel," Andy yelled, suddenly realizing the words were music to his own ears.

"Great. Don't you pass out. How can I help you?" Kelly shouted back.

Moments later, he was out of the tunnel. Andy slumped down on the pile of dirt that Dong had so furiously dug from the ceiling, and leaned back to rest. He was so completely exhausted he could hardly think, but knowledge of the success of their mission kept him alert.

"Just sit tight there a while, and I'll find some sticks, and some twine from the cabinet. Once it's held tight, the pain should ease a little," Kelly said, as he left to find the supplies.

He quickly returned, and while Andy was having a temporary splint placed on the arm, he related his story. He ended by telling how Dong had fallen backward over the ladder into the pit, and landed on his own knife.

"How thoughtful of him!" commented Kelly sarcastically.

It was a comic relief, and Andy grinned in spite of the terrible pain in his arm.

While Kelly was binding, Andy was idly pawing the loose dirt with his left hand. Dong had moved a lot of earth. As he pushed the loose pile down toward the floor, he suddenly felt something smooth, like metal. His attention was drawn to it immediately, for this was not an object dug from the ceiling of the tunnel. It was smooth metal with rounded corners, and had been completely covered by Dong's excavation.

"What's this?" Andy cried.

Quickly Kelly dug it out with his hands.

"It's Dong's briefcase," he said, with rising excitement in his voice.

Kelly helped Andy back on his feet, and together they carried the silver case to the file cabinet. The candle was still burning. Kelly fished into Andy's pocket and found the other one—still usable.

"Shall we break it open?" Andy asked.

"No, no need for that. Let me have a go at it," said Kelly, who was schooled in such things.

After a quick twist of a knife blade, the lock popped open. He lifted the lid. On top was the envelope that had been so dear to Ibu. The sealing chop in bright red China ink was still unbroken.

"To be opened only by the head of the Chou family," Kelly read. It was in English.

"Then it must go to Nhung Thi Nguyen. She is the only one we know now related to the Chou family. At least she is related to the person Dong Chou called 'Ibu,' and her papers should belong to her side of the family," Andy stated.

"Probably there is no other claimant to them, for Dong was married to the Vietcong," Kelly said with a smile.

Andy lifted the big envelope. Below it was a pile of official papers that obscured a small wooden box—a very heavy wooden box. He lifted it out, and removed the lid. The imprinted gold bar glowed in the soft candlelight with a lustrous hue.

"It's the gold," Andy whispered. "This must be the payoff kilo that meant so much to Dong that he was willing to get a lot of people killed just so he could keep it."

He set the box on top of the cabinet and shuffled through the papers. They looked like office correspondence of the minister of energy, and probably should go back to their files. Then the scored edges of fax papers caught Andy's eye. There, near the bottom of the case, lay the original of his request to Ho Bac Minh, asking for Viet Navy protection.

"That bastard! He never did pass our request on, except to the pirates of the Vietcong," Andy said.

They removed the rest of the papers in the case. In the bottom rested other gold pieces, and an envelope containing a piece of metal—a plaque. Suddenly Andy knew. In anticipation, he ripped the seal open and stood entranced. He gazed numbly at the brass registration plate from their company plane.

It was the evidence they had been looking for. Here was the proof that Dong had paid off the terrorists to blow up the World Oil company plane. Andy slumped wearily against the cabinet. He had found all that he had come for.

He felt no remorse in knowing that Dong Huan Chou was dead. His lust for the golden metal had justly taken its own revenge against the greedy yellow terrorist.

# Twenty-nine

"Kelly, we'd better not take all of these official papers from Dong's file. Let's leave them in the cabinet for the minister's boys to find later," Andy said, as they finished going through the drawers of the old file.

It was dank and smoky in the tunnel, and they needed to get outside and breathe some fresh morning air, for they were coughing badly. They had carefully sorted through the official papers, and left them in the top drawer. All of Dong's ill-gotten gold, some of it from the bottom drawer of the file cabinet, and his other family valuables were carefully stowed in the silver case.

"I think we have what we need to support Dong's incrimination in the eyes of the energy minister. It's just as well he doesn't have to answer to a court for his actions, because they'd hang him for sure," Kelly replied.

Great care had been taken to include Ibu's red China-ink, chop-sealed envelope, the plane's registration plate, and the damning copy of the fax message. Andy knew he'd need those items later that day. Both men were exhausted, but Andy knew their work was not yet complete for this new day.

"Are you able to help me carry this?" Andy asked.

"Yes, I can take the case; hold my other hand."

Kelly helped Andy struggle up the ladder, and then he pushed the case up into the burned-out house. They gulped the fresh air as though it were pure oxygen, and gradually the burning in their lungs was eased.

"Should we close the entry to the tunnel?" Kelly asked, as they both sat on the charred bench, recovering their orientation and letting their eyes adjust to the bright daylight.

"Yes, although there's nothing of value to anyone in there now, except to the energy minister. It'll keep the soldiers from prowling down there, but I'd bet they'd be afraid to go down alone," Andy stated as he grinned.

He was elated, knowing he had all of the proof in hand, and was still alive. A broken arm was a small price to pay for this night's success. Together he and Kelly pushed the heavy bookcase back across the tunnel entrance, and made it appear as it did before.

"Now you sit and rest," Kelly directed. "I'll get the car and come for you."

Andy had waited there, happy to sit on the bench with the pistol for protection and the precious silver case under his feet, just regaining his strength until Kelly returned. He heard the car move into the compound and past the whitewashed rocks, right up to the front step.

With his painful arm in a makeshift cast, he eased himself into the car. Kelly attempted to tell the soldier on duty at the gate that he should guard the house well, for the minister of energy would be coming to inspect there soon. At least they assumed he would. The guard nodded and smiled broadly, then saluted smartly as Kelly drove away across the much tortured gate. He had not understood a word, but the mention of "minister" was enough.

He would stay alert.

At the VietAmer office in the Majestic Hotel, Andy placed the silver case in his locked storage area with the Magnum. It was almost noon when he was able to check the message file, and solemnly read the report of the successful sinking of the pirate vessel by James and Pug. Andy let out a great shout.

"Hallelujah!" he yelled. "They did it! Pug and James did it!"

Kelly came running.

"They did it! They sunk the pirate boat," Andy called out again, for he could not stop himself.

"Now, that's the news we've been waiting for. How'd they do it?"

"It was with Pug's bazooka. They caught them towing a heavy cable with a mine, and blew up their gasoline supply. Then the whole damn boat burned and sank!"

For a moment, Andy's arm even quit hurting. He and Kelly were all smiles, and they were both tempted to dance around the office, had their local office manager and secretary not been watching.

"Did they get shot at?"

Andy read on quickly.

"Yeah, with burp guns and with a rocket launcher."

It took some time to digest the long, explicit message.

"Uh-oh. James was wounded. Sounds like he picked up some blast effect from a rocket, and suffered a bad leg injury."

"Just how bad is he?"

"They say he's getting on well, but needs a hospital. He'll be here on tomorrow's crew-change copter. Pug's OK, and is staying on the job," Andy continued.

Both he and Kelly were greatly relieved that there were no more serious injuries. Their company and friends had suffered enough damage.

"Were there any survivors from the pirate boat?" Kelly asked.

"They picked up three, and the survivors quickly admitted to Pug that the NLF hired them." Andy was ecstatic.

"I'd say we came out about as well as we could, not having access to the script."

"Kelly, I'm going to sit down in the office. I need a quick rest. Ask the men to see if they can get me a direct line to the minister of energy, Ho Bac Minh."

Andy was feeling bad and even sounding weak, as he slumped into the first available chair.

The minister's secretary, hearing who was on the line, put the call through promptly. Andy quickly related the news of his encounter with Dong in the tunnel to Ho Bac Minh, describing how his former assistant had died. He heard no weeping from the minister, because he had previously been informed by the soldiers that Dong escaped.

Andy also explained his broken arm, and that he was on his way to see a doctor. A meeting was requested for later that afternoon to show him the evidence that would confirm Dong's guilt.

Ho Bac Minh was elated to hear the news, and wanted Andy to come to his office at his earliest convenience. He knew about the pirate boat's sinking from their promptly delivered communications, but Andy explained they needed to get the injured Wellman to Hong Kong by company jet as soon as possible. His request that the minister furnish him a vehicle pass into the international airport for an ambulance was readily approved. Their company jet, he explained, was waiting on the tarmac at Tan Son Nhat International airport to take James Wellman to a hospital.

On the arrival of Andy and Kelly in the minister's conference room that afternoon, they were both feeling better, for they were bathed to rid themselves of the smoky odor and cleanly dressed after short naps. Andy had a fresh cast on his arm, and a neat white sling. The officers of the Vietnam State Oil Company were already there and seated, waiting with Ho Bac Minh.

"Doctor Cheston and Mr. Johnson, we are happy to see you have come here with no greater injuries. I wish to congratulate you and VietAmer Oil's staff in your persistent efforts to operate in spite of the resistance of the

Vietcong—and in following Dong Huan Chou, to find him in his tunnel, and to persist until he met his justly deserved end. You have done us a great service."

The minister and his staff were on their feet, and all crowded around the two Americans, each in turn shaking their hands heartily. He was effusive in his praise, and he went on to compliment all of their activities.

He extended his dialogue when they were again seated, with prodigious apologies for the failure of their communications system. It had not lived up to their sincere intentions, which were to cooperate fully with VietAmer. Andy was well aware that such a congenial attitude of their officials boded well for their future operations offshore from the Mekong Delta.

"We thank you for those words of recognition," Andy replied, "but we were, perhaps, acting more in our own selfish interests, and therefore deserve no praise. Several good men were killed by Dong's actions, all friends of ours. We were glad to see that justice was done, and that his guilt has now been made obvious to everyone."

Andy then sank wearily into his seat, for he was depending on Kelly to watch over his physical well-being. He, better than anyone, knew what an ordeal Andy had come through. He carried a thin leather briefcase, from which he produced the telltale, damning faxed message. Andy took it gently and handed it to the minister. He accepted the paper and read it carefully, noting the automatically inscribed date and time on the perforated paper. He then carefully placed it in his own file.

"This damning evidence would have convicted him, were he still alive," he stated.

"Had he passed the message on, it would have saved the lives of the pirate crew, as well as avoided James Wellman's wound. It placed our entire drilling operation in great jeopardy," Andy stated.

Kelly next handed Andy the envelope they had discovered in Dong's possession, which contained the registration plate of their company's chartered plane. Andy passed it on to the minister without comment with his one good hand.

This, too, the minister examined carefully, noting that it had the make and serial numbers of the plane clearly legible.

"This is proof positive of the terrorist act. It would not have been in his possession had he not paid the ones who planted the bomb on the plane. Fortunately, there is no need for a trial here. However, an international court may need the evidence. We'll have to furnish depositions, but only after you've had a rest," Ho Bac Minh stated.

Andy requested that the brass plaque be returned to World Oil at some later date, and then he graciously accepted the airport pass. He then handed it to Kelly, who immediately filed it away deep inside the briefcase. In Vietnam, a minister's signature was a prize not to be taken lightly.

When they returned to the Majestic Hotel, Andy was happy to see that James had arrived back in Saigon on the crew-change helicopter, as scheduled. They would all have a well-deserved rest that night. Andy and Kelly were more than slightly exhausted after their tunnel ordeal, and James was just happy to get into a real bed without the noise and the perpetual vibrations of the drillship's engines.

James was almost asleep as he related his and Pug's experience with the pirates to Andy and Kelly. They had sandwiches and beer sent up, for they were all more exhausted than hungry. He explained that Pug Cox had broken the shipboard regulations to go onto the heli-deck, just to see him off. It had been the most unusual velocity survey he'd ever run, aided by medicinal alcohol.

Andy was soon asleep, but he dreamed fitfully, awakening several times with a start. He vaguely remembered the previous night during which he and Kelly had not seen a bed. He was truly happy for the first time in a year, and many of his long-term objectives were about to be fulfilled. When he finally slept soundly, he dreamed of a beautiful Oriental girl with long black hair to her waist—but when he awoke, he was smiling, and he couldn't remember that she was wearing anything at all.

It was midday before the VietAmer explorers were assembled to depart the Majestic Hotel for the airport, ready for their return to Hong Kong. Andy had sent Kelly on an errand that morning to pay their personal respects to friends who had been helpful, and to make some other personal arrangements. He had stayed in the office to relay the news of their successful activities by phone to Bill Hanby in Tokyo.

They talked for an hour, and Bill wanted to hear every detail—about his and Kelly's adventure, as well as the attack on the pirate boat by James and Pug. He had already heard about the well-logging progress. When he was thoroughly briefed on the actions, he asked that Andy send their plane back to Tokyo.

"I'm coming to Hong Kong to visit the drillship in a few days, because Gilbert Eason wants to make an inspection tour. The chairman wants to see personally how an offshore well test is run."

"OK. I'll send your plane home tomorrow evening. But I'll have to get together with Tim McAllister, and we'll vote on whether or not we can allow a visit by an outsider," Andy laughed.

They finished their conversation with assurances that their next meeting would be under much happier circumstances than they'd encountered in recent months.

Andy sent a fax to his office in Hong Kong, advising Kim to arrange transportation and hotel reservations. He also requested that he have his sister, Lin Jin, and her mother, Thi Lan, meet them at the hotel on their arrival. He had an important matter to discuss with their entire family, and he wanted to do it at a party.

Their office manager made a special arrangement for the use of an ambulance and its delivery crew. They made the necessary stops to gather the injured James from the hospital, and headed for the airport as early as they could get ready.

"Swing the ambulance right on up to the plane," Andy directed the driver as they entered the airport.

He waved the minister's pass at the gate guard as they slowed, but then continued onto the tarmac at the airport. The excited guard ran after them, toward the parked jet. The ambulance driver crossed the yellow marker lines, driving right up to the plane's wingtip. Two of the customs guards arrived beside the ambulance, somewhat upset because they had almost been ignored when they entered through the gate.

James was quickly removed from the ambulance on a gurney. As Andy had intended, they presented a very serious scene to the onlooking guards as his bed was directed to the plane by his attendants. The two bearers, accompanied by the starchy white-clad nurse, carefully wheeled him toward the World Oil jet.

The guards met Andy as he stepped down from the front seat, taking care to protect his arm in the sling. They demanded to see the exit permits for all of those who were departing on the plane. Andy produced the special vehicle entry permit, which had allowed them to drive into the aircraft parking area. When they saw the minister's signature, that seemed to moderate their anguish somewhat.

While their luggage was being loaded aboard the jet, the guards were being impressed by the fact that the pass was signed by the minister of energy himself. The driver of the ambulance carefully explained this point several times in Vietnamese before their luggage was all placed safely aboard.

Andy held the passports containing multiple exit visas for the entire group. He fumbled a bit as he showed them to the customs guards with his one good hand. Meanwhile, the little procession with the gurney had James safely aboard the plane, and he had been strapped in by Kelly and the nurse. She looked prim and officious in her starched uniform.

It was a problem for Andy to shuffle so many passports, but the customs agents did not object, for they already had heard rumors of the circumstances surrounding this flight.

They were proud to be associated with such a newsworthy activity. It would provide them a good story to tell their family and friends that evening.

When the attendants wheeled their gurney back to the ambulance, Andy was still having trouble with the passports. He again dropped the entire batch on the ground, and both of the agents hurried to assist him. Finally, he placed the passports in the crook of his arm-sling, and waved good-bye as he climbed aboard the jet. The ambulance had already pulled away as the jet's door was sealed behind him.

The sleek plane taxied to the takeoff position, and roared down the runway on its way to Hong Kong. The customs agents had not noticed that the prim nurse had failed to return to the ambulance.

* * *

The small, streamlined jet made a tight turn on its approach into the Hong Kong runway, and most of the passengers were still asleep. As they taxied in, they were awakened, to gather their belongings and prepare to deplane. They could carry all of their light luggage, and Andy toted the silver case with his one good arm. There was no reception committee waiting, for Kim had barely found enough time to phone around and make the arrangements Andy had requested. There was going to be a real celebration when they got to their hotel.

The four passengers departed the plane without the aid of an ambulance. Andy knew that James was well on his way to recovery, and could have walked before, had the ruse of nursing assistance not been needed. He was impressed by the "Western" appearance of the lady accompanying them, who had previously been dressed as a nurse. Now she looked just like the girls from Saigon, in her hip-fitted slacks and high heels.

Kelly quickly checked their ground transportation arrangements, and they were ready to depart when the customs agents were finished. Andy watched closely as the agent at the check-in window mentally noted how strange it was that the young lady had a British passport, which, although several years old, had never before been stamped. The Vietnamese government must be relenting, he had finally assumed.

Kim had done a yeoman's job of preparations for the party Andy had ordered. With the approval of his boss, Tim McAllister, he had arranged to have Andy's clothing moved from his room into a suite, and reserved rooms for Kelly and James. His sister, Lin Jin, had been contacted, and she was elated when she heard that Andy was safe. She had agreed to meet them at his hotel suite, accompanied by their mother, Thi Lan.

Tim had rounded up the off-duty employees of the company who were in town, and available. They were all invited to attend the impromptu party. There were stories that needed telling. It was not that they had been gone so long, but to Andy it had seemed like an eternity. They may as well all celebrate at once, and together, for everybody would want to hear their stories firsthand.

On their arrival at the hotel entry ramp, Kim was standing beside the doorman. Andy waited to see his expression when he became aware that his Vietnamese cousin, Nhung Thi Nguyen, was arriving with the entourage. She had a British passport, he knew, but had not been able to get an exit permit from Vietnam because her family was not in good graces with the government. Therefore, when she stepped out from the limousine, Andy watched as a grin spread across Kim's unbelieving eyes.

Kim stammered, and finally asked, "Nhung Thi, how did you get here?" He hurried to hug her tightly, and to kiss her.

"It was a simple thing," she respond, in tears. "This morning I was in the bombed apartment, wondering what the future would bring. Then Kelly came, and told me to get into a nurse's uniform. My friends helped me with that. Then with the ambulance attendants, we put James Wellman on the jet."

She was smiling and crying all at once.

"I just forgot to get off."

Andy was a little proud that he and Kelly had arranged this loving scene between the two long-lost cousins, even though they had met recently. Now they'd have time to relive their childhood together.

Nhung Thi kept saying, "I just can't believe I'm here at last."

The buildings were all too big and new and impressive for her to comprehend so soon.

"Why don't you come along with me, Nhung Thi and Kim. You can use my bedroom to freshen up until our other company arrives, and I'll go and check on the refreshments." Andy looked at Kim. "I assume you ordered the catering for a party?" he asked.

"Yes, sir; everything is set. Even the champagne," Kim replied. "Come, and I will assist you with the registration."

\*   \*   \*

The party had already started, with James and Kelly and the rest of the office crew gathered in the living area of Andy's suite. The caterer arrived on schedule, and the hors d'oeuvres were plentiful and delicious. The bar was well stocked, and James had settled in one corner to tell his story of how the pirates had been obliterated.

Andy excused himself and left the suite, for he wanted to attend to another interest.

When Lin Jin and Thi Lan stepped out of their car at the entryway, Andy saw them, as he watched from his vantage point through the glass doors. He rushed forward to meet them as they entered the foyer. Lin Jin was a strikingly beautiful woman, but Andy was never so impressed as now. It was a great relief for him, just to see her statuesque and poised body in action again.

He had been busy with the business of drilling an oil well, and she had not encouraged him to visit. In fact, she had been keeping her distance while she attempted to sort out their family relationships, not even calling him or accepting his calls.

Andy could not fathom how Lin Jin knew about the importance of this day, but something had happened between them. It was an ESP like that he sometimes enjoyed with his twin sister, Beth. Perhaps it resulted from his release from his sworn obligation to repay the NLF for their dirty deeds in Harold Blanton and the others' memory, he thought.

His relationship with Lin Jin had suddenly become a thing of urgency. There was no longer a great gulf of family pride between them. His relieved attitude was reflected in her very appearance, for now they were thinking of their respect for each other's intentions, without regard for family ties. He saw it in her eyes in the moment they met.

Andy took Lin Jin in his arms, and kissed her carefully on each cheek. Neither could let the other go, so they stood there in the lobby entryway for several seconds. Suddenly, he realized that Mother Thi Lan was standing quietly, trying to be unobtrusive. But that did not embarrass Andy in the slightest. He had not intended to be rude, and he turned immediately to greet her as well with a proper hug and a kiss on each cheek.

"Lin-san and Thi Lan, I'm so happy to see both of you again. This week has been a rough one, and thank God it is now behind us. I wanted you both to come to our party, and join in our happy reunion. We can tell all our tales of adventure when we get upstairs, and hope to make some sense out of the events of the past year," Andy said, as he guided them toward the elevator.

"Andy-san, darling, I was so worried about you," Lin Jin said softly. "I spoke to Kim at the office every hour, but he had little information about you. Now that you are here and I can see you, I can be alive again."

Great tears streamed down her cheeks and were quickly wiped away, only to be replaced by others.

"I had not intended to worry you, Lin-san," Andy repeated the theme, still holding onto her arm.

"I was worried because I knew of your sworn intention to repay your obligation to the terrorists. But I was so afraid for you. The devil Dong had long arms, and many dark influences to call upon and set against you."

Lin Jin was gradually getting over her need to cry.

"VietAmer may take a long time in achieving a balance with the Viet government, but this episode has brought out an interesting conclusion. We can work with those Vietnamese in power, such as Ho Bac Minh, to achieve our common goal of successful oil production," Andy concluded.

"Doctor Cheston," Thi Lan interrupted, "You must not go away on such ventures again, for my daughter is just too hard to keep busy while you are away. She worried for your safety so much."

"I assure you, that was not my intention," Andy answered, as he put his good arm around Lin Jin and led them both into the elevator. "In the future, I don't think I will allow this lovely lady to get too far away from me."

He smiled at Thi Lan as he held Lin Jin closer.

When the three of them entered the room, the party came to a sudden hush. Kim led his long-lost cousin over to his mother and sister.

"Do you recognize this lady?" Kim asked.

He need not have, for Lin Jin was already moving to gather her childhood playmate to her. She cried and laughed all at once.

The strain on Nhung Thi was less, because she had been expecting this meeting. They spent the next half hour going over the events that had led them to Hong Kong. The Hoe family had never expected Nhung Thi to be able to leave Vietnam. Every few minutes, Thi Lan or Lin Jin would find Andy, and thank him again for making this family reunion possible. Tim and

Pamela McAllister did their best to keep the caterer supplied with orders for food.

Gradually, the discussion among the Hoe family members explained the complex relationships that had grown over the years. Thi Lan explained to Lin Jin and Kim that Dong's Ibu was really his stepmother, and was actually her own sister. Lin Jin and Kim were both shocked, and soon Lin Jin was again crying.

It was a difficult fact for Lin Jin to accept, but it was readily confirmed by Nhung Thi. She had been told everything by her grandfather after her mother had died and he returned from the reeducation experience. It was at once a very sad and a happily informative discussion.

James had brought more than the story of his and Pug Cox's pirate adventure to the party. He had brought the well logs. Soon, all of the company technicians had them on a table, trying to pick the pay zones. He had news of the first test results of the well. They had set casing and drilled out with a core barrel.

Today they had received word at the office that the drillstem test indicated they already had a producing well. And they had not yet drilled all of the prospective horizons. This was, indeed, a day for celebrations!

But Andy cut his celebration short when he remembered he had some other pressing Hoe family business to discuss. He called Thi Lan, Lin Jin, Nhung Thi, and Kim to accompany Tim, James, Kelly, and him into the bedroom. The explorers had become his staunch supporters over the past year, and he wanted them to be present when they opened the case.

Andy was aware that the Hoe family had no idea why he had arranged this gathering, so obviously for their benefit, but there were facts to which they needed to be educated. The information was new to some of them, so it had to be digested one fact at a time.

He slid the silver case out from under the bed, and placed it precisely on the spread. Then he flipped the sturdy latches, and laid it open to show the treasures that Dong had so carefully amassed for his future life in retirement. The heavy balsa-wood box was opened, and the stamped gold ingot was lifted out for everyone to see.

Its luster had not diminished, for "gold is forever, and knows not its owner." It was a solid block of magic—and indeed a small fortune. But to whom did it belong now?

"This gold ingot, and probably these other pieces as well, came indirectly from the coffers of the Vietcong," Andy stated. "By Lam Thang's information, we know it was authorized to be taken from the bank by Dong. It paid for the terrorist act against World Oil's plane. Dong then retrieved the bar from robbers, and hid it in his tunnel. I believe all of this belongs to the Hoe estate, as there can be no other claimants."

Andy made the statement in preparation for opening Ibu's sealed envelope. She was Dong's stepmother, and Thi Lan's sister. She had lost her life trying to retrieve the documents from the fire.

"Thi Lan, you have my deepest sympathy in the death of your relative. I hope you will not think badly of me for having been present at the fire. Please believe me the fire was set by the soldiers. They did their best to prevent her from returning to the burning house, but she acted like a madwoman and broke away from them. She thought this envelope was that important."

Andy spoke as kindly as possible.

"Doctor Cheston, Andy-san, I do not blame you for the events that occurred. She and I had long ago grown apart, since she took her second husband and began to rear the boy, Dong."

Thi Lan, Little Orchid, was suddenly crying.

"They belonged to a different political group, and we could never agree on a way of life after that marriage. I thought she came to hate me. That is why I have kept our relationship a secret from my own children, although others in the family knew. Li Hong Hoe, as well as Lam Thang, already knew, and he must have told Nhung Thi before he died."

She finished with a long sob.

"Yes, that is true. He told me everything," Nhung Thi added.

"Thank you for that," Andy said. "Now let's see what the envelope contains." He broke the seal with its bright red, China-ink chop, and extracted a sheaf of papers. They were well worn, and almost brittle. Carefully, he unfolded them and laid them out on the bed.

Thi Lan immediately began to cry in great sobbing gasps. She recognized the clippings and knew their significance. She was trying to read in Vietnamese between the tears.

"What does the paper say?" Andy asked, looking first at Thi Lan and then at Lin Jin.

The four family members pored over the documents; finally, Lin Jin took her sobbing mother aside, and tried to comfort her. It seemed everyone knew why they were crying except for the American explorers, and no one wished to explain. It was as though they must guard the secret of Ibu's folder a little longer.

Nhung Thi was the first to realize their need to know, and finally began to explain.

"The papers are police documents and newspaper clippings from before the war. They say that Thi Lan was raped by a soldier of the French Army, during their occupation of Saigon. Her husband reared her resulting child as his own, and as a sister to younger Kim. Those two are actually half-brother and sister."

Kim, too, was teary-eyed.

"I never knew we were only related by our mother. Now I can see where your finer features are developed. But still you are my sister. I will love you no less."

He had his arms around Lin Jin as he spoke.

"Now I understand what Lam Thang was trying to tell me as he died," said Nhung Thi. "He was trying to say that Thi Lan was raped by a French soldier. Now it is clear. He did not wish to die with that knowledge on his conscience. He was afraid, according to Vietnamese lore, that he could not close his eyes if his vengeance wish was not fulfilled. Really, he wanted you to know this, Ange-san," Nhung Thi lisped his name again.

"But why, after all these years and all of the events of war, did Ibu want to preserve this information? Did she think it would make a difference?" Andy looked to each of the members of the family.

"I was so ashamed, and I did not know if it would make a difference between Lin Jin and me. She preserved the secret for my sake," Thi Lan said. "That is why I sent the children away to school with the nuns. I wanted them to learn the truth of the church, instead of the truth of the way people sometimes act and live."

"Does it make a difference, Andy-san?" asked Lin Jin pointedly. This answer was very important to her, for she had always believed deeply in maintaining family confidences.

"None whatsoever!" Andy replied with vigor. "You grew up as a family, and your love is deeper than anything that could be separated by a document."

As the family discussed their newfound relationship, Lin Jin was holding her mother, and assuring her she did not blame her for keeping the secret all through these years. Now she understood many of the family moves and business relationships that had previously seemed abnormal. Her grandfather, Li Hong Hoe, had been trying to protect her against what might happen if she did find out about her mother's secret. Lin Jin kept reassuring Thi Lan that the guilt was not hers.

There was another document, which Kelly had been quietly trying to decipher. Finally he took it to Kim, and asked him to translate it for all of them. He took the paper and read over it to himself, knitting his brow intensely for several minutes.

"This is Ibu's will," he finally announced. "It says that everything she owns, which is the entire estate, belongs to her only living relative, Thi Lan Hoe."

Thi Lan gasped.

"But I thought she hated me," she sobbed.

Kim continued, "She had this drawn up because she did not trust her stepson, Dong. She knew that without the will, he would keep the entire Hoe estate for himself. She must have had a late change of heart about the Hoe family. Had she died before him, he would have read this and destroyed it. Then he could have continued in his possession of that land. Without a will, the Vietcong would have supported him in his ownership. With this paper, the estate will continue in the Hoe family possession."

"Doctor Cheston, we must thank you for saving these documents. I see now how foolish I have been in not telling Lin Jin of her true ancestry. She was reared as a loving daughter, and now it is showing through our true relationship. We love each other, as a family should. I am truly sorry for my attitude toward my sister, Ibu. We will forever be in her debt, and yours, Andy-san."

"Kelly and I were fortunate to be in the right place at the right time," Andy replied. "Now, Nhung Thi, since you have your British passport and are out of Vietnam, what are your plans?"

"I will answer that for now!" replied Thi Lan. "She will come and live with us for the time being. With this gold, which you say belongs to the estate, I believe Nhung Thi should set up a business, and, as is our family custom, we will find a nice Oriental man to comfort her in the absence of Lam Thang."

The head of the Hoe family had spoken, and with a broad smile.

Finally, the party did break up. It was late in the evening, and no one had even thought of interrupting their discourses to go out to dinner. The food kept being replenished by the caterer, along with more ice and more champagne, and everyone wanted to hear the stories over and over. When Thi Lan finally gathered her purse, she took Nhung Thi by the hand. They were escorted toward the door by Kim Jin.

As they departed, she said, looking beyond Andy to Lin Jin, "Good night, my dearest daughter. I have had a great cloud lifted from my spirit, and I thank you for your blessed understanding."

There was another round of kisses, and Kim led his mother and cousin away as the door closed. Lin Jin gave no indication that she was ever going to leave the side of her beloved Andy-san.

The two of them strolled arm in arm to stand outside on the balcony, where they could view the magnificent skyline of Kowloon and gaze across the bay toward Victoria Peak. The Chinese characters for Hong Kong translated to "Fragrant Harbor." As Andy held the lovely Lin-san up in his arms, he knew this city would be the haven of their future together—it would remain their "Fragrant Harbor."

He looked deep into her black, starry eyes, and said, "Were it not for my cast, my darling Lin Jin, I'd carry you over the threshold, and straight into the bedroom."

Lin Jin smiled, and replied, "That would do no good, sir, for there's a silver case filled with pirates' gold lying there."

# Epilogue

Bill Hanby called Elizabeth Halstead in California, and explained all that had occurred to her brother and VietAmer Oil in an hour-long phone conversation. She, in turn, explained that she had written a long letter of apology to Lin Jin Hoe, saying she had been wrong to attempt to force her girlfriend's advances on Andy. Now she realized she had been unable to give proper attention to her own twin brother's expression of his heartfelt feelings because of her misunderstanding of the Oriental culture.

The chairman of World Oil, Gilbert Eason, went to Hong Kong with Bill Hanby to congratulate Andy on their oil discovery, and the well completion. He appreciated the methods of operation of the VietAmer Oil Corporation, and the procedures under which they were operating. He recognized their newfound ability to associate honestly with the Vietnamese government on their own turf.

Andy was advised that he would receive a substantial bonus in stock options for the wholly-owned VietAmer Corporation. If VietAmer continued to find and develop oil fields, he would soon be a very rich and important business leader. He also explained that if the U.S. government relented, and allowed them to rejoin World Oil, he would be welcome into an appropriate senior position.

Elizabeth Halstead arrived in Hong Kong to visit her twin brother, accompanied by her girlfriend, Leslie Bicknell, much to James Wellman's delight. After meeting the Hoe family on their own territory, Beth became a friend of Lin Jin and her mother and brother. Her attitude toward Orientals had made a complete reversal after she had become better acquainted. She then understood her brother's adoring feelings completely, as only a twin can.

The wedding for Lin Jin and Andy was held in the spring, in the garden of the Halstead estate near Sausalito, California. It was well attended by members of both the Hoe family and the World Oil staff. In the double-ring ceremony, the bride gave the groom a yellow golden ring, inscribed, "Lin-san will always love Andy-san."